Geographies and Moralities

RGS-IBG Book Series

The *Royal Geographical Society (with the Institute of British Geographers) Book Series* provides a forum for scholarly monographs and edited collections of academic papers at the leading edge of research in human and physical geography. The volumes are intended to make significant contributions to the field in which they lie, and to be written in a manner accessible to the wider community of academic geographers. Some volumes will disseminate current geographical research reported at conferences or sessions convened by Research Groups of the Society. Some will be edited or authored by scholars from beyond the UK. All are designed to have an international readership and to both reflect and stimulate the best current research within geography.

The books will stand out in terms of:
- the quality of research
- their contribution to their research field
- their likelihood to stimulate other research
- being scholarly but accessible.

For series guides go to www.blackwellpublishing.com/pdf/rgsibg.pdf

Published

Geographies and Moralities
Edited by Roger Lee and David M. Smith

Military Geographies
Rachel Woodward

A New Deal for Transport?
Edited by Iain Docherty and Jon Shaw

Geographies of British Modernity
Edited by David Gilbert, David Matless and Brian Short

Lost Geographies of Power
John Allen

Globalizing South China
Carolyn L. Cartier

Geomorphological Processes and Landscape Change: Britain in the Last 1000 Years
Edited by David L. Higgitt and E. Mark Lee

Forthcoming

Domicile and Diaspora
Alison Blunt

The Geomorphology of Upland Peat
Martin Evans and Jeff Warburton

Fieldwork
Simon Naylor

Putting Workfare in Place
Peter Sunley, Ron Martin and Corinne Nativel

Natural Resources in Eastern Europe
Chad Staddon

Living Through Decline: Surviving in the Places of the Post-Industrial Economy
Huw Beynon and Ray Hudson

After the Three Italies: Wealth, Inequality and Industrial Change
Mick Dunford and Lidia Greco

Publics and the City
Kurt Iveson

Geochemical Sediments and Landscapes
David Nash and Susan McLaren

Driving Spaces
Peter Merriman

Geographies and Moralities

International Perspectives on Development, Justice and Place

Edited by
Roger Lee and David M. Smith

Blackwell
Publishing

BLACKWELL PUBLISHING
350 Main Street, Malden, MA 02148-5020, USA
108 Cowley Road, Oxford OX4 1JF, UK
550 Swanston Street, Carlton, Victoria 3053, Australia

First published 2004 by Blackwell Publishing Ltd

Library of Congress Cataloging-in-Publication Data

Lee, Roger, 1945-
  Geographies and moralities: international perspectives on development, justice, and place/Roger Lee and David M. Smith.
    p. cm. — (RGS-IBG book series)
Includes bibliographical references and index.
  ISBN 1-4051-1636-6 (hardcover: alk. paper) — ISBN 1-4051-1637-4 (alk. paper)
  1. Regional disparities. 2. Distributive justice. 3. Geography—Moral and ethical aspects.
I. Smith, David Marshall, 1936—II. Title. III. Series.

  HT388.L44 2004
  305.5—dc22

                                                                              2004006261

A catalogue record for this title is available from the British Library.

Set in 10/12 plantin
by Kolam Information Services Pvt. Ltd, Pondicherry, India
Printed and bound in the United Kingdom
by TJInternationalLtd,Padstow,Cornwall

The publisher's policy is to use permanent paper from mills that operate a sustainable forestry policy, and which has been manufactured from pulp processed using acid-free and elementary chlorine-free practices. Furthermore, the publisher ensures that the text paper and cover board used have met acceptable environmental accreditation standards.

For further information on
Blackwell Publishing, visit our website:
www.blackwellpublishing.com

Essays in honour of David M. Smith

Contents

Series Editors' Preface

The RGS/IBG Book series publishes the highest quality of research and scholarship across the broad disciplinary spectrum of geography. Addressing the vibrant agenda of theoretical debates and issues that characterize the contemporary discipline, contributions will provide a synthesis of research, teaching, theory and practice that both reflects and stimulates cutting edge research. The Series seeks to engage an international readership through the provision of scholarly, vivid and accessible texts.

Nick Henry and Jon Sadler
RGS-IBG Book Series Editors

Notes on Contributors

Stuart Corbridge teaches at the University of Miami and the London School of Economics. He works in rural eastern India, on questions of government, empowerment and environmental politics. He is the author, with John Harriss, of *Reinventing India: Liberalization, Hindu Nationalism and Popular Democracy* (Polity Press, 2000); with Sarah Jewitt and Sanjay Kumar, of *Jharkhand: Environment, Development, Ethnicity* (Oxford University Press, 2003); and, with Glyn Williams, Manoj Srivastava and Rene Veron, of *Seeing the State: Governance and Governmentality in Rural India* (Cambridge University Press, 2004). He is interested in 'geographies and moralities' in the context of the needs and rights of distant strangers, the policing of the debt crisis, and poorer people's encounters with the state.

Priscilla Cunnan received a working-class school education under the apartheid system in South Africa. She holds three degrees from the University of Durban-Westville, where she was also employed as a researcher and teaching assistant. She completed a PhD in the geography of health at Queen Mary, University of London, focused on the health of poor women street traders in Durban. Her research interests include working with marginalized and deprived communities in South Africa and more recently in London. She is currently Assistant Director of the Science and Engineering Foundation Programme at Queen Mary, University of London.

Sarah E. Curtis is Professor of Geography at Queen Mary, University of London. She has extensive international research experience in the geography of health and health services, especially on inequalities of health and access to health care, and on the assessment of health needs and impacts. She is currently conducting research funded by Research Councils and NHS agencies on health impact assessment of urban regeneration schemes, the relationship of social and physical environments to variations in health and well-being of adolescents, variation in use of mental health services, and therapeutic aspects of design of mental health facilities. Her latest book is *Health and Inequality: Geographical Perspectives* (Sage, 2004).

Peter Dicken is Professor of Geography at the University of Manchester. He has held visiting appointments at universities and research institutes in Australia, Canada, Hong Kong, Mexico, Singapore, Sweden and the United States. He is an Academician of the Social Sciences, a recipient of the Victoria Medal of the Royal Geographical Society (with the Institute of British Geographers) and of an Honorary Doctorate of the University of Uppsala, Sweden. His major research interests are in global economic change, as reflected in his book *Global Shift: Reshaping the Global Economic Map in the 21st Century* (Guildford Press, fourth edition, 2003).

Bolesław Domański is Professor of Geography and head of the Department for Regional Development at the Jagiellonian University in Cracow, Poland. He has recently been working on social dimensions of local and regional development, effects of foreign direct investment and activity of transnational corporations, restructuring of old industrial regions, and urban and regional inequalities. He is the author of *Industrial Control over the Socialist Town: Benevolence or Exploitation?* (Praeger, 1997), as well as of numerous publications on post-socialist economic and social transformation in various European journals and books.

Donna Easterlow is Honorary Research Fellow, Department of Geography, University of Durham. Her research interests centre on the relationships between geography, inequality and public policy in contemporary Britain. Her work explores the impact of welfare restructuring on the 'health divide', or the increasing importance of health status as an axis of social and geographical inequality. This includes studies of access to public and private housing, employment and life insurance for people experiencing long-term ill-health. The results have been published in a range of academic journals, including *Policy & Politics*, *Housing Studies*, *Health & Place* and *Public Health*.

Shlomo Hasson is a professor at the Hebrew University of Jerusalem, where he teaches in the Geography Department and the Institute of Urban and Regional Studies. His fields of interest are cultural and political geography and urban planning. He is the author of *Urban Social Movements in Jerusalem* (State University of New York Press in cooperation with The Jerusalem Institute for Israel Studies, 1993), *Neighbourhood Organizations and the Welfare State* (with David Ley; University of Toronto Press, 1994), *Divided Regions: A Comparative Perspective* (with Moshe Hirsh and Alexander Weingrrod; The Jerusalem Institute for Israel Studies, 2000),

The Struggle for Hegemony in Jerusalem: Secular and Ultra-Orthodox Jews in Urban Politics (The Floersheimer Institute for Policy Studies, 2001) and *State, Religion and Society in Israel: Possible Futures* (The Floersheimer Institute for Policy Studies, 2002).

Jean Hillier is Professor of Town and Country Planning at the University of Newcastle. Her main research interests lie in praxis-based planning theories and in discursive and relational analyses of participatory planning strategies. Underlying most of her research is a deep concern with issues of social exclusion, and the impact of planning decisions on women and marginalized groups and on nature. Publications include *Shadows of Power: An Allegory of Prudence in Land Use Planning* (Routledge, 2002), *Habitus: A Sense of Place* (edited with Emma Rooksby; Ashgate, 2002) and *Consensus and Consent* (edited with Denis Cryle; University of Queensland Press, 2004).

Rex Honey is Professor of Geography and Associate Director of the Center for Human Rights at the University of Iowa. He is former chair of the Ethics, Justice and Human Rights Speciality Group of the Association of American Geographers, and is Secretary of the International Geographical Union's Commission on Geography and Public Policy. His research interests focus on public policy and human rights. He has ongoing research programmes in West Africa, the Middle East, the South Pacific, Western Europe and the United States.

Ron Johnston is a professor in the School of Geographical Sciences at the University of Bristol, having worked previously at Monash University (Australia), the University of Canterbury (New Zealand) and the Universities of Sheffield and Essex. He has written widely on aspects of the recent history of human geography, including *Geography and Geographers* (Edward Arnold), first published in 1979 (sixth edition co-authored with James Sidaway; 2004), and two major co-edited books – *The Dictionary of Human Geography* (with Derek Gregory, Geraldine Pratt and Michael Watts; fourth edition, Blackwell, 2000) and *A Century of British Geography* (with Michael Williams; Oxford University Press, 2003).

Avery Kolers is Assistant Professor of Philosophy at the University of Louisville, Kentucky. He earned his PhD at the University of Arizona. His primary research interests are political philosophy and ethics. He is currently writing a book on the justification of territorial claims and the role of territorial rights in the theory of global justice, and intends to apply the theory not only to international territorial disputes, but also to problems associated with globalization and indigenous land rights.

Roger Lee is Professor of Geography and immediate past head of the Department of Geography at Queen Mary, University of London. An Academician of the Social Sciences, he is an editor of *Progress in Human Geography*, a former editor of the *Transactions of the Institute of British Geographers* and founder of electronic *Transactions*. His interests lie in the connections between economic life and its social understanding. His latest book, *Alternative Economic Spaces* (Sage, 2003), is a volume of research essays co-edited with Andrew Leyshon and Colin Williams, and he is currently working as a co-editor (with A. Leyshon, L. McDowell and P. Sunley) on a compendium of economic geography to be published by Sage in 2006.

William S. Lynn is Research Scholar and Executive Director at the Centre for Humans and Nature in New York. He received his doctorate from the University of Minnesota, where he studied the philosophy of geography, critical landscape geography, practical ethics, interpretive social science and qualitative methods. With research foci in animal ethics and global ethics, he is the principal investigator for the People, Animals and Nature Initiative, a founding editor of the journal *Ethics, Place and Environment* and Research Associate at Vasser College. He is currently finishing a book, *Practical Ethics: Moral Understanding in a More Than Human World*.

Brij Maharaj is Professor and head of Geography (Pietermaritzburg) and Research Director at the Centre for Civil Society (Durban), University of Natal. He serves on the International Geography Union Commission on Geography and Public Policy, was Faculty Fellow at the University of Illinois, and is a life member of the National Association of Geographers of India. In 1998 he was awarded Fellowship of the Society of South African Geographers. He has published extensively on issues relating to segregation, land dispossession and restitution, and urban processes in South Africa.

David M. Smith is Emeritus Professor of Geography at Queen Mary, University of London, where he has worked since 1973. He held earlier appointments at the Universities of Manchester, Southern Illinois, Florida, Natal, the Witwatersrand and New England (Australia), and has made numerous research visits to Israel, Poland, South Africa, the former Soviet Union and the United States. His books include *Human Geography: A Welfare Approach* (Edward Arnold, 1977), *Geography and Social Justice* (Blackwell, 1994) and *Moral Geographies: Ethics in a World of Difference* (Edinburgh University Press, 2000).

Susan J. Smith is Professor of Geography at the University of Durham. Her work concerns the role of housing and the organization, institutional-ization and meaning of space in structuring social inequality. She has published on the indignity of victimization and fear of crime, the affront of racism and gender inequality, and the challenge to housing, employment and financial services for people experiencing ill-health. This work has an interdisciplinary focus (engaging with debates in social policy, social medicine and housing studies) and a practical edge (with links to central and local government, financial service providers, interest groups and communities).

Nigel Spence is Professor of Geography at Queen Mary, University of London. Previously he was Casel Reader in Economic Geography at the London School of Economics. His interests are in urban and regional economic planning and he has published widely in journals of this field. His books are *British Cities: An Analysis of Urban Change* (Pergamon, 1982) and *Regional Policy Evaluation* (Gower, 1983). He has three monographs in *Progress in Planning* and has authored an HMSO report on Infrastructure and Industrial Costs. He has undertaken research for UK Government Departments and European agencies such as the Commission and the Court of Auditors.

Gill Valentine is Professor of Geography at the University of Sheffield, where she teaches social and cultural geography and research methods. She has published widely on a range of topics including geographies of sexuality, consumption and children, youth and parenting. Gill is a (co)author/editor of ten books, most recently *Cyberkids: Children in the Information Age* (FalmerRoutledge, 2003) and *Key Concepts in Geography* (Sage, 2003). She is also a co-editor of two journals: *Gender, Place and Culture* and *Social and Cultural Geography*.

Grzegorz Węcławowicz is Professor and head of the Department of Urban and Population Studies in the Institute of Geography and Spatial Organization of the Polish Academy of Sciences in Warsaw. His current research is on urban issues, particularly during the post-socialist transformation, involving social exclusion and segregation at the regional and intra-urban levels in Poland and Central Europe. He has written one book in English: *Contemporary Poland: Space and Society* (UCL Press, 1996). His most recent book, *Urban Social Geography: The Socio-spatial Differentiation* (PWN, 2002), was published in Polish.

Foreword

Revaz Gachechiladze

Professor of Human Geography, Tbilisi State University
Georgian Ambassador to the State of Israel

From the authors of antiquity we learned that morality and ethics might have a spatial dimension. They sometimes compared their own countries with those of barbarians. And these comparisons always led to the conclusion that the other countries and peoples were without ethics and immoral while the *polis* of the author was a model of ethics and morality!

Leaving aside these not quite fair comparisons of ancient authors, really scientific geographical research on social behaviour, which actually distinguishes societies from each other, began in the last three to four decades of the previous century. And within the constellation of the researchers of such issues the name of David M. Smith is one of the brightest.

I remember well the 1970s, when Western approaches to social geography reached the Soviet Union, where there was a taboo on geographical research on 'non-standard problems'. Soviet people were to be equally happy everywhere, no spatial differences in welfare could exist. Together with some sociologists, we had to overcome a host of obstacles to prove that social problems ought to be studied geographically and to publish the first book in the USSR on the geography of crime. For the young (in those days) geographers the inspiration was provided by the works of Western European and North American authors, David Smith's books not least among them.

Later I met personally with David and understood almost instantly that he is a person who has the right to speak about morality in a way that would not be considered hypocrisy. I knew that David studied certain countries, for instance South Africa under apartheid. My desire was to persuade him to turn my Georgia into a subject of his scientific research. I must confess that efforts in this direction appeared to be futile. But I succeeded in making David Smith a true friend of my country. And we are not alone: David hosted a lot of young scholars from different countries, and helped them to acquire knowledge. Many people are grateful to him.

David first arrived in Georgia together with his unforgettable wife, Margaret, in June 1991. The country had already declared formal independence, but was not yet recognized as such by any state. David and Margaret fearlessly travelled in the Caucasus mountains, steadily becoming rather dangerous in those days. We visited places where one could already feel the heavy breath of forthcoming civil wars. He came to Georgia again, together with a group of British scholars, in 1993 when a civil war was raging in the country. Despite this we managed to start the British–Georgian Geographical Seminars, which actually substituted for the British–Soviet Seminars, continuing in London in 1995. He again visited my country in 1997 to co-organize with me the third such seminar.

The Georgian Geographical Society, which claims its origins from the Caucasian Branch of the Imperial Russian Geographical Society established in 1850 in Tbilisi, Georgia, has bestowed its Honorary Membership upon David Smith, a great scholar, a great friend, a great man.

The fact that this collection, which gathers together articles by the best British and international authors, originated as a tribute to David Smith is no surprise. It would only be surprising if we did not appreciate his most valuable contribution to geography, to which he has added a moral dimension.

Preface

Geographies and Moralities is a set of research essays reflecting on the links between geography, ethics and morality. Although such links are inherent and ever-present, their explicit investigation and reflexive incorporation has, until recently, been surprisingly rare in geographical scholarship. The purpose of this book is, then, to demonstrate this inherency in a wide variety of contexts and so to advance and encourage further critical reflections on its implications for geography.

In this, the book marks and celebrates the achievements and widespread contributions and influence of David M. Smith, who, after four decades of research leadership in human geography, continues to demonstrate and proselytize issues of morality and ethics and so to disrupt certain tacitly accepted norms and to open up a range of research questions and the politics associated with them. This work goes on – arguably with ever more urgency under contemporary global and local geo-economic and geo-political circumstances – and so the book is not a backward-looking assessment but a contribution to an agenda for a more explicitly morally and ethically informed geography in the future.

And in that, the book also points up the centrality of geographical scholarship itself for a credible understanding of the contemporary world. This is a world riven with the consequences of a widespread, even wilful, lack and neglect of geographical understanding of the continuous construction, and subsequent consequence, of difference along a range of interlocking dimensions – both social and environmental.

Thus *Geographies and Moralities* contributes to a range of fundamental questions vital to the sustainability of the contemporary world. It does so in a special way through the contributions of leading scholars who have come together in a collaborative endeavour. This, as much as the substantive individual contributions to the volume, demonstrates the way in which it is not merely academic work that may be sustained through critically empathetic collaboration, but the very making of the geographies and histories through which human life itself is, and may continue to be, developed.

Roger Lee

Acknowledgements

Geographies and Moralities begins and ends with David Smith. He is, quite simply, a wonderful colleague, constantly disrupting the intellectual status quo – and hence thoughts about the political status quo – and engaging others with his thought and argument. This, I take it, is the point of academic work. Typically, this book reflects David's great influence not only in its contribution to the emergence of a field of study but very much in the nitty-gritty of its production.

The countless colleagues, some of whom are contributors to this book, who are, quite remarkably, prepared to persuade – if not to convince – me that whatever contribution I may make to such academic work is worth doing, remain a delightful and selfless source of support. Peter Dicken (and here the book comes doubly full circle) remains a personal and intellectual inspiration.

All the contributors to this book have been more formative than they know. Their constant belief in the project and their will to see it through was both extraordinarily heartening and so effective. Nick Henry was as generous, direct and modest as ever in encouraging a submission to this series of books and then to take the project on. All the anonymous reviewers made very full and highly perceptive comments on the proposal, and I can only apologize for my failing to respond to them in a way fitting of their insight. However, the generous comments made by the anonymous reader of the completed manuscript reflected their earlier sympathetic critiques. The further critically perceptive points made by the reader on individual chapters and on the organization of the book as a whole have enhanced the finished product even further. The shape of the book owes more to reviewers and readers than to anyone. In this creative – but demanding – process, Angela Cohen and her team at Blackwell have combined sympathy and pressure in superbly judged measure. Both editors would like to thank Justin Dyer for his superb work as copy editor.

Finally, the book reflects not only David Smith's wide and ongoing influence in critical human geography but also the unique academic environment created by my colleagues in the Department of Geography at Queen Mary, University of London. It is they, and all their co-workers elsewhere, who will make something of whatever this book has to offer.

Roger Lee
London
June 2004

This volume provides the opportunity to thank some of those who gave me various kinds of assistance over my half-century's involvement with geography. At Solihull School, thanks to Guy King-Reynolds for starting me off; at the University of Nottingham, to Eric Rawstron for showing me the way; at the University of Manchester, to Peter Dicken and Peter Lloyd for helping to shape new directions; at Southern Illinois University, to Don Eggert for my first radical encounters, and to Denis Fair for arousing my interest in development; at the University of Florida, to 'Dick' Dickinson for sharing his ecological and social concerns; and to Bruce Young, Keith Beavon and Ian Douglas, for invitations to join their departments at the Universities of Natal, the Witwatersrand and New England.

Returning to Britain, at Queen Mary, University of London, thanks to Eric Rawstron (again) for supporting my appointment, to subsequent heads of the Department of Geography (Bruce Atkinson, Murray Gray, Philip Ogden, Nigel Spence and Roger Lee), and to other colleagues past and present, for sustaining an academic environment conducive to my independent creative spirit while not neglecting the performance indicators. And I also thank those of my former post-graduate students who fulfilled expectation (including contributors to this volume: Peter Dicken, Jean Hillier and Priscilla Cunnan), along with generations of undergraduates on whom I tested the contents of successive books.

While based at Queen Mary I have been able to take up short-term posts facilitating research in countries that have provided material for case studies. The following are a selection of those to whom I am grateful for providing academic support, research material, friendship and hospitality. In the United States: Sandy Bederman (Georgia State University), for assistance with research in Atlanta; Tom Boswell and Peter Muller (University of Miami), for making me welcome in their department; Jim Proctor (University of California at Santa Barbara), for a fruitful collaboration on geography and ethics. In the former Soviet Union: Mark Bandman and Alexander Novoselov (Economics Institute, Siberian Branch of the

Academy of Sciences), for arranging visits to Akademgorodok; Natasha Barbash, Veniamin Gokhman and Yuri Medvedkov (formerly Geography Institute, Academy of Sciences), for revealing different facets of Moscow; Revaz Gachechiladze, Alex Rondeli (Tbilisi State University) and their colleagues, for making links with Georgia so exciting; Oksana Dmitrieva (St Petersburg University of Economics and Finance), for invitations to what became a favourite city. In Poland: Piotr Korcelli, Grzegorz Węcławowicz, Marek Jerczińsky and their colleagues (Institute of Geography and Spatial Organization, Polish Academy of Sciences), for congenial visits to Warsaw; Sylwia Kaczmarek (University of Łódź), for helping me to see her city; Bolek Domański (Jagiellonian University), for introducing me to Cracow; Iwona Sagan (University of Gdansk), for enabling me to return to Poland. In South Africa: Ron Davies (University of Cape Town), colleagues in various departments at the University of Natal, and Keith Beavon again (Wits), for time in the field and home as well as the office; Brij Maharaj (University of Natal), Dhiru Soni, Vadi Moodley and their colleagues (University of Durban-Westville), for their company and support on repeated visits; Denis Fair again, for many years of regularly renewed friendship; Marie Huchzermeyer and colleagues (School of Architecture and Planning, University of the Witwatersrand) and Gustav Visser (Free State University), for invitations to return after what I thought was my last visit. In Israel: Shlomo Hasson and Arie Shachar (Hebrew University of Jerusalem) and Amiram Gonen (Floersheimer Institute for Policy Studies), Yehuda Gradus, Avinoam Meir, David Newman and Oren Yiftachel (Ben Gurion University of the Negev), and Yoram Bar-Gal and Stanley Waterman (University of Haifa); these and others were generous with their time and hospitality.

My travels have been funded in part by opportunities to teach in host departments. I have also been assisted by grants from the Academic Study Group on Israel and the Middle East, the British Academy, the British Council, the Economic and Social Research Council, the Leverhulme Trust, the Central Research Fund and Hayter Fund of the University of London, and sources within the countries concerned. Thanks to them all.

I am enormously grateful to those who have contributed to this book. They have all enriched my professional life, and I am privileged to consider many of them as friends. I am touched by their generous references to my work, and especially to its influence on theirs. I am particularly grateful that almost all our original selection of authors were able to hang on in there until we found a publisher as distinguished as Blackwell, and that they went on to meet demanding deadlines. As initiator and original sole editor of this book, Roger Lee generously allowed me to share the work, as a finale to thirty years of scholarly association which has been one of the highlights of my time at Queen Mary.

Finally, to members of my family, who often accompanied me on my travels and into the field. Margaret shared so much that our roles were at times inseparable; no conventional form of acknowledgement can convey what she gave me, how she made my life – she was just there, part of us. Margaret met most of the contributors to this volume, at home or abroad, and I am grateful to them all for agreeing the dedication to her memory. My deepest thanks go to Michael (with Paula) and Tracey, for their loving care and support, and for being who they are.

David M. Smith
Loughton, Essex
June 2004

to the memory of

Margaret Smith
1937–2002

I miss her now. Properly. Not with anger, or because I want to avenge or undo the past, but just because I'd like to see her again. I know she's out there somewhere, or perhaps inside, in a place where the air is verdigris. I guess time doesn't mean much where she is, and she'll come back when she's good and ready. Sometimes I think I can feel her, staying playfully out of reach. Getting closer by the minute, building up speed to pull me free.

Tomorrow I'm going to pack a bag and get in the car and drive down the Baja. I'm going to check into Quintas Papagayo, and collect enough drift-wood for a fire, then take a shower and walk into Ensenada. If I start early enough I'll get there while the streets still teem with tourists buying rugs and bangles and pottery animals, and the sky over the harbour is still thick with birds squabbling for scraps of fish: early enough to wander for an hour in a bright afternoon sun which hazes land and sea into one.

Maybe later, as the light begins to change and the crowds thin out, I'll start to feel something, to believe again in nights of shadows and distant shouting. And perhaps as I walk the streets towards Housson's, past the dark store-fronts, I'll find the corner I've always looked for, and turn it, and she'll be there.

Michael Marshall Smith, *One of Us*
(HarperCollins and Bantam Books, 1998, reprinted by permission)

1

Introduction: Geographies of Morality and Moralities of Geography

Roger Lee and David M. Smith

That geography and morality are strongly interconnected may not be immediately apparent. Human geographers have become familiar, over the years, with the subject matter of such disciplines as economics, politics and sociology, with culture also looming large. On the physical side, geology was once an essential foundation for the field, now linked to a range of other environmental sciences. But morality has not attracted anything like the same attention. Indeed, there have been periods in the history of geography when a yearning for scientific status has generated reverence for supposedly value-free objectivity, with any normative inclinations yielding to positivism. Such was the case during the 'quantitative revolution' and the era of human geography as 'spatial science', which preoccupied much of the 1960s and 1970s. And when, some years ago, the then Secretary of State for Education in a British Conservative government (Kenneth Clark) pronounced that geography should be about facts and not opinions, he was reflecting a common understanding of the field as essentially descriptive, as well as perhaps suspicion of the subversive nature of some of the opinions that geographers might hold.

However, as soon as we raise issues like spatial inequality and its social, economic and political consequences, the normative dimension becomes clear. Universal ideals of development and justice may, for example, be reduced to a concern for economic growth, with its attendant problems for those left behind. There is also the more critical issue of normative ethics: to what extent are uneven development and social inequality just? The resolutions of such questions are both reflected in, and constitutive of, the moral values of particular people in particular places. And these particularities both reflect local circumstances and practices and condition the ways in which these have been formed and transformed over time by the mutually interactive relations between 'local' and 'non-local' influences and norms. Thus the reference to pluralities of 'geographies' and 'moralities' in our title expresses the spatial and temporal path dependence, variation and difference in what we mean by geography and morality. Furthermore, a recognition that there are 'moralities of geography', as well as 'geographies of morality', adds to our concerns the normativity of the practice of geography, and of geographers, customarily referred to as professional ethics. What is 'good geography' or a 'good geographer' is not merely a matter of technical virtuosity, theoretical refinement or disciplinary integrity; moral values, such as social relevance and political purchase, are always involved.

As the terms 'ethics' and 'morality' tend to be used rather indiscriminately, often interchangeably, let us be clear about our own understandings at the outset. Put as simply as possible, we distinguish between ethics as moral theory, and morality as practical action (see, for example, Rauche, 1985, pp. 252–3). Thus ethics, as the subject of moral philosophy, involves reflection on moral values, their origin, meaning and justification. Morality refers to what people believe and what they do in pursuit of, or merely as a reflection of, their own conceptions of the right and the good. This distinction would not be endorsed by all moral philosophers, and some of our contributors may work from different understandings. However, it helps to highlight a further aspect of geographical variability: while ethics might claim a broader reach than morality, both can be specific to place (as well as to time), and have to be understood in this context. They are, in short, social constructs.

The Social Construction of Morality in and between Places

The motto of the co-educational grammar school near Manchester, northwest England, in which one of us (Roger Lee) received an education in the latter half of the 1950s and early 1960s was 'manners maketh the man'. In what was a geographically very significant manoeuvre, the motto had been borrowed from William of Wykeham (1324–1404), Bishop of Winchester and founder of Winchester College. This joint derivation – from the discourse of Christianity, often assumed to be centrally concerned with morality, as well as from an ancient and esteemed southern English public school – must have done wonders for the missionary instincts of those who chose the motto. Unfortunately, it seemed to pass by the northern industrial youths, female and male, to whom it was directed, at this particular place and time. Other (im)moral influences tended to prevail.

Nevertheless, Wykeham's motto begins to suggest the significance not merely of moral engagement for social life but also of the geographies and politics through which this is formulated and practised. First, the motto implies that manners are pre-existing things, to be achieved by 'man'. And yet manners, and the morality that they represent, are made by people situated in place and time, and so are geographically and historically constituted. To take a trivial example: for some in France it is rude to sit at the dining table with hands held in laps, whereas in (parts of middle-class) England sitting with elbows on the table is more than likely to be censored. While alternative table manners may appear insignificant compared with, say, differences over human rights or conceptions of social justice, they are aspects of the common concern for a morality in shaping both self-image and attitudes towards others. The behavioural distinctions relate to a culturally differentiated historical geography about which, nevertheless, conversations are possible around the commonalities. The practices reflecting such differences may be criticized, but the right to articulate them is to be defended and the purpose of democratic politics is to enable their free expression as well as debate.

Secondly, the story of the school motto points to a normative notion of moralizing: of defining norms to which individuals, aspiring to be good or right, should conform. It points, in short, to the very process of social construction exemplified by questions of etiquette such as table manners. One reading of such moralizing would be dismissive, reducing it to preferred patterns of socialization to which the moralizers would wish to subject the masses, whether school children or the population at large. However, while extra-terrestrial authority may sometimes be imputed, morals are socially constructed and, as such, are constituted in the geographies through which they take place. They may chime with the aspirations of people in particular places, or they may be challenged, rejected and replaced. Supposedly universal notions of morality, like those sometimes associated with development and justice, are constantly reshaped on the stubborn anvil of geographical practice and particularity.

Thirdly, the story raises the question of the relationship between moralities and human being. The capacities to think normatively and to imagine are widely regarded as distinguishing humans from other forms of animate life (and from its electronic competitors, clever at dynamic and responsive learning though they may be). The questioning as well as the practice of what are intrinsically contested moral values is an inescapable part of being human. This is why a state of a-morality is so difficult to imagine. Moral thought is both pervasive, even if often only implicitly, and overriding, or frequently taken to be – at least in defence of social action. Further, the existence and constant transformation of geographies and temporalities of moralities reveals less a form of moral relativism than the universality of the profound influence of geography and time on how human beings understand their lives, and what they make of them. That the ethics devised in the process can itself be time- and place-specific is illustrated by such expressions as 'ancient' and 'Enlightenment' ethics, and in the distinction sometimes made between 'Anglo-American' and 'continental' philosophy. This specificity is also revealed in the great ethical traditions featured in Blackwell's *A Companion to Ethics* (Singer, 1991), for example, which include Indian and Chinese ethics as well as those associated with Buddhism, Judaism, Christianity and Islam – all of which have their own distinctive geography.

Reasserting the Normative

As the final decade of the twentieth century dawned, Francis Fukuyama (1992) famously pronounced 'the end of history', with the demise of socialism leaving liberal capitalism triumphant. But in a world in which some see the contingencies of geography as well as of history finally resolved, through neoliberal economic and political practice and the un-problematic effects of globalization, issues of morality and ethics become increasingly significant. Capitalist social relations are indeed becoming universalized, but there is no equivalent universalization of development and justice beyond those embedded in capitalism, declarations of universal human rights notwithstanding. The reality is of an increasingly differenti-ated world, in the sense of unequal life chances at the local, national and global scales, and of growing fragmentation into sharply divided peoples and places.

There are at least two broad and related implications of this increasing significance of normative issues. One is the question of politics. If all the world really is becoming the same, and human life individualized, what is the basis for political engagement rather than disillusionment with politics? Connected to this is the problematic construction of political-economic difference in a world allegedly converging on a universally accepted set of norms, and the consequent appeal to such reputedly timeless values as community and family, and to identity – often defined in terms of brands, for example, and capable of construction through market transactions. And yet, questions of difference still give rise to major social and geo-political conflicts whilst, paradoxically, morality and ethics are often utilized as unproblematic (i.e. given, unquestioned and universally agreed) in certain forms of political rhetoric, whereas they are both highly contextualized social constructs. For Chantal Mouffe (1998) these issues of difference and of unproblematic ethics and moralities are related. She argues that antagonism is inherent in social relations and so, even if the world has been geographically flattened or historically 'ended', politics is still concerned primarily with conflict. There can be no 'third way'.

The second question is that of universalism vs particularism. Is cultural difference still a justification for the differentiation of moral norms, or are some kinds of behaviour beyond the pale anywhere and everywhere? We may accept distinctive table manners and certain other customs as part of a local or national culture, but hardly the torture of prisoners or the exclusion of women from public life. And, again relatedly, how is the increasing material significance of moral or ethical evaluation, and of inequality, connected to the resolution of questions of economic organization, reproduction and development, and political-economic practice? The relationships between universalism and particularism have, in one guise or another, teased geography and geographers throughout the intellectual history of the discipline. But the distinction is inescapable for consideration of ethical and moral issues – as it is in all attempts to understand social relations – because it refers to the extent to which the differences between human beings should enter into moral judgements by them, and about them, and into the practices to which these judgements give rise.

The truth of descriptive ethical relativism or particularism – that moral values vary from place to place, as well as from time to time – is too obvious to require much illustration. Taking a topical British example, some people in the countryside approve of fox-hunting, while others elsewhere find it morally objectionable. Bull-fighting is part of Spanish culture, but torturing animals to death for public entertainment strikes people in many other countries as wrong. More generally, such frequently asserted human rights as free speech and freedom from hunger are taken more seriously in some countries than others. The different emphasis given to different moral values is reflected in institutional arrangements. Thus, the United States has a Bill of Rights upholding individual liberty, which some would like Britain to emulate, but it has no welfare state; Britain still has a National Health Service available to all irrespective of ability to pay, which is envied by some Americans but stigmatized by others as 'socialized medicine'.

However, some moral values might appear to be universal. Such human virtues as honesty, courage and care are valued in all societies. Their particular manifestations may vary from place to place and time to time, but it is hard to imagine a society functioning for long if its people were dishonest, cowardly and uncaring. A version of the so-called 'Golden Rule' of treating others as one would wish to be treated is found in virtually all the world's major ethico-religious traditions. But even this requires a context, a process of people coming to terms with living together in mutually supportive social relations, theologians or philosophers capable of systematizing and propagating such a rule, and a politics and set of institutions able to translate these social ideas into practice. As Jürgen Habermas (1990, p. 208) explains, moral universalism is itself 'a historical result'. We might add that it also arose in a particular geographical context, of an expanding 'known' world carrying unequal power relations, in which parochial partiality no longer provided an adequate ethical basis for social relations involving ever more distant and different others. More topically, population movement within the expanding European Community will test to the limit universalist expectations of the right to seek work and social security. The right to change one's place by crossing international borders is fiercely contested in the contemporary world of sharply differentiated life chances and rising national chauvinism; it remains the right we are not ready for (Nett, 1971). Again, both geography and history are involved, in the discourse which has turned the once welcomed political 'asylum seeker' into a pariah.

Geography's Moralities

The implications of these kind of features of moral discourse and construction for such social practices as development and justice are the prime subject matter of this book. The disciplinary context within which we write is that of a strong (re)engagement of geography with normative issues in recent years, involving what has been referred to as a 'moral turn' (Smith, 1997). The first substantial challenges to geography's prevailing positivist orientation came in the aftermath of the quantitative revolution, most powerfully in the exploration of social justice by David Harvey (1973) and of values in geography by Annette Buttimer (1974). A resurgence of the humanist tradition brought further contributions, notably treatments of morality and the good life by Yi-Fu Tuan (1986, 1989). The revitalization of cultural and social geography has had a distinctively normative tone, including arguments for the application of a 'moral lens' to human geography and for (re)connecting its inquiries to moral philosophy (Philo, 1991). The notion of 'moral geographies' ('landscapes' or 'locations') as a rubric for a distinctive kind of thick descriptive ethics has subsequently attracted much attention (Smith, 2000, pp. 45-53). The 1990s saw the return of social justice to the geographical agenda (Smith, 1994; Harvey, 1996), while Robert Sack (1997) has made morality central to his exposition of *homo geographicus* and to his understanding of place (Sack, 2003).

Philo's injunction to engage moral philosophy was given substance by the first edited collection of papers exploring the interface of geography and ethics (Proctor and Smith, 1999). This was followed by one of these editors' book examining some of the implications for ethics of the geographer's world of difference, considering the moral significance of those familiar geographical concepts of landscape, location and place, proximity and distance, space and territory, along with justice, development and nature (Smith, 2000). Links between geography and political philosophy were explicit in discussions of development ethics (e.g. Corbridge, 1998). Connections were also made with environmental ethics (Light and Smith,

1997). These and other concerns have also been reflected in, for example, the content of the journal *Ethics, Place and Environment*, as well as in longer-established periodicals (see, for example, reviews in *Progress in Human Geography*).

Of course, geography did not discover ethics in intellectual isolation. There has been a normative turn in the social sciences at large (Sayer and Storper, 1997), impacting on economics, political science and sociology, as well as in such hybrid fields as cultural, urban and development studies. This itself reflects a growing range of issues challenging the contemporary world, in which the pace of technical innovations seems constantly to be outstripping advances in the ethical understanding required, literally, to evaluate humankind's increasingly complex interaction with nature as well as changing social relations. Talk of moral crisis hardly seems exaggerated. That geography is central to so many contemporary concerns crying out for fresh ethical thinking with a sharp critical edge is part of the motivation for this book.

Geographies and Moralities

Through the medium of a series of studies drawn from across the broad field of human geography, and from an international range of local contexts, this book addresses a number of issues related to development, justice and place.

1 If moralities are inescapable, distinctions like those between positive and normative thought start to look distinctly chaotic. Even the choice of subjects for such thoughts are exposed to moral pressures emanating from a variety of sources: cultural, economic, political and social. It was not chance or whim which shifted the attention of human geographers from location theory to social justice in the era of so-called 'radical geography', and to such issues as race, gender, disability and sexuality more recently. Similarly, the increasing importance of qualitative as opposed to quantitative research methods has an ethical dimension

2 Moralities are profoundly geographical products of the uneven development of social relations among people and between people and nature. Such differentiations, the distinctions that they both reflect and induce, and the tensions that are created through them, together constitute the very source of moralities. Moralities are, in short, constructed through geographically articulated social interaction. The interesting questions which arise here concern not so much the distinction between the 'moral' and the 'immoral', but how 'moral' and 'immoral' come to be defined, practised and reproduced in distinctive ways across space and time. Thus the transcendence of, or retreat towards, forms of nationalism or more local

partiality (e.g. ethnic chauvinism) raises profoundly geographical questions about the nature of human being and how it may be constructed.

3 The ways in which moralities are both constituted through economic, political and social processes and shape the nature of such processes raise questions around the complex and multifaceted nature of these influences upon social life and how they are themselves formatively related to each other. The growing realization, within the social and natural sciences and the humanities, that the economic, the social, the cultural and the natural are inseparable extends even more forcefully and formatively to include the moral and the ethical. Nevertheless, these various domains of human action cannot be reduced completely to each other. There is, therefore, an important issue here of the extent and nature of over-determination in understanding the complex and mutually formative relationships between the 'economic' and the 'cultural', for example, or between the ethical and the social.

4 The transformation of issues of social (in)justice into matters of social exclusion implies an unquestioned norm (the condition from which exclusion is sustained), rather than a contested process which may be judged by certain criteria to be just or unjust. A discourse of social exclusion, which posits as a universal a set of circumstances and relationships that are in fact a highly particular form of social life, serves to sustain and enhance existing inequalities of power around what are represented as unproblematic norms. For example, the reminder by Michael Walzer (1983, p. 105) of Lee Rainwater's axiom that money buys membership of industrial society invites reflection on the normativity as well as the sociology of the kind of commodity fetishism which inevitably excludes people lacking, literally, purchasing power. And the generalization of social exclusion that puts paid to other forms of alterity is a wider implication of the unproblematic normalization of the increasingly insistent ethics of neoliberalism (see, for example, Leyshon, Lee and Williams, 2003).

Debates and conflicts over questions of morality and ethics are not a mere product of millennial angst. Rather, they inform the very nature of the human condition. Furthermore, as argued above, the nature of morality and ethics is itself profoundly related to geography and difference. This book, written by an international range of authors working in and on five continents, sets out to explore ways in which geographically shaped questions of ethics, morality and justice infuse social interaction and development in a variety of contexts. As such, it is concerned less with arguing the case for the inclusion of moral and ethical considerations in the scholarly understanding of spatial relations (not least as such a case has been made elsewhere: Proctor and Smith, 1999; Smith, 2000), than with demonstrating the inseparability of ethics, morals and geography in a variety of situations.

Specifically, the individual chapters are, in their own contexts of moralities and geographies, intended to allow a focus on the specifics of circumstance. In this way, they may address the complex issues involved in the interplay between the constraints of relations of power in the constructions of moralities, and the tensions between intrinsic notions of morality – with associated claims of universality – and human difference. Each chapter is written by an author who has been obliged to engage with moral and ethical issues in the substantive work in which she or he is engaged. This raises issues of both personal and professional ethics, not as incidental but as central to the reflexive practice of scholarship.

Structure of the Text

Within the framework outlined above, the contributors have exercised freedom to address aspects of development, justice and place as they wished. Each chapter is quite capable of standing on its own, and speaking for itself. While we have hesitated to impose our own editorial structure on the contributions as written, the arrangement of chapters under five broad headings indicates our sense of their coherence, further drawn out in short introductions to each part of the book. The sequence runs through the central issues of development, justice and place (Parts I, II and III), on to the conduct of research (Part IV), and concludes with the moral context of professional practice (Part V).

Part I provides illustrations of moral geographies of uneven development, at different geographical scales – global, European, national and intra-national. Peter Dicken points to the complex, interrelated forces determining 'who gets what *where* and how' in the changing global economic map, resulting in uneven development at the international scale and within countries. Nigel Spence explores contradictions between uneven development among national and regional economies in the European Union (EU) and the policy urge for convergence and cohesion; eastward expansion of the EU raises important moral issues, concerned with what the new Europe should be like. In the first of two contributions from Eastern Europe, Bolesław Domański criticizes the image of East-Central Europe as a morally, culturally and politically inferior periphery of Western Europe, pointing to some fallacies in research on post-socialist societies and arguing that the periphery should be included in a common European future. Grzegorz Węcławowicz draws on Polish experience to consider uneven development at the regional and intra-urban scale, in conditions of societal transformation; he asks whether Poland's accession to European integration will enhance social and spatial justice, in the sense of smoothing rather than further sharpening disparities in living conditions.

Part II moves on to issues of distribution: social justice, welfare and human rights. Sarah Curtis considers the relationship between social exclusion, health and health care, in the context of the National Health Service (NHS) in England, elaborating the problems posed by inequalities involving particular population groups. Susan Smith and Donna Easterlow challenge neoliberal critics of welfare, pointing out that the tendency for welfare-state solutions to poverty to be replaced by market-based policies is leading to more unequal societies. Moving on to rights, Rex Honey uses Nigeria as an illustration of cultural struggles over human rights and the question of scale in moral geography, against a background of colonial rule, post-colonial military government and contemporary forces of globalization. Avery Kolers explains that rights to land, or the just distribution of territory, require approaches which recognize how people relate to land in ways which defy the crude calculations of the market. Shlomo Hasson provides an illustration of conflict over space, in the city of Jerusalem, where the problem is how to resolve apparently irreconcilable moral-political claims to the same territory. Brij Maharaj considers rights to land in South Africa, following dispossession on a racial basis under apartheid. He argues that land restitution is an opportunity to heal scars from the past.

Part III provides cases of moral practice deeply embedded in particular places, their culture and material conditions. Stuart Corbridge takes queueing (or waiting in line) as a quintessentially geographical phenomenon ordering time and space; cultural differences may be observed in the practice of queue-jumping, but he prefers an interpretation which recognizes the production of scarcity in the economic and political realms. Gill Valentine discusses the role of the school as a place in which young people learn about sexuality; she goes on to examine the attempt of the Scottish parliament to repeal legislation which bans the promotion of homosexuality in schools, showing how protagonists have drawn on different moral discourses about Scottishness to argue their cases. Jean Hillier challenges traditional theoretical approaches to local land-use planning, which suggest that officers make technical recommendations to elected representatives who take neutral decisions; evidence from Western Australia reveals the local communicative behaviours involved in planning decision-making practice.

Part IV addresses issues of research method and practice which arise when geography engages with ethics. We deliberately juxtapose two rather different contributions, one theoretical and the other applied, connected by recognition of the significance and demands of qualitative research. William Lynn explains that causal explanation in human geography cannot depend on models and measurement alone; it must apprehend the meanings embodied in human agency, which requires qualitative inquiry.

He argues that this is an indispensable element of the metatheoretical rationale for ethics as an internal and legitimate endeavour of geography. Priscilla Cunnan provides an illustration of ethically informed research, involving methods which required carefully considered interaction with people whose lives she wished to understand, consistent with an underlying ethic of concern and respect for them.

In Part V, two concluding chapters consider moral context and professional practice. Ron Johnston explains that David Smith's career as a professional geographer covers four turbulent decades during which the nature of the discipline was the subject of much debate and contestation. David's own career trajectory mirrors these, and an evaluation of the influence of external forces on him, and of his influence on the discipline, provides insight into these events. Finally, David Smith himself considers his journey, from location theory to moral philosophy. If there is anything to give this coherence, it is an abiding concern with the normative, with the role of scholarship in seeking to identify and to create a better world; hence the focus of this volume.

REFERENCES

Buttimer, A. (1974) *Values in Geography*, Commission on College Geography, Resource Paper 24, Washington, DC: Association of American Geographers.

Corbridge, S. (1998) 'Development ethics: distance, difference, plausibility', *Ethics, Place and Environment* 1, 35–53.

Fukuyma, F. (1992) *The End of History and the Last Man*, London: Penguin Books.

Habermas, J. (1990) *Moral Consciousness and Communicative Action* (trans. C. Lenhardt and S. W. Nicholsen), Cambridge: Polity Press.

Harvey, D. (1973) *Social Justice and the City*, London: Edward Arnold.

Harvey, D. (1996) *Justice, Nature and the Geography of Difference*, Oxford: Blackwell.

Leyshon, A., Lee, R. and Williams, C. (eds) (2003) *Alternative Economic Spaces*, London: Sage.

Light, A. and Smith, J. M. (eds) (1997) *Space, Place, and Environmental Ethics, Philosophy and Geography* 1, London: Rowman and Littlefield.

Mouffe, C. (1998) 'The radical centre: a politics without adversary', *Soundings* 9, 11–23.

Nett, R. (1971) 'The civil right we are not ready for: the right of free movement of people on the face of the earth', *Ethics* 81, 212–27.

Philo, C. (compiler) (1991) *New Words, New Worlds: Reconceptualising Social and Cultural Geography*, Lampeter: Department of Geography, St David's University College.

Proctor, J. D. and Smith, D. M. (eds) (1999) *Geography and Ethics: Journeys in a Moral Terrain*, London: Routledge.

Rauche, G. V. (1985) *Theory and Practice in Philosophical Argument*, Durban: Institute for Social and Economic Research, University of Durban-Westville.

Sack, R. D. (1997) *Homo Geographicus: A Framework for Action, Awareness, and Moral Concern*, Baltimore and London: Johns Hopkins University Press.

Sack, R. D. (2003) *A Geographical Guide to the Real and the Good*, New York and London: Routledge.

Sayer, A. and Storper, M. (1997) 'Ethics unbound: for a normative turn in social theory', *Environment and Planning D: Society and Space* 15, 1–17.

Singer, P. (ed.) (1991) *A Companion to Ethics*, Oxford: Blackwell.

Smith, D. M. (1994) *Geography and Social Justice*, Oxford: Blackwell.

Smith, D. M. (1997) 'Geography and ethics: a moral turn?', *Progress in Human Geography* 21, 583–90.

Smith, D. M. (2000) *Moral Geographies: Ethics in a World of Difference*, Edinburgh: Edinburgh University Press.

Tuan, Y-F. (1986) *The Good Life*, Madison, Wis.: University of Wisconsin Press.

Tuan Y-F. (1989) *Morality and Imagination: Paradoxes of Progress*, Madison, Wis.: University of Wisconsin Press.

Walzer, M. (1983) *Spheres of Justice: A Defence of Pluralism and Equality*, Oxford: Blackwell.

Part I

Moral Geographies of Uneven Development

Uneven development has been a prominent theme in geography for more than a quarter of a century. Development is a deeply normative concept, closely connected with conceptions of human good, or how we should live on planet Earth. But the active processes of development and underdevelopment – and, indeed, their very definitions – are reflections of social norms. These are incorporated, consciously or unconsciously, into the conduct of social life, and necessarily embody certain ethical positions and moral practices. The frequent failure in analyses of uneven development to recognize the power of social relations, through which norms are set and practised, reduces development to a purely positive rather than a normative concept.

Similarly, the identification of development problems, and the practice of development planning, often tends to be largely a technical exercise, with underlying moral values left implicit. For example, it may be assumed that the state of development can be measured in material terms, with development as a process defined by the prefix 'economic'. Insofar as social structure and culture are concerned, it is frequently assumed that 'underdeveloped' countries are impeded by their own ways of life, and that they need to 'modernize' or 'Westernize'. That value judgements are involved in these positions is obvious, hence the interest in development ethics in recent years. Old hands have recognized the importance of moral issues (e.g. Friedmann, 1992), and links have been forged with environmental ethics in such contexts as sustainable development (Smith, 2000, Chapters 8 and 9).

The four contributions in this part of the book cover various moral aspects of uneven development, at different spatial scales. Peter Dicken (Chapter 2) begins with the global economy, pointing out that it generates both 'goods' (like employment, income and access to products and services) and 'bads' (like unemployment, poverty and environmental pollution). It also generates 'winners' and 'losers', because the goods and bads are unequally distributed. He recognizes that global inequalities are a moral outrage – often made more outrageous by their reduction to distributions and patterns – thereby raising the question of what the future *should* be like, and how such a vision might be achieved.

One possible route is through imaginative and practically effective political action. For example, the Treaty of Rome, which established the European Economic Community in 1958, set out as its task to improve throughout the Community harmonious development of economic activities, along with a continuous and balanced expansion. However, focusing on uneven development in what became the European Union (EU), Nigel Spence (Chapter 3) identifies a north-western core and a periphery comprising the less successful post-socialist economies. The aspiration of convergence and cohesion among the European economies as the EU is enlarged confronts evidence that the tendency appears to be one of divergence, or increasing inequality among countries and regions. The issues raised include the moral responsibility of the richer countries to assist those that are less well founded. And this responsibility is the more pressing in that the process of European integration over the past twenty years or so has involved the choice between, and subsequent interpretation and practice of, very different forms of social relations.

Thus, in Chapter 4, Bolesław Domański suggests that the perception of East-Central Europe (ECE) as a peripheral post-socialist wilderness involves a discourse of moral superiority on the part of the Western European core. The view that ECE should take Western Europe as a development model is reminiscent of the way the modernization perspective has been applied to the Third World. Domański accepts the empirical reality of ECE as poor in terms of economic development, but challenges the broader image of moral, cultural and political inferiority. His interpretation recognizes tensions between residual egalitarian values inherited from socialism, solidarity forged in opposition, and the competitive individualism intrinsic to capitalism.

Domański refers to the shock of multifaceted transformation, to which East-Central Europe has been exposed. In Chapter 5, Grzegorz Węcławowicz describes some of the outcomes in Poland, in terms of the winners and losers to which Dicken draws attention. Evidence for the scale and distribution of poverty among regions and within cities highlights particular localized population groups which have become disproportionately victims of poverty and social exclusion, along with the emergence of a new rich, with implications for social stability as well as for social justice. The question arises as to whether, within the state of civil society, there can emerge institutions and practices capable of moralizing the new political-economic order and so construct relations of cooperation and mutuality from the strongly individualistic reaction to the supersession of state socialism. The changing nature of such institutions and practices is the focus of Part II of the book.

REFERENCES

Friedmann, J. (1992) *Empowerment: The Politics of Alternative Development*, Oxford: Blackwell.

Smith D. M. (2000) *Moral Geographies: Ethics in a World of Difference*, Edinburgh: Edinburgh University Press.

2

Globalization, Production and the (Im)morality of Uneven Development

Peter Dicken

Introduction

The intrinsic geographical unevenness of development and social well-being has been a recurring theme in David Smith's academic work. Thirty years ago, in developing his 'welfare approach' to human geography, he identified the key geographical question as 'Who gets what *where* and how?' (Smith, 1974). His 1979 book, *Where the Grass is Greener: Living in an Unequal World*, mapped various dimensions of inequality at different geographical scales, foreshadowing today's interest in multi-scalar processes and outcomes. This chapter is written very much in that spirit, but within the context of contemporary globalization debates. It is a chapter, therefore, written in the discourse of a 'globalizing' world but which does not attribute causality to 'globalization'.[1] As Hay and Marsh (2000, p. 10) argue,

> ... the concept of globalization may give the impression of explanation, but it cannot in itself explain anything. It is in fact merely to redescribe, and to redescribe in the most imprecise and obscurantist terms at that, the object of our attentions. It is in short a redescription masquerading as an explanation. As such, our critical hackles should rise whenever globalization is appealed to as a causal factor.

Undoubtedly, there are major transformative forces at work reshaping the global economic map and, in the process, determining 'who gets what *where* and how'. But they are extremely complex, interrrelated forces. Globalization, in fact, is a *syndrome* of processes and outcomes (Dicken, Peck and Tickell, 1997; Mittelman 2000) that are manifested very unevenly in both time and space. It is neither an inevitable, all-pervasive, homogenizing end-state nor is it unidirectional and irreversible. It is certainly not deterministic. As Hart (2001, p. 655) argues, it is not 'unfolding teleology or immanent process, but ... multiple, non-linear interconnected *trajectories*'.

The chapter is organized into three major sections. In the first section, current developments in the geographies of production are briefly outlined. In the second section, some key aspects of the resulting unevenness of development at the global scale are described. In the third section of the chapter, some of the major current debates on the social implications of 'globalization' are explored, particularly from the perspective of the poorest countries in the world.

Changing Geographies of Production

Despite the claims of sceptics like Hirst and Thompson (1999), there have, indeed, been very substantial quantitative and qualitative changes in the global economy, which have created a significantly different situation from that which prevailed in the late nineteenth and early twentieth centuries. Most of all, it is changes in the *how*, as well as in the *where*, of the material production of goods and services that demonstrate the kinds of transformations that are taking place. The major difference is in the *nature* and the *degree* of integration and in its primary drivers. There has been both a *stretching* and an *intensification* of economic relationships (Held, McGrew, Goldblatt and Perraton, 1999, p. 15). International economic integration before 1914 – and even until only about four decades ago – was essentially *shallow* integration, manifested largely through arm's-length trade in goods and services between independent firms and through international movements of portfolio capital and relatively simple direct investment. Today, we live in a world in which *deep integration*, organized primarily within and between geographically extensive and complex transnational production networks and through a diversity of mechanisms, is becoming increasingly pervasive.

These developments are the result of complex interactions between transnational corporations (TNCs), states and technological change. TNCs, as capitalist enterprises, are constantly seeking ways of reducing costs, increasing sales and, therefore, enhancing their profitability. In that framework, they see the world as their oyster. But their ability to expand geographically, to take advantage of geographical differences in the cost and availability of resources (in the broadest sense) and to switch and re-switch their operations between locations is constrained – or facilitated – by the actions of states. They are constrained by regulations that inhibit entry to national spaces or impose rules of operation on firms located there. They are facilitated by processes of de-regulation (of trade, of ownership of assets) and of enticements to firms to relocate. Finally, of course, techno-logical changes have been significant *enabling* factors, especially those which transform time-space relationships and those which allow produc-tion processes to be fragmented and reorganized geographically. The result is the increasing salience of *global production networks* (GPNs):

> ... the nexus of interconnected functions and operations through which goods and services are produced, distributed and consumed ... [have] ... become both organizationally more complex and also increasingly global in their geographical extent. Such networks not only integrate firms (and parts of firms) into structures which blur traditional organizational boundaries ... but also integrate national economies (or parts of such economies) in ways which have enormous implications for their well-being. (Henderson, Dicken, Hess, Coe and Yeung, 2002, pp. 445–6)

The result has been a significant reshaping of the global economic map, especially during the half-century since the end of the Second World War in 1945. Although the world economy continues to be dominated by a small group of 'core' economies, there have been substantial global shifts in production, trade and investment. Such shifts, however, have been geo-graphically selective and, therefore, extremely uneven. At the global scale, only a small number of developing countries have experienced really sig-nificant economic growth. The most spectacular cases, of course, are the newly industrializing economies (NIEs) of East Asia, including, most recently, the truly potential giant, China. Notwithstanding the effects of the financial crisis of the late 1990s, the East Asian region undoubtedly represented the biggest single geographical change in the global economy during the twentieth century. In comparison, the experience of most other developing countries (with a few exceptions) has been far less favourable. Most notably, of course, Africa remains the world's biggest and most intractable problem region.

'Goods' and 'Bads', 'Winners' and 'Losers' in the Global Economy

The processes of production, distribution and consumption generate both 'goods' and 'bads'. They produce 'goods' in the form of employment opportunities, incomes and access to an increasing variety of consumer products, services and cultural artefacts. They also produce 'bads' in the form of unemployment, poverty, resource depletion, environmental pollu-tion and cultural damage. The extent to which the 'goods' exceed the 'bads' is a contested issue, as is the issue of who are the 'winners' and who are the 'losers',[2] because such goods and bads are, themselves, highly unequally distributed both geographically and socially.

To those with a Panglossian[3] view of the world (essentially the neo-liberals), the answer is straightforward:

> Globalization is a savage process, but it is also a *beneficial one, in which the number of winners far outnumbers that of the losers.* (Micklethwait and Wooldridge, 2000, p. ix, emphasis added)

To its critics, the effects are very different:

> Today, when we hear or read about the global economy, it is usually in terms of the trillions of dollars of goods, services, and investment that circle the planet, with the great increases in national wealth that accrue to states that adopt open policies. But there are other data that usually go unnoticed in these discussions. We hear less about the 100 million citizens in the industrial countries who are classified as living below the poverty line. We hear less about the 35 million in these same countries who are unemployed. We hear less about growing income inequality. And we hear still less about the 1.3 billion people in the developing world whose income level is under $1 per day. For all these people, the global economy has not yet brought either material gifts or the hope of a better life. (Kapstein, 1999, p. 16)

Nevertheless, it is certainly true that the growth of the global economy during the past few decades has dramatically increased the material well-being of many people. This should certainly not be forgotten amidst the clamour of anti-globalization rhetoric. But the evidence does not support the assertion that 'the number of winners far outnumbers that of the losers'. On the contrary. Geographically, the contours of the geo-economic map show a landscape of great unevenness and irregularity; a landscape of staggeringly high peaks of affluence and deep troughs of deprivation interspersed with plains of greater or lesser degrees of prosperity. The development gap is stunningly wide. The United Nations Development Programme (UNDP, 1999, p. 3) shows that, by the end of the 1990s, the 20 per cent of the world's population living in the highest income countries had:

- 86 per cent of world GDP – the bottom 20 per cent had only 1 per cent of world GDP;
- 82 per cent of world export markets – the bottom 20 per cent just 1 per cent;
- 68 per cent of foreign direct investment – the bottom 20 per cent had just 1 per cent;
- 74 per cent of world telephone lines – the bottom 20 per cent had just 1.5 per cent.

The contours of world poverty

There are good reasons for seeing poverty as a deprivation of basic capabilities, rather than merely as low income. Deprivation of elementary capabilities
can be reflected in premature mortality, significant undernourishment (especially of children), persistent morbidity, widespread illiteracy and other
failures.

Sen, *Development as Freedom* (1999), p. 20

Not only is the development gap stunningly wide but also it has been
getting wider. Despite considerable advances in some parts of the world,
one in five people (around 1.2 billion) live on less than $1 per day. Nearly
70 per cent of these utterly impoverished people live in South Asia and
Sub-Saharan Africa. Of course, that doesn't mean that no country has
improved its position. Some – especially in East Asia – certainly have.
The number of people in East Asia and the Pacific living on less than
$1 per day fell by around 140 million between 1987 and 1998.

In general, however, the winners – and the losers – have been the usual
suspects. The already affluent developed countries have sustained – even
increased – their affluence, some developing countries have made very
significant progress, but there is a hard core of exceptionally poor countries
that remains stranded. Most strikingly, it is the countries of Sub-Saharan
Africa and parts of South Asia which have benefited least. In both cases, the
number of people living on less than $1 per day increased very substantially.
In social terms, the clear winners are the elite transnational capitalist class.
While transnational elites are clear winners, women – at least in many parts
of the world – tend to be losers in the global economy. Of the 1.2 billion
people living on less than $1 per day, a staggering two-thirds are women.

The major source of income (for all but the exceptionally wealthy) is
employment, or self-employment. A key factor in poverty, therefore, is
availability of work. Hence, the question of 'where will the jobs come
from?' is a crucial one throughout the world. People strive to make a living
in a whole variety of ways: for example, exchanging self-grown crops or
basic handcrafted products; providing personal services in the big cities;
working on the land, in factories, or in offices as paid employees; running
their own businesses as self-employed entrepreneurs, and so on. For the
overwhelming majority of people, employment (full- or part-time or as self-
employment) is the most important source of income. However, not only
are there not enough jobs 'to go round' – one estimate from the mid-1990s
suggested that 400 million new jobs will need to have been created by 2006
just to absorb newcomers to the labour market (FIET, 1996, p. 16) – but

also the volatility of employment opportunities appears to be increasing. At the end of 2000, there were approximately 160 million people unemployed in the world economy (and this figure refers only to 'open' unemployment – it does not include the millions of people suffering from 'hidden' unemployment who are not measured in the official figures).

Developed countries in the global economy: increasing affluence – but not everybody is a winner

At a global scale the developed countries in general are clearly 'winners' in the global economy. They continue to contain a disproportionate share of the world's wealth, trade, investment and access to modern technologies. But, if we refocus our lens to look at what is happening *within* the developed world, we find wide variations in economic well-being, both between and within individual countries, even though most people in developed countries are significantly better off than in the past.

Throughout the long economic boom of the 1960s and early 1970s, there was both a progressive increase in incomes in developed countries and a general reduction in the income gap between the top and bottom segments of the population. For the first twenty-five years or so after the Second World War, the general trend was for the earnings gap between the top and the bottom segments of the labour force to narrow whilst, at the same time, the overall level of per capita income increased substantially. In other words, most people became better off. This is no longer the case, especially in the United States but also in the United Kingdom.

In 1995, the ratio of the earnings of the highest 10 per cent of the labour force to that of the lowest 10 per cent rose in the United States from 3.2 to 4.4 and in the United Kingdom from 2.4 to 3.4. The average income of the top 5 per cent of US households was roughly seven times that of the bottom 40 per cent of households in the early 1970s. In the mid-1990s, the top 5 per cent earned on average ten times more than the bottom 40 per cent. As in the case of employment, it is the less-skilled workers who have been most adversely affected. The pattern is more mixed across other industrialized countries. The same degree of increasing income dispersion within the labour force has not occurred in many of the continental European countries. In some cases, indeed, the gap has narrowed rather than widened. On the other hand, these countries have experienced much higher levels of unemployment than the United States in particular and even the United Kingdom. This suggests that labour market adjustments are occurring in different ways in different countries. In the United States and the United Kingdom adjustment has been primarily in the form of a relative lowering of wages at the bottom of the scale and a consequent *increase in income inequality.* In Western Europe, on the other hand, such wage levels may have been maintained at the expense of jobs with an increase in unemployment.

Developing countries in the global economy: some winners – but mostly losers

The position of the developing countries in the global economy is, to some extent, the obverse of that of the developed countries. Developing countries as a whole contain a disproportionately small share of the world's wealth, trade, investment and access to modern technologies (especially of information technologies). But if we refocus our lens to look at what is happening *within* the developing world, we find wide variations in economic well-being particularly between the relatively small number of countries that have grown spectacularly, and become highly integrated into the global economy, and the majority which remain, to varying degrees, marginalized, at least in terms of the benefits of globalization.

The success stories are confined to a relatively small number of developing countries. The spectacular economic growth of the NIEs of East Asia has been one of the most significant developments in the post-war world economy. In particular, the first generation East Asian NIEs 'succeeded in industrializing and joining the ranks of middle-income, emerging market countries in the span of 30 years. This is a performance unmatched in the 19th and 20th centuries by Western countries and, for that matter, by Latin American economies' (Ito, 2001, p.77). The spread of the growth processes to encompass some other East Asian countries during the 1980s and 1990s has meant that

> already, in little more than a generation, hundreds of millions of people have been lifted out of abject poverty, and many of these are now well on their way to enjoying the sort of prosperity that has been known in North America and Western Europe for some time. . . . While some groups have been obliged to bear the negative consequences of development far more than others . . . it seems clear that the development project in the Asia-Pacific region holds out the promise of a scale of generalized prosperity unknown in human history. (Henderson, 1998, pp. 356–7)

At the other end of the spectrum, the poorest sixty or so developing countries are poor not just in terms of income but also in virtually every other aspect of material well-being. They are the countries of the deepest poverty. There is no single explanation for the deep poverty of low-income countries. But in the context of the global economy, one factor is extremely important: an over-dependence on a very narrow economic base together with adverse conditions of trade. The overwhelming majority of the labour force in low-income countries is employed in agriculture. This, together with the extraction of other primary products, forms the basis of these countries' involvement in the world economy. Approximately 80 per cent of the exports of developing countries are of primary products compared with less than 25 per cent for the developed economies. Although the terms of trade do indeed fluctuate over time, there is no doubt that they have generally and systematically deteriorated for the non-oil primary-producing countries over many years.

A second problem facing the world's poorest countries is that they attract very little foreign direct investment. Neither do these countries attract much portfolio investment, because there are few attractive investment opportunities in the domestic economy. Yet, although the world's poor countries receive relatively little financial investment, many of them still face a crippling external debt problem.

The 'double exposure' problem

In this discussion of outcomes of globalization processes we have focused on one set of issues: those to do with economic well-being. Of course, there are many others, and these may interact in such a way as to change the identity of winners and losers. This is the issue identified as a 'double exposure' problem by O'Brien and Leichenko (2000, 2003) in their analysis of the dual, and related, effects of economic globalization and climate change:

> Both climate change and economic globalization are ongoing processes with uneven impacts, and both include implicit winners and losers.... Double exposure refers to cases where a particular region, sector, ecosystem or social group is confronted by the impacts of both climate change and economic globalization. It recognizes that climate impacts are influenced not only by current socioeconomic trends, but also by structural economic changes that are reorganizing economic activities at the global scale.... different outcomes emerge when the two processes are considered together. (O'Brien and Leichenko, 2000, p. 227)

Their analysis explores these issues from several perspectives: regional, sectoral, social, and in terms of ecosystems. Regionally, they show, for example, that although Africa is a 'double loser' overall, the situation is more varied than this generalization suggests. Sectorally, they show in the case of Mexican agriculture that 'farmers who are trying to compete in ... international markets as well as agricultural wage labourers . . . are . . . likely to be double losers in terms of climate change and globalization' (O'Brien and Leichenko, 2000, p. 229).

Among the most vulnerable social groups affected by double exposure are the poor residents of cities in both the developed and developing worlds:

> At the same time that globalization is contributing to the economic vulnerability of disadvantaged residents of US cities, climate change may increase the physical vulnerability of these groups to weather-related events. Climate change may increase mean summer temperatures in Northern cities, and may also increase the frequency and magnitude of summer heat waves, consequently increasing heat-related illnesses and deaths. . . . Residents of poor, inner-city communities are among the most vulnerable to heat waves due to lack of resources to pay for air conditioning or to leave stifling central city areas. . . . Globalization and climate change thus represent a dual threat to these groups.
>
> For poor residents of cities in the developing world, the double impacts of globalization and climate change may be even more severe. . . . In conjunction with increased financial vulnerability as the result of globalization, poor residents of developing world cities are also among the groups that are most vulnerable to climatic change. Many of the urban poor live in shantytowns and squatter settlements located in precarious areas such as on hillsides. . . . Such areas are especially vulnerable to mudslides or flooding as the result of severe storms, events that may increase in both frequency and magnitude as the result of climate change. In addition to direct physical hazards, the urban poor are also vulnerable to climate change related health-hazards, particularly outbreaks of diseases such as cholera and malaria, both of which increase with warm spells and heavy rains. (O'Brien and Leichenko, 2000, p. 229)

The argument, therefore, is that different sets of winners and losers from globalization may emerge when the effects of the two sets of global processes are superimposed on both those who are vulnerable and those who may benefit.

To be 'Globalized' or Not to be 'Globalized'

> The main losers in today's very unequal world are not those who are too much exposed to globalization. They are those who have been left out.
>
> Kofi Annan, Secretary-General of the United Nations,
> Speech to UNCTAD Meeting in Bangkok, 2000

> Is the problem actually globalization or not-globalization? Is the difficulty being part of the system or not being part of it? How can globalization be the source of problems for those excluded from it?
>
> Mittelman, *The Globalization Syndrome* (2000), p. 241

It is abundantly clear that the relationship of many of the world's poorest countries is highly marginal in terms of the global economy. The usual prescription for those developing countries poorly integrated into the global system is that they should open their economies more: for example, by positively encouraging exports and by liberalizing their regulatory structures.

> For policymakers around the world, the appeal of opening up to global markets is based on a simple but powerful promise: international economic integration will improve economic performance. As countries reduce their tariff and non-tariff barriers to trade and open up to international capital flows, the expectation is that economic growth will increase. This, in turn, will reduce poverty and improve the quality of life for the vast majority of the residents of developing countries.
> *The trouble is . . . that there is no convincing evidence that openness, in the sense of low barriers to trade and capital flows, systematically produces these consequences. In practice, the links between openness and economic growth tend to be weak and contingent on the presence of complementary policies and institutions.* (Rodrik, 1999, pp. 136–7, emphasis added)

'Openness', then, is the name of game. But this will only work if the playing field is relatively level – which it clearly is not. And it also has to work both ways – which clearly it does not. Tariffs imposed by the developed countries on imports of many developing country products remain very high. It is common for tariffs to increase with the degree of processing (so-called 'tariff escalation'), so that higher-value products from developing countries are discriminated against. At the same time, agricultural subsidies make imports from developing countries uncompetitive. In other words, the odds are stacked against them (see UNCTAD, 2002).

> The human costs of unfair trade are immense. If Africa, South Asia, and Latin America were each to increase their share of world exports by one per cent, the resulting gains in income could lift 128 million people out of poverty. . . .
> When developing countries export to rich-country markets, they face tariff barriers that are four times higher than those encountered by rich countries. Those barriers cost them $100bn a year – twice as much as they receive in aid. (Oxfam, 2002, p. 1)

Simply opening up a developing economy on its own will almost certainly lead to further disaster. There is the danger of local businesses being wiped out by more efficient foreign competition before they can get a toehold in the wider world. Hence a prerequisite for positive and beneficial engagement with the global economy is the development of robust internal structures.

The severity of the situation facing the developing countries in general, and the low-income, least-industrialized, countries in particular, has led to successive demands, over the past three decades, for a radical change in the workings of the world economic system. In fact, very little progress has been made on most of these demands. The very poor developing countries, those at the bottom of the well-being league table, have benefited least from the globalization of economic activities. Both their present and their future are dire. Ways have to be found to solve the problems of poverty and deprivation.

In such a highly interconnected world as we now inhabit, and as our children will certainly inhabit, it is difficult to believe that anything less than global solutions can deal with such global problems. But how is such collaboration to be achieved? Can a new international economic order be created or is the likely future one of international economic disorder? There can be no doubt that the present immense global inequalities are a moral outrage. The problem is one of reconciling what many perceive to be conflicting interests. For example, one of the biggest problems facing the older industrialized countries is unemployment. Many in the West believe that imports from low-cost developing countries are a major cause of such unemployment. In such circumstances, the pressure on Western governments to adopt restrictive trade policies becomes considerable.

The alternative is to adopt policies that ease the adjustment for those groups and areas adversely affected and to stimulate new sectors. But this requires a more positive attitude than most Western governments have been prepared to adopt. For the poorer developing countries it is unlikely, however, that industrialization will provide the solution to their massive problems. Despite its rapid growth in some developing countries, manufacturing industry has made barely a small dent in the unemployment and underemployment problems of developing countries as a whole. For most, the answer must lie in other sectors, particularly agriculture, but the seriousness of these countries' difficulties necessitates concerted international action. This, in turn, is part of a much larger debate about the overall governance of the world economy.

The macro-structures of the global economy are, essentially, the institutions, conventions and rules of the capitalist market system. These are, of course, not naturally given but socially constructed – in their present form predominantly as a neoliberal political-economic ideology. The rules and conventions of the capitalist market economy relate to such phenomena as private property, profit-making, resource allocation on the basis of market signals, and the consequent commodification of production inputs (including labour). The IMF, the WTO and the World Bank, together with the various 'G' meetings, are the most obvious manifestations of global institutions, although there are, of course, a myriad of other, more specific, bodies such as industry-specific regulatory agencies (see Braithwaite and Drahos, 2000).

What we do not have, of course, is a coherent system of global governance; rather, we have a 'confusion' of institutions. The institutions that do exist are, however, only a part of the broader socio-cultural matrix of practices, rules and conventions that shape how the world works. Neither, despite the phenomenal recent growth of civil society organizations (CSOs),[4] do we have a truly – or even a partial – global civil society. Although the proliferation of transnational social movements has 'unquestionably projected the globalization debate into the popular political consciousness in important ways... the movements themselves have a severe democratic deficit: representing humanity ultimately requires legitimation through some sort of people's mandate' (Taylor, Watts and Johnston, 2002, pp.15–16). But there is little consensus on these issues, as shown by the difference between Monbiot's (2003) position that only a truly *global democratic* reform process will suffice and that of Hines (2000) and Goldsmith and Mander (2001) based on a fundamental *local reconfiguration* of human activities.

So, the key question is not so much what the world might be like in the future but what it *should* be like. After all, 'globalization is not a force of nature; it is a social process' (Massey, 2000, p. 24). The major global challenge is to meet the material needs of the world community as a whole in ways that reduce, rather than increase, inequality and which do so without destroying the environment. That, of course, is far easier said than done. It requires the involvement of all major actors – business firms, states and international institutions – in establishing mechanisms to capture the gains of globalization for the majority and not just for the powerful minority.

Such a system has to be built on a world trading system that is *equitable*. This must involve reform of such institutions as the WTO, the World Bank and the IMF. The exercise of developed country power through the various kinds of conditionality and trade-opening requirements imposed on poorer countries has seriously negative results. Without doubt, trade is one of the most effective ways of enhancing material well-being. But it has to be based upon a genuinely fairer basis than at present. The poorer countries must be allowed to open up their markets in a manner appropriate to their needs and conditions. After all, that is precisely what the United States did during its phase of industrialization, as did Japan and the East Asian NIEs in a later period. At the same time, developed countries must operate a fairer system of access to their own markets for poor countries. Even the journal *Business Week* acknowledges this when it states that 'the flaws of trying to force every country into the same template have become clear... it is time to forge a more enlightened consensus' (*Business Week*, 2000, p. 45).

Of course, this will cause problems for some people and communities in the developed countries and these should not be underestimated. They are reflected most clearly in the various lobbying groups that attempt to influence government trade policy. Often they succeed in doing so, as showed by the Bush administration's implementation of tariffs on steel imports in 2002, and as demonstrated by the EU's continuing distortion of agricultural trade through its common agricultural policy. It is highly paradoxical that the two major trading groups at the forefront of demands for a more open trading system are also all too ready to protect their own markets.

There are, indeed, many losers in the otherwise affluent economies. Their governments must design and implement appropriate adjustment policies for such groups if such trade policies are to be acceptable politically. Equally, governments of developing countries must engage in their own internal reforms: to strengthen domestic institutions, enhance civil society, increase political participation, raise the quality of education and reduce internal social polarization. Although difficult, such policies are not impossible if the social and political will is there. The imperatives are both practical and moral. In practical terms, the continued existence of vast numbers of impoverished people across the world – but who can see the manifestations of immense wealth elsewhere through the electronic media – poses a serious threat to social and political stability. But the moral argument is, I believe, more powerful. It is utterly repellent that so many people live in such abject poverty and deprivation whilst, at the same time, others live in immense luxury. This is an argument not for levelling down but for raising up. The means for doing this are there. What matters is the will to do it. We all have a responsibility to ensure that the contours of the global economic map in the twenty-first century are not as steep as those of the twentieth century.

NOTES

1 This chapter draws extensively on Dicken (2003, Part IV; 2004).
2 See O'Brien and Leichenko (2000, 2003) for a discussion of the distinction between absolute and relative winners and losers.
3 Dr Pangloss was the tutor in Voltaire's eighteenth-century satirical novel *Candide*. Although Candide lives in a world of immense suffering and hardship, Dr Pangloss insists that it is 'the best of all possible worlds, where everything is connected and arranged for the best' (Voltaire, 1759, p. 8).
4 The term 'CSOs' (civil society organizations) is preferable to the more commonly used, but narrower and less appropriate, 'NGOs' (non-governmental organizations). Glasius, Kaldor and Anheier (2002) provide a comprehensive discussion of CSOs in the context of global civil society.

REFERENCES

Braithwaite, J. and Drahos, P. (2000) *Global Business Regulation*, Cambridge: Cambridge University Press.

Business Week (2000) 'Global capitalism: can it be made to work better?' *Business Week* 6 November.

Dicken, P. (2003) *Global Shift: Reshaping the Global Economic Map in the 21st Century* (4th edition), London: Sage Publications; New York: Guilford Press.

Dicken, P. (2004) 'Geographers and "globalization": (yet) another missed boat?' *Transactions of the Institute of British Geographers* 29, 5–26.

Dicken, P., Peck, J. A. and Tickell, A. (1997) 'Unpacking the global', in R. Lee and J. Wills (eds) *Geographies of Economies*, London: Edward Arnold.

FIET (1996) *A Social Dimension to Globalization*, Geneva: FIET (International Federation of Commercial, Clerical, Professional and Technical Employees).

Glasius, M., Kaldor, M. and Anheier, H. (eds) (2002) *Global Civil Society 2002*, Oxford: Oxford University Press.

Goldsmith, E. and Mander, J. (eds) (2001) *The Case Against the Global Economy and for a Turn Towards Localization*, London: Earthscan.

Hart, G. (2001) 'Development critiques in the 1990s: *culs de sac* and promising paths', *Progress in Human Geography* 25, 649–58.

Hay, C. and Marsh, D. (2000) 'Introduction', in C. Hay and D. Marsh (eds), *Demystifying Globalization*, London: Macmillan.

Held, D., McGrew, A., Goldblatt, D. and Perraton, J. (1999) *Global Transformations: Politics, Economics and Culture*, Cambridge: Polity.

Henderson, J. (1998) 'Danger and opportunity in the Asia-Pacific', in G. Thompson (ed.), *Economic Dynamism in the Asia-Pacific*, London: Routledge.

Henderson, J., Dicken, P., Hess, M., Coe, N. and Yeung, H. W.-c. (2002) 'Global production networks and the analysis of economic development', *Review of International Political Economy* 9, 436–64.

Hines, C. (2000) *Localization: A Global Manifesto*, London: Earthscan.

Hirst, P. and Thompson, G. (1999) *Globalization in Question: The International Economy and the Possibilities of Governance* (2nd edition), Cambridge: Polity.

Ito, S. (2001) 'Growth, crisis, and the future of economic recovery in East Asia', in J. E. Stiglitz and S. Yusuf (eds), *Rethinking the East Asia Miracle*, New York: Oxford University Press.

Kapstein, E. (1999) *Sharing the Wealth: Workers and the World Economy*, New York: W. W. Norton.

Massey, D. (2000) 'The geography of power', in B. Gunnell and D. Timms (eds), *After Seattle: Globalization and its Discontents*, London: Catalyst.

Micklethwait, J. and Wooldridge, A. (2000) *A Future Perfect: The Challenge and Hidden Promise of Globalization*, London: Random House.

Mittelman, J. H. (2000) *The Globalization Syndrome: Transformation and Resistance*, Princeton, NJ: Princeton University Press.

Monbiot, G. (2003) *The Age of Consent: A Manifesto for a New World Order*, London: HarperCollins.

O'Brien, K. L. and Leichenko, R. M. (2000) 'Double exposure: assessing the impacts of climate change within the context of economic globalization', *Global Environmental Change* 10, 221–32.

O'Brien, K. L. and Leichenko, R. M. (2003) 'Winners and losers in the context of global change', *Annals of the Association of American Geographers* 93, 89–103.

Oxfam (2002) *Rigged Rules and Double Standards: Trade, Globalization and the Fight Against Poverty*, London: Oxfam.

Rodrik, D. (1999) *The New Global Economy and Developing Countries: Making Openness Work*, Washington, DC: Overseas Development Council.

Sen, A. (1999) *Development as Freedom*, Oxford: Oxford University Press.

Smith, D. M. (1974) 'Who gets what *where* and how: a welfare focus for human geography', *Geography* 59, 289–97.

Smith, D. M. (1979) *Where the Grass is Greener: Living in an Unequal World*, Harmondsworth: Penguin.

Taylor, P. J., Watts, M. J. and Johnston, R. J. (2002) 'Geography/globalization', in R. J. Johnston, P. J. Taylor and M. J. Watts (eds), *Geographies of Global Change: Remapping the World*, Oxford: Blackwell.

UNCTAD (2002) *Trade and Development Report, 2002: Developing Countries in World Trade*, New York: United Nations.

UNDP (1999) *Human Development Report, 1999*, New York: United Nations.

Voltaire (Arouet, F-M.) (1759) *Candide* (trans. J. Butt), London: Penguin, 1947.

3

Regional Inequality, Convergence and Enlargement in the European Union

Nigel Spence

Introduction

The subtitle of this volume claims the outlining of international perspectives on development, justice and place. This contribution is firmly grounded in such a purpose, focusing on the uneven development of the European Union (EU) in the context of the 2004 enlargement. Conceptualizing inequality in levels of development is a particular forte of David Smith, and his Penguin *Where the Grass is Greener* (1979) is a masterpiece in this respect. This is not just my view, for in my copy – a 1982 edition published by Johns Hopkins – David Harvey, in his preface, praises Smith's efforts to instruct us on how to conceive of such inequality and figure out the forces that promulgate it at a variety of spatial levels. Now, I think that it is fair to say that Smith is more 'at home' with social and economic inequalities within the US and within and between socialist countries than within the EU, but his book cited above does make mention of regional differentiation within Britain and Poland (as well as some other newly accessing countries of the EU), so there is some link with the present chapter.

Before pointing up the tasks of this chapter, we need briefly to remind ourselves of the purpose, geographical scale and evolution of that supranational level of government, the European Union. In 1957 the Treaties of Rome set up the European Economic Community (known familiarly as the EEC or the Common Market) and six countries were founder members – Belgium, France, Germany, Italy, Luxembourg and the Netherlands. These same six countries had previously collaborated in the form of the European Coal and Steel Community, set up in 1951. The Common Market was expanded in 1973 with the accession of the UK, Ireland and Denmark to become a community of nine, followed by Greece in 1981 to make ten. Next came Spain and Portugal in 1986 to total twelve, and then Austria, Finland and Sweden in 1995, bringing the membership to fifteen. Then, in 2000, the Nice Treaty paved the way for the current and ongoing enlargement, where it was agreed that Cyprus, the Czech Republic, Estonia, Hungary, Latvia, Lithuania, Malta, Poland, Slovakia and Slovenia would all be able to join, which they did on 1 May 2004. This brought the number of seats at the table to twenty-five. And there are a number of potential members still waiting in the wings, including Romania, Bulgaria and Turkey. This brief overview simply records the evolution of the membership of the club. It says nothing about the way the rules and policies of the club have changed over time, from being primarily focused on realizing the benefits of a common market in economic terms to the more recent attempts at full economic and, just as important, political union – the Treaty of Maastricht in 1992 on a closer union and the draft constitution published in 2003 being perhaps the most significant steps.

So much for the historical institutional context – what of the perspectives on development, justice and place? Well, this chapter is concerned first to explore the nature of development inequalities within Europe broadly, sometimes between nations and sometimes within them, and this will raise the fundamentally important issue of convergence. Given such developmental inequality over the places that constitute the EU territory, the aim of the chapter next is to consider the nature and effectiveness of the policies that have been designed to confront this injustice. All this leads to a concluding comment on the current debate concerning the implications of the present ongoing enlargement encompassing a wider Europe.

Regional Development Disparities and Convergence in Europe

Long-term growth performance of individual countries within the broader Europe

At the national level it is instructive to understand that unequal development amongst European countries is long-seated and probably best viewed in core–periphery terms (Berend, 2003). Largely as a result of the way world trade evolved in response to industrialization, north-western Europe developed as the core and Mediterranean, Nordic and central-eastern European countries as the periphery. The contrast between the modern industrial economies of the core and the traditional agricultural-based economic systems of the periphery were plain to see and provided the basis for a growing developmental gap in the early part of the last century. Scandinavian countries were the exception, and for a variety of reasons rapidly caught up with and indeed joined the core. Much was changed following the First World War when some peripheral counties eschewed free market competition with core countries, instead turning inwards to focus on import-substituting industrial policies as a basis for development. The consequence was the rapid growth in central and eastern European countries of those manufacturing sectors declining in the core, such as textiles, in true product/process life-cycle fashion. Of course, some peripheral countries were unable to join this catch-up club, and Italy, Greece and Spain in particular failed to match the growth rates of either the core or the emerging industrial periphery in the inter-war years.

Enter the next Kondratieff long-range industrial cycle and the picture changed again. Deployment of new technology in capital-intensive industrial pursuits was the key to this economic phase. Not unnaturally the core was best placed to benefit from these advances, although even in these countries the necessary restructuring was by no means straightforward. The peripheral countries found the demands doubly difficult as both human and physical capital was lacking in comparison with the core. The reaction again was to focus inwards and sever connections with core markets, and the result over the longer term was to be a widening of the existing development gap. The consequences of the Second World War served to complete the separation of the main peripheral economies in central and eastern Europe with those of the core, and this important part of the periphery began to modernize the Soviet way. The result was that impressive and rapid urban and industrial growth occurred in this post-war phase. But it was a growth that did not engender further technological advance, and because of the institutional context, it was growth that did not prepare for what was to come.

In the core, too, only more so, during the immediate post-war years there was rapid growth. New technology was implemented, new production methods were managed, mixed economies thrived almost everywhere, and countries specialized and traded. It was at this time that the European Common Market was founded. Interestingly these years saw peripheral Mediterranean countries achieve some of the most rapid growth rates of all, but even after two post-war decades they still lagged way behind the core. Italy was the exception, becoming part of the core after the war, primarily based on the industrial development in the north of its territory.

De-industrialization heralded more structural change in the core, after oil crisis shocks in the seventies and early eighties. High-technology sectors became the manufacturing engines of growth and the service sector developed at the expense of manufacturing generally. Core countries adjusted to the new demands, helped by the expanding markets of an enlarging European Community. Peripheral member countries – the cohesion countries of southern Europe and Ireland – benefited greatly from market access and from investment assistance from central funds. Although it is true to say that development levels are by no means the same across member countries of the EU, all may now be considered as part of the core. In contrast, the central and eastern European part of the periphery has undergone severe economic crisis, failing to adjust and restructure such that inflation and increasing debt has been commonplace, resulting in the eventual collapse of state socialism at the turn of the nineties. Not surprisingly this period saw the gap between the core and periphery (now only represented by central and eastern Europe) increase considerably. Some of the post-transformation economies on the western rim of this area did rather well in the final decade of the twentieth century, although they clearly have some considerable way to go to integrate with the core. But the current development differential between the core and those other peripheral countries in this part of Europe is better described as a chasm than a gap.

Contemporary national and regional economic performance within the EU

Even within the current core there are wide variations in growth performance and, as a consequence, in economic well-being. A more detailed and contemporary look into the economic fortunes of EU nations is provided by Melachroinos and Spence (2001), in this case for manufacturing activity. The time frame is 1978 to 1994 and the data (much richer for states than is ever possible for regions) are derived from the OECD (1998).

Manufacturing everywhere in the EU, of course, in recent times has been subject to severe de-industrialization forces, but, despite this, manufacturing output and labour productivity has been rising and making contributions to economic growth and well-being. Productivity is key to economic performance whatever the spatial scale, and therefore productivity differences provide good pointers to inequalities in levels of well-being. Underpinning those productivity differences are important contributing forces such as capital stock, technological advance and labour force competences. It is also often argued that productivity differentials provide a more informed measure of competitiveness between places than anything else, for example differential trade balances. Productivity is also an important measure used in understanding the dynamics of economic convergence (or otherwise).

The measurement of productivity is by no means unproblematic. It is never easy to find appropriate data let alone grapple with the economic subtleties of model choice. Melachroinos and Spence (2001) used the concept of total factor productivity (TFP) to take a grip on these important economic issues. The notion of TFP is based on an aggregate production function, where change in value added (for a nation, say) is equated with changes in input shares of capital and labour and changes in a residual parameter that represents TFP. Now TFP contains a variety of ingredients, amongst others being innovation and technical change, organizational and institutional change, changes in demand and changes in social attitudes. In other words it contains all the things that might be conceived of as additional to the proportionate changes in the shares of the conventional input factors of production – capital and labour. This approach is not without its problems and the interested reader can follow these up: for example, Hulten (2000) provides an impressive review. But given time-series data on capital stock and measures of labour used in the production process, it is possible to measure TFP and thereby achieve some helpful insights into what might be the cause of differential economic growth.

Some thirteen EU countries were looked at in this way – the EU of the fifteen, excluding Ireland and Luxembourg, where data were insufficient. Further, these countries were classified into those constituting 'large' economies (France, Germany, Italy, Spain and the UK), in contrast to the remaining eight, making up 'small' economies; and additionally classified into those constituting 'southern' economies (Greece, Italy, Portugal and Spain), compared to the other nine 'northern' members.

In this time frame, output growth in simple terms has been faster in small and southern economies (greater than 2 per cent per annum) compared to large and northern economies (about 1 per cent per annum). Potentially this indicates rather encouraging signs for convergence. However, if this is unpacked it appears that although TFP growth is the main driver of rising output, there is hardly any difference in TFP contributions between the north and the south. The real story here is that growth in capital stock in the south is double that in the north and that employment decline is vastly less. Much the same, although less marked, applies to differences in performance between large and small economies. In other words, the main differences in growth rates between these constituencies of nations arise from the varying contributions of inputs.

What, then, can be said about change in the levels of geographical inequality? This research confirms other evidence giving little weight to the view that that there is a process of convergence in the performance of EU economies. This is especially true in recent times. Simple calculation of coefficients of variation in TFP levels over the thirteen countries, repeated over time, shows that in reality it is divergence in performance that is the name of the game. Furthermore, inter-country variation in performance is clearly greater for the critical TFP measure compared to other indicators such as labour productivity or capital to labour ratios. In other words, it is the differences in the ways that input production factors are used, no doubt dependent on differing levels of technological development, that underpin spatial inequalities in manufacturing across the EU. The small economies as a whole, it is true, have been improving in TFP over the period studied, but still they have some way to go (15 percentage points) to catch the large economies group. As for the contrasts in TFP between the north and the south, they are quite simply huge – a factor of five difference – and there are few signs of a narrowing of the gap. In summary, it is technical change that represents the principal discriminant between manufacturing growth performances across the EU, and this is very much a function of advanced versus lagging economies.

Any treatment of economic performance at a national scale invariably involves the averaging and smoothing of regional growth differentials, which are of absolutely vital importance to the people who live there. Despite the relative paucity of key data available at such regional scales (it is impossible to undertake a comprehensive TFP analysis, for example), a large literature has evolved in an EU context attempting to measure and understand processes of regional economic convergence, as demonstrated in Armstrong and Vickerman's (1995) collection.

Martin and Tyler (2000) select employment growth as a suitable variable for descriptive treatment at the level of the NUTS 2 regions of the EU. This is a spatial scale approximating usually to small clusters of counties in the UK – a scale one tier below that of the Standard Region (of which there are eleven). If cumulative employment change is calculated for these regions against an aggregate EU average and simply graphed for each country against time from 1976 to 1998, a remarkable picture emerges. Each member state is characterized by divergence of regional performance. This is the case even for those nations that have achieved high national rates of employment growth. In some cases the divergence is more marked than in others, with the greatest regional differentials being seen in Italy, Spain, the UK and Greece.

Other studies, too, seem to generate conclusions pointing in the same direction. After early optimism that regions in the EU were on course for economic convergence in the sixties and seventies, the more recent picture seems to be the reverse or, at best, one of imperceptible change (Dunford, 1993, 1996; Armstrong, 1995; Neven and Gouyette, 1995; Fagerberg and Verspagen, 1996; Cappelen, Fagerberg and Verspagen, 1999). It is, however, certainly the case that measuring convergence itself is no straightforward task. There are several methods, each one focusing on a slightly different dimension of change. A recent study by Lopez-Baso, Vaya and Mora (1999) employing new methods and new data concludes that at this scale much depends on the nature of the indicator variables selected. Rodriguez-Pose (1999), too, adopts a similar stance, preferring to explore the subtleties of difference at the detailed regional level rather than using a simple overall measure of convergence over many diverse regions. Magrini

(1999), on the other hand, also uses new methods but concludes that divergence in regional performance is the more likely bet.

Policy Initiatives Designed to Combat Unequal Worlds

European regional policies – Structural and Cohesion Funds

For many years now the EU has set aside a substantial fraction of its budget for regional policy purposes. There is a series of excellent periodic reports that chart the progress and success of the policies that have been deployed (e.g. Commission of the European Communities, 1999a). For the current period (2000–6) these regional funds amount to one third of the total budget – some 213 billion euros. Of this, the lion's share (195 billion euros) is allocated through the four Structural Funds, principally the European Regional Development Fund and the European Social Fund. The remaining 18 billion euros is spent by the European Cohesion Fund in the four cohesion countries of Greece, Ireland, Portugal and Spain (Commission of the European Communities, 1999b).

The Structural Funds are spent on clearly defined objectives. Some 22 per cent of the population of the EU live in so-called 'Objective 1' regions. These are areas, often but not exclusively in the south of Europe, whose levels of economic development may be thought of as lagging behind the rest. They receive some 70 per cent of the funding. Objective 2 regions, on the other hand, are those that are facing structural difficulties of economic and social transition from one economic regime to the next. About 18 per cent of the population live in such areas, which are often, but again not exclusively, highly urbanized and located in the old industrial areas of northern Europe. Some 11.5 per cent of the Structural Funds budget is spent here. A further 12.3 per cent is spent on Objective 3 regions, where polices to promote training and employment creation outside Objective 1 regions are administered. Then, lastly, mention should be made of the four Community initiatives designed to tackle specific problems and spending 5.4 per cent of the total budget. Interreg III deals with cross-border issues, Urban II covers sustainable redevelopment in cities, Leader + is focused on rural development, and, finally, Equal comprises a number of projects aimed to improve access to the labour market.

So much for the objectives, what is the money actually spent on? Much of it is spent on the public infrastructure, especially energy and transport. Although not always in the public domain, another dimension concerns the provision of telecommunications. Assistance to help industry invest and the training of the workforce are two further dimensions of expenditure.

Finally, increasing funds are used to transfer technology and information to those areas perceived as lacking in these respects. Almost all the Cohesion Fund is spent on environmental (especially water) and transport infrastructure. There is one aspect of this fund that is particularly apposite to this chapter and that is the sum set aside for Structural Policies pre-Accession (ISPA). This, too, is for environmental and transport initiatives in the ten new member countries (plus Bulgaria and Romania) of the Community. The ISPA funds are joined by funds for the PHARE programme designed to improve institutional and administrative arrangements, and the SAPARD programme for agriculture and rural development in accession countries. Together these three funds amounted to 40 billion euros for the 2000–2 planning period.

These are the current policies but initiatives similar to these have been in place for many years now. In the early days of the Community emphasis was placed on alleviating the problems in areas of industrial decline. Then, as new countries from southern Europe joined, emphasis switched to promoting economic development in areas previously underdeveloped. The obvious question to pose is: have the policies had any effect? Regional disparities are still plain to see, so perhaps it should be said that the policies have had little or no success. But the logic in this line of argument is deficient in one important respect, and that is that it fails to take account of what might have happened in their absence. Regional policy evaluation is a large, sophisticated, but difficult, field of study and there are many reports that point to important successes in such policies, as demonstrated in Johansson, Karlsson and Stough's (2002) collection. The provision of public goods, such as infrastructure, has undoubtedly aided the development of many regions in the Community that otherwise would have lagged even further (Commission of the European Communities, 2001).

Enterprise policies in Enterprise Europe

It almost goes without saying that enterprise is the key to economic and social development of any contemporary society (Rovolis and Spence, 2000). Development depends on wealth creation and this does not occur in the absence of enterprising behaviour by human beings. That such behaviour is best fostered in marketplaces as far as possible free from restriction reflects the contemporary political consensus.

The most obvious manifestation of enterprise can be seen in the creation of new businesses. New business starts are usually small in scale, although not necessarily so, and arise for a whole variety of reasons associated with industry profits and growth, scale economies, capital intensity, product differentiation, research and development as well as innovation, emerging market opportunities and the availability of entrepreneurial skills, not to mention venture capital. Sometimes, it is the individual appetite for business that is important and, sometimes, new businesses are started out of sheer necessity via the unemployment register. The second dimension of enterprising behaviour can be found within already existing business. Now clearly, simply for businesses to survive, and be able respond to the ever-changing economic climate, requires enterprise. But, more important, for business to prosper, entrepreneurs must continually seek to exploit new business opportunities in terms of either product or process innovation (or both), and even then this presupposes that any new value that is added can be realized in the competitive marketplace.

In essence, whether enterprise can be found in new business start-ups or new initiatives within existing business, the prime objective of all such behaviour is to enhance levels of production and productivity, broadly interpreted (Krugman, 1994). All that is consumed has to be produced, utilizing the various input factors. Obviously, if more can be produced using the same input factors, then such productivity improvements can raise levels of economic and social well-being in society.

It was at the March 2000 Lisbon Economic Council that the foundations for the new EU enterprise policy were put in place against the context of contemporary global economic forces and the evolution of knowledge-based economies. A new strategic goal was set to position the EU 'to become the most competitive and dynamic knowledge-driven economy in the world, capable of sustainable economic growth with more and better jobs and greater social cohesion'. The overall objective of the new EU enterprise policy is to achieve the goal of Enterprise Europe – a phrase coined by President Prodi. It is widely felt that this will be the key to the sustainable development of the Community territory and the well-being of all of its citizens, future as well as present. Enterprise and cohesion, then, are inextricably linked.

Enterprise Europe is an impressive goal and one that will not be achieved without a fundamental change in the culture of enterprise that has come to characterize some parts of the EU economy. The key to success in such a changing economic context is enhanced entrepreneurial and innovative behaviour. It is envisaged that the prime contributors to the development and growth of this new economy, both in terms of the value added and jobs, will be small and medium-sized enterprises (SMEs). To come anywhere near achieving this ambitious goal, action will be required across the sectoral spectrum, although it is expected that the majority of new initiatives will stem from the service sector and e-commerce. There can be little doubt, however, that the new information technologies behind the knowledge-driven economy will be key to the economic fortunes of most, if not all, sectors of the future economy.

The overall goals for European enterprise policy are to be achieved via the Commission's deployment of the *Multiannual Programme for Enterprise and Entrepreneurship 2001-2005* (Commission of the European Communities, 2000). The total expenditure for the full five-year period, however, is small and amounts to 230 million euros.

Enterprise and cohesion

What will be the effects of the new enterprise policies on those parts of the EU territory that are characterized by lagging levels of economic development, variously interpreted? The first issue to confront in attempting such an evaluation is the fact that the new enterprise policy, as designed, has no specific spatial dimension. It applies to the whole of the EU territory. This is not in any way unusual, unacceptable or unexpected, for the overall aim is to facilitate the development of Enterprise Europe as a whole. But what, logically, are the implications for economic and social cohesion? To begin to approach this question it is necessary to understand the nature of spatial economic convergence. This is no easy task.

In a growing literature on convergence it is clear that there is much to be learned, and some pointers have been given above. This is the case even for the apparently simple task of understanding whether or not the process is actually taking place. When it comes to understanding the causalities, few things are certain. Some commentators seek to understand whether conventional neoclassical economic processes such as capital accumulation, factor movements and technology transfer are the main influences on the patterns of convergence observed or whether more specific forces such as promoted by explicit regional polices are the cause. EU integration initiatives of various kinds also figure prominently as potentially important influences, but with these many have yet to have their full effect. Contemporary economic theorizing, however, rarely points to such simplistic processes and out-turns. Spatial market imperfections and scale economies are such that some would argue for the exact opposite of convergence as a natural tendency for regional economic systems. The expectation is that those regions that have a good developmental start, through whatever comparative advantage, tend to retain and build upon that advantage and thereby draw away from their competitors. The result is divergence, and this forms the *raison d'être* for development policy intervention to improve the fortunes of those regions that are lagging, usually in the form of spatially discriminatory policies.

What, then, can be envisaged from a new enterprise policy delivered essentially in a spatially non-discriminatory way across the whole of the EU territory? The positive side of the argument is that the new policies are such that they will remove a whole raft of so-called 'barriers to entry' to the economy. A considerable amount is known about such barriers, and all of the evidence points to their existence in areas that lag in developmental terms (Fotopoulos and Spence, 1999). In the short term, at least, the expectation is that the releasing of latent potential and the removal of barriers to enterprise (widely interpreted) existing in lagging areas will be a force for cohesion. It is highly likely that enterprise is being stifled in lagging regions by the lack of a suitable operating environment. If enterprise policy touches all parts of the regional economic system in all countries, then this lack can be overturned and opportunities provided. However, on a somewhat more cautionary note, once these opportunities have been provided and the latent potential has been taken up, whether or not convergence continues to take place will be dependent on the operation of a whole range of forces of which enterprise policy is but one. It very much depends upon what view of the convergence–divergence theory is subscribed to. Many of the new enterprise policies do, of course, have parallels in spatially discriminatory policies delivered by the EU via the Structural Funds. When this is the case, then the expectation must be that such policies would work in favour of convergence and cohesion.

Enlargement: Economic Reality, Policy and Justice

Enterprise and enlargement

An equally difficult question to answer concerns the effects that the new enterprise policy might have on economic and social cohesion in the circumstances arising from the enlargement of the Community. This is difficult because the new policies are being played out over some national territories that are relative newcomers to the capitalist mode of production. There can be little doubt that in the newly accessing countries there is considerable latent entrepreneurial potential previously subjugated by decades of economic repression engendered by planned economic systems. Policies designed to promote a new enterprise culture are likely to fall on far from deaf ears in such countries. In this sense and following the logic of the argument, it is likely that there will be impressive responses in these countries to the call for more entrepreneurial behaviour. This is because in several senses the policy will be 'flowing with the tide' of newly acquired economic freedom and opportunity.

Information is scarce about the likely outcomes of EU accession for the newly admitted countries. Poland is something of an exception, and well-considered ideas about the nature and future roles of SMEs have recently become available (Konopielko and Bell, 1998; Miller, 2000). It is now apparent that in Poland's economic transition SMEs have played a key role in contributing to economic growth in output and the alleviation of unemployment through enhanced job generation. This process of the development of the SME sector has been sufficient to lead some observers to estimate that SMEs increased their number by over 30 per cent during the nineties and now contribute over 40 per cent of GDP and 60 per cent of all jobs in Poland. These are rapid and important increases by any standards and add some empirical weight to the above judgement that there is a considerable potential for catch-up in the newly accessing countries. Furthermore, much of this achievement has been based on intervention through bilateral aid schemes from a number of sources, not least from the EU. Part of the remit of the Enterprise Directorate-General is to manage efficient relations in the business sphere with third countries, including the candidates for enlargement. The Enterprise Directorate-General specifically helps with sectoral and technical expertise in trade policy activities; it manages some Mutual Recognition Agreements and also assists newly accessing and applicant countries with the implementation of some aspects of Community legislation. In evaluation terms, then, EU aid has already begun to achieve closer cohesion between Poland and the other EU member states.

In terms of the cohesion of the enlarged community, these forces, and the enterprise policies that underpin them, should prove beneficial. This will be especially so in the early years when there will be considerable scope for catch-up by the newly accessing countries. The gap, although wide and continuing, should begin to close and convergence become apparent at least when viewed at national scales and in the short term. However, what is much less certain is whether enterprise policies that do not discriminate between new member countries and those existing member countries will continue to be an effective force for cohesion in the longer term.

Enlargement and cohesion

This is where the real debate about spatially discriminating policy is. We have already seen that the Cohesion countries benefit greatly from their status and so, too, do those regions designated as falling within policy Objectives 1 and 2. These nations and regions are deserving of their support because they fall short of the EU norms in terms of their wealth creation. It is plain to see that with enlargement these parts of the EU territory are experiencing a transformation of their relative position in the Community as they move away from the bottom of the league table. There are new countries and regions to support. One estimate is that the pre-enlargement levels of regional disparities will more than double (Cal, 2003). The demands on resources are likely to be greater than ever before.

Those that currently receive are unlikely to remain untouched by the increased demands. Those that currently give are unlikely to be able to support all at the same levels that are provided now. It is said that there will be, in fact, three types of member state in the enlarged Community. The first group will comprise most of the newly accessing countries, with a GDP only some 40 per cent of the EU average. The second group will be the cohesion countries (minus Ireland but plus Cyprus, Slovenia and the Czech Republic), with a GDP about 80 per cent of the Community norm. And last there will be the remaining countries, enjoying a GDP per capita of around 120 per cent of the EU average.

The debate in Europe currently is about the form that future cohesion policy will take. What is its role in fostering convergence in an enlarged EU of twenty-five countries? How can Community policies become more coherent in allowing other initiatives, such as enterprise policy, to play roles in enhancing cohesion? How should cohesion policy approach territorial cohesion to take cognizance of the marked spatial imbalances that the new enlarged Europe will bring? How can cohesion policy be directed towards those drivers that will have high added value for the well-being of citizens? What should be the priorities for balanced and sustainable territorial development? How should the convergence of lagging regions be encouraged? What policies are needed for those regions in the vanguard of wealth creation and development? How should the funds be divided up between regions and states for purposes of cohesion? What should be the underlying principles of Community intervention in the development of its territory? What should be the overall response to the clear increased economic, social and territorial needs that enlargement will bring?

These are political issues for sure. But they are also moral ones. Just what are the limits to the moral responsibilities of rich EU countries and regions to assist in the development of those neighbours less well founded? Just what are the moral responsibilities of the not-so-rich countries and regions well used to receiving help but who now may be called upon to assist those less fortunate than themselves? What should the newly accessing countries expect from membership of the club they have joined? Just how should all member countries view the potential for even wider club membership in the future? And we have not even begun to raise the question of attitudes to those territories that will never be eligible to join this elite club. It is a fascinating debate and the outcomes will be real.

REFERENCES

Armstrong, H. (1995) 'Convergence among regions of the European Union, 1950–1990', *Papers in Regional Science* 74, 143–52.

Armstrong, H. and Vickerman, R (eds) (1995) *Convergence and Divergence among European Regions*, London: Pion.

Berend, I. T. (2003) 'Past convergence within Europe: core–periphery diversity in modern socio-economic development', in G. Tumpel-Gugerell and P. Mooslechner (eds), *Economic Convergence and Divergence in Europe: Growth and Regional Development in an Enlarged European Union*, Chelternahm: Edward Elgar, pp. 9–23.

Cal, V. (2003) 'Economic and social cohesion in an enlarged European Union', in G. Tumpel-Gugerell and P. Mooslechner (eds), *Economic Convergence and Divergence in Europe: Growth and Regional Development in an Enlarged European Union*, Chelternahm: Edward Elgar, pp. 421–4.

Cappelen, A., Fagerberg, J. and Verspagen, B. (1999) 'Lack of regional convergence', in J. Fagerberg, P. Guerrieri and B. Verspagen (eds), *The Economic Challenge for Europe*, Cheltenham: Edward Elgar, pp. 130–48.

Commission of the European Communities (1999a) *Sixth Periodic Report on the Social and Economic Development of the Regions of the European Union*, Luxembourg: Office for Official Publications of the European Communities.

Commission of the European Communities (1999b) *The Structural Funds and Their Co-ordination with the Cohesion Fund: Guidelines for Programmes in the Period 2000–06*, Luxembourg: Office for Official Publications of the European Communities.

Commission of the European Communities (2000) *Challenges for Enterprise Policy in the Knowledge-Driven Economy*, COM (2000) 256, Luxembourg: Office for Official Publications of the European Communities.

Commission of the European Communities (2001) *The Second Report on Economic and Social Cohesion*, Luxembourg: Office for Official Publications of the European Communities.

Dunford, M. (1993) 'Regional disparities in the European Community: evidence from the REGIO databank', *Regional Studies* 27, 727–43.

Dunford, M. (1996) 'Disparities in employment, productivity and output in the EU: the roles of labour market governance and welfare regimes', *Regional Studies* 30: 339–57.

Fagerberg, J. and Verspagen, B. (1996) 'Heading for divergence? Regional growth in Europe reconsidered', *Journal of Common Market Studies* 34, 431–48.

Fotopoulos, G. and Spence, N. (1999) 'Spatial variations in new manufacturing plant openings: some empirical evidence from Greece', *Regional Studies* 33, 219–29.

Hulten, C. R. (2000) 'Total factor productivity: a short biography', Working Paper No. 7471 NBER Working Paper Series, Cambridge Mass.: National Bureau of Economic Research.

Johansson, B., Karlsson, C. and Stough, R. R. (2002) *Regional Policies and Comparative Advantage*, Cheltenham: Edward Elgar.

Konopielko, L. and Bell, J. (1998) 'Reinventing aid for SMEs in Eastern Europe lessons from the implementation of the STRUDER programme', *Regional Studies* 32, 290–4.

Krugman, P. (1994) *Peddling Prosperity*, New York: W. W. Norton.

Lopez-Baso, E., Vaya, E. and Mora, A. J. (1999) 'Regional economic dynamics and convergence in the European Union', *Annals of Regional Science* 33, 343–70.

Magrini, S. (1999) 'The evolution of income disparities among the regions of the European Union', *Regional Science and Urban Economics* 29, 257–81.

Martin, R. and Tyler, P. (2000) 'Regional employment evolutions in the European Union: a preliminary analysis', *Regional Studies* 34, 601–16.

Melachroinos, K. A. and Spence, N. (2001) 'Manufacturing productivity growth across European Union states', *Environment and Planning A* 33, 1681–703.

Miller, D. (2000) 'Paving the way for EU accession: regional development and support for SMEs in eastern Poland', *Regional Studies* 34, 586–92.

Neven, D. and Gouyette, C. (1995) 'Regional convergence in the European Community', *Journal of Common Market Studies* 33, 47–65.

OECD (1998) *The OECD STAN Database for Industrial Analysis 1970–1997*, Paris: OECD.

Rodriguez-Pose, A. (1998) *The Dynamics of Regional Growth in Europe. Social and Political Factors*, Oxford: Clarendon Press.

Rovolis, A. and Spence, N. (2000) *Impact of Community Enterprise Policy on Economic and Social Cohesion*, DG Regional Policy: European Commission.

Smith, D. M. (1979) *Where the Grass is Greener: Living in an Unequal World*, Baltimore: Johns Hopkins University Press; US edition, Baltimore: Johns Hopkins University Press, 1982.

4

Moral Problems of Eastern Wilderness: European Core and Periphery

Bolesław Domański

Introduction

The inspiration for this chapter comes from two strands of David Smith's activity: first, his moral concern, and, second, his interest in East-Central Europe (ECE). It comes at a time of profound changes throughout Europe, which, in turn, result from broader economic and political challenges and attempts to deepen the integration of the EU and broaden its geographic scope. With the accession to the EU of ten new members, including eight post-socialist countries, there is growing political and academic debate as to what the emerging new Europe means.

Faced with this enlargement of the European Union, some West European politicians have argued for the forging of a new core that would exclude new members. They have received support from prominent intellectuals. In the aftermath of the Iraq war, Jürgen Habermas argued in an article co-authored with Jacques Derrida that there is a wide gap between 'the core Europe' (*Kerneuropa*) and candidate countries from behind the Iron Curtain. It is the core Europeans who share essential values and achievements which constitute 'European identity' transcending national-ity. 'Only the core states of Europe ... are able to agree on a common definition of their own interests' (Habermas and Derrida, 2003, p. 33); therefore they should institutionalize the avant-garde core of the EU. Others can join once they have accepted European identity and interests represented by the core.

The view that countries east and south-east of Germany do not embody fundamental European values reveals deeper beliefs concerning the nature of Europe within the academic and political establishment. The interpret-ation of the cultural, economic and political differentiation of Europe, and its moral and practical implications, deserves consideration.

Three groups of problems are critically examined in this chapter. Initially, it focuses on the image of East-Central Europe (ECE) as periphery and its consequences for the understanding of the EU.[1] This is followed by a discussion of certain fallacies of the research on post-socialist societies, their moral meaning and possible effects. Finally, the moral dimension of problems faced by these societies is addressed.

Core and Periphery

The idea of core (centre) and periphery has a long history and there is no room to explore it here. We can, however, discuss a number of forms in which the belief in the peripheral status of ECE countries appears.

These countries belong to 'emerging markets' or 'frontier markets' (Sidaway and Pryke, 2000). What follows is that turbulence in one country often leads to capital flight from all markets assigned to these high-risk categories. As a result of their peripheral status, these countries have a heightened dependence on the verdicts of international rating institutions. Budget deficits in the United States or Germany do not undermine the trust of the business community in these economies, which their international rating is said to reflect, but the macro-economic difficulties of, say, Romania, may have disastrous effects for its rating and hence its treatment in the world of finance. The cost of being part of the periphery is in this case very real.

The metaphor of 'cathedrals in the desert' has become popular in the interpretation of post-socialist economic development. It was originally applied by Grabher (1994) to some German industries in the early years of unification, and is now used to reflect the contrast between disembedded foreign investment or enclaves of growth in the region of economic decline. It conveys the image of general post-socialist wasteland, where success, usually built on Western capital, can only be a local and probably temporal phenomenon. ECE can contribute little to the world economy, except for providing new markets, raw materials and cheap labour. This view is explicit or implicit among a number of devoted proponents of neoliberal economy and its staunch critics.

Areas east of Berlin and Vienna are peripheral not only economically, but also politically. This finds profound expression in the notion of 'shatterbelt'. It is interesting that the 'shatterbelt' includes long-standing states such as Hungary, which is more than 1,000 years old, but it does not refer to Germany, which has functioned as a united nation-state for a relatively short time, and was involved in two great wars and major boundary changes. The ECE countries are regarded as territories of chaos that could pose a threat to the stability of the European core.

Furthermore, there are cultural roots to the categorization of ECE as a periphery. The Iron Curtain severed this part of Europe from the core. It removed the people of the East from the eyes of those in the West. The former lived beyond the limits of the world of the latter. Their absence or insignificance was evident in many prominent geographical and historical books which claimed to deal with the world or Europe as a whole, for example *History of Western Civilization* (McNeill, 1986), *A World in Crisis?* (Johnston and Taylor, 1989) and *Europe: A History of Its People* (Duroselle, 1990).[2] The people of ECE have now emerged from nonexistence and appear to be strangers who adhere to pre-modern beliefs. They represent some sort of 'wilderness' and need to convert to proper values before they are treated as moral equals and can be offered their say in the discussion concerning Europe. This bears a striking similarity to the view that there are some untamed people beyond the spatial and cultural limits of our civilization. Smith (2000) shows that spatial separation and/or ignorance allow us to treat others as 'uncivilized barbarians' who belong to an inferior culture.

The geographical image of the ECE periphery is related to a selective view of European history. It is all too easy to reduce the heritage of ECE to ethnic and religious conflicts, political oppression, and so on. Habermas (2001) denies the broader significance of the revolution which brought ECE societies from totalitarianism to democracy. Many authors try to make us believe that no lesson can be learned from the socialist experience of ECE and its rejection.[3] How widespread is the sentiment for the world order based on the Iron Curtain as the foundation of stability? The latter is reminiscent of the criticism voiced by some Western politicians against pre-1989 opposition activity in the East, which they saw as a 'threat to world peace'.

On the whole, the heritage of the periphery may be regarded as irrelevant to members of the superior culture. Neoliberals may ignore the specificity of the region as a result of their universalistic belief in the free market and perceive economic 'transition' as a technical task. Post-Marxists may grieve the departure from an attempt to establish an alternative to capitalism. Many people can share a belief in linear or dialectical historical development, where modernization or progress, whatever either means, spreads from the economic or intellectual core to the periphery. Perhaps ECE simply comprises backward societies which have not developed a modern economy and/or progressive outlook. It therefore follows that they have to catch up and adopt features and/or views that the core has already embraced. The implication is that they do not know what is good (lack correct values) and in particular do not understand what is good for them. The core cannot learn much from the periphery, unless treated as a threat or curiosity.

This leads to a specific understanding of the Eastern expansion of the European Union. First, this is an act of benevolence on the part of Western Europe. Second, it is done to stabilize an area of political and economic chaos. Third, new members are claimants and recipients of the wealth produced in the core. It follows that they should learn and accept correct values. The core is both a benefactor and a mentor.

This contrasts with the perspective on the accession in ECE. It is seen as an act of justice and the realization of local aspirations (this may also lead to claimant attitudes). It confirms being a part of European culture: something which has always existed, though it used to be politically denied. We never left Europe; Western Europe left us.

British historian Norman Davies (1996, p. 28) says:

> Eastern Europe is no less European for being poor, or underdeveloped, or ruled by tyrants. In many ways, thanks to its deprivations, it has become more European, more attached to the values which affluent Westerners can take for granted. Nor can Eastern Europe be rejected because it is 'different'. All European countries are different. All *West* European countries are different. And there are important similarities which span the divide. A country like Poland might be very different from Germany or from Britain; but the Polish experience is much closer to that of Ireland or of Spain than many West European countries are to each other.

It would require a long discussion to consider what ECE can contribute to European values in the forging of a 'new Europe'. Conflicts should not obscure ages of co-existence and intermixing of people of different languages and religions, including Jews. For inhabitants of many regions here, European identity may seem a natural, everyday experience (Batt and Wolczuk, 2002). There have been multi-national federal traditions: for example, four centuries of the voluntary union of Lithuania and Poland, and pre-imperial republics such as Novgorod the Great in Russia. A quest for fundamental values and collective goods was manifest in the Prague Spring of 1968. The spirit of solidarity constituted the foundation of the mass 1980–1 civil movement in Poland, which transcended narrow group interests and operated on a territorial rather than an occupational basis. Moreover, in the light of their historical experience, post-socialist societies may now be suspicious of utopian ideologies and moral justification of any rule that delivers stability and saves them from chaos. Yet, despite these positive experiences from which the whole of Europe could draw, there has generally not been much attempt to understand the experience of the periphery. The roots of European universalism should be limited neither geographically nor historically to the present wisdom of few nations (see Unwin, 1998; Gerner, 2001). Both the Eastern and the Western lung are crucial to the integrity of European culture, to use John Paul II's metaphor (cited by Kukliński, 2001).

It is not the empirical validity of describing ECE as a periphery in terms of its level of economic development and dependence on core economies which is questioned here. It is a broader image of moral, cultural and political inferiority of this part of Europe together with a deterministic interpretation of existing differences. Such a categorization has moral and political implications. It represents a paternalistic attitude to ECE and legitimizes exclusionary political action, a sort of social closure on the part of Western Europe.

What we see are attempts to reproduce the old or create new divisions in Europe: first, an internal divide within the extended EU; and, second, the rift between the EU and the rest of East-Central Europe. One could argue that both divisions are to a certain extent unavoidable. It would be unrealistic to expect that the integration of new members into an established community could escape temporary barriers which protect the 'old' members. It is beyond the scope of this chapter to discuss which of the barriers are justified. As Smith (2000) observes, capital can already move freely, while labour has to accept limitations. However, we can dispute the justification for the establishment of core Europe demanded by some politicians and academics. This would mean the institutionalization of an internal periphery within the extended EU in order to allow 'core Europeans' to define 'common' European interests and make decisions shaping the future of Europe without the interference of second-rate European citizens. What is at stake is the sharing of power.

Another pressing problem is the external periphery of the EU, where third-rate Europeans have to live. It is morally and politically disastrous to accept such a category as a long-term reality. There is an urgent need to forge new relations between these countries and the EU in order to prevent their further marginalization. Their strategic role within Europe is open to debate. Double political and moral standards are sometimes applied to Russia and other countries. This stems from both its position as a nuclear power and the long tradition of the tolerant approach to imperial Soviet or Russian ambitions. The Balkans tend to be perceived as a distinct breed (Todorova, 1997; A. Smith, 2002). For many people in the West, it is difficult to accept the existence and aspirations of Ukrainians, one of the largest European nations, which is a shocking legacy of imperial or Cold War thinking.[4] Central Europeans may hold attitudes similar to those criticized above towards their Eastern or Southern (Balkan) neighbours. As a Ukrainian woman who has worked in Poland for three years says:

> We come from a neighbouring country, but people sometimes ask questions as if we came from the Moon. They ask if we have a TV at home or whether

children go to school. As if we were some sort of savages. They do not understand that we are the same people, and that we only lack money. And it is worst when we are called Russians. (cited in Machcewicz, 2003)

The vision of the EU as a fortress, refusing responsibility for people outside its bounds, is unacceptable and contradicts moral ideas of extended care advanced by Smith (1998, 2000).

Land of Hope or Despair! Remarks on the Responsibility of Our Research

Positioning of some people at the periphery may not only legitimize their paternalistic treatment and denial of participation in dialogue and decisions, but also deprive them of hope. One of the major shortcomings of some geographical research on ECE, both in the East and West, is a one-sided portrayal of post-socialist economies as falling apart with no clear alternative. This may be a fatalistic view of European geography and history. 'Cathedrals' of modern capitalism cannot become embedded in the 'desert'; they will have little impact on barren surroundings. The roles of core and periphery appear immutable. The East is doomed to failure as the periphery exploited by global capital.

Does this foster active attitudes and social mobilization or rather promote a sense of hopelessness and passivity? The practical lesson for young people might be to flee to the West or adopt a claimant's attitude to the state and the EU. The dismal picture and lack of prospects may become a self-reinforcing prophecy, contributing to the reproduction of the peripherality of ECE.

We cannot forget about moral responsibility for the practical consequences of the academic interpretation of reality. Cloke (2002, pp. 596–7), discussing Hannah Arendt's views, emphasizes the crucial role of the capacity for action: 'a gloomy acceptance of an inability to change things represents an abrogation of the responsibility to recognize the extent of this capacity for action'.

The deterministic slant can reflect the theoretical perspectives adopted. Some interpretations fall little short of old functionalist explanations. On the one hand, the gap between the core and the periphery is confirmed by economic decline in parts of ECE. At the same time, growth in other countries is explained by their function within the global capitalist system – it serves the core through the profits of transnational corporations (TNCs), which expand to new markets and exploit new labour. Consequently, the growth in the periphery reinforces its peripherality. The problem with such an interpretation is not the empirical validity of individual facts, but the circular nature of theoretical reasoning. The observed phenomena are explained by the reproduction of core and periphery, while this duality is in turn proved by the same phenomena. Such an approach does not allow change in the position of the areas categorized as periphery and hence precludes empirical search for symptoms of such change.

Similarly, it is difficult to accept an assumption that these societies would have been better off if they had continued their non-capitalist endeavour. Such speculation is rarely based on an analysis of ECE socialist mechanisms, so it fails to point out which of them are worth maintaining.

Neoliberal economists preach an optimistic, though intrinsically narrow, gospel of the positive effects of the market economy. The comparison of economic performance of various post-socialist countries shows that the thorough installation of basic market institutions has been a precondition for economic growth. Still, post-socialist society has a complex set of problems to resolve that go beyond these basic mechanisms and/or are brought about by them. The variety of capitalist societies in Western Europe suggests numerous options, but the impact of local determinants and traditions is considerable.

Some authors attribute the different economic performance of transition countries largely to their geographical location (Sachs, 1997). This scarcely captures the cultural, social and economic background behind the relative success of economies contiguous to Western markets such as Slovenia, Hungary, the Czech Republic or Poland, nor does it leave much room for local agency. More importantly, the concept of the diffusion of Western ideas, investment and trade links primarily on the basis of physical proximity inevitably carries overtones of geographical determinism, which may deprive more 'distant' countries of hope.

There is a salient problem of distinguishing well-founded hope from false hope or utopia. We ultimately learn which expectations are realistic and which solutions are plausible *ex post*. However difficult it may be, a striving for values, meaning and hope is a moral endeavour and an obligation to the people of any studied area.

There are several other fallacies in the research on post-socialist societies. They can only be indicated briefly here:

- Many studies are static, focusing on the state of affairs, while ignoring processes. Some interpretations are totally ahistorical: history begins about 1990, contemporary phenomena are severed from earlier structures and mechanisms, which is justified by their alleged 'erosion', 'deregulation' and the impact of exogenous forces.
- The explanations of local development play down the role of endogenous factors: labour, small business, town authorities and local

communities may be perceived as passive recipients of whatever effects large enterprises and state policy bring about.

- Low costs of labour are sometimes put forward as the principal factor of foreign investment,[5] or even economic growth in general. It is occasionally part of a broader argument of 'social devaluation', according to which countries or places compete predominantly on the basis of lowering their social standards.
- The myth of post-socialist deregulation underlies disregard for social costs and benefits of the vast systems of regulation devised and implemented in each of these countries since 1990.
- The state is often treated as a single entity and a 'black box', rather than as a network of institutions with varying spheres of influence, goals and practices.

One may find papers and chapters where the introduction is full of lip service paid to local heritage, labour agency, path dependency, and so on. What follows may be a narrow, ahistorical case study, ignoring the broader social and geographical context as well as longer historical processes. Scanty empirical material may contrast with general conclusions, which may simply reflect the author's preconceptions.

The Moral Dimension of the Social Transformation of Post-socialist Europe

East-Central European societies have been exposed to a shock of multiple transformation. They have had to cope with technological modernization and its social effects in parallel to the (re)introduction of liberal democracy, the transition to a market economy, globalization and, in some cases, European integration. This has faced them with new technological, social and political problems as well as previously unknown moral dilemmas.

The functioning of democratic and market mechanisms is contingent on moral values, which may take specific forms in this part of Europe. There are, for example, issues of business ethics in societies where private economic activity used to operate on the fringes of the law, environmental ethics in places where ecological improvement is in conflict with job protection, and work ethics of people who were subjected to large-scale wastage of results of their work and now meet a stringent performance-oriented approach and lack of employment security.

The past experience of the imposed collectivist ethics of duty can make individualistic ethics of rights appear very attractive. This can be accompanied by mistrust of other people propagated by Marxist-Leninist ideology and suspicion of public institutions as a legacy of socialist state practices. Rapid, unexpected and pervasive changes in ECE are a source of 'trauma', which may reinforce distrust, anxiety or even moral panic (Sztompka, 1999). Giddens (1990) identifies 'cynical hedonism' as one social reaction to risk. A claimant's attitude towards the state and a sense of being wronged are deeply ingrained. The distinction between the private and the public may be blurred, which can fuel corruption. Emphasis on responsibility and duty, rather than individual rights, may come from religion, a tradition of extended family and social collaboration, which helped people to survive economic hardships and provided a basis for civil mobilization against previous regimes.

Moral ambiguities are also visible in the domain of social inequalities. They are influenced by a divergence between egalitarian values and social practice under state socialism, the current increase in the extent of disparities, their conspicuousness and new origins. The inequalities are generated by mechanisms well-known from capitalist societies. Two groups of problems related to inequality, which are somewhat specific in post-socialist societies, are considered here, namely change of ownership and state regulation.

The redistribution of property rights to existing assets became a key issue after the fall of socialism. Different privatization methods were adopted: for example, mass privatization in the Czech Republic and a case-by-case approach in Poland and Hungary (Williams and Baláž, 1999). The Czech investment funds reveal difficulties arising from the lack of real owners. In Hungary, firms were mostly put to open tendering, which resulted in a high share of foreign ownership. Poland saw various forms of privatization with strong preferential treatment of insiders: employee-buyout schemes, which above all favoured local managers, and the distribution of 15 per cent of the stock to the workforce in the case of selling the enterprise. Insider privatization was entirely dominant in Russia.

There are a number of moral issues relevant here. First, as Smith (1994) points out, it would be proper to have equal opportunities at the start, which was obviously not the case. The effects were conversion of political into economic capital by the *nomenklatura* and the rise of a new class of domestic owners on the basis of early capital accumulation. The latter has partly been socially approved, which is not the case with the former. Secondly, there are problems of compensation for socialist expropriation, which may also concern foreign citizens, for example Germans in the Czech Republic. Public attitudes to these claims vary but are often negative. Most countries, except for Poland and Belarus, have enacted certain property restitution programmes (Jeffries, 2002). Thirdly, mass privatization may represent equality of opportunity. By contrast, there is little moral justification for a rental windfall to small groups which benefit from free shares or assets leased to insiders. This excludes the vast majority of citizens and reflects 'buying off' support for privatization or privileges granted by the state.

It is necessary to challenge a widespread fallacy of the general deregulation of post-socialist states. First, it ignores the enormous role of the state in modifying and introducing complex systems of regulation. Second, it diverts attention from the serious social and moral question of who benefits from the post-socialist regulation.

The vast scope of legal and institutional change in the systems of regulation in ECE raises the issue of how much this regulation is grounded in the moral norms of society. This is a problem of a relationship between the *ius* and the *lex*. The more the regulation departs from socially accepted norms, the less legitimate it is. This may be illustrated by the Polish example.

The Polish state has failed to meet its obligation to provide a transparent and stable legal and institutional framework for economic activity. The intricate system of regulation with more than thirty controlling institutions is neither unequivocal nor durable. This allows for different interpretations by various bodies and encourages informal activities. Under-financed courts are a bottleneck which has helped the parasitical operation of firms that avoid paying their suppliers, thus contributing to bankruptcies, job losses and illegal profits.

The costs of the state apparatus are on the rise, while expenses on public services and social welfare are being cut. Substantial resources go to numerous governmental agencies and funds which pursue their autonomous goals with weak control and limited social benefits. The powerful lobbies operating in a few state-owned sectors of coal, steel and railways consume immense direct and indirect subsidies (unpaid social security contributions, taxes and environmental fees) and run up debts to suppliers and banks without the risk of bankruptcy. This serves political, managerial and union elites as well as narrow groups of labour. A growing share of pension funds and bank capital is frozen in government bonds, which reduces the amount of financing available for firms. Indigenous private enterprises are part of lobbies built on personal, politically embedded networks. TNCs tend to strike individual bargains with public institutions. Thus, *some* domestic and foreign enterprises profit from the system.

To sum up, the post-socialist Polish state, similarly to its socialist predecessor, reveals unequal treatment of its citizens, favouring well-organized pressure groups and discriminating against others, including the deprived, who lack adequate mechanisms for interest representation. Such a system defies both the universalistic idea of impartial regulation, which treats broad categories of people and firms in the same way, and a redistribution to the benefit of weak groups. The costly state is incapable of coping with social deprivation and fostering economic development. Moreover, inequalities in state practices undermine public trust in the law and the state. It is a case not of insufficient regulation, but of its departure from moral norms and poor quality in some areas: orientation to group interests and ineffectiveness, which is the central problem of several post-socialist states.

An honest and accountable state, committed to fair treatment of its citizens, is essential for social activity which can overcome ECE peripherality. The proliferation of social movements and success of local governments constitute countervailing forces to the deficiencies of the state apparatus and put civil pressure on the improvement of regulation in Poland. There are areas where relatively effective, transparent and stable regulation is already in place, for example environmental law.

Last but not least, the complex history of ECE gives special significance to the discourse on local heritage. This is very much a normative issue. It includes a complex problem of 'cultural ownership'. This can be illustrated by a debate aroused by the secret removal of Bruno Schulz's murals from the Ukrainian town of Drohobych to Israel a few years ago. Who has moral rights to the works of this writer and painter of Jewish descent who became a prominent figure in Polish-language literature in the 1930s, portrayed Jewish culture in his homeland of Galicia, the vast part of which is now Ukraine, and lost his life in the Holocaust? Can anybody claim exclusive rights to his works at all?

Conclusion

Post-socialist Europe has recently emerged from a sort of oblivion, which entails redefinition of its relationships with the rest of the world. It is worth considering how and why East-Central Europe may pose a moral problem to people in the West and what moral problems are faced in post-socialist societies. This chapter is neither a systematic overview of various perspectives on ECE, nor an account of its current problems. It is a personal critique of certain attitudes and assumptions concerning this part of Europe found among politicians and academics, together with their moral underpinnings and implications. It rests on a belief that open discussion of such issues is relevant in contemporary European debate.

The arguments of the moral superiority of core Europe can be challenged on two grounds. First, it would be in line with widespread anti-essentialism to question any claim to the superiority of some values to others. This is not the approach taken here. This contribution is rather meant to cast doubt upon the validity of ideas that underlie such claims.

There seems to be an ingrained belief in the perennial peripherality of ECE as an area of political instability, economic desert and cultural wilderness, where backward ideas abound. However, this peripherality is not an outcome of some impartial, abstract social forces, but is reproduced by the discourse and regulation of various actors. Western Europe is confronted with the East as a threat and demand: economic (to share wealth), political (to share power) and cultural (to enter into dialogue). The idea that 'new' Europeans are admitted to 'our' Europe, so they should endorse 'our' moral and political perspective, is paternalistic. Respect to others may be shown in proportion to their affinity to ourselves. Habermas and Derrida (2003) define their European outlook as opposed to American 'hegemonic unilateralism'. One may ask how many people from Ireland to Russia could identify with their supposedly universalistic view of Europe? A Hungarian author, Péter Esterházy (2003, p. 13), comments sarcastically: 'Earlier I had been an Eastern European, then I advanced to the group of Central Europeans. . . . A few months ago I became a new European but even before I have accustomed to this, I learn that I am not a genuine European.'

The elements of the beliefs discussed appear in various forms and may be rooted in imperial, liberal or Marxist ideologies. The exclusion of people who are perceived as different Europeans may represent what Sibley (1988) calls 'purification' of social space by keeping out certain others. Moral development means the capacity to overcome narcissistic tendencies and narrow parochialism and to adopt wider perspectives (Sack, 1997). 'If the human capacity of putting one's self in the place of others is to be an effective wellspring of morality, this requires understanding that place, as well as those others' (Smith, 2000, p. 214). This entails learning the complex experience of the whole of Europe, parts of which are easily discarded or stereotyped.

There are a growing number of publications on ECE, many of which are in-depth or comparative studies based on comprehensive research which broaden our understanding of these societies. Still, there are also case studies and synoptic papers which offer general conclusions built upon a limited empirical base and doubtful theoretical assumptions. They are distinguished by their ignorance of the broader historical and geographical context of the phenomena discussed. A common fallacy is a passive view of ECE societies, which appear as recipients of external influences. The vital issue of local capacity for action may be neglected.

It is not argued that the criticized approaches are predominant. Everybody can judge for him- or herself how far these are explicitly or implicitly present in the way ECE is studied, explained to students and understood by politicians. We need critical research that could capture and interpret various processes: ones that reproduce core–periphery relationships and ones that alter them. If we avoid morally doubtful stereotypes, simplistic determinism and fatalistic conclusions, our work can be academically better, morally responsible and politically relevant. Main arguments against the challenged views are of a moral and practical nature: they deny opportunities for change and deprive people of hope – a basic human need. The aim is to foster processes of social mobilization based on the development of social and cultural capital, rather than pessimism and social apathy leading to destruction and marginalization (Sztompka, 1991).

There are many developmental paths of ECE countries, which arise from the past trajectories and contemporary choices of various social actors (Bradshaw and Stenning, 2003; Turnock, 2003). A lot can be learned from the effects of different social models in Western Europe, even though there is no simple process of their diffusion and adoption in the East. If we believe in Europe as a 'unity in diversity', there is room for a dialogue on European past and future. This means renouncing a stance of moral superiority, which legitimizes the political status quo of a disempowered ECE periphery, while European values and interests can be defined and represented by self-contained 'core Europeans'. It is crucial to seek ways of including within the common European future those people who remain outside the extended EU, rather than pursuing the creation of a new core.

NOTES

I am grateful to Krzysztof Gwosdz, Iwona Sagan and Alison Stenning for their helpful comments on an earlier draft. The responsibility for all opinions and errors lies solely with the author.

1 Some ideas discussed here were originally presented at the RGS-IBG Annual Conference in London (September 2003).
2 The latter met strong criticism from Greece, whose contribution was largely neglected.
3 See critique by Michalak and Gibb (1992), Bivand (1997) and Domański (1997).
4 There are other issues not discussed in this chapter, for examle Turkish aspirations and relations with non-Europeans.
5 TNC managers, who follow their efficiency-minded approach world-wide, may perceive more local assets that serve their goals than do economists who interpret their activity.

REFERENCES

Batt, J. and Wolczuk, K. (eds) (2002) *Region, State and Identity in Central and Eastern Europe*, London: Frank Cass.

Bivand, R. (1997) 'Imaginative geographies: spaces beyond the horizon?', in A. Kukliński (ed.), *European Space, Baltic Space, Polish Space*, Part Two, Warsaw: European Institute for Regional and Local Development, University of Warsaw, pp. 213–20.

Bradshaw, M. and Stenning, A. (eds) (2003) *East Central Europe and the Former Soviet Union: The Post-socialist States*, London: Pearson.

Cloke, P. (2002) 'Deliver us from evil? Prospects for living ethically and acting politically in human geography', *Progress in Human Geography* 26, 587–604.

Davies, N. (1996) *Europe: A History*, Oxford: Oxford University Press.

Domański, B. (1997) *Industrial Control over the Socialist Town: Benevolence or Exploitation?* Westport: Praeger.

Duroselle, J. B. (1990) *Europe: A History of Its People*, London: Viking.

Esterházy, P. (2003) 'Wir Störenfriede: Wie gross ist der europäische Zwerg?', *Süddeutsche Zeitung* 11 June, p. 13.

Gerner, K. (2001) 'Europe, globalization and the grand historical choices of the 21st century: a new historical perspective', in H. Bünz and A. Kukliński (eds), *Globalization: Experiences and Prospects*, Warsaw: F. Ebert Stiftung, pp. 210–25.

Giddens, A. (1990) *The Consequences of Modernity*, Cambridge: Polity.

Grabher, G. (1994) 'The disembedded regional economy: the transformation of east German industrial complexes into western enclaves', in A. Amin and N. Thrift (eds), *Globalization, Institutions, and Regional Development in Europe*, Oxford: Oxford University Press, pp. 177–95.

Habermas, J. (2001) *The Postnational Constellation: Political Essays* (trans. M. Pensky), Cambridge, Mass.: MIT Press.

Habermas, J. and Derrida, J. (2003) 'Nach dem Krieg: Die Wiedergeburt Europas', *Frankfurter Allgemeine Zeitung* 31 May, p. 33.

Jeffries, I. (2002) *Eastern Europe at the Turn of the Twenty-first Century: A Guide to the Economies in Transition*, London: Routledge.

Johnston, R. J. and Taylor, P. (eds) (1989) *A World in Crisis?* (2nd edition), Oxford: Blackwell.

Kukliński, A. (2001) 'What will Polish EU membership mean for EU and for Europe at large? Preliminary reflections', in H. Bünz and A. Kukliński (eds), *Globalization: Experiences and Prospects*, Warsaw: F. Ebert Stiftung, pp. 459–81.

Machcewicz, A. (2003) 'Jestesmy takimi samymi ludzmi' [We are the same people], *Rzeczpospolita* 19 April, p. 8.

McNeill, W. H. (1986) *History of Western Civilization* (6th edition), Chicago: University of Chicago Press.

Michalak, W. Z. and Gibb, R. A. (1992) 'Political geography and eastern Europe', *Area* 24, 341–50.

Sachs, J. (1997) *Geography and Economic Transition*, Cambridge, Mass.: Harvard Institute for International Development. Available at *www.cid.harvard.edu*

Sack, R. D. (1997) *Homo Geographicus: A Framework for Action, Awareness, and Moral Concern*, Baltimore: Johns Hopkins University Press.

Sibley, D. (1988) 'Purification of space', *Environment and Planning D: Society and Space* 6, 409–21.

Sidaway, J. and Pryke, M. (2000) 'The strange geographies of "emerging markets"', *Transactions of the Institute of British Geographers* 25, 187–201.

Smith, A. (2002) 'Imagining geographies of the "new Europe": geo-economic power and the new European architecture of integration', *Political Geography* 21, 647–70.

Smith, D. M. (1994) *Geography and Social Justice*, Oxford: Blackwell.

Smith, D. M. (1998) 'How far should we care? On the spatial scope of beneficence', *Progress in Human Geography* 22, 15–38.

Smith, D. M. (2000) *Moral Geographies: Ethics in a World of Difference*, Edinburgh: Edinburgh University Press.

Sztompka, P. (1991) *Society in Action: The Theory of Social Becoming*, Cambridge: Polity.

Sztompka, P. (1999) *Trust: A Sociological Theory*, Cambridge: Cambridge University Press.

Todorova, M. (1997) *Imagining the Balkans*, New York: Oxford University Press.

Turnock, D. (2003) *The Human Geography of East Central Europe*, London: Routledge.

Unwin, T. (1998) 'Ideas of Europe', in T. Unwin (ed.), *A European Geography*, Harlow: Longman, pp. 1–16.

Williams, A. M. and Baláž, V. (1999) 'Privatization in Central Europe: different legacies, methods, and outcomes', *Environment and Planning C: Government and Policy* 17, 731–51.

5

Where the Grass is Greener in Poland: Regional and Intra-urban Inequalities

Grzegorz Węcławowicz

Introduction

'Human beings have moral values.' This is not a quotation from the Pope or any other Polish Catholic bishop's sermon. It is the opening sentence of David M. Smith's (2000) book *Moral Geographies: Ethics in a World of Difference*. This sentence reminds us that geography is not a value-free science and that the product of our research should have more social relevance. It is quite relevant at the end of the euphoria of democratic transformation in Poland and in Central Europe, particularly when inequality has become one of the key issues, as a basic ingredient of quality of life.

The new model under construction, of an efficient property-owning democracy, has become an alternative to that of inefficient communism. The expected shift of the whole society towards increased social well-being has been constrained by an increase of inequality and the 'injustice' of the market economy. In the perception of some social groups, and in the light of all economic indicators, the whole of Polish society can be categorized as gainers or losers during the transformation. Associated with this, the traditional structure of regional prosperity has changed.

One of the purposes of this chapter is to shed some light on the spatial distribution of poverty in Poland, considering it a by-product of the transformation, and of spatial and regional policy. I do not try to distinguish between social determinants and spatial determinants of poverty, assuming that the spatial are to a large extent the result of social determinants.

The Hierarchy of Explanation and the Level of Analysis

Several years ago while trying to explain the intra-urban differentiation of the socialist city, a hierarchy of explanation was adopted starting from the political level, to the levels of ideological, economic and living conditions (Węcławowicz, 1988, 1996). The most important phenomenon was the struggle for maintaining political power. Since power was monopolized by the communist group, it had a monopoly on judgement concerning which ideological principles were correct and which not. The main strategy of this group for achieving social and political support was nationalization of the economy and forced industrialization. Having control of the national economy and industrialization, this group modified the economic processes and industrialization to safeguard the maintenance of power. The modification of those processes had roots in the ideological principle of the formation of an egalitarian society and the supporting social group of the working class. The main means was the control of distribution of living conditions. So the explanation of socio-economic disparities and their spatial structure based solely on the description of the spatial differentiation of living conditions provides only a partial answer to the question of the intra-urban differentiation of the socialist city.

The level of socio-spatial disparities up to 1989 in Poland was partly a by-product of the communist political system. The central allocation of better or worse living conditions on a regional scale had been treated as a reward or as a punishment for the inhabitants of a particular region or town. So the regional injustice of the socialist state had roots in inefficient economic management and policy, inherited from pre-war times but also produced by the communist system. The communist maxim of 'to everyone according to their need', under the ideal of the equal spatial allocation of productive forces, had been implemented in regional policy only at the beginning. The shift to the new maxim: 'to everyone according to their work', and next, 'to everyone according to impartial principles of social justice', had indicated a tendency to change the selective allocation of production forces. In particular, the supposed impartial principles had throughout been determined by the ruling group, according to participation in supporting the existing power structure. The achievement of regional equalization of the standard of living was impossible due to the fact that regional planning was part of ideologically determined social engineering. In addition, the gradual formation of interest groups, defined regionally and by economic sector, and the increase in their power, had contributed to the increase of regional disparities.

In spite of the radical changes in everyday life in Poland, the hierarchical structure of most important processes has remained the same for the decade and more of transformation. The most general level, however, we should now recognize as globalization and European integration. To a great extent, all economic and social processes could be perceived as subordinated to the logic and requirement of globalization. This subordination to globalization is imposed by the market mechanism, not by direct political subordination, as in the previous communist system. So in the socio-spatial analysis we usually undertake on variations in living conditions, we should bear in mind that the roots of spatial patterns are to be found in this highest level of explanation.

Transformation in the Social Structure of Poland

The increase in social differentiation is one of the most frequently described phenomena of market transformation, not only in Poland but also in all post-communist countries. As noted above, all citizens could be classified as gainers or losers in the transformation. In Poland a large-scale process of class recomposition had started after 1989, involving the changing structure of ownership, the distribution of income and wealth, consumption, cultural behaviour, political significance and prestige. The radical shrinking of some social classes and the expansion of others are very evident. From the very beginning of the transformation it became obvious that the main pre-existing social groups – workers in large state industrial plants and peasants (particularly in state farms) – had little chance of surviving in the market system. The demands of the market system, and particularly the new rules of the labour market, have introduced changes in wages and in the earning capacity of particular professions and the demand for particular skills.

The distribution of income between social and occupational groups has been changing (Table 5.1). In the first years of the transformation, income mobility was high, due to the increase of economic opportunities in the new expanding private sector, and to basic recession in the public sector. As a result some socio-occupational categories have had relative upward mobility, but for other categories the economic situation has deteriorated. Managers and state administrators have made the greatest progress, their monthly income per family member increasing to three times the average level. Relative improvement can also be noted in the case of the intelligentsia, engineers, private businessmen and administration in general. All manual social groups, however, particularly unskilled workers and peasants, experienced a relative decline.

In very general terms the process of the formation of three large social groups is underway: the elite, the middle class and the poverty class.

The current elite group has been constructed from the former communist elite, *nomenklatura* members, part of the former anti-communist

Table 5.1 Monthly family income per person (zlotys), in relation to national average in 1987, 1993 and 1998

Socio-occupational categories	1987	1993	1998
Managers and higher state administrative officials	145	317	223
Non-technical intelligentsia	145	226	175
Engineers	123	134	128
Technicians	104	101	120
Middle-grade clerks	112	129	118
Lower-grade clerks	103	105	109
Businessmen	146	144	160
Employed in sales and service	98	91	87
Foremen	100	85	119
Skilled workers	95	79	92
Unskilled workers	91	68	76
Manual workers in service	80	63	75
Employed in farming	77	58	67
Farm owners	88	57	68

Source: Domański, 2000, 2002.

opposition and the intelligentsia. In very rare cases members of the former working class or peasants were recruited to this elite. The middle-class group, still under formation, is recruited from former communist upper- and lower-grade *nomenklatura* members, part of the anti-communist opposition leadership and the intelligentsia (Węcławowicz, 1996).

The poverty group is emerging from all social categories losing from the transformation. Above all it involves the unemployed, some unskilled workers, the majority of the rural population (particularly former peasant workers) and owners of small farms, and even part of the lower-level intelligentsia. A large segment of the unskilled working class are also on the losers' side. This also involves the majority of elderly people. The huge share of people employed in the administration or dependent on the state budget is highly differentiated and generally badly paid, creating a group who regard themselves as losers. The cities, particularly the biggest ones, have become very expensive to live in for an increasing share of their citizens. These people can still survive, however, with a niche in the informal sector of the economy. This phenomenon contributes substantially to an increase in social polarization, having its impact on spatial segregation.

To describe this phenomenon, the concept of an underclass has been adapted to the current vocabulary describing social differentiation in Poland (Domański, 2000). This social category is segregated at the regional and intra-urban scales. First of all it involves regional concentration in the rural areas dominated by the former state farming sector and underdeveloped private farming. The second geographical concentration involves, in particular, declining industrial towns, small towns in rural areas and, at the intra-urban scale, some housing estates from the early 1950s and 1960s.

The Scale of Poverty

The multidimensional living condition survey conducted by the Central Statistical Office in 2001 (GUS, 2002) revealed the significant inequality of Polish households. This inequality, particularly in income, is showing a tendency to increase. Currently, according to this research, around 5 per cent of households do not have money for the cheapest food and clothing, around 33 per cent cannot get recommended medicines, and 10 per cent of households with children in primary and secondary school could not afford to buy manuals (textbooks). In addition, around 8 per cent of households had arrears in housing payments. This research shows also that 34 per cent of households are not satisfied with their economic situation.

In the Central Statistical Office research the scale of poverty by nearly all criteria had steadily increased since 1993 (Table 5.2). At the regional scale the worst conditions are in the region of the current administrative units (voivodships) of Świętokrzyskie, Lubelskie, Łódzkie, Warmińsko-Mazurskie and Podkarpackie. The level of poverty is also related to the size of settlement (Table 5.3).

Alternative sources of information are based on *Social Diagnosis 3*, which describes the quality of living conditions of Poles (Czapiński and Panek, 2003). Poverty is part of a much larger social problem of exclusion. The highest risk of exclusion involves first of all the inhabitants of rural areas, families with large numbers of children, unemployed elderly persons, those without good education and those without access to modern means of information like the Internet and digital TV. Adopting two methods of poverty estimation, objective and subjective, in Poland in March 2003, 25 per cent of households were below the objective poverty line, whereas, according to subjective criteria, the figure was 57 per cent. The worst situation involves no-salary households, that is, pensioners and recipients of various benefits, with over 61 per cent and 87 per cent respectively in poverty. The next worst affected categories were peasant households (56 per cent and 78 per cent), the unemployed (50 per cent and 78 per cent) and households with three or more children (53 per cent and 78 per cent).

In spite of the fact that research from *Social Diagnosis 3* (Czapiński and Panek, 2003) is representative only at a very general scale of size of the settlement, it indicates that in March 2003 the larger percentage of household in poverty was in the smaller settlements. It was also possible to

Table 5.2 Different criteria and the scale of poverty in 1993–2002

Poverty definition	1993	1994	1995	1996	1997	1998	1999	2000	2001	2002
Relative (50% monthly spending of households)	12.0	13.5	12.8	14.0	15.3	15.8	16.5	17.1	17.0	18.4
Legislative	–	–	–	–	13.3	12.1	14.4	13.6	15.0	18.5
Minimum of subsistence	–	6.4	–	4.3	5.4	5.6	6.9	8.1	9.5	11.1
Subjective	40.0	33.0	30.8	30.5	30.8	30.8	34.8	34.4	32.4	30.4

Source: Warunki życia ludności w 2001 r., Staudia i analiza statystyczne. Główny Urząd Statystyczny Departamant Statystyki Społecznej, Warsaw, 2002, p. 203, *http://www.stat.gov.pl/*

Table 5.3   Poverty rates in percentage of persons in households by different definitions of poverty and by place of residence (size of settlements) in 2001

Size of settlement in no. of inhabitants	Social minimum	Subsistence minimum	Relative poverty line	Legislative poverty line
Total country	57.2	9.5	17.0	15.0
Total towns	49.0	5.9	11.2	9.7
500,000 and over	31.8	2.1	4.2	3.7
200,000–500,000	43.5	4.2	8.4	7.0
100,000–200,000	49.5	6.2	11.3	9.9
20,000–100,000	52.9	5.8	11.6	9.9
20,000 and over	62.2	10.4	18.7	16.7
Villages	69.6	15.0	25.8	22.9

Source: Warunki życia ludności w 2001 r., Studia i analiza statystyczne. Główny Urząd Statystyczny Departamant Statystyki Społecznej, Warsaw, 2002, p. 200 *http://www.stat.gov.pl/*

identify among the sixteen administrative region of Poland (voivodships) the regions with highest objective poverty (32–4 per cent), that is, Warmińsko-Mazurskie, Podlaskie and Podkarpackie.

Regional Differentiation of Poverty Iindicators

Along with the increase in social differentiation, an increase in spatial disparities is also a phenomenon characteristic of the market transformation. The new regional structure under formation is shaped by two basic trends: the collapse of the old industrial regions and deepening underdevelopment of already underdeveloped areas. The formation of new prosperous regions with production adapted to the requirements of the new economic conditions, that is, competitive domestic and international markets, is underway. The traditional disparities between rural and urban areas and between small and larger cities, however, have substantially increased.

The most accessible indicators since the beginning of the 1990s are the set of data concerning the evolution of the labour market, particularly the regional structure of unemployment rates. Other indirect indicators for spatial analysis could be the distribution of gross domestic product (GDP), earnings, gender discrimination, commercial law partnerships or standardized school exams.

The distribution of GDP, as the most aggregated indicator of regional differentiation, can reveal or hide many aspects of disparities. For example in the analysis based on the sixteen administrative regions (voivodships), the differentiation is one to two (Figure 5.1). Analysis based on forty-four spatial units for Poland (NUTS-3 level) shows the disproportion jumping

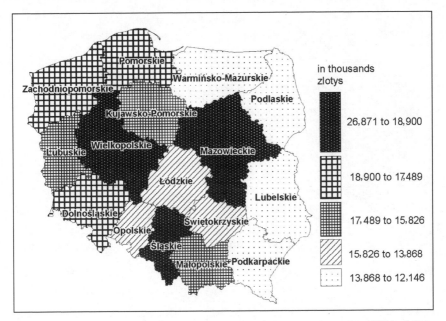

Figure 5.1   Gross domestic product in 2000 by sixteen voivodships (administrative regions; NUTS-level 2) in thousand zlotys per capita. Source: *Statistical Yearbook of the Regions - Poland 2002*, Central Statistical Office, Warsaw.

to the level one to four (Figure 5.2). This level of disparities is assessed as very large; however, in comparison with other European countries, it is relatively small (Węcławowicz, 2002).

A less aggregated indicator of disparities than GDP is income, particularly remuneration from work. Any spatial analysis of the distribution of average earning, for example at the county level, will reveal first of all the differentiation between urban and rural areas (Figure 5.3). The best situation is in the large agglomerations and in counties with industry, the worst is in rural areas dominated by small private land-holders and the former state-owned farms.

The close association of poverty with unemployment, particularly with long-term unemployment, creates a situation in which the regional structure of poverty follows the regional structure of unemployment (Figure 5.4).

The increasing share of young unemployed and people permanently (more than one year) without employment could create a more serious problem of poverty, particularly because the same groups have lost their unemployment allowance. The threat of unemployment, however, has become not only a new factor of social consciousness, but also an additional indicator of poverty.

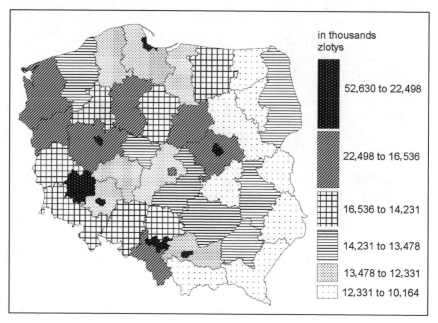

Figure 5.2   Gross domestic product in 2000 by forty-four statistical units (NUTS-level 3) in thousand zlotys per capita. Source: *Statistical Yearbook of the Regions - Poland 2002*, Central Statistical Office, Warsaw.

The specific Polish correlate of poverty, inherited from the communist and centrally planned economy, is the disproportionately high percentage of elderly people, or households of pensioners, in poverty. This involves particularly households associated with agriculture.

The most drastic situation is in rural areas. A large share of current poverty is the inherited result of communist policy toward the agricultural sector. Ideological pressure on the private sector resulted in the conservation of traditional farming at an inefficient and underdeveloped stage of agriculture. A large number of legal and bureaucratic barriers maintained the private sector in an unmodernized and backward state, with poor infrastructure facilities compared even to other socialist countries. As a result, Polish peasants entered the market economy absolutely unprepared and with very limited assets. This lack of assets concerns in particular the low level and poor quality of the technical infrastructure, low educational levels, lack of investment capital and the shrinking possibility of additional jobs in non-agricultural sectors. Peasant-workers were usually the first social category to be made redundant in the industrial sector and forced, at the beginning of the transformation, to return to a single job in agriculture.

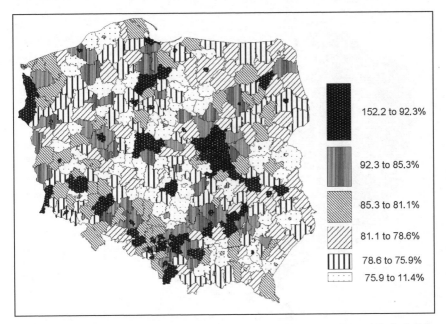

152.2 to 92.3%

92.3 to 85.3%

85.3 to 81.1%

81.1 to 78.6%

78.6 to 75.9%

75.9 to 11.4%

Figure 5.3   Average monthly gross wages and salaries (per cent) in 2001. Source: *Statistical Yearbook of the Regions - Poland 2002*, Central Statistical Office, Warsaw.

One of the most important components of the underclass in Poland currently is the group of former state farm workers. Under the communist system state-owned farms represented 18 per cent of arable land. At the beginning of the transformation (1989), it had involved 474,000 employees, that is, when families are included, around 2 million people were dependent on this sector (Zgliński, 2003). Employment, however, was reduced by 346,000 up to the year 2000.

In former state farms the concentration of social infrastructure, kindergartens, health centres, sports grounds and cultural facilities subsidized formerly by state budgets has been liquidated. Former employees have been trapped in housing estates, having neither jobs nor financial means for covering the full cost of maintenance. The new Agency for Agricultural Property of the State Treasury had conducted privatization by selling all assets and land to private investors. This was the first reason for the unemployment, pauperization and gradual impoverishment of rural workers unprepared for the transformation. In addition, the former employees have been excluded from the opportunities provided by privatization and from compensation available to other employment categories, for example miners, telecommunication workers or other industrial

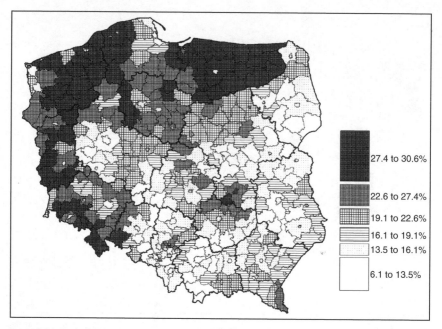

27.4 to 30.6%

22.6 to 27.4%

19.1 to 22.6%

16.1 to 19.1%

13.5 to 16.1%

6.1 to 13.5%

Figure 5.4   Unemployment rate (per cent) in 2002. Source: *Statistical Yearbook of the Regions - Poland 2002,* Central Statistical Office, Warsaw.

employees. The most common reaction of such rural households was the reduction of their needs, which, together with low access to education and jobs, resulted in apathy and the reproduction of poverty and social pathology. Currently only around 20 per cent have a job, and for the rest the receipt of welfare benefits like unemployment, disability and retirement pensions are a main source of income.

An important element of social disparities is the rapidly changing position of women in the labour market. It is most visible in income disparities representing gender discrimination. At the regional scale, the divergence in sex structure is strongly marked, particularly between urban and rural areas. The urban areas are differentiated according to their economic functions: for example, towns dominated by the textile industry are more dominated by women, while in the heavy industrial towns the sex balance is more even. In rural areas, particularly in northern and eastern territories, a shortage of women has emerged as a result of greater female urban migration. This has had serious social and economic consequences because of the limited number of marriages and the reduced chance of creating new family farms.

The research on earnings undertaken by the Central Statistical Office is representative of private and public companies employing more than five people. For the first time the information concerning individual personal earning can be directly cross-tabulated with gender, age and socio-economic position (GUS, 1997). So the question of a place of different characteristics in determination of individual earnings can be established. In general, men have 11 per cent higher earnings than the national average, while women have 12 per cent lower earnings; altogether women earn 26.2 per cent less than men.

The position of women is worse in all classifications. In terms of age, for example, the worst position is in the age groups 65 and older (where women earn 46.3 per cent less than men) and 35–44 years old (30.4 per cent). According to working period, the worst position is for women who have working experience of between ten and nineteen years, where the gap in earnings is 30.7 per cent; however, for those working less than five years, the gap is only 21.7 per cent. Much higher disparities exist according to education. For people with higher education the gap is 37.9 per cent in favour of men, and in extreme case rises to 45.2 per cent for those with only basic vocational education.

At the regional scale gender disparities are much stronger. For example, in the industrial region of towns like Katowice, Konin, Legnica and Piotrkowskie the disparity between a large proportion of badly paid women and much better paid men is highest. Traditionally, Silesian mining families dominated in this region, a pattern that post-war immigrants adapted to and one that was little changed even by the imposition of communism and its egalitarian ideology. The situation of women in Katowice differs substantially from the situation of women in other regions and is strongly connected with the stereotype of woman as a housewife of the traditional miners' working class.

At the national scale different occupational patterns of women's employ-ment are 'responsible' for the earnings differential. Differences in earnings within the country originate from the economic character of the region and the differentiated proportion of women working in the dominant economic sector.

Standardization of school examinations, which was at the national scale for the first time in 2002, has provided the newest indirect statistical indicator of regional differentiation. Since the first analysis (Bański, Kowalski and Śleszyński, 2002), all research has indicated a regional struc-ture based on cultural and material conditions, and also dependent on the local socio-economic and family environment. In urban areas there is a significant correlation between a district's better school results and the higher social status of its inhabitants.

Among the cities the best results are in Warsaw, Wrocław and Cracow (i.e. the largest centres of science and research in Poland). The worst results involve pupils from Bytom and Sosnowiec (industrial towns in Upper

Silesia) and Szczecin. So there is a distinction between those cities with good universities and prosperous economic situations, on the one hand, and those with mono-functional, industrial and deteriorating economic situations, on the other.

Increase of Intra-urban Disparities

The socio-spatial structure of the socialist cities in Poland has been documented by several factorial analyses (Węcławowicz, 1975, 1988; Dangschat and Blasius, 1987). However, full comparative studies showing how deep an impact the transformation has had on the urban structure will be possible when the National Census 2002 results become available.

The economic and socio-political crisis of the late 1970s and early 1980s led to the identification of additional factors determining socio-spatial disparities. These involved, first of all, the existence of numerous privileges in access to new housing, and the existence of very rich but relatively small elite areas in contrast to the vast gloomy and modest working-class housing estates in which poverty and pathology were endemic. As a result, socio-spatial disparities had substantially increased before the transformation.

In a more detailed analysis one can observe the increase in concentration of workers in selected areas. For example, the segregation index for workers in 1988 in Warsaw was estimated at the 31.75 level. It is much higher than for any other segregation index, for example for individual educational groups. The central part of Warsaw is characterized by a very low percentage of workers, as in 1931, and 1970. The segregation index of the population with higher education (26.67) indicates the strongest spatial separation of this category in comparison to people with secondary education (18.89) and vocational and primary education (17.59 and 18.41, respectively). The distribution of the population with higher education indicates a concentration of this group in the southern part of the city.

In the formation of the social structure of the city in the 1990s, the new social group of the middle class independent of the state sector was the result of privatization and the booming development of the private sector. The increase of the self-employed and the diminution of working-class groups are two opposite social tendencies which are slowly gaining very visible spatial expression.

The widening of the poverty stratum in Warsaw and other Polish cities has been very evident, and consists of homeless persons and elderly pensioners. In addition the huge number of people employed in administration or dependent on the state budget are highly differentiated and generally badly paid.

For new poor immigrants, Warsaw and other Polish cities have either become inaccessible, or permit only a marginal existence in very badly paid jobs and poor housing in emerging slum areas. This generates a 'shadow economy' in terms of employment and production.

Another important situation disclosing socio-spatial disparity is housing. The quality of existing stock as well as the accessibility of new dwellings is quite low. Intra-city discrepancies in housing quality are growing. This involves particularly the lack of rehabilitation of 'old' public stock, on the one hand, and visible improvement of the quality of estates built in the 1990s, on the other.

The housing finance system has in principle been adjusted to market conditions, but persistent high inflation makes it unaffordable to the population. The rationalization of the maintenance of communal dwellings has been introduced by the implementation of new legislation on rents and housing allowances. This market-oriented rent reform, the rent increase in cooperative and municipal dwelling, and partial withdrawal of subsidies, together with the lowering of the income of numerous families, has led to the emergence of a rent arrears problem.

Conclusions

The increase of poverty in the regional and urban space of Poland can be treated as a result of the radical changes in social relations. Its contribution to the increase in spatial disparities has also arisen from the abandonment of regional policy at the beginning of the transformation, and a nearly 'ideological' belief in the 'invisible hand' of the free market.

The prophecy expressed by public opinion (Public Opinion Survey) at the beginning of the transformation was that the introduction of the free market would be merely an opportunity for rich people, and that disparities between rich and ordinary citizens would increase in the future (question-naire studies: September, October, November 1992). At that time only 5 per cent of respondents believed that all people would have more wealth, whereas 88 per cent believed that ordinary people would become increas-ingly poorer; that is, a tiny group would be more and more wealthy. The majority considered themselves to be part of the group that would be poorer in future. In some regions of Poland this prophecy or belief became reality.

We can identify two main causes of the poverty: system error and per-sonal error. The first involves a majority of the elderly population, mostly pensioners and retired, with very low income determined by long-term government policies inherited from the communist system. Social workers indicated in the interviews that the social minimum is enough to cover constant expenditures (like housing and electricity) but leaves nothing for food and other maintenance expenditures. The 'system' – state policy – can be blamed also for an increase of poverty in the case of a majority of unemployed or under-paid employees in the public sector. The second cause, based on personal error, involves long-term pathological groups and individual choice or social inertia.

So where is the grass less green? First of all in the areas dominated by long-term unemployment and a low level of education and educational achievements. In the rural regions it involves areas deteriorating economically and dominated by an elderly population; also by peasants working on inefficient small farms, and workers in agricultural jobs with low wages in the former state farms. In the urban areas, it is parts of the city dominated by the working poor in manual and lower-grade clerical and service jobs with low wages, and in those cities which had an industrial base and are now facing basic restructuring problems.

The formation of areas of poverty, at both the regional and intra-urban scale, is generating political tension, particularly in a society with still very egalitarian attitudes, but it also generates more active attitudes in opposition to the passivity and the claim culture inherited from the previous system.

The largest disappointment from the transformation is that still, and sometime to a greater extent, poverty has become inherited, which has its spatial dimension in the preservation of several backward regions and the formation of new ones.

The journal *Gazeta Wyborczo* has summarized the emerging new dimensions of differentiation in Polish society as between those who are in Europe and those who are in the Third World. This is similar to the pre-war division between Poland 'A' and 'B' (west and east).

The expectation ascribed to the liberal and free market economy after a decade and a half of experience has become more and more dissatisfied. The regional disparities and the boundaries between rich and poor have become more visible instead of less, in all social and economic terms. There is a threat that social and economic protests and dissatisfaction expressed regionally will became abused by populist politician; however, this is already evident in voting behaviour.

As European integration dawns, once more the old question concerning social and spatial justice appears: will accession bring a smoothing or sharpening of regional and urban disparities in living conditions and opportunities for human development?

REFERENCES

Bański, J., Kowalski, M. and Śleszyński, P. (2002) *Zarys problemów związanych z uwarunkowaniami zróżnicowań przestrzennych winików sprawdzianu dla uczniów szkół podstawowych w 2002 r.*, Warsaw: Opracowano dla Centralnej Komisji Egzaminacyjnej w Warszawie, IGiZ PAN.

Czapiński, J. and Panek, T. (2003) *Diagnoza Społeczna 2003: Warunki i jakość życia Polaków*, Warsaw: Wyższa Skoła Psychologii i Zararządzania.

Dangschat, J. and Blasius, J. (1987) 'Social and spatial disparities in Warsaw in 1978: an application of correspondence analysis to a socialist city', *Urban Studies* 24, 173–91.

Domański, H. (2000) *Hierachie i bariery społeczne w latach dziewięćdziesiątych*, Warsaw: Instytut Spraw Publicznych.

Domański, H. (2002) *Ubóstwo w społeczeństwach postkomunistycznych*, Warsaw: Instytut Spraw Publicznych.

GUS (1997) *Rocznik Statistyczny Województw 1997*, Warsaw.

GUS (2002) *Zróżnicowanie warunków życia ludności w Polsce w 2001 r. Raport analityczny z badania ankietowego*, Warsaw: GUS Departament Statystyki Społecznej.

Smith, D. M. (2000) *Moral Geographies: Ethics in a World of Difference*, Edinburgh: Edinburgh University Press.

Węcławowicz, G. (1975) *Struktura przestrzenio społeczno-gospodarczej Warszawa w latach 1931 i 1970 w świetle analizy czynnikowej*, Wrocław: Ossolineum.

Węcławowicz, G. (1988) *Struktury społeczno-przestrzenne w miastach Polski*, Wrocław: Ossolineum.

Węcławowicz, G. (1996) *Contemporary Poland: Space and Society*, London: UCL Press.

Węcławowicz, G. (2002) *Przestrzeń i społeczeństwo współczesnej Polski, Staudium z geografii społeczno-gospodarczej*, Warsaw: Wydownictwo Naukowe PWN.

Zgliński, W. (2003) 'Wpływ transformacji PGR na przemiany rolnictwa i obszarów wiejskich w Polsce', in B. Górz and C. Guzik (eds), *Wspóczewsne przekształcenia i przyszłość polskie wsi*, Warsaw: Komisja Obszarów Wiejskich PTG, pp. 39–55.

Part II

Moral Geographies of Distribution: Justice, Welfare and Rights

---

Social justice has been a central theme in human geography since the influential exposition of David Harvey (1973). The intervening years have seen the emergence of alternative perspectives to the liberal egalitarianism of John Rawls (1971), from which Harvey drew his initial inspiration (Smith, 1994). To the injustice of the class relations of capitalism, as a central feature of Marxism, have been added social and cultural forces making for discrimination against particular population groups on such grounds as race, ethnicity and gender. So, when Harvey (1996) returned to social justice, his new inspiration was the politics of difference popularized by Iris Marion Young (1990). Social justice is concerned with human welfare, as both a condition and a policy response. Human rights are prominent in the discussion of welfare, and of the significance of citizenship. Rights to place and space have also become an issue (see, for example, Mitchell, 2003), with assertions of entitlement to particular territory implicated in some of the most intractable conflicts in the contemporary world.

The six contributions to this part of the book illustrate various aspects of justice, welfare and rights, as exercises in the moral geography of distribution (or redistribution). Sarah Curtis (Chapter 6) argues that the National Health Service (NHS) in England seems a striking example of a system set up on universalist and egalitarian principles of equity. However, there are still inequalities in health status and access to care, disproportionately affecting certain population groups and places. She argues that concern with territorial social justice in resource allocation needs to be supplemented by attention to the injustice of restricted access to particular services. Susan Smith and Donna Easterlow (Chapter 7) retain a British focus, posing the problem of changing understanding of 'welfare'. They point out that market mechanisms are increasingly preferred to state welfare provision. However, their own research shows that the allocation of housing (a welfare resource) according to health status (a measure of need) can improve people's health and life quality, while market provision of housing falls short of the ideal of distribution according to need. They challenge neoliberalism, calling for a societal (re)commitment to an ethics of care. Here again the power of underlying social relations to define and structure notions of ethics and morality is laid bare. Such social relations are not simply given, but can be transformed by political and social struggle.

Human rights are often taken to be universal, but Rex Honey (Chapter 8) explains that the rights which actually exist in international and domestic agreements are socially constructed. It is not the rights themselves that are permanent features of life, but cultural struggles involving conflict over what constitutes a just society. Rights actually recognized can change over time, as they do from place to place. Nigeria provides an illustration of cultural struggles over human rights, among population groups within the country and in relation to external standards, demonstrating the significance of geographical scale to moral geographies.

The other three chapters address rights to land. Avery Kolers (Chapter 9) is concerned with 'territorial justice' in the sense of the just distribution of territory. Overcoming what he terms the 'Anglo-American ethnogeography', which views land as merely a passive resource to be allocated by market forces, leads to recognition of the kind of broader claims to territory which should be taken seriously in the resolution of disputes. Shlomo Hasson (Chapter 10) describes a particularly demanding case of conflict with a territorial basis, in the city of Jerusalem, not only between Jews and Palestinian Arabs but also between Jews of different religious orientation. He argues for an ethical approach which avoids absolute winners and losers, in favour of recognition of the rights of both sides. Brij Maharaj (Chapter 11) turns to reparation as an aspect of social justice, raising issues of rights in relation to dispossession of land in South Africa under apartheid. He examines the policies and mechanisms developed to address land reform and restitution, as part of a process of societal healing.

The very question of human rights, let alone their realization in thought and practice and the establishment of institutions devoted to their implementation, is far from unproblematic in the contemporary world. The notion of human rights reminds us in the most direct fashion that human life is social and that such rights are socially constructed – and, in part at least, socially structured in terms of what might be possible in any context. Here morality and ethics are very evident; their inherent spatiality is clear and their uneven and dynamic geography is all too apparent.

REFERENCES

Harvey, D. (1973) *Social Justice and the City*, London: Edward Arnold.
Harvey, D. (1996) *Justice, Nature and the Geography of Difference*, Oxford: Blackwell.
Mitchell, D. (2003) *The Right to the City: Social Justice and the Fight for Public Space*, New York and London: Guilford Press.
Rawls, J. (1971) *A Theory of Justice*, Cambridge, Mass.: Harvard University Press.
Smith, D. M. (1994) *Geography and Social Justice*, Oxford: Blackwell.
Young, I. M. (1990) *Justice and the Politics of Difference*, Princeton, NJ: Princeton University Press.

6

Social Exclusion, Health and Health Care: The Case of the National Health Service in England

Sarah E. Curtis

It is an honour and a pleasure to add to this collection to celebrate the huge contribution made by David Smith to fields of geography which are concerned with human welfare and social justice. Like many other colleagues represented in this book, I was very much impressed and influenced at an early stage in my academic career by his book entitled *Human Geography: A Welfare Approach* (Smith, 1977), and his subsequent publications have continued to provide a touchstone and key reference in geographical discussion of variation in health and welfare, for me and for many other researchers around the world. His inspiration continues to be crucial for the continuing stream of research at Queen Mary, University of London, relating to inequalities in human health and health care, some of which is referred to in this chapter.

Introduction

This chapter considers the relationships between social exclusion, health and health care from the perspective of geographical notions of social justice, including those expounded by David Smith. It uses the example of access to the National Health Service (NHS) in England as an illustration, but this is not meant to imply that access to health services is the only factor which is important for health of socially excluded groups in the country. As discussed below, much of the health disadvantage experienced by socially excluded groups is the result of factors apart from the health care they receive. However, this does not absolve the NHS from responsibility to do as much as possible to reduce health inequalities. The following discussion considers why, although, in some respects the NHS is organized in a way that might be expected to maximize the potential for health services to limit health inequalities, in practice it faces major challenges in this respect. Some of these relate to geographical processes that contribute to health difference.

The Nature of Social Exclusion

There could be some debate over what 'social exclusion' comprises. Smith (1994, pp. 182–5) discusses, for example, the concept of an 'underclass', and he cautions against interpretations invoking notions of a 'culture of poverty', whereby the most disadvantaged groups are represented as being themselves responsible for a self-reproducing marginalization from values and lifestyles approved by the moral majority. Smith argues instead for perspectives that recognize that social exclusion operates through a complex set of structural social and economic processes affecting individual agency. Some disadvantaged populations differ from the majority population because they do not have the same access to means to satisfy their 'basic needs' (including the means to promote and protect good health as far as possible). They are therefore excluded from full and equal participation in 'mainstream' social and economic systems of social production, economic production and consumption. Shaw, Dorling and Davey-Smith (1999) also discuss literature relating to the exclusion of certain groups from the civil or legal rights assumed for the majority in society. Those people who are affected by these forms of social exclusion are often (but not always) living in places with high levels of poverty and disadvantage which may compound the challenges they face. An important theme below concerns the extent to which poverty and marginalization of places contributes to the health experience of individuals living in them (for example, where health service provision is not proportionate and responsive to the basic needs of the local population).

An important aspect of social exclusion is that it is not a condition which is entirely limited to some sort of single, monolithic social group, and nor is it restricted only to certain localities. Social exclusion can affect widely diverse populations in a variety of settings, and in this discussion space only allows consideration of various examples. The same processes are not important in all instances of social exclusion, and this makes it difficult to write a comprehensive account of the geographical factors involved. However, there are some common themes that frequently recur in discussions of the geography of health and social exclusion, such as: the difficulty of obtaining accurate information on the welfare of these groups; the failure of welfare systems to provide them access to the means of meeting basic needs; and the ways in which key institutions in society may add to the experience of exclusion. These issues are the focus of attention here, since they are probably relevant, in some way, to many different marginalized populations.

A further debatable feature of discussions of health of socially excluded populations is the frequent emphasis on their 'vulnerability' to disadvantage. This is usually meant as a reference to the impact of structural processes of exclusion, which are not within their control. However, it is unhelpful to label socially excluded populations as 'vulnerable' if it leads to an underestimation of the considerable resources of resistance and resilience which they often display. Some aspects of social and economic exclusion, such as rejection of some of the social norms and behaviour preferred by the majority population, could be interpreted as rational adaptations to their particular circumstances on the part of socially excluded populations.

A Universal Concept of a Socially Just and Inclusive Health Care System?

David Smith (1994, p. 294) argues in support of a view that '[t]he provision of what people require to satisfy basic needs constitutes a minimal case for the impartial treatment of everyone, whoever and wherever they may be.' He also makes a strong case (p. 288) that health care is one of those spheres of provision for basic needs for which it is possible to argue for 'the principle of strict equality according to need ... And no locational advantages, such as better ... hospitals in places inhabited by richer people. ... Truly egalitarian services should be publicly provided, with no possiblity for private practice.' He therefore concludes that universal (rather than relative) principles of need and provision are required for services such as health care, and appears to support the case for what Wimberly (1980) has described as the TCC (total, compulsory and comprehensive) model of health care.

According to the type of universal principle of social justice for which Smith is arguing, an ideal model for a national health system would therefore be one which:

- treats health care as a public good, allocated in relation to medical need, rather than ability to pay, social position or geographical location;
- is designed to provide a universal and comprehensive service;
- uses resources allocated in ways which are equitable (i.e. proportionate to needs and not necessarily in equal shares);
- is designed to favour those who are most disadvantaged in terms of health;
- is acceptable to society as a whole because there is general agreement that risks and costs of ill health requiring medical services should be shared collectively.

The NHS in England: Health Care Based on Universal Concepts of Social Justice

The National Health Service appears in many respects to be a particularly striking example of a health care system set up to meet these requirements of a universal concept of social justice in provision of medical care. In the following discussion, reference is made specifically to the NHS in England because it is administratively distinct and is treated as such in the policy literature. However, similar points apply to NHS services in Scotland and Wales.

The NHS is a comprehensive health care system, covering the full range of medical services for the totality of the British population. It is also compulsory in the sense that for those required to contribute to the costs it is not possible to opt out of participation in this collective health care system, and although there is a significant and growing sector based on private health insurance, it is relatively small compared with many other countries. The vast majority of British people rely at least partly on the NHS for their medical care. The costs of health care for the patient, at the point of use, are low in the NHS and eligibility does not depend on insurance cover. Although there are fees and charges for some health care under the NHS (e.g. charges for prescriptions and dental checks), patients are not charged at the point of use for care by doctors or nurses or for hospital treatment. More than 80 per cent of the costs of NHS services are met through general taxation, so that costs are shared collectively among taxpayers and distributed 'progressively' in a way that is proportional to ability to pay, because richer people pay higher taxes.

There is a high level of central control in the NHS and considerable emphasis is placed on trying to ensure that access to health care is not variable in relation to place of residence or social group. The NHS has been a world leader in strategies that aim to allocate national resources for health geographically in a fair manner. In the 1970s, the Resource Allocation Working Party (Department of Health and Social Security, 1976) established the principle that resources for NHS running costs should be allocated to different parts of the country in a way that would reflect variations in population need for care, rather than on an incremental basis, according to what had been spent in previous years. This was an important innovation in application of ideas of territorial and social justice in a welfare service, and the principle has endured (even though, in operation, the procedures used to determine a fair allocation of resources have been the subject of intense debate and frequent changes, as discussed below).

Another feature of the NHS that makes it consistent with a model of a socially just health system, accessible to all, is the emphasis on primary health care as the lynchpin of the system. The NHS differs from other national health systems in that access to most hospital services (and many community based health services) is through referral by a general practitioner (GP). Patients are registered on the practice list of a particular GP (and are able choose their doctor and to change to register with a different practitioner). This means that one particular GP is responsible for ensuring that their primary medical care needs are met and for directing patients through the health care system for other services they may need. The gatekeeper role of the GP, through the referral process, makes the primary care doctor pivotal for the whole health care system. It is generally accepted that primary health care is the most important basic health care service and that it is essential to meet objectives of 'health for all' promoted by the World Health Organization (1998). Primary medical care (treatment of illness, illness prevention and promotion of good health through services generally provided outside hospitals) is especially important for disadvantaged populations, who may have the greatest risks of ill health. The fact that the British NHS has such an integrated and universal primary health care system should help to meet the basic health care needs of all the population.

The Independent Inquiry into Inequalities in Health (Department of Health, 1998, p. 111) reiterated the commitment to equity enshrined as a founding principle in the NHS and identified 'several interlinked responsibilities' relating to health inequalities. The NHS is expected to:

- provide equity of access to effective health care;
- work in partnership with other agencies to improve health and tackle causes of health inequalities;
- stimulate the development of health policies beyond the boundaries of the NHS.

Furthermore, this document states the mission of the NHS in ensuring equity in health as follows:

> The principle of equity includes several important elements: ensuring that health care services serving disadvantaged populations are not of poorer quality or less accessible, that the allocation and application of resources are in relation to need; and ensuring that positive efforts are made to achieve greater uptake and use of effective services by making extra efforts to reach those whose health is worse. (Department of Health, 1998, p. 111)

Challenges to Equity in the NHS: Geographies of Inequality of Health Care

However, in spite of all these features of the NHS, and the clear policy intent to address issues of equity, socially excluded populations still experience inequitable differences in health care, as compared with other social groups in England. These include differences in access to and use of health care as well as in health outcomes. Average measures of the general health of the English population have continued to improve over the last twenty or thirty years, with reductions in mortality, for example, and longer life expectancy. However, variation in health has not shown the same improvement.

Persistent health inequalities have been demonstrated geographically in analyses of trends in health of rich and poor areas. Several studies have pointed to widening geographical disparities in mortality and life expectancy during the 1980s and 1990s, due to more rapid health improvement in affluent areas, while in the poorest areas health has improved more slowly, or even got worse (Shouls, Congdon and Curtis, 1996; Raleigh and Kiri, 1997; Shaw, Dorling, Gordon and Davey-Smith, 1999). Shouls et al. (1996) showed, for example, that in affluent semi-rural areas of England and Wales, mortality among males aged 45–64, was better than the national average, and it improved by 27 per cent between 1981 and 1992. In contrast, in deprived northern areas and in some socially mixed areas of London, mortality rates were higher than average at the beginning of the 1980s and improvement was only 19 per cent and 12 per cent, respectively.

There are also marked differences between social groups in England, which have not diminished in recent decades and may have increased. Health disadvantage has also been noted for certain social groups, defined in terms of occupational social class. For example, the Acheson report (Department of Health, 1998) reported mortality rates among professionals of 280/100,000 in 1991–3 compared with 806/100,000 for unskilled workers. In 1970–2 these rates had been 500/100,000 and 897/100,000, respectively. Thus while mortality levels had improved to some extent for all groups, the improvement had been much greater for the more privileged professional group than for the unskilled manual group, which includes the largest proportion of people who are most likely to experience social and economic exclusion. There is also a large literature on the health disadvantage of unemployed people (e.g. reviewed by Bartley, Ferrie and Montgomery, 1999).

Health disadvantage has also been documented for some social groups defined in terms of their housing status, ethnic status or political status, who are often depicted as especially at risk of social and economic exclusion. For example, there is discussion about the health of people who are homeless, travellers, refugees, belong to certain minority ethnic groups, and who have marginalized lifestyles, such as illicit drug users. The fact that these groups are often missing from mainstream and routine statistical systems for monitoring and measuring population health makes it more difficult to evaluate their health status reliably. Also *ad hoc* qualitative studies may not reach these groups unless specifically designed to do so, since there are special challenges in including such groups effectively in study designs. Where evidence is available, it is not always as rigorous in scientific terms as the data available for the majority population; however, it often indicates that the health experience of these groups is relatively poor.

There is not space here to review all of this literature in detail, but illustrations include reviews produced by the Health of Londoners Project (Bardsley, Jones, Kemp, Aspinall, Dodhia and Bevan, 1998) relating to the links between housing and health in London, which showed that homeless adults had increased risk of mental illness, respiratory diseases, poor access to health promotion and primary care, and that low birthweight, infant mortality and problems of child development were more common among children of families who were homeless or in temporary housing. Aldous, Bardsley, Daniell et al. (1999) also reviewed the evidence concerning health of refugees in London, mainly deriving from several *ad hoc* studies in particular parts of the city. Some health risks for refugees were associated with conditions in their country of origin (e.g. various mental and physical post-traumatic stress disorders associated with experience of conflict or torture and risks of infectious diseases contracted abroad where these are more common in the population). However, the review also reports some evidence that the general health of refugees tends to worsen the longer they are in Britain, which suggests that some aspects of conditions here are damaging to their health.

Research on the health status of travellers in England include studies by Van Cleemput and Parry (2001), who found comparative levels of health which were similar to more deprived urban populations and worse than the national average. Feder, Vaclavik and Streetly (1993) also report on relatively low levels of preventive health care in traveller populations. These findings are fairly typical of the situation reported for travellers in other parts of Europe (Hajioff and McKee, 2000). Studies of more settled minority ethnic groups in England have also identified aspects of health difference compared with other social groups; these were reviewed, for example, by the Department of Health (1998), which pointed to relatively high mortality rates for most (but not all) immigrant populations and higher levels of some forms of illness in minority ethnic populations (examples are high prevalence of diabetes and coronary heart disease among South Asian groups, high rates of diabetes and hypertension among African Caribbeans, higher suicide rates for South Asian women, and high, increasing tuberculosis infection rates among Pakistani, Bangladeshi and Black African populations). However, death certificates report country of birth rather than ethnic group membership and so mortality data relate to those born outside Britain rather than minority ethnic groups more generally. Also, Nazroo (1997) has demonstrated that disparities in health seem to a large extent associated with the poor living conditions and the economic exclusion experienced by many people in these groups, rather than with cultural differences as such. Furthermore, for some minority ethnic groups, some health indicators are more favourable than for the majority population (e.g. lower lung cancer death rates among migrants from Asia, the Caribbean and Africa).

Thus, much of the evidence suggests that the health of the groups at greatest risk of social exclusion in England have different health experiences to those of the majority in society, even though it would be misleading to argue that social exclusion is associated with health disadvantage in every respect. Studies which have examined the explanations for these health disparities suggest that the differences can be partly understood in terms of fundamentally geographical processes. In the following sections of this chapter some of these will be discussed, making particular reference to research in the geography of health that has illustrated how some of this health difference may be associated with failure of the NHS to provide a truly equitable service for socially excluded groups in England.

Challenges to Ensuring Equity of Access to Services of Good Quality

Variability in access to health care is an extremely complex phenomenon. Various conceptual models have been proposed to represent the range of factors that influence access to health care and use of services. Some of these have focused mainly on individual characteristics that are important for care (e.g. Rosenstock, 1966), and others emphasize aspects of health service organization, especially at the local level (Penchansky and Thomas, 1981). From a geographical point of view, the more interesting models are those which situate the individual, and his or her interaction with particular parts of the health service, within the wider context of the ideology and organization of the national health care system as a whole. For example, Fielder (1981) and Puentes-Markides (1992) propose models showing how the wider social structure and political economy influence access to, and use of, health services. Curtis (2004) argues that individual health service use can be seen as embedded within national and local dimensions of administrative structures, social milieux and the disposition in space of the physical infrastructure for provision of care.

Geographical factors are only part of this complex web of causation, but they are given particular emphasis in the following discussion. This focuses on two examples of essentially geographical challenges for the NHS: in ensuring territorial justice in resource allocation between different areas of the country; and, at the finer scale, in making spaces of care inclusive and therapeutic for all social groups.

Challenges in Ensuring Territorial Justice in Resource Allocation

Various studies have drawn attention to the evidence concerning what Tudor-Hart (1971) referred to as 'the inverse care law' of service provision in the NHS, which describes a situation in which the quantity or quality of service provision is inversely related to the level of need for heath services in the population. Authors like Knox (1978) contributed to the growing critique of the NHS during the 1970s (reviewed subsequently, for example, by Jones and Moon, 1987) which pointed out that by incrementally providing most health care resources to areas which had always used most resources in the past, the NHS was contributing to geographical inequities in the distribution of funds, facilities and personnel. This meant that access to care was not, as intended, proportionate to needs in a way which was independent of place of residence. Furthermore, some of the most disadvantaged places in England and Wales had poorer levels of health service provision (for example, those declining industrial areas in the north and west of the country which were marginalized economically by post-industrial economic developments, and more deprived areas of many inner cities, where there were likely to be relatively large concentrations of disadvantaged and socially excluded populations). This means that for socially and economically excluded populations in some parts of the country, their health disadvantage may have been compounded by poor resourcing of NHS services relative to needs in the places where they were living.

To tackle this problem, the Resource Allocation Working Party (Department of Health and Social Security, 1976) proposed what is now a well-known system of allocating resources for the running costs of NHS hospital services in a way which was more proportional to measures of population need for health care in geographical areas. The 'needs formulae' used for this process have been subject to frequent change (e.g. Royston, Hurst, Lister and Steward, 1992; Carr-Hill et al., 1994; Smith, Sheldon, Carr-Hill, Martin, Peacock and Hardman, 1994). There has also been intense debate over the method of calculating population need for health care and whether or not this should be completely independent of the existing pattern of use of hospital services (Mays, 1987; Sheldon and Smith, 1997). Thus there is continuing disagreement over how a relative indicator of 'need' should be determined and which indicators it should contain. Curtis and Bebbington (2002) have also argued that, apart from this controversy about how geographical variation in 'need' might be measured across the country as a whole, there are further questions about whether such a general approach to measuring national variation in relative need can be sufficiently sensitive to local differences in the way that population variables relate to need for care. Carr-Hill et al. (1994) tried to deal with this problem by using multi-level modelling strategies which allow for local variability in the relationships between hospital use and population measures of health and socio-economic conditions. However, Curtis and Bebbington (2002) argue that given present techniques and data, it is unlikely that standard resource allocation formulae can simultaneously reflect average patterns of need for hospital care in the country as a whole, while at the same time expressing the extreme levels of 'need' and demand for services associated with the particular combinations of circumstances affecting the most severely disadvantaged areas, such as those found in poor inner cities.

National spending formulae may also be rather poor at measuring the needs of other types of marginalized places. It is often argued, for example, that problems of isolation and sparsity in remote rural areas are not very well reflected in national needs formulae. Watt and Sheldon (1993) discuss these costs of rural sparsity and argue that they should be factored into central NHS calculations of the resource needs of rural areas. Haynes and Gale (1999) discuss a further problem involved in trying to use geographical methods to assess the health care needs of poor populations in rural areas. Because poor residents are thinly distributed across the countryside in small numbers, information on them does not have much impact on average data for whole areas in rural regions. In contrast, the large and highly concentrated disadvantaged populations in poor urban areas are much more visible in population statistics and they tend to attract proportionately more funding as a result.

Bloor and Maynard (1995) have also criticized previous revenue allocation mechanisms in the NHS because they have been applied mainly to hospital services, rather than to primary care. Parallel methods for directing additional funds to general practices with large numbers of patients from deprived areas were also developed, mainly based on area indicators proposed by Jarman (1983). Although these 'deprivation payments' may have helped to offset the costs of higher workloads for GPs in some disadvantaged areas, some commentators suggest that the indicators used have shortcomings because of the combination of variables they contain or the ways that they have been applied (e.g. Senior, 1991; Moon and North, 2000).

A weakness of area-based revenue allocation formulae in the NHS is that they do not take into account effectively the needs of populations with high levels of service need services who are also very geographically mobile (e.g. Department of Health, 1998; North East London Health Authority, 2002). As noted above, high levels of residential instability are a characteristic of some groups that are socially excluded. Homeless people, travellers and refugee populations, for example, frequently lack fixed residential locations, are under-enumerated in the population census, and are hard to track and record in population surveys. In areas where such populations tend to be concentrated, such as poor districts of major cities, the total size of the population needing to use NHS services is therefore underestimated, and this means that the service is under-resourced for all local users, as well as for mobile populations. These groups are also more likely to be unregistered with a regular general practitioner for NHS services, so that the main 'gateway' to health care is not easily open to them and they tend to rely heavily on alternative sources of emergency care such as accident and emergency departments. Providing preventive health care and health promotion services to these very mobile populations is also challenging for the conventional primary care services because some normal procedures for sustaining continuing links with patients (e.g. mailing invitations for health checks or vaccination to the patient's place of residence, health monitoring visits at home) are inappropriate and it may not be possible to have quick access to these patients' medical records in the same way as for those patients who are registered. Special provision may need to be made to bring these services to such groups (Feder, Salkind and Sweeney, 1989; Feder et al., 1993).

As authors such as Powell (1990) and Mohan (1995) have argued very cogently, the inverse care law is concerned with the quality as well as the quantity of health service provision relative to needs. The central system of management in the NHS has left largely to local health agencies the responsibility for using NHS resources to deliver services that are well adapted to the needs of the population in terms of quality and the quantity. Especially since local powers and incentives given to local and regional NHS agencies are relatively weak in this respect, there remain large questions over whether they are able effectively to prioritize the needs of the most marginalized and disadvantaged service users. An illustration is provided by a study in northern England by Gatrell, Lancaster, Chapple, Horsley and Smith (2002), who demonstrated relatively low uptake of heart bypass surgery in areas with large Asian populations, which did not appear to be consistent with patterns of need.

Furthermore, central government targets which local health services are required to meet may conflict with the needs of populations most at risk of social exclusion. Thus, for example, national targets to reduce waiting times for elective hospital treatment are particularly hard to juggle with relatively high levels of demand for emergency hospital care arising in disadvantaged populations, or with the obstacles to discharging patients in good time, when poor housing and difficult family circumstances make it more difficult for them to recuperate at home. Similarly, in an area like East London, national targets to reduce illness and death due to conditions like cardiovascular illness or cancer have to be considered alongside other health problems, such as tuberculosis and HIV/AIDS, that are not prioritized to the same extent nationally, but which are especially important for some groups in the local population, such as homeless people or for some minority ethnic groups. These perspectives highlight the local specificity of health service needs and they bring into question the potential to achieve justice in service provision for socially excluded populations using 'mainstream' managerial solutions in the NHS that are not sensitive to the local context.

It is evident from the discussion above that central control over territorial resource allocation in the NHS is quite influential. The central NHS executive has made much use of geographical information to assess likely variation in relative need for health care, and to allocate resources in proportion to need, in ways which are intended to be consistent with principles of territorial justice. However, technical and conceptual difficulties have meant that the results have not been fully effective in targeting resources towards the most disadvantaged or socially excluded populations.

Health Care Facilities: Therapeutic Healing Spaces or Spaces of Exclusion?

Geographical research has also highlighted other ways in which NHS provision may (albeit unintentionally) have negative effects on the health or well-being of socially excluded populations. Some geographers have paid attention, for example, to the nature of the spaces in which health care is provided (a particular kind of 'moral geography'). Gesler (1992, 1993) has offered a conceptual framework for considering therapeutic landscapes, arguing that non-medical, as well as medical, aspects of the places in which patients are treated are important for the healing process and for their well-being. Importantly for this discussion, therapeutic healing landscapes may be distinguished by certain physical, social and symbolic features which make them, for example, comfortable, refreshing, homely, welcoming, peaceful or positively stimulating, and consistent with patients' sense of moral and spiritual values. Gesler (1996) has also identified the potential for equal participation as important for a healing setting.

Gesler, Bell, Curtis, Hubbard and Francis (2004) have reviewed recent commentaries on hospital design in Britain and discussed how these relate to ideas about therapeutic landscapes and healing places. However, hospital design in recent decades has often been criticized for over-emphasizing the requirement to facilitate clinical models of treatment, and for neglecting other aspects of what Francis and Glanville (2001, pp. 62–3) refer to as 'architectures of personal care'. A more balanced approach to hospital design and management would pay greater attention to creating healing social and symbolic environments that accord with the values of patients as well as clinical staff, integrating the hospital within the community, ensuring good public access for patients and visitors. Some contemporary and older hospital buildings have been explicitly constructed with these principles in mind. However, we also have to consider that many of these principles are based on the views of social groups who are dominant in 'mainstream' society (architects, doctors, managers, middle-class patients). There still remains a question about whose principles are most relevant if we are concerned about the therapeutic and healing properties of hospital design for socially excluded groups of users.

It is therefore important to consider geographical accounts of the power relationships which are manifested in settings used to deliver health care. Philo (e.g. 1997) has provided comprehensive analyses of the social relationships reflected in hospital buildings and regimes. His work has drawn especially on historical examples of institutional provision for psychiatric patients. These reflected the dominance of the medical establishment and middle-class ideas about treatment and the organization of these institutions. Parr (e.g. 2000) has also reviewed how social inclusion and exclusion operate in more contemporary, non-institutional settings for care of people with mental illnesses. She found that in some cases patients themselves sought to exclude some people whose behaviour was not considered acceptable for the majority of users. Another example of this type of analysis is provided by Gillespie (2002), who comments on the power relations expressed through the architecture and organization of a family planning clinic, finding, for example, that the clinic seemed to exclude or discourage use by some groups, such as women with disabilities, and that the treatment of users in the public spaces of the clinic sometimes seemed to impose upon them a subordinate power relationship to staff. This could present barriers especially for users who suffer social exclusion in other areas of life and find it relatively difficult to act assertively towards people seen to be in authority.

Geography has therefore begun to contribute to a significant debate about how spaces of care are organized both physically and socially and whether more could be done to make these spaces fully responsive to the needs of some populations who need to use them but may find them intimidating, unsympathetic or inaccessible.

Conclusion: The Challenge of Social Justice in Practice

This discussion has focused very selectively on certain aspects of NHS care in England that seem likely to undermine attempts to provide a truly comprehensive and inclusive health service. As indicated above, access to health care is only one of many factors that affect the health of socially excluded populations. The issues reviewed here seem important, however, because they highlight the challenges faced in practical implementation of the ideals of social justice that David Smith has argued for so persuasively. Even within the NHS in Britain, which was built upon an ideology which seems to accord quite well with Smith's ideals of social justice, there remain major obstacles to be overcome before provision can really meet the basic health care needs of the most disadvantaged and socially excluded populations in society. This makes it all the more important to stress the need to continue to strive towards a goal of universal social justice in health care.

The examples here are also of interest from a geographical perspective. They show how a range of different types of geographical research on health, ranging from systematic and quantitative studies to intensive qualitative analyses, have begun to explain why social justice is often not achieved in health care. David Smith has set an agenda for research in geography that has been fundamental to a significant stream of work on health and health care inequalities and seems set to continue for some time in the future.

REFERENCES

Aldous, J., Bardsley, M., Daniell, R., Gair, R., Jacobsen, B., Lowdell, C., Morgan, D., Storkey, M. and Taylor, G. (1999) *Refugee Health in London. Key Issues for Public Health*, London: Health of Londoners Project.

Bardsley, M., Jones, I. R., Kemp, V., Aspinall, P., Dodhia, H. and Bevan, P. (1998) *Housing and Health in London: A Review*, London: Health of Londoners Project.

Bartley, M., Ferrie, J. and Montgomery, S. (1999) 'Living in a high-unemployment economy: understanding the health consequences', in M. Marmot and R. Wilkinson (eds), *Social Determinants of Health*, Oxford: Oxford University Press, pp. 81–104.

Bloor, K. and Maynard, A. (1995) *Equity in Primary Care*, Discussion Paper 141, York: University of York Centre for Health Economics.

Carr-Hill, R., Sheldon, T., Smith, P., Martin, S., Peacock, S. and Hardman, G. (1994) 'Allocating resources to health authorities: development of method for small area analysis of use of inpatient services', *British Medical Journal* 309, 1046–9.

Curtis, S. (2004) *Health Inequality: Geographical Perspectives*, London: Sage.

Curtis, S. and Bebbington, A. (2002) 'Geographical variations in health and welfare and their significance for equity and efficiency in resource allocation', paper presented at Festschrift for Professor Bleddyn Davies, 18 September, London School of Economics.

Department of Health (1998) *Independent Inquiry into Inequalities in Health*, London: Stationery Office.

Department of Health and Social Security (1976) *Sharing Resources for Health in* England, Report of the Resource Allocation Working Party, London: DHSS.

Feder, G., Salkind, M. and Sweeney, O. (1989) 'Traveller gypsies and general practitioners in East London: the role of the traveller health visitor', *Health Trends* 21, 93–4.

Feder, G., Vaclavik, T. and Streetly, A. (1993) 'Traveller gypsies and childhood immunization: a study in East London', *British Journal of General Practice* 372, 281–4.

Fielder, J. (1981) 'A review of the literature on access and utilization of medical care with special emphasis on rural primary care', *Social Science and Medicine* 15C, 129–42.

Francis, S. and Glanville, R. (2001) *Building a 20/20 Vision: Future Health Care Environments*, London: Nuffield Institute.

Gatrell, A., Lancaster, G., Chapple, A., Horsley, S. and Smith, M. (2002) 'Variations in use of tertiary cardiac services in part of North-West England', *Health and Place* 8, 147–53.

Gesler, W. (1992) 'Therapeutic landscapes: medical geographic research in light of the new cultural geography', *Social Science and Medicine* 34, 735–46.

Gesler, W. (1993) 'Therapeutic landscapes: theory and a case study of Epidauros, Greece', *Environment and Planning D: Society and Space* 11, 171–89.

Gesler, W. (1996) 'Lourdes: healing in a place of pilgrimage', *Health and Place* 2, 95–105.

Gesler, W., Bell, M., Curtis, S., Hubbard, P. and Francis, S. (2004) 'Therapy by design: evaluating the UK hospital building program', *Health and Place* 10, 117–28.

Gillespie, R. (2002) 'Architecture and power: a family planning clinic as a case study', *Health and Place* 8, 211–20.

Hajioff, S. and McKee, M. (2000) 'The health of the Roma people: a review of the published literature', *Journal of Epidemiology and Community Health* 54, 864–9.

Haynes, R. and Gale, S. (1999) 'Mortality, long-term illness and deprivation in rural and metropolitan wards of England and Wales', *Health and Place* 5, 301–12.

Jarman, B. (1983) 'Identification of underprivileged areas', *British Medical Journal* 286, 1705–9.

Jones, K. and Moon, G. (1987) *Health, Disease and Society: An Introduction to Medical Geography*, London: Routledge & Kegan Paul.

Knox, P. (1978) 'The intra-urban ecology of primary medical care: patterns of accessibility and their policy implications', *Environment and Planning A* 10, 415–35.

Mays, N. (1987) 'Measuring morbidity for resource allocation', *British Medical Journal* 295, 764–7.

Mohan, J. (1995) *A National Health Service? The Restructuring of Health Care in Britain since 1979*, Basingstoke: Macmillan.

Moon, G. and North, N. (2000) *Policy and Practice: General Medical Practice in the UK*, London: Macmillan.

Nazroo, J. (1997) *Ethnicity and National Health*, London: Policy Studies Institute.

North East London Health Authority (2002) *Funding: The Case for East London*, London: NELHA.

Parr, H. (2000) 'Interpreting the "hidden social geographies" of mental health: ethnographies of inclusion and exclusion in sem-institutional places', *Health and Place* 6, 225–38.

Penchansky, R. and Thomas, J. (1981) 'The concept of access: definition and relationship to consumer satisfaction', *Medical Care* XIX, 127–40.

Philo, C. (1997) 'Across the water: reviewing geographical studies of asylums and other mental health facilities', *Health and Place* 3, 73–89.

Powell, M. (1990) 'Need and provision in the National Health Service: an inverse care law?', *Policy and Politics* 18, 31-7.

Puentes-Markides, C. (1992) 'Women and access to health care', *Social Science and Medicine* 35, 613-617.

Raleigh, V. and Kiri, V. (1997) 'Life expectancy in England: variations and trends by gender, health authority, and level of deprivation', *Journal of Epidemiology and Community Health* 51, 649–58.

Rosenstock, I. (1996) 'Why people use health services', *Milbank Memorial Fund Quarterly* 44, 94–127.

Royston, G., Hurst, J., Lister, E. and Steward, P. (1992) 'Modelling the use of health services by populations of small areas to inform the allocation of central resources to larger regions', *Socio-economic Planning Sciences* 26(3), 169–80.

Senior, M. (1991) 'Deprivation payments to GPs: not what the doctor ordered', *Environment and Planning C* 9, 79–94.

Shaw, M., Dorling, D., Gordon, D. and Davey-Smith, G. (1999) *The Widening Gap: Health Inequalities and Policy in Britain*, Bristol: Policy Press.

Shaw, M., Dorling, D. and Davey-Smith, G. (1999) 'Poverty, social exclusion and minorities', in M. Marmot and R. Wilkinson (eds), *Social Determinants of Health*, Oxford: Oxford University Press, pp. 211–39.

Sheldon, T. and Smith, P. (1997) 'Equity in the allocation of health care resources', *Health Economics* 9, 571–4.

Shouls, S., Congdon, P. and Curtis, S. (1996) 'Geographic variation in illness and mortality: the development of a relevant area typology for SAR districts', *Health and Place* 2, 139–55.

Smith, D. M. (1977) *Human Geography: A Welfare Approach*, London: Edward Arnold.

Smith, D. M. (1994) *Geography and Social Justice*, Oxford: Blackwell.

Smith, P., Sheldon, T., Carr-Hill, R., Martin, S., Peacock, S. and Hardman, G. (1994) 'Allocating resources to health authorities: results and policy implications of small area analysis of use of inpatient services', *British Medical Journal* 309, 1050–4.

Tudor-Hart, J. (1971) 'The inverse care law', *Lancet* 27 February, 405–412.

Van Cleemput, P. and Parry, G. (2001) 'Health status of gypsy travellers', *Journal of Public Health Medicine* 23, 129–34.

Watt, I. and Sheldon, T. (1993) 'Rurality and resource allocation in the UK', *Health Policy* 26, 19–27.

Wimberley, T. (1980) 'Toward a national health insurance in the United States: an historical outline 1910–1979', *Social Science and Medicine* 14C, 13–25.

World Health Organization (1998) 'Health for all: origins and mandate', *http://www.who.int/archives/who50/en/health4all.htm*

7

The Problem with Welfare

Susan J. Smith and Donna Easterlow

Introduction

As many as twenty-five years ago, David Smith (1977, 1979) carved a niche for a new generation of welfare geographers by addressing a range of questions on the theme of 'who gets what, where, how and why?' He paved the way for those concerned with issues of social justice to argue that, where some got less than others – less than they needed or deserved – there should, in caring societies, be both the will and the means to redress this inequality. Just, care-full welfare geographies could and should be aspired to.

Today the idea of welfare remains a question of geography. Welfare provision lies at the intersection between global economics and local politics. The principles and practices of welfare also bridge the divide between social and cultural geographies, on the one hand, and economic geographies, on the other. However, the idea of welfare is no longer in vogue. 'Welfare geography' has ceased to be a keyword in the main academic journals; 'welfare transfers' have slipped out of the political vocabulary. In much of the developed world, what was a solution to poverty and inequality in the 1960s – a comprehensive system of universal services, coupled with compensation in cash or kind for those excluded from reasonable access to resources and life chances – became a scapegoat for the inequalities of the 1980s. By the turn of the millennium, a commitment to social welfare was no longer part of the civic way of life – especially in neoliberal economies like the USA, Britain and New Zealand. Instead, the north-west European vision of a collectively funded social contract has been eclipsed in the political imagination by a trend towards labour market flexibility, low social protection and the 'mixed *economy*' of welfare.

There is no dearth of ethical or theoretical interest in the injustice which liberalized economies and restructured welfare states have wrought; and no doubt that this itself is a matter for geographers – this is at the core of important works by Harvey (1996, 2000), Merrifield and Swyngedouw (1996) and David Smith (1994, 2000). Nor is there any shortage of research showing that inequalities in incomes and employment, and in who gets what, where, persist despite – indeed because of – 'reforms' in servicing and the commitment to 'a modern welfare state' (there is an enormous literature on this). But the practical political challenge posed by the demise of the welfare ideal is rarely squarely addressed. The question of who gets what is routinely answered by governments with reference to market principles and provisions, rather than welfare ideals and services. The notion that a viable way to deal with poverty and inequality might be to suspend or amend the price mechanism, in order to distribute goods and services according to need, funded by a system of collective insurances, has lost its place on the agenda. The 'how' of who gets what, where, is taken for granted: markets are preferable to, or more practical than, states. In this chapter, we ask whether this change of tack – this drift to the market – was logical, inevitable or just, and whether it is sustainable. What *is* the problem with welfare?

Global Matters

Perhaps the most influential critique of the idea of welfare is the claim that collectively funded social transfers are a luxury that we can no longer afford. As Britain's Prime Minister has noted, 'We are all globalists now' (Blair, 1998), living in an integrated international economy which, so the argument goes, works in a particular way. This is an economy in which states have (no choice but) to compete with each other for shares of transnational investment, and for trade in goods and services. In this neoliberal 'competition world', labour costs have to be low, and public spending has to be minimized. Welfare transfers are therefore regarded as a burden which may cause unemployment, price labour out of the global market, prompt disinvestment by foreign firms, and trigger speculation against national currencies.

This line of reasoning is evident in the steer given to states by the supranational agencies that oversee global capitalism. Welfare protection, they imply, is not a cost-effective enterprise: 'The slowdown in the growth of the OECD economies in the past 26 years', claims the OECD itself, 'has been accompanied by fears about the sustainability of current systems of economic protection' (OECD, 1996, p. 2). The 'danger' is greatest for the north-west European welfare states, who are urged to 'alleviate the burden on their budgets of regimes of unemployment benefits or social security

which are no longer suited to the present world, and which are of a very
high cost' (Michel Camdessus, Managing Director of the IMF, G7 meeting, Hong Kong, September 1997, cited in Atkinson, 1998, p. 2). The
British government has taken a lead in heeding these warnings. As the
Chancellor of the Exchequer puts it: 'There is no safe haven, no easy escape
for any country from global competition without putting at risk long-term
stability, growth and employment' (Brown, 2003). This explains why even
a healthy economy should be protected from welfare ideals. 'Just as you
cannot spend your way out of a recession, you cannot, in a global economy
simply spend your way through a recovery either' (Brown, 1997, p. 297).
The argument is that having any kind of welfare state can jeopardize a
nation's competitiveness, thereby compromising both incomes and standards of living. In this environment, welfare states, as we have known them,
are things of the past; competitive states are the future, and the two are not
compatible. It is economics rather than politics which set the terms of the
welfare debate.

This is such a powerful set of ideas – steeped in 'common sense' and
fuelled by fiscal uncertainty – that for some years the 'one (neoliberal)
globalization' thesis seemed self-evident. The fact that 'globalization'
more or less took over from 'privatization' during the 1990s as a label for
market-based 'reforms' of what were once welfare, or publicly owned,
services is a marker of just how effective that thesis was. And there is
undoubtedly a set of vested interests – among governments and the economists who advise them – in having 'one' global economy run on certain,
neoliberal, lines (with the model of welfare that this implies). Exercising
these interests, moreover, and behaving politically as if the world is operating in this way, and must do so, has a self-fulfilling tendency (Piven, 1995;
Kelly, 1999; Miller, 2002).

But notwithstanding the power of some governments to keep a particular
worldview – a particular economic metageography – in place, there is an
equally compelling critique of this 'apocalyptic' version of globalization.
This critique exposes the 'problem' with welfare as a political vision rather
than an inevitable outcome of an economically integrated world (Peck,
2001). There are three planks to this argument.

First, there is a growing literature questioning most claims relating to all
the key phenomena of the 'one (neoliberal) world' thesis: the mobility of
skilled labour; the movement of the terms of trade towards the newly
industrializing economies; and the decline of wage rates to internationally
low levels (Jordan, 1998). The global economy is not a single integrated
labour force or marketplace – and while geography and history matter, it
never could be.

Second, scholars are increasingly critical of the role of organizations like
the IMF and the European Commission which have promoted a particular

discourse of globalization as a means of justifying the (reductions in) social policy which they consider appropriate to a globalized world (Deacon, 2001). There is, moreover, a growing scepticism in the literature – from economics through political science and international relations – towards the idea that nation-states and governments have little control over either the global economy or their own economies and welfare futures (Palier and Sykes, 2001; Stiglitz, 2002). The discourse of globalization may have been used by governments as a 'convenient alibi' to defend a particular strategy for welfare, but this is a political choice rather than an economic constraint (Hay 2001; Kelly, 1999; Watson and Hay, 2003).

Finally, while it has not been popular among mainstream economists to challenge the idea that having a well-developed system of social protection comes at the expense of economic growth, some, most notably Tony Atkinson (1995, 1998), find the empirical evidence – which so many quote as definitive – to be at best inconclusive. Assessing the evidence linking poor economic indicators with a range of welfare transfers, Atkinson (1998, p. 20) argues: 'If this were a court of law, and the welfare states were charged with undermining competitiveness, then I would put it to the jury that the case has not been proven beyond reasonable doubt.' Indeed he takes this a step further, using economic ideas to illustrate that welfare transfers can work with, rather than against, the grain of economic growth. His claim is that welfare state mechanisms might as easily have positive as negative consequences for economic performance (see also Atkinson and Sinn, 1999).

Similarly, with reference to standards of living and quality of life, Wilkinson (1996), for example, has built a sustained and convincing evidence-based case that income inequality depresses life expectancy, and that it is the most egalitarian, rather than the richest, societies which (in the more economically developed world at least) have the best physical and mental health prospects. Will Hutton (2002) enlarges on this, arguing that while the economic ill-effects of regulation, taxation, public provision and welfare are routinely exaggerated, the benefits conferred by high-quality universal education, health care and income guarantees are rarely mentioned. There is a case, then, for arguing that welfare provision is not only compatible with national economic success in the context of world development, but that it is also socially desirable and ethically imperative.

Furthermore, even as mainstream political parties in most countries of the world are claiming that that there is no (feasible) alternative to worldwide free markets and their attendant welfare regimes, John Gray (1998) has argued powerfully to the contrary, pointing to a future in which the protective function of states is likely to expand rather than wither away as citizens demand shelter from the effects of a move towards global liberalism. Even the OECD (1999, p. 137) now recognizes not only that 'one of the effects of globalization could be to increase the demand for social protection', but also that 'globalization reinforces the need for some social protection'. Rodrick (1997), in fact, shows that those European countries most exposed to free trade (Luxembourg, Belgium and the Netherlands) have experienced strongest demands for a more active government role in the provision of social insurance. There is, then, an argument that governments can, and indeed may be forced to, promote a different vision of how the world works (Bonoli, George and Taylor-Gooby, 2000). The recent flurry of popular anti-globalization books – which, as John Kay (2003) has pointed out, may be the *only* books on business and economics that have been selling well in Europe – and the birth of anti-capitalist social movements underline this point. It seems that, far from having too little room to manouvre in a new world order, governments who insist their hands are tied have missed key opportunities to promote alternative visions of what globalization is about (Hay, 1998, 2001).

There is no space in this chapter to adjudicate among the complex arguments running through the economic globalization literature. However, there is no need to do so. For our purposes it is enough to make the point that the 'problem' with welfare which attracts by far the most attention – the possibility that it is unaffordable and disadvantageous in a globalizing economy – is unproven. Global markets may serve to fracture societies and weaken states, but competent governments do have a margin of freedom within which to act. The social costs of failing to use economic growth to fund social protection are increasingly well documented; meanwhile, there is no evidence that the economic limits for social policy and redistributive justice have yet been reached.

Principles and Practicalities

So far, we have argued that although governments may appeal to global processes to legitimize the demise of welfare, the basis of this appeal is questionable. We now consider a range of other discourses against welfare which, though they are not played out on a global stage, are equally potent in undermining public support for collective strategies of social protection. Here we provide a brief critique of three interlinked but increasingly questionable ideas: that the welfare ideal is flawed in principle; that it is unworkable in practice; and that 'price' is a more just and effective principle than 'need' when allocating goods and services.

All of these ideas stem from a charge that the welfare experiment has been tried in a number of societies and that it has failed. The claim is this: welfarism has failed to alleviate poverty, redistribute resources or guarantee individual security; it has failed to extend the rights of citizenship to those who qualify for them; it has denied people the choices and opportunities for self-determination and improvement that a civilized society might expect. Worse still, such safety nets dampen enterprise and foster dependence on the state. It follows that suspending the price mechanism – allocating goods and services according to need rather than ability to pay – simply does not, and crucially cannot, work. This line of reasoning is rooted in the most persuasive of Hayek's writings, in the most popular of Friedman's polemics, and in the rhetoric of neoliberal governments around the world, whose faith in monetarism as the holy grail of economic stability has barely been shaken by recent world events.

To consider this set of arguments – arguments against the idea that governments can or should intervene substantially in, let alone provide alternatives to, markets – we draw on the example of housing, which has been the focus of much of our own research. Housing is, of course, central to studies of social justice, (in)equality and geography (S. J. Smith, 2000). Housing has also been the fulcrum for political and scholarly debates on the relative efficacy of states and markets in delivering services and resources (Clapham, Kemp and Smith, 1990). This is especially true in Britain, which is a good example for the purposes of this chapter: it is a country with a strong welfare tradition which was the world's guinea pig for the application of monetarist ideas; and the UK led the developed world's U-turn into inequality towards the end of the twentieth century (Harrison and Bluestone, 1988; Alderson and Nielson, 2002; Atkinson, 2003). In Britain, it is in relation to housing provision that monetarist experiments – experiments aiming to minimize the state's involvement in markets – were first (and most extensively) conducted (Forrest and Murie, 1988). Encouraging tenants in socially provided and managed properties to buy their homes, so expanding owner occupation (the market) at the expense of public renting (the state), set off the wave of privatizations and quasi-marketizations which dominated the agenda of Conservative governments in Britain throughout the 1980s. So it is that the British housing system provides a litmus test for the welfare ideal, welfare practices and market alternatives.

Welfare in principle

In Britain, the welfare arm of the housing system has, since it was first created in 1919, allocated homes according to need rather than ability to pay, and bridged the payment gap with a range of subsidies and benefits. The provision of social rented housing has been part of the project of making welfare transfers in cash or kind to compensate for the inequalities which arise in the marketplace. It has also sought to meet and manage needs which markets do not (and have never been required to) service at affordable prices. The 1970s and 1980s saw the completion of an impressive series of empirical studies documenting the achievements and limitations of this process. Disturbingly for the welfare tradition, the findings indicated that, far from ironing out social inequalities – around class, race and gender in particular – attempts to suspend the price mechanism and allocate homes according to need were actively reproducing these divides. This body of research was largely undertaken by the academic Left, was based on sound evidence, and was only possible because the providers of social housing were so open to scrutiny from researchers. It is therefore ironic that the findings chimed in so neatly with the neoliberal political climate. Far from solving social problems, it seemed as if the welfare state was creating them, confirming politicians' suspicion that welfare interventions have too few checks and balances, rarely meet their aims, and fail to address inequality.

There is no doubt that some people's needs are not met by the way welfare states have been organized. Low-income groups, single parents (especially single mothers) and racialized minorities, for example, have been unjustly marginalized across a range of social and market institutions, not just in housing. However, in order to gauge whether there is a problem with the *principle* of social welfare, there is a case for looking at the experience of those whose needs have historically been more squarely *in*cluded in welfare societies. People with health-related needs, for example, have always been constructed in British social policy as most 'deserving' of welfare assistance.[1] This is born out in studies of social housing allocation systems which were, from the 1960s to the 1990s at least, driven by the idea of housing for health (Smith, 1990; Smith and Mallinson, 1997). Here, then, is a space in which to consider whether it is ever possible to suspend the price mechanism and distribute resources according to need.

Given the centrality of health, and more recently also of physical and sensory impairment, to needs-based housing allocations systems, it is surprising how little systematic attention this has received in studies of housing provision. Our work in this area is based on what was the first (and which remains the only) large-scale study of the conduct and effectiveness of what was then termed 'medical rehousing' in Britain (Smith, 1993; Easterlow, 1998). The research included a survey of over 800 households at various points in the rehousing cycle. Interviewees' experiences suggest that when housing is allocated in order to meet accessibility and/or health-related needs, it can (though it does not always) provide access to healthier environments, it may secure both palliative and therapeutic outcomes, it reduces demands on (yet enhances access to) formal and informal care, and it is associated with improvements in people's quality of life (Smith, Alexander and Easterlow, 1997). The allocation of a key welfare resource – *housing* – according to a measure of need – *health* – can work. Indeed, it can surpass what is conventionally expected of it. This, we argue, challenges the idea that housing cannot, in principle, be allocated (rather than bought), and it undermines the notion that public services are inherently cumbersome and unresponsive to demand. Indeed some of the most imaginative and innovative ways of making social renting work have come from the sphere of housing for health. Furthermore, some of the most imaginative – and effective – strategies of housing for health have originated in the social rented sector of the housing system (Easterlow and Smith, 2003).

Welfare practicalities

There are, of course, practical problems involved in the project of housing for health. The greatest of these is almost certainly posed by the reduced capacity of a housing system which is administered by market processes to enact a welfare role (Smith and Mallinson, 1997). This aside, however, there is still a practical argument against welfare, rooted in the ostensibly reasonable charge that it is far more challenging to find a way to distribute resources according to need than it is to sell them for a price. The argument here is that prioritizing needs is too difficult to operationalize justly.

It is, of course, fair to argue that if the welfare ideal doesn't work for some, and might only work for a minority of others, something must be wrong. The question, though, is: what? The neoliberal argument is that the world is made up of complex, plural societies in which it is difficult (and perhaps immoral and exclusionary) to recognize some needs and not others, and to prioritize some needs above others. At best the practical task of suspending the price mechanism might be too large and complex to manage. In the case of housing, for example, who is to say how accessibility needs should be prioritized relative to needs arising from living in over-crowded conditions; and who is to say that a ground-floor flat is an appropriate match to some kinds of needs, while a house with a garden is more suitable for others? And even if we agree a 'conception of the good' – a set of allocative criteria – how do we match people to resources in such a complex world?

Too much has been written on conceptions of both need and the 'good life' to do justice to these ideas here. However, one of the biggest concerns about systems which attempt to put these welfare-linked ideals into allocative practices has been located in the exercise of discretion. Discretion refers to the extent to which social managers are trusted to make decisions about which needy people receive what kind of social resource. Discretion is, in effect, one solution to the practical difficulty of suspending the price mechanism in the interests of social welfare. But it is a solution which has, by all accounts, gone badly wrong. In the case of public housing allocations, for example, research has suggested that discretionary decisions conflate what people need with what they are presumed to deserve; and that who deserves what tends to be indexed instead by certain social and demographic characteristics. The net result is that even when an organization believes itself to be committed to equal opportunities, people get quicker access and better offers more because of who they are than because of what they need (Henderson and Karn, 1984; Jeffers and Hoggart, 1995). Because of this, the exercise of discretion has been regarded as one of the major, possibly insurmountable, problems with the practice of welfare.

Again, however, some findings from the housing for health project provide a different perspective. Smith and Mallinson (1996) draw together materials from nine detailed case studies to show that discretion cannot fairly or realistically be 'defined' out of systems of resource allocation. Instead, they outline a range of practical options for balancing discretion with accountability, and for working with trust in the delivery of public services. They argue that, far from discretion being inherently problematic, it is a fundamental necessity for a welfare-rich society. It can be (made to be) a resource rather than a technical failure. To say this does not get around the problem that the world and the states within it are systematically unequal (divided by incomes and wealth, and by ideas about race, gender and other social categories). Neither does it deny that these inequalities frame the way conceptions of need are defined and managed (by individuals and organizational rules) within key institutions. However, this different take on discretion, which we would now see as providing one basis for a social democratic approach to equality and diversity, could be a pathway to confronting rather than reproducing the problem of social inequality.

Unfortunately, in a neoliberal economic climate, the failure of state institutions to act more quickly has only increased the political attractiveness of something completely different, on the grounds that, whereas the discretion that infuses all welfare adjustments reproduces social inequality in systematic ways, the way markets work does not. This is because markets are amoral mechanisms, dealing dispassionately with transactions among individuals on the uncontestable criterion of ability to pay. Markets are theoretically neutral between different conceptions of what is good, fair and just. Conceived of in this way, they are not just a financial necessity; they are a practical solution to the problem of unequal resources – a problem which has been constructed as the consequence of over-intervention by the state. So if the practical problem with welfare is that it can't be comprehensively 'designed in' by what the British Prime Minister once dubbed 'the intrusive hand' of the state (Blair, 1998), the 'logical' solution is that at least some measure of welfare could be achieved anyway by the celebrated, if invisible, hand of the market. In the case of housing, almost twenty-five years has passed since this 'solution' was enacted. To what extent has it worked?

Welfare markets?

We can address this question by extending the housing and health example to consider how well the market sector works, and cares, for people when their health is compromised. The potency of key political discourses against welfare and in favour of markets is nowhere better illustrated than in the example of housing. Owner occupation is just one aspect of the market for housing, but it accommodates most people in the more developed world, and it has been celebrated and sought after by the British public because it appears to combine ample residential choice with an opportunity to store and accumulate wealth. It is also prized as an arena in which people can control their living space, engage in their own projects, and have a secure base from which to plan their lives and futures. As a result, home ownership – the largest segment of the housing market – has expanded so much in Britain in the last twenty years that as well as accommodating the majority of the middle and upper classes, it is home for half the poor, and for a growing proportion of people whose physical and mental health is at risk, and/or who have physical and sensory impairments. This raises the question of how people who might once have turned to the state, not just on account of their incomes, but also because of their health, fare in a market-dominated system. We have sought to answer this, at least in part, in a second round of housing for health research (developing an agenda set out in Easterlow, Smith and Mallinson, 2000) based on qualitative research which aims to track households' trajectories though home ownership.

The research draws on in-depth accounts from households in three areas of the UK to show how home ownership has been made as attractive to people experiencing a variety of limiting long-term illnesses as it has to anyone else. Indeed, the work identifies several reasons why this sector might currently be more attractive to them on welfare grounds than social renting. This chapter is not the place to detail all the very individual events and circumstances that a range of different people with a variety of health experiences encounter in the housing marketplace. It is, however, appropriate to sketch the story of some things they have in common.

The first part of this story is concerned with the extent to which people are able to choose a home from the market in order to meet housing needs (i.e. as a route to welfare) as well as for financial gain (this is discussed in Smith, Easterlow and Munro, 2004). The indication here is that when people's health is at risk, particularly if their incomes are at the lower end of the spectrum for home owning, their market choices can be limited by two crucial factors. First, there is a shortage of suitable affordable properties to buy: the market does not routinely provide for changing mobility and accessibility needs, for care-giving and -receiving relationships, and so on. This shortage is compounded by the limited relevant information provided by some key intermediaries in the buying and selling process. Second, people report difficulties in translating their incomes into adequate housing finance if, for example, they have the 'wrong' kinds of wealth (notably incomes which include benefits), or the 'wrong' kinds or sequences of employment. The upshot is that because markets are geared to prices not needs, and because financial services are offered in line with this – and are moreover, as rationed by discretionary judgements as any state service – people already experiencing poor health can, even if they succeed in buying a home, end up living in the wrong kinds of spaces for home owning to act in a health-promoting way. These are, furthermore, the kind of spaces which may limit people's options to use housing investments to store and accumulate wealth. There are, in short, grounds to suggest that health inequalities may be at best reproduced and at worst amplified by the way markets work.

The second part of the story considers the extent to which housing markets can or should 'care' for those who use them (Easterlow and Smith, 2004). Study participants set considerable store by the 'freedom' they have as owners to maintain, alter and adapt their home to their changing physical and emotional needs. They also regard home owning as a source of stability or security, protecting them from future uncertainties. Although these are complicated issues, a recurrent theme among the home owners and buyers who participated in our research concerns the lengths people go to in order to make their spaces in the housing market into safe, secure and care-full places. Owner occupiers have actively bought in to the idea that markets deliver in ways that state bureaucracies do not, and have done their best to make the most of this. But there are limits. Failing health is often incompatible with the 'do-it-yourself' culture that markets rely on. Living with chronic or limiting illnesses can be costly, and help with home repairs and maintenance may not be top of the list. In the wake of some health experiences, homes can become disabling, and where poor health is associated with loss of earnings, the financial as well as physical limits to owner occupation may quickly loom large. The irony here is that while owners try hard to make markets work in socially desirable, as well as financially manageable, ways, governments do not. They *are* committed to 'making markets work for all', but the assumption is that public interests are best served by less not more regulation. The mantra 'market solutions to market failures' means, for example, that whereas social tenants can benefit from a variety of state safety nets if their incomes fail, home buyers cannot. Private rather than social insurances are their first port of call. Since these are largely insurances against accident, sickness and unemployment, it is not hard – even though the issues are complex – to spot the problem for those already experiencing ill health.

Britain is a society which has argued for market solutions to the problems of accommodating the majority of the population – including the majority of those who might be described as poor or vulnerable. In the area of housing and health – which we have argued provides a litmus test for the problem of welfare – markets fall short of the ideals they embody. They do so, of course, for the same kinds of reasons that social renting compromised welfare ideals. Markets are as riddled with practical difficulties as any other distributive system. The difference is that, for this fault, welfarism was all but dismantled; it was certainly 'radically reformed' in ways that markets never have been. Even now the government makes far more demands of the (declining) social sector than of the increasingly pervasive institutions of the market. In housing, for example, a variety of targets are set (and funds earmarked) for social landlords, and rights extended to social tenants, without parallel in the market sector. In this policy environment, far from challenging or changing market mechanisms, governments actively look to them for inspiration. Choice-based lettings and the possibility to purchase equity shares, for instance, are now being offered to social tenants as an example of the merits of transferring 'best practice' from the market into the social sector. Interestingly, there is no mention anywhere of the merits of transferring imaginative, innovative ideas developed by state institutions in the direction of the market.

Market solutions are still the answer to welfare failures; and they are the answer to market failures too. Yet this whole edifice is built on the assumption that the pursuit of welfare is a project which is flawed in principle and practically unworkable. We have argued that these charges are not only contestable, but are as applicable to the institutions of the market as to any other method of resource allocation. Where does this leave the problem with welfare?

From Welfare States to Caring, Creative Societies?

The words 'problem' and 'welfare' seem inextricably linked. Welfare transfers have been (constructed as) problematic because they are too costly in a global economy; the notion of states intervening in markets is (regarded as) problematic because the principle is held to be flawed; the practice of suspending the price mechanism and allocating resources according to need has been (defined as being) problematic because it is so hard to operationalize. Having constructed the problem in this way, governments throughout the neoliberal world have adopted the 'obvious' solution: that is, to cut budgets, 'target' resources, limit eligibility, replace dependence on the state with enterprise in the market, and, most recently, introduce market principles into the social sector.

In this chapter, we have challenged this line of reasoning by arguing that the most commonly cited 'problems' with welfare are at best contestable. Together they form a powerful discourse of legitimacy for particular visions of a market economy. However, they do not amount to a coherent argument against the idea of using collective resources to meet social needs. In the remainder of the chapter, we go on to suggest that – because of this – the most fundamental problem with welfare is not among the issues raised so far. Indeed the root of the problem is so far removed from the neoliberal agenda that it is rarely articulated. It is not that welfare aims are unrealistic, but that welfare goals have been designed with too little imagination. It is not that states have overstretched themselves, but that they have shown too little ambition in defining their sphere of influence. It is not that too much has been expected of the welfare ideal, but rather that too little has been extracted from the many organizations and institutions which have a bearing on social well-being. We conclude, then, with a question: if the problem with welfare is that its scope is too narrow, what are the alternatives; what other welfare imaginaries might work?

Consistent with the bulk of the chapter, we address this question with reference primarily to the British experience of making the transition from a welfare state to a neoliberal market economy. One argument sometimes mounted from the ('old') Left is that to the extent that the welfare experiment failed it did so because it was never properly tried. Taking the case of rehousing for health, or for other social needs, for example, it could be argued that housing managers have never been able to put the principle into practice, precisely because the service has never been adequately resourced. The same argument could be made for other public services, particularly the National Health Service, especially when British public spending is compared with that of its European neighbours. It is possible that the problem with welfare is that there was never enough state ownership, management and involvement in key socially relevant institutions, and that the real costs were never covered. One welfare imaginary could be to tackle this: to go 'back to the future' in pursuit of welfare aims.

A different take on this, and the one we wish to develop here, is that welfare experiments were always limited because the social democratic Left, like the neoliberal Right, assigned a role to states which conceived of their activities as essentially separate from (and often incompatible with) the workings of markets. Looking to the origins of the British welfare state, for example, the clear impression is that welfare consisted of two elements. On the one hand, the 'social services' were established to provide an *alternative* to market provisioning. This was the idea developed by Marshall and Titmuss: states would move into the gap left by markets, in the interests of fairness and equality. On the other hand, because markets were conceived of as something outside, beyond and autonomous from society, the role of the state in managing these – assuming it had a role at all – was conceived of as a process of *intervention* in, or *correction* of (or, more recently, regulation of), the failures or imperfections in a mechanism which would otherwise 'work' of its own accord. This is the position associated with Keynesian economics. The welfare state was, then, part of a world which was (and to a large extent remains) irreconcilably divided into economies and societies, driven by markets and kept together by states.

Our concern is that while scholars have spent entire careers debating the extent (and end) of a post-war welfare consensus in British politics, most overlook the really enduring point of agreement in these debates, namely the assumption about what markets are. Put crudely, the Left has argued that markets do one thing (adjust supply to demand for those who can pay) while states do another (service unmet needs). The Right has argued for markets to do most things (dispense a wide range of goods and services) while states ensure they are free to achieve this. Either way, it is the role of the state that is open to debate; the work of the market is not. It is intriguing that this vision of the marketplace – which has been in place far longer than the vision of the global economy we outlined earlier – has attracted so little critique.

Our preferred welfare imaginary is, nevertheless, one which contests the entrenched dualism of state and market. It questions the idea (the ideology) of what markets are, and challenges the essentialism which economists, social policy analysts and generations of politicians have invested in them. Our argument is that resorting to this distinction has always allowed governments to place limits on what a caring society could achieve. An essentialist take on markets, for example, is why the new 'socially responsible globalization' promoted by organizations such as the IMF and World Bank (Deacon, 2001), or embedded in the OECD's quest for a 'Caring World', are still oriented to the demands of global capitalism for a healthy, educated and skilled labour force. It is why arguments for a global social policy are still about combining workfare policies with private safety nets in the management of risk, and it is why they remain set in an individualistic and competitive frame of reference. These innovations sound appealing, but at root they remain part of that shift from Keynesianism to Schumpeterianism whose purpose is mainly 'to subordinate social policy to the needs of labour market flexibility and/or to the constraints of international competition' (Jessop, 1994, p. 24)

In Britain, for example, the Prime Minister's claim that 'radical reform is the route to social justice' (Blair, 2002) is in practice about how states no longer need to be the first port of call when markets fail, and about how those serviced by the state have most to gain by being exposed to the ideas of the market. This strategy may appear to be merging the spheres of the state and the market – which is precisely what we are arguing for – with a goal we can only applaud: to create 'the good society, where we live in an atmosphere of solidarity, tolerance and respect' (Blair, 2003). However, in practice this version of how to align the institutions of the state with those of the market extends a particular ethos (around competitive individualism), rooted in a particular conception of how markets work, into a sphere of provision (the world of welfare) which has traditionally nurtured rather different visions of how lives could be lived and societies might operate.

By using market principles to create a new 'welfareplace' in the social sector, the government is ensuring that competition rather than co-operation, self-interest rather than collective good, are the touchstones for all aspects of life, not just those serviced by market institutions. This dissolution of what states have traditionally stood for (their mechanisms, their values and their ethos) into the way markets work is encapsulated in Cerny's (1990) idea of the transition from the 'welfare state' to the 'competition state'. But there is more to it than this. Principles of competition *have* been introduced to the public sector as a way of working, and as a way of structuring social relations between service providers and individuals in terms of contractual relations. However, these principles also structure relations between individuals themselves in every sphere of life. Parents are encouraged to compete to secure the best private or public education for their children. Households are encouraged to find and 'choose' the best hospitals and professionals, within and beyond the National Health Service, in order to maximize their own quality of care. Managers and employees are rewarded for being enterprising, rather than for being supportive, caring, or simply capable in the world of work, whether this is in the public or private sectors. There is, in short, what Rodger (2003) calls a 'vocabulary of motives' infusing British society which is rooted in competitive individualism and is negative to the principle of welfare. The consequence, as Staeheli and Brown (2003) and Haylett (2003) have argued, is that the reform of welfare has been about more than pursuing neoliberal economic aims or conservative political goals; it has also been an attack on the ethics of care.

This ethics of care is currently being (re)promoted in the academic literature, opening up the new frame of reference which one of us (over)-optimistically predicted some years ago (Smith, 1989). It is an ethics, moreover, whose importance was recognized by the early architects of welfare states. Their most fundamental point was that the realization of care-full societies depends on institutionalizing caring principles and setting up caring structures (Miller, 1987). For Richard Titmuss, for instance, the 'social services' could only work if they were built around those principles of altruism, mutual responsibility and reciprocity that epitomize the best of what he termed 'family' life (referring to close, mutually supportive, social relations). These are *feelings*, as well as principles and practicalities, and they are not just about setting targets and working hard to meet them. Rather they refer to an ethos that could infuse the whole of society (Titmuss, 1967). This ethic depends on co-operation rather than competition, and values burden-sharing rather than the pursuit of self-interest. It connects, in short, with a range of social values which are quite different to those attached to current constructions of the market.

We suggest, then, that the main 'problem' with welfare today is that the ethics of care has been eclipsed not just by the expansion of an essentialized market into the wake of a restructured welfare state, but also by the idealization of market principles as a way of going on even in the social sector. The 'solution' to this kind of problem is to extend an ethics of care (and perhaps a range of other values) into the operation and regulation of markets. To achieve this, it may be time for governments to recognize, with a growing coterie of economic geographers and sociologists, that it is *visible* not invisible hands which shape the way that all institutions work, including those of the market (Swedberg and Granovetter, 2001; Peck, 2003). By working with and through these 'visible hands', both analysts and governments could develop new ways of thinking, new conventions and expectations, about what so-called 'market processes' can achieve. That is, success in reshaping societies in the way governments claim they will depends on a different way of thinking about what markets are, and how they work.

John Gray has shown in a careful and perceptive analysis that 'free' markets have to be created by sustained political effort (that is, by significant 'interventions'). If this is the case, it follows that other kinds of 'market' could also be devised by the exercise of political will. As Gray (1992, p. 74) has argued: 'market institutions are social constructions, artifacts which we may not have designed, and which are for us historical inheritances, but which we may properly alter and reform so that they better contribute to human aims'. This means that just as one vision of how markets work dominated both social and economic life in the late twentieth century, it is possible to imagine how, in the twenty-first century, a different set of values – around a caring society underpinned by a welfare philosophy – could be compatible with the workings of a whole range of institutions and organizations, whether these are currently labelled as being 'public' or 'private'. Indeed, by transcending the dualism of state versus market with this idea in mind, a very different vision of the good life is possible. This might, in the end, produce a society which recognizes and rewards those who 'care', as much as it values those who 'work'. It might be a society which has the institutional infrastructure as well as the social capital not only to support family, friends and community, but also to exercise respect and concern for strangers, to feel for 'distant others'. It will certainly be a society which has relinquished an obsession with making markets work in favour what David Smith (1998) has recognized as an extension of the social and spatial scope of societies' capability to care.

NOTE

1   It is, of course, important not to overdo this claim. The differences between 'sick' and 'healthy', as well as between 'able' and 'disabled', are essentialized in the same way as gender difference, age and race. And as the tide turns against the welfare ideal, people whose health is at risk are as vulnerable as any other to being constructed as 'undeserving' for policy purposes. Our own research, for example, suggests that people experiencing a range of common illnesses face discrimination in a variety of walks of life.

REFERENCES

Alderson, A. S. and Nielson, F. (2002) 'Globalization and the great U-turn: income inequality trends in 16 OECD countries', *American Journal of Sociology* 107, 1244–99.

Atkinson, A. B. (1995) 'The welfare state and economic performance', *National Tax Journal* 48, 171–98.

Atkinson, A. B. (1998) 'Can welfare states compete in a global economy?', *Discussion Papers in Public Sector Economics no. 98/1*, Public Sector Economic Research Centre, University of Leicester.

Atkinson, A. B. (2003) 'Income inequality in OECD countries: data and explanations', revised version of Working Paper 881, prepared for the CESifo conference 'Globalization, inequality and wellbeing' (Munich, November), downloaded from the author's website (*http://www.nuff.ox.ac.uk/economics/people/atkinson.htm*), August 2003.

Atkinson, A. B. and Sinn, H.-W. (1999) *The Economic Consequences of Rolling Back the Welfare State*, Cambridge, Mass.: MIT Press.

Blair, T. (1998) 'Europe's left-of-centre parties have discovered the "third way"', *The Independent*, 7 April.

Blair, T. (2002) *The Courage of Our Convictions: Why Reform of the Public Services is the Route to Social Justice*, London: The Fabian Society.

Blair, T. (2003) 'Our mission: to govern for long-term progress', speech at Garston Urban Village Hall, Liverpool, 4 July.

Bonoli, G., George, V. and Taylor-Gooby, P. (2000) *European Welfare Futures*, Cambridge: Polity.

Brown, G. (1997) 'Speech to the Labour Party Conference', in M. Powell (ed.), *New Labour, New Welfare State?* Bristol: Policy Press, pp. 281–99.

Brown, G. (2003) Speech by the Chancellor of the Exchequer at the Global Borrowers and Investors Forum, London, 17 June.

Cerny, P. G. (1990) *The Changing Architecture of Politics: Structure, Agency, and the Future of the State*, London: Sage.

Clapham, D., Kemp, P. and Smith, S. J. (1990) *Housing and Social Policy*, Basingstoke: Macmillan.

Deacon, B. (2001) 'International organizations, the EU and global social policy', in R. Sykes, B. Palier and P. M. Prior (eds), *Globalization and European Welfare States*, Basingstoke: Palgrave, pp. 59–77.

Easterlow, D. (1998) *Housing and Health: A Geography of Welfare Restructuring*, unpublished PhD thesis, University of Edinburgh.

Easterlow, D. and Smith, S. J. (1997) 'Fit for the future? A role for health professionals in housing management', *Public Health* 111, 171–8.

Easterlow, D. and Smith, S. J. (2003) 'Housing policy and health in Britain', in P. Gill and G. de Wildt (eds), *Housing and Health: The Role of Primary Care*, Oxford: Radcliffe Medical Press, pp. 1–16.

Easterlow, D. and Smith S. J. (2004) 'Housing for health: can the market care?', *Environment and Planning A* 36, 999–1017.

Easterlow, D., Smith, S. J. and Mallinson, S. (2000) 'Housing for health: the role of owner occupation', *Housing Studies* 15, 367–86.

English, J. (1979) 'Access and deprivation in local authority housing', in C. Jones (ed.), *Urban Deprivation and the Inner City*, London: Croom Helm, pp. 113–35.

Forrest, R. and Murie, A. (1988) *Selling the Welfare State: The Privatization of Council Housing*, London and New York: Routledge.

Gray, J. (1992) *The Moral Foundations of Market Institutions*, London: IEA Health & Welfare Unit.

Gray, J. (1998) *False Dawn*, London: Granta.

Harrison, B. and Bluestone, B. (1988) *The Great U-Turn*, New York: Basic Books.

Harvey, D. (1996) *Justice, Nature and the Geography of Difference*, Oxford: Blackwell.

Harvey, D. (2000) *Spaces of Hope*, Edinburgh: Edinburgh University Press.

Hay, C. (1998) 'Globalization, welfare retrenchment and "the logic of no alternative": why second-best won't do', *Journal of Social Policy* 27, 525–32.

Hay, C. (2001) 'Globalization, economic change and the welfare state: the "vexatious inquisition of taxation"?', in R. Sykes, B. Palier and P. M. Prior (eds), *Globalisation and European Welfare States*, Basingstoke: Palgrave, pp. 38–58.

Haylett, C. (2003) 'Class, care and welfare reform: reading meanings, talking feelings', *Environment and Planning A* 35, 799–814.

Henderson, J. and Karn, V. (1984) 'Race, class and the allocation of public housing', *Urban Studies* 21, 115–28.

Hutton, W. (2002) *The World We're In*, London: Little, Brown.

Jeffers, S. and Hoggart, P. (1995) 'Like counting deckchairs on the *Titanic*: a study of institutional racism and housing allocations in Haringey and Lambeth', *Housing Studies* 10, 325–44.

Jessop, B. (1994) 'The transition to post-fordism and the Schumpeterian welfare state', in R. Burrows and B. Loader (eds), *Towards a Post-Fordist Welfare State?* London: Routledge, pp. 13–37.

Jordan, B. (1998) *The New Politics of Welfare*, London: Sage.

Kay, J. (2003) *The Truth About Markets*, London: Penguin.

Kelly, P. S. (1999) 'The geographies and politics of globalization', *Progress in Human Geography* 23, 379–400.

Merrifield, A. and Swyngedouw, E. (1996) *The Urbanization of Injustice*, London: Lawrence & Wishart.

Miller, D. (2002) 'Conclusion: a theory of virtualism', in J. G. Carrier and D. Miller (eds), *Virtualism*, Oxford and New York: Berg, pp. 187–215.

Miller, S. M. (1987) 'Introduction: the legacy of Richard Titmuss', in B. Abel-Smith and K. Titmuss (eds), *The Philosophy of Welfare. Selected Writings of Richard M. Titmuss*, London: Allen & Unwin, pp. 1–17.

OECD (1996) *Beyond 2000: The New Social Policy Agenda*, Paris: OECD.

OECD (1999) *A Caring World: The New Social Policy Agenda,* Paris: OECD.

Palier, B. and Sykes, R. (2001) 'Challenges and change: issues and perspectives in the analysis of globalization and the European welfare states', in R. Sykes, B. Palier and R. M. Prior (eds), *Globalisation and European Welfare States,* Basingstoke: Palgrave, pp. 1–16.

Peck, J. (2001) 'Neo-liberalising states: thin policies/hard outcomes', *Progress in Human Geography* 25, 445–55.

Peck, J. (2003) 'Economic sociologies in space', paper presented to the workshop 'A Dialogue with Economic Geography and Economic Sociology: Post-disciplinary Reflections', Nottingham University. Available from the author (*http://www.geography.wisc.edu/faculty/peck.htm*).

Piven, F. F. (1995) 'Is it global economics or neo-laissez-faire?', *New Left Review* 213, 107–15.

Rieger, E. and Leibfried, S. (1998) 'Welfare state limits to globalization', *Policy and Society* 26, 363–90.

Rodger, J. J. (2003) 'Social solidarity, welfare and post-emotionalism', *Journal of Social Policy* 32, 403–21.

Rodrick, D. (1997) *Has Globalization Gone Too Far?* Washington, DC: Institute for International Economics.

Smith, D. M. (1977) *Human Geography: A Welfare Approach*, London: Edward Arnold.

Smith, D. M. (1979) *Where the Grass is Greener: Geographical Perspectives on Inequality,* London: Croom Helm.

Smith, D. M. (1994) *Geography and Social Justice*, Oxford: Blackwell.

Smith, D. M. (1998) 'How far should we care? On the spatial scope of beneficence', *Progress in Human Geography* 22, 15–38.

Smith, D. M. (2000) *Moral Geographies: Ethics in a World of Difference*, Edinburgh: Edinburgh University Press.

Smith, S. J. (1989) 'Social geography: social policy and the restructuring of welfare', *Progress in Human Geography* 13, 118–28.

Smith, S. J. (1990) 'Health status and the housing system', *Social Science and Medicine* 31, 753–62.

Smith, S. J. (1993) 'Housing provision for people with health and mobility needs', *Findings* 86, York: Joseph Rowntree Foundation.

Smith, S. J. (2000) 'Housing studies', in R. J. Johnston, D. Gregory, G. Pratt and M. Watts (eds), *The Dictionary of Human Geography* (4th edition), Oxford: Blackwell, pp. 346–9.

Smith, S. J., Alexander, A. and Easterlow, D. (1997) 'Rehousing as a health intervention: miracle or mirage?', *Health and Place* 3, 203–16.

Smith, S. J., Easterlow, D. and Munro, M. (2004) 'Housing for health: does the market work?', *Environment and Planning A* 36, 579–600.

Smith, S. J. and Mallinson, S. (1996) 'The problem with social housing: discretion, accountability and the welfare ideal', *Policy and Politics* 24, 339–57.

Smith, S. J. and Mallinson, S. (1997) 'Housing for health in a post-welfare state', *Housing Studies* 12, 173–200.

Staeheli, L. A. and Brown, M. (2003) 'Guest editorial: Where has welfare gone? Introductory remarks on the geographies of care and welfare', *Environment and Planning A* 35, 771–5.

Stiglitz, J. E. (2002) *Globalization and Its Discontents*, London: Penguin.

Swedberg, R. and Granovetter, M. (eds) (2001) *The Sociology of Economic Life*, Boulder, Colo.: Westview.

Titmuss, R. M. (1967) 'Welfare state and welfare society: lecture delivered at the British National Conference on Social Welfare, London', in B. Abel-Smith and K. Titmuss (eds), *The Philosophy of Welfare. Selected Writings of Richard M Titmuss*, London: Allen & Unwin, 1987, pp. 141–56.

Watson, M. and Hay, C. (2003) 'The discourse of globalisation and the logic of no alternative: rendering the contingent necessary in the political economy of New Labour', *Policy and Politics* 31, 289–305.

Wilkinson, R. G. (1996) *Unhealthy Societies*, London: Routledge.

8

Struggles over Human Rights in Nigeria: Questions of Scale in Moral Geography

Rex Honey

Introduction

In the aftermath of the carnage of the Second World War, sobered by the inhumanity of the Holocaust, the General Assembly of the United Nations approved the Universal Declaration of Human Rights on 10 December 1948 (United Nations, 1948). Representatives of the world's independent states, citing the common humanity of all people, recognized a series of rights that people should have simply because they are people. The citizens of Nigeria had no voice of their own in the General Assembly that day because they were struggling to gain political sovereignty. They were struggling for their own rights, rights the General Assembly said they should share with all others simply because they, too, were people. More than five decades on, those struggles continue. In Nigeria they continue for two reasons. One is that all societies struggle over human rights, claims of universality notwithstanding, as they debate the nature of the just society, as they wrestle over competing ideals and their implementation. The other is that Nigeria – in common with most African countries – has additional struggles for its people, both internal and external. These struggles are a consequence of the economic and political disadvantages befalling former colonies in a world that has increasing rather than decreasing gaps between rich and poor (Onimode, 1984). They are also a consequence of the perversely negative impact oil has had on Nigerian development (Sala-i-Martin, 2003), leaving a fractured country with a damaged polity and a damaged environment.

Let's consider Nigerian struggles over human rights, beginning with an examination of cultural struggles over human rights at various scales, then turning to Nigeria to see how those struggles have occurred and are occurring, not only within and between cultures but also between Nigeria and the forces of globalization. These struggles provide poignant evidence of the role of scale in a moral geography. At the scale of a particular culture they encapsulate the debate over what is right, what is fair, what is moral. In a multi-cultural country like Nigeria, with different cultures dominating different spaces within the country, struggles over human rights between cultures illustrate another scale. These struggles involve political movements encompassing the entire country rather than just a part of it. They influence the kinds of cultural compromises necessary as various interests compete over determination of the country's moral geography. Finally, at the global scale, the struggles between international forces, on the one hand, and local and national forces, on the other, involve a moral geography that is world-wide with national and local imprints.

Cultural struggles over human rights

Though advocates claim that human rights are 'universal' – applying in all places at all times – the rights that exist in international and domestic agreements are of course socially constructed rather than given (Brown, 2000; Honey, 2004). They are the culmination of considerable struggle. Struggle over what is just, what is fair. Struggle over entitlements. Struggle over obligations. Struggle over protections. Eventually, struggle over what is encoded as a right that all people should have because of their common humanity. Hence despite the claim of universality, the list of internationally recognized human rights is changing rather than fixed, fluid rather than permanent.

Literally scores of human rights are codified internationally. Since 1948, many were delimited in the two major covenants in 1966 (United Nations, 1966a, 1966b). Others are embodied in a series of additional agreements, such as those dealing with women's rights and children's rights (United Nations, 1979, 1989). Not only do the lists themselves change, but so do interpretations of rights and adherence to international agreements. Hence, what are permanent are the cultural struggles over human rights, not the rights themselves. This is true for all three 'generations' of human rights: the first generation political and civil rights; the second generation economic, social and cultural rights; and the third generation solidarity rights (Weston, 2003).

Scales of cultural struggles

Cultural struggles over human rights occur at three discernible scales. They are struggles within a culture, struggles between cultures within a country, and struggles between a culture or cultures and the forces of globalization, whether resistance to the global human rights movement, on the one hand, or resistance to global forces that deny human rights, on the other.

Struggles over human rights within a culture essentially have to do with how that culture conceptualizes justice, how it deals with differences, and the procedures it establishes for achieving fairness and resolving conflicts. These include struggles within a culture over what constitutes a just society. These struggles are ageless, including struggles that led to the Magna Carta and the American Declaration of Independence. More recently they include the struggles for racial and gender equality as well as the end of discrimination based on sexual preferences or disabilities. These struggles involve the full spectrum of human rights, from the political and civil rights embodied in the American Bill of Rights, through the economic rights codified in the standards of the International Labour Organization, to the solidarity rights written into the global Land Mine Treaty. They involve debates over cultural change aimed at reducing oppression, even when that oppression is deeply sedimented within the practices of a culture. For example, seeing domestic violence as a human rights violation rather than as the right of a man to maintain control over his home requires a major shift in thinking, a shift accomplished in much of Europe in the third quarter of the twentieth century but following later elsewhere. Indeed, some cultures seem to be only beginning to struggle to overcome the abuses of unbridled patriarchy even now. Another example is the struggle over the death penalty. Again, most European countries have abolished the death penalty. Indeed, its abolition is a requirement for membership in the European Union. By contrast, only twelve of the fifty American states prohibit use of the death penalty, though a number of states that officially permit the penalty do not in practice apply it. The issue is a locus of struggle in the United States. In much of Africa and Asia debate over the death penalty has hardly begun. In those societies judicial execution remains not only the law but also the well-supported cultural norm.

Cultures or sub-cultures within a country also struggle against each other – or against the prevailing morality enforced by the state – over human rights, both because the cultures have different conceptualizations of the just society and because of power struggles between the cultures. Conflict between cultures is a particularly acute problem in post-colonial states defined externally, including most African states and many Asian states. India exemplifies the problem. Hindu nationalists, empowered by the rise to power of the Bharatiya Janata Party, favour the implementation of legislation establishing a single civil code for the country in place of the multiple civil codes in place as a recognition of the religious diversity of the country (*Times of India*, 20 July 2003, p. 1). Predictably, the Muslim community in particular rails against what it sees as cultural oppression.

Each side has its view of how society, particularly a multi-cultural society, should be governed. Each in effect has its view of what constitutes a just society. Each struggles on behalf of its view. A nuanced interpretation is that in addition to the struggles within each culture, India has struggles between those cultures. Similar struggles take place elsewhere, covering such issues as language rights for the Welsh, Quebecois, Flemish and Bretons, or over religious freedom for minorities in such predominantly Christian countries as Ireland, Poland, Russia and such predominantly Muslim countries as Iran, Algeria and Sudan.

The third category of cultural struggles cuts both ways with countries resisting global forces deriding the countries for their human rights violations and with countries resisting the human rights violations stemming from global forces. Examples of the former would be patriarchal cultures resisting global pressures for recognition of women's and children's rights. Examples of the latter would be the imposition of sweat shops by external economic interests. All too often governments of poor countries are dually complicit. They resist the recognition of rights because the implementation of those rights would threaten the foundation of oppressive power. And they co-operate with global economic interests, either covertly or overtly, to the detriment of local workers and the fouling of domestic environments (Smith, 2003).

Nigerian Human Rights Struggles

Nigerian cultures have experienced mammoth change over the last three centuries, largely because of the imposition of external influences but also because of efforts to adjust those externally generated changes to indigenous values and perspectives. Those changes can be grouped into three distinct and significant periods: before formal colonial status; the colonial period; and the post-colonial period.

The major forces for change in the pre-colonial period were the slave trades (both trans-Atlantic and trans-Saharan), Islam from the desert north and Christianity from the coastal south. The trans-Saharan slave trade began at least as far back as the early centuries of the second millennium (Crowder, 1968). It provided contact with the Muslim cultures of North Africa and Southwest Asia, including both the Levant and the Arabian Peninsula. This contact over time led to the adoption of Islam in the Sahel south of the Sahara.

The trans-Atlantic slave trade, extending from the late sixteenth century to the early nineteenth century, had two major impacts (Blaut, 1993). One was demographic, with the removal of considerable labour power. The other was in social organization, particularly with the adoption of firearms.

It also led to the establishment of a series of European fortresses along the coast.

The momentum for change increased significantly in the nineteenth century, first with the so-called 'Fulani Jihad', led by the charismatic Usman Dan Fodio, spreading and reinforcing Islam particularly across the north of what became Nigeria in the century's first decade (Johnston, 1967). The Fulani, a largely pastoral people, adopted Hausa as their language and spread its use as the vernacular language, displacing scores of other languages while consolidating both political power and the pre-eminence of Islam in the areas they came to dominate (Otite, 1990). The second major external influence was an increase in European (by then British) presence, first from the fortress settlement of Lagos (begun as a Portuguese colony and named after a small port on Portugal's south coast) and eventually across all of what became southern Nigeria. This presence included not only the military and trading interests but also Christian missionaries. In addition to Christianity, the missionaries introduced Western education, a catalyst for major cultural change. Within a generation of the Berlin Conference, at which European powers divided Africa into sets of spheres of influence – with no African voice present – Britain consolidated its control over the colony it named 'Nigeria' (Crowe, 1942; Crowder, 1967).

Before the colonial period, the area that became Nigeria was inhabited by a great range of polities, societies and economies: political systems ranging from very powerful monarchies to what were essentially republics; social systems ranging from highly stratified class systems with variations of slavery to quite egalitarian structures; and economies ranging from sophisticated trading and farming communities to quite rudimentary hunting and gathering bands.

British policy during the colonial period, which lasted until 1960 when Nigeria gained its political sovereignty, reduced the variation in political, social and economic systems in the country, but it accentuated the differences between the North and South. Using the system of indirect rule that had been successful in the Indian Raj, the colonial power opted to work with local rulers, even where none existed before, reducing political variation in the process (Crowder, 1967). Britain forced all regions to adopt cash economies by imposing taxes, again reducing variations. On the other hand, by limiting the movement of Christian missionaries to the South, effectively limiting Western education to the South as well, Britain drove a wedge between the North and South. The colonial masters cut a deal with the northern emirs, prohibiting missionaries from proselytizing in the North in exchange for administrative co-operation. Hence most of the southern population adopted Christianity while most northerners retained or adopted Islam. (The majority also retained their traditional African beliefs, according to Udo [1970].)

Furthermore, southern Nigerians gained substantial economic advantages over their northern compatriots. This is partly because Lagos became the country's major city, playing the multiple roles of the colony's transportation, commercial, industrial and administrative capital. It is also because educated southerners, increasingly literate in English as well as their vernacular languages, took the jobs in the burgeoning civil service and emerging commercial economy.

Among the lessons southern Nigerians learned from the British were those of political liberty and human rights. They pushed for those rights before, during and after the Second World War, to the alarm not only of their British rulers but also of northern Nigerians, who feared being dominated politically as well as economically by southern Christians.

When Britain did grant independence to Nigeria, closing the colonial period, it did so in a way that protected the interests of the northern elites. It also did so by dividing the country into three regions, a unified one for the entire North and divided ones for an East and a West in the South, and it did so by (to the everlasting scepticism of southerners) defining more parliamentary constituencies in the North than the combined East and West. This allowed northern interests to dominate electoral politics. It also guaranteed a volatile political structure with constant cultural struggle, foremost between the Christian South and Muslim North but also among the more than 300 ethnic groups in Africa's most populous country (Otite, 1990).

A few crucial factors have influenced cultural struggles over human rights in post-independence Nigeria, specifically the persistence of military rule, the global impacts of the Cold War, and the windfall (for the government) of oil. Foremost is the dominance of the military, which ruled Nigeria from 1966 through 1979 and again 1983 through 1999, meaning twenty-nine of its first thirty-nine years as an independent country. With its major benefactors – Britain, the United States and France – looking the other way during the Cold War, the Nigerian military amassed the hardware and finances necessary to intimidate the Nigerian people. It amassed the hardware because its benefactors were willing to sell. It amassed its wealth because Nigerian oil came on line in the early 1970s, just when the price of petroleum sky-rocketed on global markets. The easy wealth allowed the military to rule without having to tax the people, essentially allowing the government to exist separately from the people as it ruled over them. Only after the end of the Cold War did the major global powers echo the global human rights movement by demanding democratic rule and responsive government in what should have been a rich African country. It was not, however; rather, the military squandered Nigeria's oil wealth, simultaneously despoiling large tracts with devastating, uncompensated oil damage. Through this period Nigeria became what Richard Joseph (1987) dubbed a 'prebendal' state, operating on graft and threats rather than anything approaching the ideal of a government of the people, by the people and for the people.

During the decades of military rule, successive military governments bought political support through the provision of funds to those who would support them. They co-opted most traditional rulers by providing modest stipends. They gained additional support by creating new states, increasing the number from the original three to thirty-six by 1996 (Kraxberger, 2005). The state creation process allowed the government to draw attention away from failed policies.

Correcting the human rights abuses of three decades is a daunting task, one that has fallen on Olusegun Obasanjo, elected President of Nigeria in 1999 and again in 2003. His administration, among other things, is coping with sometimes virulent cultural struggles over human rights. These struggles involve all three generations of human rights: civil and political; economic, social and cultural; and solidarity. They are effected by the uniform interest of Nigerian cultures to get their share of the national pie, meaning their share of the oil wealth that for so long was treated as the prerogative of the military.

Human rights struggles within Nigerian cultures

Nigeria has more than three hundred self-defined, recognized cultures, largely stemming from the typical differentiator of language distinctions (Otite, 1990). These cultures have their own mores and norms. With external influences challenging tradition, all Nigerian cultures faced internal struggles over human rights. An example is struggle over the roles of traditional rulers as political rights were extended to commoners. Most Nigerian cultures had some form of a traditional ruler, often but not exclusively from royal lineages. Global human rights norms call for the rights of individuals to choose their rulers. Successive military governments in Nigeria co-opted traditional rulers by offering a range of benefits in exchange for public support. Typically, Nigerian chiefs succumbed to the temptation, providing a modicum of respectability to the parade of military regimes. That duplicity has cost traditional rulers some of the support they could formerly assume from their subjects.

Another area of struggle over human rights within cultures has been marriage rights. Traditionally, young Nigerians married the partners chosen for them by their parents. Particularly in the South, the voice of the individual has become increasingly important in determining marriage partners. Even in the North, public opinion has been rising against the practice of arranged marriages for girls in their early teens (*Guardian* [Nigeria], 28 August 2003). Likewise, most Nigerian cultures have struggled over more general rights for girls and women, including access to education, property rights and protection from abusive rights of passage, including imposition of female genital mutilation (FGM), also known as female circumcision or female cutting. The practice has gradually lost favour as increasing numbers of cultures decide that the procedure is neither necessary nor appropriate.

Education has also been a theatre of struggle within Nigerian cultures. International standards have recognized the right to education, from 1948's Universal Declaration through 1966's Covenant on Economic, Social and Cultural Rights, through the Convention on the Rights of the Child. In the late nineteenth century, when mission schools were diffusing across the Nigerian South, parents quickly sensed the significance of education for their children. A major Nigerian critique against the performance of military governments was the disarray of the educational system, from the most rudimentary level through the most sophisticated.

Nigerian cultures tend to place a great deal of emphasis on a person's ancestral home, traced through the patrilineal line. People tracing their ancestries to a particular place are 'indigenes' of that place, whether they live there or have ever been there. If they live away from this ancestral home, they are settlers or strangers – settlers if they have not maintained their ties with the place of origin, strangers if they have. A person is an indigene not only of a village, city or town but also of one of Nigeria's thirty-six states. Typically, only indigenes have full rights in a place, whether social or political, locality or state. Unlike the situation in Western democracies, with a citizen of a country able to move to another part of the country with full rights soon if not immediately, some rights for Nigerians tend to be tied to the place of origin. Applying for a national university, for example, is done from the state of origin, not the state of residence. Local privileges, including honorary titles (a big issue in Nigeria), are generally limited to indigenes rather than residents. Recognizing the divisiveness of the indigene tradition, human rights activists have called for extension of full social and political rights to Nigerian citizens wherever in the country they live.

The indigene/settler/stranger distinction even pertains within an ethnic group. This is particularly important for Igbos and Yorubas because they can be residents of states dominated by their ethnic groups and still be strangers or settlers if they are from another state. In such cases, the struggles for full rights are struggles within a culture. Of course when people are living in a state dominated by another ethnic group, these become human rights struggles between cultures.

Human rights struggles between Nigerian cultures

As extensive as changing attitudes towards human rights have been within Nigerian cultures, the struggles between cultures gain much more publicity and public attention. This is partly because the contestation is more public and more heated, even violent. Recent years have witnessed pitched battles between Tiv and Jokun forces in the east central part of the country, Itsikiri and Ijaw forces in the Niger Delta, and Hausa and Yoruba forces in both the South and the North. Consistently, the violence has been generated by perception of oppression and exploitation, that is, the perception that basic human rights have been violated.

Human rights struggles between Nigerian cultures also include disputes over the implementation of *sharia*, or Islamic law. Since colonial times, Nigeria has had a dual court system with separate civil codes for Muslims, Christians and practitioners of traditional African religions (Ostien, 1999). In a move interpreted as provocative by southern Christians, twelve northern states adopted *sharia* after the election of civilian governments in 1999. Non-Muslim complaints involve the extension of *sharia* to criminal law rather than just civil law. The highly publicized case of Amina Lawal is illustrative. The fact that she gave birth as a single woman proved, according to a judicial interpretation, that she was an adulteress. An Islamic court sentenced her to death by stoning, though the same court dismissed charges against the father of the child because the requisite number of people had not witnessed the sexual union that led to the birth. Southern Nigerians, along with people across the world, were outraged at the judicial decision, both for its brutality and for its blatant gender bias. In the face of world-wide demands for immediate intervention, President Obasanjo, who happens to be a southern Christian, called for patience, asking for the judicial process to be allowed to run its course before his government would intervene. Eventually his patience proved wise, with the *sharia* court throwing the case out on a technicality (*Guardian* [Nigeria], 12 July 2003). His patience allowed the judicial process to work as designed, without premature action by the federal authorities in a state judicial matter. Had the woman actually been executed, the country would have experienced a serious, perhaps fatal, rift. However, the country still faces the divisive issue of having *sharia* implemented in northern criminal courts.

Women's rights also figure prominently in other human rights struggles between cultures within Nigeria. One of these involves the continuing practice of FGM, still the norm in many communities, which regard the procedure as necessary to assure female chastity, constituting a blatant sexist double standard. Many Nigerian cultures regard FGM as a rite of passage for pubescent girls. They justify the procedure on mistaken ideas about hygiene. The actual procedure is usually performed without anesthesia by older women who themselves underwent the procedure in their own youth. Aside from the issue of unjustifiable suffering, the procedure amounts to brutalization (Klouba and Muasher, 1985).

Still another arena of conflict is the practice, mainly in the North, of arranged marriages for girls in their early teens. Aside from the violation of the right to marry or not – Article 16 in the Universal Declaration of Human Rights – the practice often leads to physical harm of the brides because they give birth at such an immature age that their urinary systems are damaged to the point of incontinence, with the consequence that their usually much older husbands send them back to their families in need of surgery. The Nigerian government has a concerted campaign to stop early marriage, but the practice continues to flourish, especially among the poor in the North. Part of the problem is a cultural view that a father is obligated to find a husband for each of his daughters, with his obligations to them then ending. By arranging early marriages, a father is able to fulfil his obligation before he dies. If he were to die with unwed daughters, especially daughters at puberty, he would be abrogating his responsibility because if he were not around to protect them and control their sexual behaviour, they might become sexually active and therefore ineligible for marriage.

The rapidity of culture change, coupled with a growing recognition of the importance of human rights, means that struggles between cultural groups over those rights is the Nigerian norm.

Of course Nigerian cultures also compete for the national petroleum income. Petitions for state creation were often ethnically – culturally – based (Kraxberger, 2005). This is because having a state meant access to a share of the treasury without having to provide the state budget from within the state. With the return to civilian rule, and with increasing transparency of governance, responsibility for local and state budgets will be shifted gradually to the local and state levels, diminishing the attractiveness of gaining a state of one's own.

Nigeria and the global human rights community

Nigeria also experiences a number of struggles between its cultures and the global human rights community. Clearly, human rights were of little concern to the succession of military governments that ruled Nigeria for most of its independent existence. Just as clearly, the rest of the world – other than such human rights organizations as Human Rights Watch and Amnesty International – took little notice until after the Cold War. Only in the 1990s did a number of European nations, in conjunction with the United States and Canada, begin to cajole the Nigerian military to move toward democracy. Sadly, the apparatus of the Nigerian state developed violent cultures of its own, cultures difficult to eradicate in a few years of civilian rule.

Consequently, one of the current global charges against the Nigerian government is continued violence by the military and police. Human Rights Watch (2003) cites several recent instances of extrajudicial killings by Nigerian forces. These have occurred in all regions of the country, for example Kaduna in the North, Ogoniland in the East, Ondo in the West. Human Rights Watch criticizes the civilian government of Nigeria for failing to corral the violent tendencies of its military and police. A particularly disturbing case involves a Jokun military officer who used the military to attack Tiv people involved in land disputes with the Jokun in Benue State (*Guardian* [Nigeria], 23 September 2002, p. 1). Human Rights Watch castigates the government for inadequately investigating the attack. Insufficient transparency in governance keeps Nigerians in fear of the government apparatus, even under civilian rule.

A major focus of global human rights attention in Nigeria is the plight of the people in the oil-producing areas of the Niger Delta. When oil production began in Nigeria, the military government of the day took control of the resource, denying a consequential role to those who lived in the oil-producing areas. The oil companies worked closely with the government, clearly more concerned about their business interests than the environmental or political interests of local inhabitants. Resistance movements began in the Delta, some calling for a more environmentally attentive approach, others for a political voice for the residents. At times the resistance included sabotage. The governmental and corporate response was to control the region through the state's power of coercion, including shooting people, or, as in the famous case of the late Ken Saro-Wiwa and his cohorts, convicting and executing leaders on trumped-up charges (Sierra Club, 2003). The global human rights movement continues to press Nigeria's civilian government to redress the injustices perpetrated against the residents of the oil-producing areas.

The international human rights movement also continues to pressure the Nigerian government to improve the status of women in this highly patriarchal country (Jenda, 2002). Nigerian custom denies women equality in several important areas as well as subjecting women to physical abuse. Examples are the limitation of inheritance rights to males in a number of cultures, the widespread acceptance of domestic abuse as a husband's prerogative, and a tendency to focus parental rights in fathers rather than mothers, particularly in the instance of divorce.

Some reaction in Nigeria obviously supports the positions of the global human rights movement. Indeed, Nigeria has evolved a series of effective human rights organizations of its own, among them the Civil Liberties

Organization, the Constitutional Rights Project and the Committee for the Defence of Human Rights (University of Minnesota Human Rights Library, 2003). Other Nigerians and Nigerian organizations have resisted these external pressures, sometimes using the pejorative language of neo-colonialism to fend off critiques, at other times using the language of human rights to do so. In the former case, supporters of traditional Nigerian cultures decry the imposition of external values – external values from morally bankrupt places at that – to replace the time-honoured traditions of their cultures (An-Na'im and Deng, 1990). Clearly, Nigeria has many struggles to endure before it is a global examplar of human rights.

Nigerian struggles against external violations of human rights

Just as clearly, the violations of human rights in Nigeria are not just a consequence of cultural intransigence. Rather, many of those violations are the product of external forces of exploitation and oppression. Nigerian human rights struggles include struggles against global forces, past and present, limiting the well-being and freedom of people in Nigeria.

Just as the United States continues to suffer the legacy of slavery – with an underclass that is disillusioned, often anti-social, ill educated and ill prepared for the complexities of the digital economy – Nigeria continues to suffer several legacies, particularly those of colonialism, the Cold War and military rule. The country is, consequently, an easy target for global forces that are at worst pernicious and at best indifferent. It is ill prepared to compete successfully in the global political economy because of under-investment in human capital, on the one hand, along with corruption and over-investment in the military, on the other. Human rights are not fulfilled in Nigeria, not just because of a collective unwillingness to fulfil them but for structural reasons that are the product of past and present global forces.

The colonial period was a time when Nigeria was 'underdeveloped' in the sense that its economy was placed in a dependent, inferior position in a global economy stacked in favour of the wealthy nations (Onimode, 1991). The major multilateral institutions that steer the global economy – the International Monetary Fund, the World Bank, the World Trade Organization and even the United Nations – are creations of the dominant players in the that economy, not African countries, even a relatively powerful African country such as Nigeria. These organizations were formed while Nigeria was still a colony. Their rules were defined by their creators, meaning Nigeria was voiceless. The country would not have agreed to the current rules, to wit its call for a permanent seat on the United Nations Security Council (*Guardian* [Nigeria], 12 July 2003, p. 1).

As explained earlier, colonialism produced a divided Nigeria, one split between a Muslim North with political power and a Christian South with economic power. With the minor exception of a caretaker here or there, the list of Nigerian heads of government consists entirely of people who either call themselves 'haji' because they are well-heeled Muslims who made the pilgrimage to Mecca or 'general' because they attained that rank in the Nigerian military. The colonial experience exacerbated this North/South schism, reinforcing the distinctions with differential educational pro-grammes and religious policies.

The schism bears much of the responsibility for the onset and longevity of military rule. The first military coup was generated by Igbo officers as a response to what they saw as marginalization of their people by a govern-ment dominated by northerners. A counter-coup returned power to north-erners, only they were from the military rather than civilians. The divisions led to a catastrophic but ultimately futile secessionist war (the Biafran War) costing two million lives from mid-1967 to early 1970.

Military rule had many deleterious consequences for Nigeria. A major one is the establishment of a political culture of corruption and duplicity instead of one of mutual interests and fair play. Joseph (1987) characterizes the resulting political structure in which politicians are judged by how much they gouge the treasury for the benefit of their home communities. They have been expected to enrich themselves. Few failed to live up to expectations. Changing these expectations is difficult. After civilian govern-ments were returned to power at the federal and state levels in 1999, the United States Agency for International Development held a number of workshops for newly elected officials, cautioning them to govern on behalf of their constituents rather than as a means of looting the treasury. The general reaction among those elected was one of disdain. In most states legislators squandered the budget by providing accommodations and trans-portation (meaning houses and cars) for themselves. Nigeria has yet to evolve a sense of sufficient public responsibility among elected officials. This augurs poorly for addressing human rights issues effectively because doing so requires transparency in political processes and responsibility among elected officials.

Conclusions

Human rights are social constructions, the products of decades, gener-ations and even centuries of struggle. That struggle really amounts to cultural reconsiderations of what constitutes just and appropriate societies, as well, of course, as simple efforts to throw off the yoke of oppression. The struggles happen at three discernible scales: within a culture over how that culture conceptualizes a vision of justice as well as how the culture implements its conceptualization; between cultures as cultures change at different speeds and as power relationships change; and between a culture and global forces, either global forces demanding attention to human rights or global forces violating human rights.

Each scale of struggle is evident in Nigeria, a country with an historical geography that has left it struggling more than most. This is because its place within the global political economy has left it vulnerable to external exploitation abetted by self-interested leaders unable or unwilling to resist the temptations offered by wealthy, powerful outsiders.

REFERENCES

A-Na'im, A. A. and Deng, F. M. (1990) *Human Rights in Africa: Cross-cultural Perspectives*, Washington, DC: Brookings Institute.

Blaut, J. (1993) *The Colonizer's Model of the World: Geographical Diffusionism and Eurocentric History*, New York: Guilford Press.

Brown, C. (2000) 'Philosophy of human rights', in R. Patman (ed.), *Universal Human Rights?* Basingstoke: Macmillan, pp. 22–34.

Crowder, M. (1968) *West Africa under Colonial Rule*, London: Hutchinson.

Crowe, S. E. (1942) *The Berlin West African Conference*, London: Guilford Press.

Honey, R. (2004) 'Geography of human rights', in C. Willmot and G. Gaile (eds), *Geography at the Dawn of the 3rd Millennium*, New York: Oxford University Press, pp. 732–42.

Human Rights Watch (2003) *http://www.hrw.org/africa/nigeria.php*

Jenda (2002) *http://www.jendajournal.com/jenda*

Johnston, H. A. S. (1967) *The Fulani Empire of Sokoto*, Ibadan: Oxford University Press.

Joseph, R. (1987) *Democracy and Prebendal Politics in Nigeria*, Cambridge: Cambridge University Press.

Klouba, L. and Muasher, J. (1985) 'Female circumcision in Africa: an overview', *African Studies Review* 12, 95–110.

Kraxberger, B. (2005) 'Geo-historical trajection of democratic transition: the case of Nigeria', *Geojournal* 60, 167–79.

Onimode, B. (1984) 'Imperialism and underdevelopment in Nigeria: the dialectic of mass poverty', *Review of African Political Economy* 14, 110–13.

Onimode, B. (1991) *The IMF, the World Bank and the African Debt*, London: African Alternatives Press.

Ostien, P. (1999) *A Study of the Court Systems of Northern Nigeria with A Proposal for the Creation of Lower Sharia Courts in Some Northern States*, University of Jos.

Otite, O. (1990) *Ethnic Pluralism and Ethnicity in Nigeria*, Ibadan: Shaneson.

Sala-i-Martin, A. (2003) 'Addressing the national resource curse: an illustration from Nigeria', Working Paper w9804, National Bureau of Economic Research, Lagos.

Sierra Club (2003) *http://www.sierraclub.org/human-rights/nigeria/background/*

Smith, W. (2003) *The Conflict between Neoliberalism and a Human Right to Water*, PhD dissertation, University of Delaware.

Udo, R. K. (1970) *The Geographical Regions of Nigeria*, Berkeley: University of California Press.

United Nations (1948) *Universal Declaration of Human Rights*, New York: United Nations.

United Nations (1966a) *International Covenant on Economic, Social and Cultural Rights*, New York: United Nations.

United Nations (1966b) *International Covenant on Civil and Political Rights*, New York: United Nations.

United Nations (1979) *The Convention on the Elimination of All Forms of Discrimination against Women*, New York: United Nations.

United Nations (1989) *The Convention on the Rights of the Child*, New York: United Nations.

University of Minnesota Human Rights Library (2003) *The Status of Human Rights Organizations in Sub-Saharan Africa: Nigeria*, Minneapolis: University of Minnesota Press.

Weston, B. (2003) 'Human rights', *Encyclopedia Britannica* (*http://www.britannica.com/*).

9

Valuing Land and Distributing Territory

Avery Kolers

When Nuñez Balboa stood on the shoreline and took possession of the South
Sea and all of South America in the name of the crown of Castille, was this
enough to dispossess all the inhabitants and to exclude all the princes of the
world? On that basis, those ceremonies would be multiplied quite in vain. All
the Catholic King had to do was to take possession of the universe all at once
from his private room, excepting afterwards from his empire only what
already belonged to other princes.

Rousseau, *On the Social Contract* (1762), p. 28

Introduction

Ignoring material obstacles (including, particularly, human ones) to the
realization of philosophical theories is a venerable tradition. Even Rousseau, despite castigating Nuñez Balboa, infamously coined the phrase
'forced to be free'. At the same time, new material conditions often change
philosophical agendas, a fact to which recent interest in transnational or
global justice attests.

More than any other event, the fall of the Berlin Wall led philosophers to
raise their sights beyond nation-state borders, ushering in the exuberance of
cosmopolitan political thought. Recently renewed attention to global poverty and starvation has dampened the exuberance, but entrenched the
cosmopolitanism. Yet even as material circumstances shape philosophical
theory, a studied *in*attention to the material world has characterized much
of the very same philosophical work. Current theories of global justice and
equality most often assume away the effects of *place*, and with them,
relationships between landscape and social organization. But, raising the
questions of territorial justice – who should be where, how much they

should have, what should be the scope of their jurisdiction, who, if anyone, should be entitled to police the limits of jurisdiction – forces us to face the material world head-on.[1]

In my view, progress in the theory of territorial justice requires that philosophers engage geographers, for at least two reasons. The first is obvious: geographers study many of the things that theories of territorial justice would have to address. In particular, dynamic, bi-directional relationships between people and places, which to my mind are crucial for understanding and justly resolving territorial disputes, have been the central object of study in human geography. The second reason is that early crossover work has already rendered disciplinary boundaries almost as porous as international ones. By increasing these boundaries' permeability, we further our own understanding while guarding against the illusion that the material world, or the moral world for that matter, is immaterial.

Even as philosophical engagement with geography is crucial and fruitful, among philosophers it has so far had its primary impact outside political philosophy. That may be changing, though, thanks in large part to the contributions of David Smith. Smith's decades-long engagement with ethics, which has happily accelerated since the publication of *Geography and Social Justice* (1994), has brought a geographer's sophistication to many of the same issues that exercise political philosophers. Without downplaying other aspects of his work, I want to emphasize two key parts of Smith's contribution which have urgent relevance for political philosophy: the search for universal principles in a world of difference and displacement; and the development of a constrained egalitarianism focused on basic needs. The first point suggests a way to get beyond the debate between moral 'universalists' and 'particularists'. Whereas particularists deny the existence of transnational principles that might solve territorial disputes, universalists typically ignore or undervalue plurality (Walzer, 1983, pp. 42–51; Pogge, 1992, p. 69; Miller, 1995, pp. 49–51; Moellendorf, 2002, p. 49). Smith's search for pluralistic universal principles is the most promising way forward.

The second point – constrained egalitarianism – follows on from the first. Philosophical work on the question 'What is equality?' (Dworkin, 2000, Chaps 1–2) tends to speak in a universalistic language that precludes accommodating two kinds of diversity: geographic diversity and diversity in the ways people interact with land. The result is actually inegalitarian. Smith's notion of 'justice as equalization', with a focus on basic human needs or capabilities, again points a way forward (Smith, 2000, Chap. 7).

This chapter attempts to understand the nature of territorial justice and move toward – what Smith has sought – universal principles that respect plurality and especially geographic diversity. Cosmopolitan political theorists have failed to recognize geographic constraints upon global institutions. Their failure is a symptom of a deeper problem: the tacit endorsement and universalization of an Anglo-American 'ethnogeography', or conception of land. As a result, cosmopolitans end up making some of the same mistakes as the 'statists' they have superseded. One key to territorial justice is to broaden the range of 'ethnogeographies' that global institutions can accommodate.

When informed by human geography, the most plausible approach to territorial justice vindicates Smith's contribution. When *not* informed by human geography, philosophers theorizing about global justice risk becoming latter-day Nuñez Balboas, or, worse, so many 'Catholic Kings'.

From Traditional to Cosmopolitan Statism

During the three decades bookended by John Rawls's *Theory of Justice* (1971) and *Law of Peoples* (1999), it became virtually impossible for philosophers to assume that distributive justice ended at national boundaries, or that such boundaries served as morally significant barriers to anything much at all. 'Statism' ran out of steam. Whereas few people complained when Rawls's first book casually assumed away not only international justice but also international migration, *Law of Peoples* has been widely criticized for its failure to demand robust principles of transnational distributive justice (Pogge, 1994; Tesón, 1998, pp. 105–26; Buchanan, 2000; Moellendorf, 2002, Chap. 2). At first, philosophers treated political boundaries as the limits of our moral world; now, however, the smart money is 'cosmopolitan' (Beitz, 1999; O'Neill, 2000).

'Statism' is the view that the state is the fundamental site of justice, political organization and solidarity. Statism is committed to the proposition that having (full membership in) a state is a fundamental good for individuals and groups, and one's compatriots constitute one's primary moral community. Statists' traditional inattention to the moral consequences of international organization has doubly distorted the theory of domestic justice: first, because international relations affect domestic institutions; and, second, by assuming away internal diversity, or, at best, treating that diversity as irrelevant to justice. Recently, statists have sought to overcome the second distortion, but the first persists (Kymlicka, 1991; Rawls, 1991).

Cosmopolitans instead start from the assumption that all individuals everywhere have an initially equal claim on our moral attention (Barry, 1999, pp. 12–13; O'Neill, 2000, p. 169; Pogge, 2001, p. 16; Moellendorf, 2002). The historical connection between states and nations exacerbates cosmopolitans' suspicions about statism, since nations are never found without invidious internal hierarchies and vulnerable minorities in their midst (Buchanan, 1997). And though states may be provisionally useful as sites of limited democracy and minimal social justice, globalization decreases their effectiveness even in this respect. Cosmopolitans tend to endorse a proliferation of levels and forms of government, though most are content to leave some power at the state level provided states earn their moral keep (Buchanan, 1999; Moellendorf, 2002).

But on territorial justice, the two views have perhaps more in common than cosmopolitans should like to admit: neither group has much to say. That statists fail is unsurprising; for them, territory is a presupposed backdrop of no moral or political importance. Extant borders are arbitrary but taken for granted. More surprisingly, cosmopolitans also tend simply to assume away territory, treating land as identical to its constituent natural resources, and therefore subject to distribution just like any other resource. Indeed cosmopolitanism is arguably more accurately viewed as a *branch* of statism, not an alternative to it, because cosmopolitan justice merely renders the international domestic. Many cosmopolitans thus fall victim to the second flaw of traditional statism: ignoring genuine internal diversity. Not only is distance ignored, but it is assumed that there is only one global politico-economic system within which all currencies of distribution are commensurate.

Consider Darrel Moellendorf's defence of the principle of fair equality of opportunity as necessary but not sufficient for international justice. In his view, such equality requires that 'a child growing up in rural Mozambique would be statistically as likely as the child of a senior executive at a Swiss bank to reach the position of the latter's parent' (Moellendorf, 2002, p. 49). (And, one imagines, vice versa.) But why should Mozambicans have to move? Why insist that they be capitalists? What about Mozambique's 1.6 million Muslims, whose religion condemns the taking of interest? Moellendorf could limit his point to earnings rather than to the particular job, though this concession would undermine fair equality of opportunity, which requires equal access to influential offices and positions, not just to money. But even limiting the point to earning power presupposes a single, all-encompassing cash economy, a single system of education and qualifications, and so on.

In other words, cosmopolitan equality of opportunity requires a single world-wide economy with no borders. Their failure to deal with territory is thus a sign not of how successfully cosmopolitans have *shed* the statist straitjacket, but of how thoroughly straitened by it they remain. For most cosmopolitans, levels of government are nested parts of a single constitutional realm; the economy is a seamless world-wide system of exchange. The state is simply expanded to comprehend the whole world. To be sure, cosmopolitans do not usually defend a 'world state'. But if there is one economic system, one federalized system of governance, and effectively one political culture, then cosmopolitans are statists whose country is the United States of Earth.

Cosmopolitans fail to develop a theory of justified claims to territory because they fail to leave statism behind. But this failure is itself explained by another: the universalization of an Anglo-American conception of land. To develop a plausible conception of global justice we must, rather, reject this universalization and accommodate a multiplicity of relationships with nature. This shift, in turn, generates independent principles of territorial justice.

Anglo-American Ethnogeography

When political theorists forget the diversity of relationships between people and land, they are presupposing and universalizing an 'Anglo-American ethnogeography'. An ethnogeography is a culturally specific conception of land, the story that an *ethnos* tells itself about place and landscape.[2] Distinct ethnogeographies contain competing ontological claims about the nature of land and the relationships between people and land.

The *Anglo-American* ethnogeography is that tradition of understanding land – epitomized by Locke, Dworkin and the dominant strain of Anglophone political philosophy in between – according to which land is a passive instrument of the human will, essentially worthless until value is inserted into it by 'mixing labour' (Hargrove, 1980; Locke, 1988; Russell, 2003). Because value is imbued in land solely through economic or instrumental activity, land is taken to have importance only as a store of natural resources or economic potentialities:

> For 'tis *Labour* indeed that *puts the difference of value* on every thing. . . . I think it will be but a very modest Computation to say, that of the *Products* of the Earth useful to the Life of Man 9/10 are the *effects of labour*: nay, if we will rightly estimate things as they come to our use, and cast up the several Expences about them, what in them is purely owing to *Nature*, and what to *labour*, we shall find, that in most of them 99/100 are wholly to be put on the account of *labour*. (Locke, 1988, p. 296)

Critics have challenged Locke's maths and his failure to see land and labour as having interactive rather than additive effects (Cohen, 1996, p. 179). But the view is not internally inconsistent (Russell, 2003), so the problem lies in the ethnogeography, not the maths. This can be seen in the use of market value.

Market mechanisms don't *measure* values, but *obscure* and *impose* values; or, more precisely, market mechanisms measure only *after* imposing some values and obscuring others. Indeed, this is the kernel of truth in neoclassical attempts to treat discoveries as creations. Before anyone discovered a use for kerosene, 'rock oil' was a smelly nuisance that reduced the land's resale value. Thereafter, kerosene was gold. Soon after that, it was just kerosene (Simon, 1998, p. 242). These fluctuations did not reveal anything about the real value of the land; they did not actualize the land's 'natural, intrinsick Value' (Locke 1988, p. 298). Rather, the market changed in some way, and that change imposed values on certain pieces of land. Any one piece of land has an infinite number of properties, and changes in social circumstances can cause the values of those properties to fluctuate. The point is not that *all* values attached to land are simply imposed, but, rather, that all *economic* values – positive or negative – are imposed, and the process of imposition obscures or distorts non-economic kinds of value.[3]

The consequences of this point are far-reaching. If markets impose rather than measure value, then it is impossible fairly to compare land holdings in the absence of a single shared economy, or fixed conventions about land values. If land holdings are *non*-comparable, though, the distributive approach to territorial justice is hopeless: there is no way to convert land into dollars and distribute it equally. To see this, consider Ronald Dworkin's resource egalitarianism, which is at the centre of an ongoing debate about the meaning of equality, and is perhaps the most powerful recent articulation of the Anglo-American ethnogeography.

Dworkin argues that everyone in a society is treated as an equal if and only if the society guarantees 'equality of resources'. Provided that all parties start out with equal resources, trade freely, and are duly insured against bad luck, Dworkin holds, market distributions embody equality. A 'resource' is any material object other than a person, and buyers themselves determine the identities of material objects – that is, they can purchase any object or part thereof, except persons. It is crucial that *persons* cannot be bought, for otherwise the market would generate the 'slavery of the talented': highly talented persons would either be purchased by others, in which case they would be slaves, or be forced to pay a high price to purchase themselves, thereby using up much of their purchasing power before they owned anything else, thence becoming wage-slaves in order to buy what the less talented already own. The focus on resources embodies the liberal commitment that people are responsible for their choices (hence, no equality of outcome), but not their unchosen circumstances. As Kymlicka (1991, p. 186) notes, 'The distinction between choices and circumstances is... absolutely central to the liberal project.'

Dworkin imagines, as a heuristic device, a group of castaways bidding on shares of an uninhabited island upon which they have been shipwrecked. This story puts off limits all questions of jurisdiction, sacred landscapes, burial grounds, long-term occupancy, staple-crop cultivation, public goods and anything else that might create or reflect non-instrumental or collective attachments to land. But such attachments are real and normatively important.

Kymlicka (1991, p. 186) shows that Dworkin's auction story presupposes that the shipwrecked persons share a culture and expect to be undifferentiated citizens of a shared polity. Kymlicka therefore tweaks the auction story to accommodate the existence of a minority culture. We might then think that an analogous strategy will work here, achieving Dworkinian territorial egalitarianism. But such a strategy would require not only people of different cultures, but also the array of different places where they had arisen – not only Bedouins, but the desert, not only sedentary farmers, but temperate plains. The most appropriate way to tweak the story is then to drop the whole idea of a shipwreck and pretend that, in a fit of conviviality, the people of the world got together to start afresh and divide the Earth equally.

Suppose, then, Bedouins bid on Arabia for the vast desert, the land that has made them who they are (*badawiyyin*, Of-the-Desert). To their chagrin, however, entrepreneurs bid on Arabia for the oil, forcing up the price. The misfortune of wanting land for cultural reasons, when others want it for economic reasons (which the Bedouins do not, by hypothesis, share), would require the Bedouins to overspend just for a place to live that supports their livelihood.[4] Having overspent for their land, the Bedouins would be required to change their lifestyle, drilling the oil in order to make up for other necessities that they could not afford because their habitat was extraordinarily expensive. But it was precisely to avoid changing their lifestyle that they bid on that land in the first place. Just as Dworkin had to put persons off-limits to avoid the slavery of the talented, this global auction will have to put *land* off-limits to avoid what we might call the 'slavery of the resource-rich'. But since all or most resources are contained in land, it is hard to see that there could be any global auction at all.

How serious is the slavery of the resource-rich? As we noted earlier, Dworkin's theory requires a distinction between choices and circumstances. If oil becomes valuable, then the Bedouins can change their way of life to take advantage of their good fortune. It is hard to see this as a burden. This challenge, though, clearly universalizes the Anglo-American ethnogeography. The existence of saleable underground oil is portrayed as good fortune, not a new burden or threat (which would be historically more accurate in most cases); furthermore, changing their nomadic, tribal way of life in order to take advantage of this 'good fortune' is portrayed as, at worst, an incidental cost, even if it requires a revolution in the Bedouins' ethnogeography. Their traditional livelihood must be portrayed as up for sale to whoever offers enough money to finance their 'modernization'. In effect, the slavery of the resource-rich means that under Dworkin's individualized egalitarianism, not only land but also livelihoods are treated as commodities.

Cosmopolitans might try to rescue the theory by initially dividing the world into different homelands, and then having each society carry out an internal auction. This answer obviously presupposes a separate method of fairly dividing the Earth into homelands. We might allocate the same amount of land, measured in hectares, to everyone, and then let them choose their homeland. The problem is that different kinds and amounts of land will count as 'equal resources' for different people who live in different ways. The nomadic Bedouin and the sedentary farmer would obviously have different prospects if given equal-sized pieces of the Arabian Desert. But even receiving equally sized plots of their *preferred* land would treat them unequally: the sedentary farmer will not get the same value from n hectares of temperate farmland that the Bedouin will get from n hectares of desert, because they live in different ways on their different lands. Ultimately, whether and to what degree any amount of land can be considered a benefit to anyone depends not on its 'intrinsick Value', but on a relational property: whether it allows people who live a certain way to live on it that way in relative security and prosperity. This point generalizes: there is no single variable equalization of which embodies equality of territory.

Dworkin could propose that parties buy insurance to protect them from being too richly resourced for their own good. Insurance compensates the unlucky for their bad luck. But this 'bad luck' is what Dworkin would call an *expensive taste*. Whether such tastes count as choices or circumstances depends on whether they are voluntary. The 'tastes' we are discussing, though, cannot rightly be treated either way. It is surely *possible* for Bedouins to 'modernize', so it is unfair to compensate them for voluntarily holding a resource that others want. They must, as Dworkin says, pay the costs of their lifestyle for others. But it is equally unfair to *demand* that they drill, and charge them for not doing so.

The problem with Dworkin's approach is its dependence on universalizing the Anglo-American ethnogeography, embodied in the desert-island heuristic. Arriving on the desert island, the castaways have no antecedent relationship to any land – have not buried their ancestors anywhere, have no cultural patterns of land use, and so on. But when we try to respect distinctive relationships with nature, Dworkin's analysis of equality collapses. Persons' interest in living in a certain way on land of a certain type can be treated only as a choice or ambition, something that must bend to the dictates of the market. Under Dworkin's theory of equality it can become too expensive to live one's own life (as, say, a Bedouin), and when it does, Dworkin must simply recommend dropping that life for another. The desert-island auction ultimately works only because, and insofar as, all the castaways share (or can be held responsible for failing to share) the Anglo-American ethnogeography.

In general, political philosophers do not recognize that they are even assuming a culturally specific conception of land, or, still less, that alternatives exist. The Anglo-American ethnogeography thus appears natural, leading cosmopolitans to universalize it.

But what is the alternative? To count as an alternative, a conception of land must deny either or both of the two tenets of the Anglo-American view: that land is the passive object of human activity, and that land has value only as far as people's instrumental interests impose it. Consider four examples. First, ecological holists deny that land's value is solely instrumental, emphasizing spiritual, moral and aesthetic value (Leopold, 1949, pp. 214–26). Second, ecological economists drop the other tenet, that land is passive, and reconceive economic theory better to respect the value added by land and natural processes, as well as the value subtracted by our current practices of allocation and use (Costanza et al., 1997, p. 253). Agrarians and ecofeminists deny both tenets. Agrarians develop an account of human flourishing in which a healthy relationship to land is indispensable; land is reconceived as active, having the power to reshape us, and its value is therefore moral, aesthetic and spiritual, as well as economic (Berry, 2002; Freyfogle, 2001). Ecofeminists *subjectify* land, treating it as one of the participants in a relationship that ought to be egalitarian and non-exploitative (Cuomo, 1996). To canvass these four views is to say nothing about the array of other ethnogeographies available around the world (Callicott, 1994).

To summarize, the Anglo-American ethnogeography, as embodied in Locke, Dworkin and nearly every mainstream Anglophone political theorist in between, treats land as the passive object of human activity, and ignores all forms of value that are not easily priced on the market. These assumptions ignore the dynamic, bi-directional relationship between people and land – the mutually formative interaction between peoples and their habitats – and therefore hide the fact that it is impossible fairly to compare the holdings of persons across economies or ethnogeographies. If this is correct, then the theory of global justice faces shipwreck, not (as Dworkin has it) on a desert isle, but on the rocks and reefs of inhabited territories.

Toward Territorial Justice

I have argued that cosmopolitan political philosophers assume an Anglo-American ethnogeography that treats land as the entirely passive and intrinsically worthless object of human activity. Any theory of global justice that applies this ethnogeography world-wide will be doomed to mistreat (among others) those who reject the Anglo-American view and have a different ontology of land.

In light of this point, we can distinguish two stages of universalizing the Anglo-American ethnogeography. In the Lockean stage, universalizers deny that those who do not share the Anglo-American ethnogeography are even using the land, licensing widespread ethnic cleansing. In the cosmopolitan stage, universalizers deny the existence of any other ethno-geography; they therefore treat dissidents as endorsers and, in a noble effort to respect everyone by 'equalizing' their holdings, actually obscure other ethnogeographies, mismeasure the values of distributive shares, force people off their lands under the guise of market choices, and ultimately commodify both land and people.[5]

But how can we avoid universalizing, when transnational justice neces-sarily requires overarching principles? Distinguish two questions: (1) 'What is the *correct* conception of land (ethnogeography)?'; and (2) 'What is the morally best way to settle disputes among groups that do not share an ethnogeography?' If we can answer (2) without answering (1), that might be good enough, so let's start there.

European apologists for the conquest of the Americas recognized only those claims that took one form – European-style enclosure and cultivation (Hargrove, 1980; Tully, 1995, Chap. 5). Such writers refused to hear or understand claims based on any other pattern of land use. Their deafness may have reflected the fear that claims are all-or-nothing, that granting the mere *existence* of Indigenous claims would grant the claimant exclusive territorial rights. The answer to question (2) must address both these issues, first by recognizing a multiplicity of kinds of claims, and, second, by weakening the force of the claims that can be made simply on grounds of being recognized. That is, instead of saying that anyone with an admissible ethnogeography has an inalienable right to set up a state in a certain place, we must say that such groups have a right of *standing*. To have standing is to be such that one's claims are justiciable – they must be admitted into a fair procedure that determines who has rights, and what their rights are. Stand-ing does not itself determine the outcome of that procedure. Such a procedure might be carried out under the auspices of a 'Territorial Court' or some other international body.

We must, then, proliferate the kinds of claims that are admissible. But how far should we proliferate? Even if we avoid universalizing one particular ethnogeography, not every claim is equally compelling. If we got to the point where 'All the Catholic King had to do was take possession of the universe all at once from his private room', we may conclude that we had gone too far. But even this obvious limit rests on an implicit conception of land – one that denies that merely mental relationships with land constitute 'use'. We therefore cannot go further in answering question (2) unless we answer question (1).

I propose to answer (1) not by seeking a single, universal ethnogeogra-phy, but by laying out a template or format within which ethnogeographies must be able to fit, if they are to ground standing in territorial disputes. The contours of this template rest in principles of human geography: cultures evolve *as* they do because they evolve *where* they do; and places evolve as they do because of who lives there. Cultures and habitats, that is, interact in mutually formative ways. This tenet treats land not as the passive object of human labour, but as an active participant in the creation of people. Nor are lands valued simply for economic reasons. Any ethnogeography may be the basis of standing *if* it can be stated in a way that emphasizes the co-evolution of peoples and lands.

The principal virtue of the approach modelled here is to broaden the range of interactions with land that can ground standing in territorial disputes. The aim is to include all and only those ethnogeographies that can be stated in this bi-directional fashion. To illustrate, three of the alternative ethnogeographies we canvassed earlier, ecological economics, agrarianism and ecofeminism, would be admissible in their current form. Ecological holism is perhaps easily fixed for inclusion; its proponents' emphasis on the inherent moral value of land, rather than the land's active character, may be more of an artefact of their debate with anthropocentrists, rather than any definite commitment to the passive character of land.[6]

Could the Anglo-American ethnogeography be included? My approach demands that those who endorse the Anglo-American ethnogeography rearticulate it in interactive terms. This is a significant demand, and may on its own remedy some major excesses of that ethnogeography. But the Anglo-American ethnogeography could also be fixed rather easily: its close initial connections with agrarianism (Montmarquet, 1985; Stewart, 1996, p. 32) bode well, as does recent work by ecological economists, who offer a corrective to the current orthodoxy in Anglo-American economics (Czech, 2000). We should not understate the change required in the Anglo-American ethnogeography. But we should also emphasize that this ethnogeography already contains the seeds of its own revision. In contrast, neither Nuñez Balboa's act of flag-planting, nor the Catholic King's claim to the entire universe, could generate standing.

We now have a principled basis for preferring the claims of, say, the Cherokee to those of the Euro-American expansionists. But at the same time, we can also understand why the emptiness of *initial* European claims to the Americas did not prevent the settlers from *generating* claims, through Europeanization of American landscapes, Americanization of European settlers, and longstanding interaction between people and land. An account that prioritizes the dynamic interactions of human agency and land makes sense of why the initial European encroachment was wrong, as well as why contemporary Euro-Americans have some kind of right to stay.

I have suggested two strategies to solve territorial disputes: weaken the kind of claim that can be made on philosophical grounds, from sovereignty to standing; and broaden the range of relationships between people and land that can be admissible in resolving territorial disputes. This two-part strategy does not use the word 'distribution' anywhere. That is a virtue. Distributive fairness would be relevant to negotiators and to the decisions of a 'Territorial Court' or other transnational body that adjudicates competing claims, once standing has been settled. Such a court could divide land spatially, temporally (e.g. seasonally), by use criteria (e.g. agriculture and hunting), or any way that was agreeable among the competing ethnogeographies of the relevant parties. Lands need not, that is, be divided in the totalizing manner of national sovereignty. In settling such divisions, arguably questions of basic needs or capabilities would be crucial, and 'justice as equalization' in Smith's sense would be a guiding principle. But standing itself – whether some group has achieved longstanding interaction with the land in an admissible fashion – is not a distributive issue.

Quite apart from its universalization, the Anglo-American ethnogeography entails a false picture of land as wholly passive; modifying or rejecting this view is an urgent matter for those within the Anglo-American social world. By naming this ethnogeography and highlighting its parochial character, however, I hope to have removed its sharpest teeth.

Conclusion

In overcoming the Anglo-American ethnogeography, I harbour no illusions about the universality of any *other* ethnogeography. But as we saw, it is impossible to be fully neutral on the question of how a group can get standing in a political dispute. It is not necessary that they be there, because diaspora claims are possible; but it is not sufficient simply to *want* to be there, because this would legitimate frantic expansionism, the 'Catholic King' taking 'possession of the universe all at once from his private room'. The trick is to proliferate the kinds of claims that can be taken seriously, while being able to exclude the 'Nuñez Balboas'. This strategy, grounded in human geography, offers a way toward territorial justice.

NOTES

An Olorunsola Award from the University of Louisville College of Arts & Sciences supported my work on this chapter. I am grateful to Dean James Brennan and Cheshire Calhoun for their support. David Smith, John Cumbler, Shlomo Hasson and David Imbroscio provided extremely helpful comments on earlier drafts. I presented a previous version at the Geography Department of Queen Mary, University of London, where audience comments were challenging and helpful.
1   Here 'territorial justice' is used in a sense different from that of Davies (1968). My concern is justice in the distribution of territorial jurisdiction itself, not in the geographic distribution of resources.
2   J. M. Blaut (1979, p. 2) defines 'ethnogeography' as 'the study of all geographical beliefs held by the members of a definite human group at a definite time'.

Ethnogeography in this sense makes no ontological claims about place or land-scape, but describes geographic beliefs without evaluating their accuracy. As I use it, the term names the *subject matter* of this study, the geographic beliefs themselves.

3   Why not say that the market *actualizes latent* values? The supposedly latent values would themselves be economic, so explanandum and explanans could not be kept separate. It is more accurate to say that the market imposes value.

4   A simpler way of putting this point is that the Bedouins have the misfortune of wanting to live on land that contains valuable resources that they do not want. But this misses the fact that the very *existence* of (these) valuable resources depends on the entrepreneurs' right to bid on them. Oil and other constituents of the land would not otherwise be 'natural resources'.

5   By analogy, see Charles Mills' catalogue of the two stages of global White Supremacy (Mills, 1998, p. 78).

6   But see Guha (1989) for a more sceptical view of the prospects for 'deep ecology'.

REFERENCES

Barry, B. (1999) 'Statism and nationalism: a cosmopolitan critique', in I. Shapiro and L. Brilmayer (eds), *NOMOS XLI: Global Justice*, New York: New York University Press, pp. 12–66.

Beitz, C. (1999) *Political Theory and International Relations* (2nd edition), Princeton, NJ: Princeton University Press.

Berry, W. (2002) *The Art of the Commonplace* (ed. Norman Wirzba), San Francisco: Counterpoint.

Blaut, J. M. (1979) 'Some principles of ethnogeography', in S. Gale and G. Olsson (eds), *Philosophy in Geography*, Dordrecht, Boston and London: Reidel, pp. 1–8.

Buchanan, A. (1997) 'What's so special about nations?', *Canadian Journal of Philosophy Supp.* 22, 283–309.

Buchanan, A. (1999) 'Recognitional legitimacy and the state system', *Philosophy & Public Affairs* 28, 46–78.

Buchanan, A. (2000) 'Rawls's law of peoples: rules for a vanished Westphalian world', *Ethics* 110, 697–721.

Callicott, J. B. (1994) *Earth's Insights*, Berkeley and Los Angeles: University of California Press.

Cohen, G. A. (1996) *Self-ownership, Freedom, and Equality*, Cambridge: Cambridge University Press.

Costanza, R., d'Arge, R., de Groot, R., Farber, S., Grasso, M., Hannon, B., Limburg, K., Naeem, S., O'Neill, R. V., Paruelo, J., Raskin, R. G., Sutton, P. and van den Belt, M. (1997) 'The value of the world's ecosystem services and natural capital', *Nature* 387 (15 May), 253–59.

Cuomo, C. J. (1996) *Feminism and Ecological Communities: An Ethic of Flourishing*, London: Routledge.

Czech, B. (2000) *Shoveling Fuel for a Runaway Train*, Berkeley and Los Angeles: University of California Press.

Davies, B. (1968) *Social Needs and Resources in Local Services*, London: Michael Joseph.

Dworkin, R. M. (2000) *Sovereign Virtue*, Oxford: Oxford University Press.

Freyfogle, E. T. (ed.) (2001) *The New Agrarianism*, Washington, DC: Island.

Guha, R. (1989) 'Radical American environmentalism and wilderness preservation: a Third World critique', *Environmental Ethics* 11, 71–83.

Hargrove, E. C. (1980) 'Anglo-American land use attitudes', *Environmental Ethics* 2, 121–48.

Kymlicka, W. (1991) *Liberalism, Community, and Culture*, Oxford: Clarendon Press.

Leopold, A. (1949) *A Sand County Almanac*, New York: Oxford University Press, 1989.

Locke, J. (1988 [1690]) *Two Treatises of Government* (ed. Peter Laslett), Cambridge: Cambridge University Press.

Miller, D. (1995) *On Nationality*, Oxford: Oxford University Press.

Mills, C. W. (1998) *The Racial Contract*, Ithaca, NY: Cornell University Press.

Moellendorf, D. (2002) *Cosmopolitan Justice*, Boulder, Colo.: Westview Press.

Montmarquet, J. A. (1985) 'Philosophical foundations for agrarianism', *Agriculture and Human Values* 2, 5–14.

O'Neill, O. (2000) *Bounds of Justice*, Cambridge: Cambridge University Press.

Pogge, T. W. (1992) 'Cosmopolitanism and sovereignty', *Ethics* 103, 48–75.

Pogge, T. W. (1994) 'An egalitarian law of peoples', *Philosophy & Public Affairs* 23, 195–224.

Pogge, T. W. (2001) 'Priorities of global justice', *Metaphilosophy* 32, 6–24.

Rawls, J. (1971) *A Theory of Justice*, Cambridge, Mass.: Belknap.

Rawls, J. (1991) *Political Liberalism*, New York: Columbia University Press.

Rawls, J. (1999) *The Law of Peoples*, Cambridge, Mass.: Harvard Univesrity Press.

Rousseau, J. -J. (1762) *On the Social Contract* (trans. Donald Cress), Indianapolis: Hackett, 1987.

Russell, D. C. (2003) 'Locke on land and labor', Pacific Division meeting of the American Philosophical Association, 27 March.

Simon, J. (1998) 'Scarcity or abundance?', in L. Westra and P. Werhane (eds), *The Business of Consumption*, Lanham, Md: Rowman & Littlefield, pp. 237–45.

Smith, D. M. (1994) *Geography and Social Justice*, Oxford: Blackwell.

Smith, D. M. (2000) *Moral Geographies: Ethics in a World of Difference*. Edinburgh: University of Edinburgh Press.

Stewart, M. (1996) *'What Nature Suffers to Groe': Life, Labor, and Landscape on the Georgia Coast, 1680–1820*, Athens and London: University of Georgia Press.

Tesón, F. (1998) *A Philosophy of International Law*, Boulder, Colo.: Westview Press.

Tully, J. (1995) *An Approach to Political Philosophy: Locke in Contexts*, Cambridge: Cambridge University Press.

Walzer, M. (1983) *Spheres of Justice*, New York: Basic Books.

10

When Two Rights Collide: Some Lessons from Jerusalem

Shlomo Hasson

> And if a geographically sensitive ethics has no more than one major message, it is...the importance of context, of understanding the particular situation: how things are, here and there. If the human capacity of putting one's self in the place of others is to be an effective wellspring of morality, this requires understanding that place, as well as those others.
>
> Smith, *Moral Geographies* (2000), p. 214

Introduction

Contrary to its biblical-prophetic image, Jerusalem is a city rife with tension and conflict. Israelis and Palestinians are engaged in a bitter national struggle over territory and sovereignty, and secular and ultra-orthodox Jews (known in Hebrew as *haredim*, that is, zealots) are involved in a cultural struggle over territorial control and political hegemony. Each group is striving to pursue its own particular moral-political goals, which are deeply rooted in its varied historical, social, political and geographic conditions. As David Smith (2000, p. 199) convincingly points out 'each of these conflicts has its own particularity, its historical and geographical context, understanding of which is crucial to any judgement of right or wrong, and any plans for peace which might pass the test of fairness'.

Though essentially different, the national and cultural conflicts in Jerusalem have much in common as they manifest contested moral-political claims to the same territory. The question which arises at this point is whether and how incompatible moral-political claims to the same territory can be resolved. Can the national and cultural differences in Jerusalem be sustained and tolerated through a moral discourse? Or perhaps when two rights collide tension and conflict are unavoidable.

These are indeed general questions that posit ethics against power. As such they transcend the specific case discussed in this chapter, resurfacing almost in any other moral-political conflict where two (or more) rights collide. To answer these questions it seems to me that one has to strike a balance between the particularities of the case involved and the universality of moral-political guidance. As several researchers have suggested, one has to be sensitive to the particular context, without falling into the trap of parochialism and relativism. This step is taken in the first section of this chapter, which describes the conflicts between Israelis and Palestinians and secular and *haredi* Jews. A subsequent and more difficult step, taken in the second section of this chapter, is to envision a moral-political approach that promotes peaceful co-existence and tolerance, which, according to Walzer (1997, p. 11), implies that people 'make room for men and women whose beliefs they don't adopt, whose practices they decline to imitate'.

The question is whether there is such a universal moral approach that is valid across cultures and social-political circumstances, or perhaps this is an unachievable task since an approach appropriate to one place is inappropriate to another. It would be useful at this point to distinguish between a universal moral principle such as tolerance or peaceful co-existence and specific political and territorial practices designed to promote these principles. I would like to suggest in this chapter that in approaching contentious groups, adherence to universal principles should be maintained while searching for context-specific moral practices.

Ethno-national Conflict: Israelis and Palestinians

Jerusalem is the centre of a bitter political and moral conflict between Israelis and Palestinians. At the heart of this conflict are two irreconcilable claims concerning the right to the land.

The context

The Palestinian population, which in 2001 numbered 215,000 people (32 per cent of the city's population), lives in the eastern section of the city. The Jewish population, which amounted to 454,000 people (68 per cent of the city's population), resides in the western part of Jerusalem (the part that has been Israeli since 1948) and in several neighbourhoods in eastern Jerusalem (the part that was under Jordan's control until 1967).

The ethnic-territorial separation is almost total, and with the exception of a small number of Jews in the Muslim and Christian quarters, there are no areas of mixed population. However, in the aftermath of the 1967 war the Israeli government has built Jewish neighbourhoods in the eastern part of the city, and a chequered pattern of urban residence has developed wherein Jewish neighbourhoods border on Palestinian neighbourhoods.

Arab Palestinians and Israeli Jews conceive of territory as a strategic asset and a symbol of historical presence and nationhood. National identity is inseparably linked to holding on to the land and is manifested in conflicting claims to the same territory. The state of Israel seeks to maintain all of Jerusalem under its sovereignty. The Palestinians wish to see East Jerusalem, Al Quds, as the capital of independent Palestine.

Contested moral claims

Each group relates to the city with its own historical and moral claims, and has its own narrative as to its relations with the land. For the Jewish people, Jerusalem is the capital city founded by King David in the tenth century BCE. It is Zion, the site of the first and second temples, a place often cited in Jewish liturgy and prayers. Religious Jews pray to God three times a day to gather the exiles and bring them back to Zion. As such, Jerusalem is a main symbol of nationhood associated with religion, history, narratives, memories and sense of belongings of the Jewish people. Jerusalem has been the capital of the state of Israel since 1949, the seat of parliament, government and the Supreme Court, and serves as a symbol of Israel's statehood.

For the Palestinians, Jerusalem is the cornerstone of their historical, religious and cultural attachment to the land. Arab armies invaded Palestine and captured Jerusalem in 638 ACE. The Arab conquest began 1,300 years of Muslim presence in what then became known as Filastin. Palestine was holy to Muslims because the Prophet Muhammad had designated Jerusalem as the first *qibla* (the direction Muslims face when praying) and because he was believed to have ascended on a night journey to heaven from the site upon which the Dome of the Rock was later built. Jerusalem became the third holiest city of Islam after Mecca and Madina. The Harem al-Sharif (the noble enclosure) with the Al-Aqsa mosque and the Dome of the Rock serve not only as religious but also as central national symbols in the Palestinian iconography.

The specific claims over Jerusalem are part of a larger moral debate between Jews and Palestinians concerning rights to the land in the country as a whole. For the Jewish people, the return to Zion has been justified on three moral grounds: return to the ancestral (biblical) land, refuge from persecutions and pogroms in Europe that culminated in the Holocaust, and an international obligation (the mandate awarded to Britain by the League of Nations in 1920), and international law (the UN resolution of 1947), to support a Jewish homeland and later a Jewish state in Palestine.

The Jewish claim to the land has been rejected by the Palestinians. What the Jewish people see as a just act of return to the ancestral land is conceived by the Palestinians as a European-like 'colonial movement', which sought to de-legitimize the Palestinians and dispossess them of their birthright (Khalidi, 1983). The Palestinians' claim to the land is grounded in their long settlement in the country and their roots in the land. International support a for Jewish homeland was interpreted as an injustice, and the UN resolution of 1947 to divide the country and give the minority Jewish group 54 per cent of the land was conceived as unjust and dishonest. The displacement of Palestinians during the 1948 war (as they were evicted or chose to leave) and the world's indifference to their plight are interpreted as an evil, which has to be amended by realizing the right of return.

Might decides: features of exclusion

In the absence of an agreement that bridges the contradictory moral-political claims, might has been exercised. To achieve its goals in Jerusalem, the state of Israel has adopted a series of strategies that aim to strengthen the Jewish presence and disempower the Palestinian population. Four main strategies can be identified in this regard: (a) territorial annexation, (b) zoning regulations, (c) residency and access restrictions, and (d) demographic control. The extension of Israeli services and social welfare benefits (National Insurance and health benefits) to the Palestinian population was the compensatory price for these measures.

Territorial annexation

In the aftermath of the 1967 war, Israel expanded the municipal boundaries of West Jerusalem by 70,500 dunams, from 38,000 to 108,500 dunams (8,500 to 27,500 acres), and extended Israel's law, juridical system and administration to East Jerusalem. In so doing, the state of Israel annexed to West Jerusalem the 6,500 dunams of East Jerusalem and another 64,000 dunams around East Jerusalem, all of which were hitherto controlled by Jordan. Of the 70,500 dunams incorporated into the city, the Israeli government expropriated 24,000 dunams to build new Jewish neighbourhoods. These neighbourhoods, which encircle the city and delineate its new boundaries, are home to 170,000 Israeli Jews, that is, just over one-third of the Jewish population of the city.

Zoning and building regulations

To curtail Palestinian growth and expansion, large tracts of land in East Jerusalem, as yet undeveloped, have been zoned as 'green areas'. In these green areas construction is prohibited. Nevertheless, two large Jewish neighbourhoods in the northern and southern sections of the city were built on green areas. Currently, the Palestinian population occupies only 13 per cent of the city's area. The Jewish neighbourhoods enjoy a much higher level of services than the Palestinian neighbourhoods; it is estimated that only 4 to 5 per cent of the municipal budget has been directed to Palestinian neighbourhoods (Hasson, 1996a). Not a single new neighbourhood was built for the Palestinian population. Indeed one Palestinian neighbourhood, the Mughrabi quarter, inside the Old City was completely demolished. Restrictions on Palestinian residential building took the form of municipal measures which withheld permits for new or expanded construction, and demolished illegal building.

Ethnic residency rights and denial of access

By separating the (newly constructed) boundaries of Jerusalem from the West Bank, access to the city was denied for Palestinians living in the greater Jerusalem area (as well as those in the West Bank and Gaza). Residency rights were restricted to those who were registered in the census of September 1967. Movement into the city, as well as benefits and property rights, was effectively barred to all Palestinians, including those who were born in the city but who failed to be present there when the census took place. Since the first Gulf War (1990), restrictions of movement into and out of Jerusalem have been imposed, and any such movement requires a special permit. In addition, new border checkpoints were established separating the city from its Palestinian hinterland.

Demographic encirclement

Politically motivated figures have occasionally been regulated by the Israeli authorities to determine the higher ceiling for Palestinian demographic growth in Jerusalem, ranging from 24 per cent in the 1970s to 33 per cent at present. Unlike most Palestinian residents of the city, Jewish residents, by virtue of being Israelis, can move in and out of the city without losing their residency rights. A Palestinian resident, on the other hand, is faced with the threat of becoming an absentee if he/she moves temporarily abroad or, indeed, even a few kilometres outside the boundaries of the municipality.

The general impact of these policy decisions, as Salim Tamari (1998) clearly demonstrates, is that Jerusalem has lost its status as a metropolitan centre for the Palestinian population of the central West Bank. Up until the mid-1980s, East Jerusalem was the major urban centre for the entire West Bank and served as a combination of a market town and religious centre, as well as an educational and cultural magnet for the country as a whole. By restricting access to the city, Israel contributed effectively to the separation of East Jerusalem from its natural geographic environment (Bethlehem to the south and Ramallah to the north), eventually undermining the city's position as a market and service centre for West Bank Palestinians.

Palestinians' counter-response

In general, as Salim Tamari (1998) argues, the Palestinian community in Jerusalem has displayed a considerable degree of apathy to its own fate. This has been the outcome of the social atomization of the population in East Jerusalem, largely made up of newcomers from the Hebron area. It also reflects Israel's welfare policy, which provides the residents with the benefits of social insurance, health services, free mobility and access to the labour market denied to the other residents of the West Bank and the Gaza Strip. Nevertheless, the residents of Jerusalem displayed some non-violent resistance to Israeli control, which took several forms.

- *Non-violent resistance.* The Palestinians never recognized Israel's authority over East Jerusalem. Palestinian residents of Jerusalem entitled to take part in the municipal elections opted by and large not to do so. In the 2003 municipal elections turnout among Palestinian voters was 3 per cent, compared with nearly 50 per cent among Jewish voters.
- *Political mobilization.* During the first decade of Israeli rule Jerusalem activists led grassroots mobilization through the network of underground political parties and professional groups based in the city. The forum that undertook this mobilization was the National Front and the Association of Professional Unions. Another vehicle for confrontation was the Higher Islamic Committee, also based in Jerusalem, which relied on religious sentiments and the spiritual status of the city to galvanize public opinion.
- *Holding on to the land.* In the struggle against the Israeli efforts, the Palestinians developed an endurance policy of holding on to the land known as *summud*. The most visible feature of the *summud* strategy is the extensive spread of illegal building activities, especially in the last decade, inside Jerusalem and on its outskirts. This strategy may partially explain why the Palestinian population more than tripled between 1967

and 2001, from about 70,000 to 215,000, climbing from 24 per cent of the total population to 33 per cent. As part of this strategy, holy places and historic sites have been transformed into major national symbols, serving as a statement of resistance and political control. The mosque of al-Aqsa has become a major symbol of resistance and defiance of Israel's authority (Abu-Amr, 1995; Jospe, 1995).

Cultural Conflict: The *Haredi* and the Secular Jewish Population

Alongside the conflict between Jews and Palestinians there is another internal cultural conflict between secular and *haredi* Jews. For many secular Jewish residents of Jerusalem this cultural conflict appears much more threatening than the national conflict with the Palestinians. In a study carried out among the different Jewish groups in Jerusalem, secular, observers, modern-orthodox and ultra-orthodox, it was found that one of the main reasons leading secular and observer Jews to consider leaving the city is the threat associated with *haredi* intolerance. Indeed the threats associated with the Jewish–Palestinian conflicts were ranked much lower and play a minor role in the decision to leave the city (Hasson and Gonen, 1997).

The context

Haredi Jews, who numbered 136,00 in 2001 (20 per cent of the city's population), live in voluntarily segregated neighbourhoods mainly in northern Jerusalem. The *haredi* population is characterized by strict adherence to religious commands, voluntary segregation and special dress: black gowns and black hats. Members of the community define themselves as anti-Zionist, do not serve in the armed forces and some of them boycott the election to the Israeli Knesset. The fertility rate of *haredi* women is quite high: 5.9 children compared with 3.0 in the Jewish population at large. Despite the large family size, many *haredi* males do not work, preferring study in the yeshiva to participation in the labour force. Consequently, most of the economic burden falls on the *haredi* women, whose rate of participation in the labour force (40 per cent) is significantly higher than that of males (30 per cent). One result of this situation has been sheer poverty, others are exemption or low payment of municipal taxes and high demands for municipal services. These unique features single out the *haredi* community in Israel from their counterparts in North America and Western Europe, where studies in the yeshiva are very often coupled with active participation in the labour force (Gonen, 2000).

The core of the *haredi* area in Jerusalem is Mea Shearim, a neighbourhood built in the late nineteenth century in the north-eastern section of the city to accommodate *haredi* Jews. Over the years, the *haredi* population has spread steadily to adjacent neighbourhoods, developing a contiguous *haredi* territory stretching from Mea Shearim in the east to Har Nof in the west (Friedman, 1991; Shilhav, 1991).

The contiguous *haredi* territory in north Jerusalem sets off the *haredim* from the rest of society. Within their confines the *haredim* have managed to develop their own separate schools, maintain their dietary laws, control the relations between the sexes, socialize the younger generation, close roads for traffic on the Sabbath and create a separate cultural identity.

The principal *haredi* spatial symbols are religious institutions: synagogues, yeshivas and ritual baths. Other symbols are associated with spatial division by gender, the closure of roads and businesses on the Sabbath and Jewish holidays, and signs and advertisements with religious content. The *haredim* have thus created a defended territorial enclave within which they can produce and reproduce what they regard as the 'holy community,' without being threatened by behavioural patterns and conduct of the surrounding secular society (Hasson, 1996b).

The reason for the spatial segregation is cultural. The *haredi* community views the secular and modern nature of the city as a threat to its existence, one that endangers it and imperils the sacred space that the *haredi* community is trying to fashion for itself. Therefore, the *haredim* strive to build walls and fences to keep out the influence of modern culture. Nevertheless, the *haredim* need the city, with its jobs, taxes, services and products. The result is an ambivalent attitude toward the city: the *haredim* are critical and insular but need to be close to the city to benefit from its resources and services (Shilhav, 1983).

Contested claims

At the centre of the conflict between *haredim* and secular Jews is a clash between two radically different ideologies. The *haredim* wish to impose the precepts of Jewish law (*halacha*) on everyday life, including conformist patterns of behaviour within the territory, whereas the secular Jewish population wish to pursue a liberal-democratic and modern way of life. The two ideologies collide on almost every aspect of daily life, including freedom of travel and shopping on the Sabbath and holidays, programmes of education, relations between the sexes, the nature of entertainment and advertisement.

The clash between the two ideologies is inevitable, and comes to the fore in the *haredi* interpretation of the Jewish *halacha* principle: 'Thou shalt love thy neighbour as thyself' (Leviticus 19:18). This ethical principle, which was indeed celebrated by Rabbi Akiva as 'a great principle in the Torah', is construed by members of the *haredi* community as an obligation imposed by the Torah law to care for their secular brethren as they care for themselves. No matter how sinful their secular brethren are, it is the *haredim* duty to show them the 'right way' by bringing them closer to Jewish life. Practically, this has a threefold implication: creating a sacred community in the *haredi* section of the city; a far-reaching intervention in secular life, including the shaping of public space and public life to bring it in line with religious life; and, finally, turning Jerusalem into a holy city.

For the secular Jews this interpretation seems to be profoundly distorted. The secular population has asserted that the freedom enjoyed by the *haredi* community (to practise its own way of life in its own districts) should not be denied to the secular population. To do otherwise would be unjust and contrary to the ethical principle of 'thou shalt love thy neighbor as thyself'. The secular population thus claims that, following the *haredi* precedent, it, too, has the right to live its lifestyle without being subject to coercion. In the absence of an *a priori* criterion to determine whose views and rules should govern the functioning of the city, the power each community wields determines how Jerusalem functions.

Force decides: features of intolerance

The clash between ideologies and moralities is manifested in a bitter conflict between secular and *haredi* Jews on the 'seam' between the two territories. It is essentially a struggle over two distinct forms of life, which are expressed in different modes of territorial organization. Experience has shown that once *haredim* move into a previously secular territory and pass a certain threshold, a radical social-territorial transformation follows. The *haredim* have transformed secular schools into yeshivas, changed the nature of local communities to suit their cultural demands (particularly separation between men and women), and exerted enormous pressure on secular residents to move out or to conform to the *haredi* way of life.

Because the *haredim* conceive of all of Jerusalem (and actually the whole country) as sacred, they have occasionally tried to control the use of public space not only within their territory but also in more distant areas. In the late 1980s, for instance, they tried to prevent the opening of theatres, restaurants and coffee shops on the Sabbath and holidays. Other conflicts between *haredi* and secular Jews were associated with the former's attempts to prevent the opening of a stadium, archaeological excavations and 'immodest' advertisements on billboards. In the past few years the *haredim* have sequestered themselves in their neighbourhoods and have abandoned the fight for more distant areas. Nevertheless, the struggle over the areas in which the secular and *haredi* populations are in contact has come to a head, especially in Ramot Allon, a neighbourhood in north-western Jerusalem, and on Bar-Illan Street, which is a thoroughfare in the northern section of the city. The *haredim* managed to close the street for prayer hours on the Sabbath and holidays, whereas most of the seculars wished it to remain open throughout.

Reacting to the *haredi* territorial sprawl, secular groups, especially those living in close proximity to the *haredi* population, mobilized their members to defend their territory. At present, Ramot Allon is the scene of the most comprehensive and extreme conflict between secular and *haredi* groups. Already in the late 1970s the secular residents of Ramot Allon successfully opposed *haredi* attempt to close the road leading to their neighbourhood. In the 1980s they built a swimming pool despite strong objections from the local *haredi* community, and they are currently struggling to maintain the secular character of the school system and the neighbourhood council.

Territorial Struggles

In spite of the profound differences in goals and objectives, the national and cultural conflicts in Jerusalem revolved around contested claims to the land. Each group struggled to create a new territory by challenging existing political structures and geographic patterns. Israel's policy to maintain the city united under its own sovereignty was confronted by Palestinian defiance. The Palestinians sought to achieve territorial partition, sovereignty, control over land and the transformation of East Jerusalem into the capital of the emerging Palestinian state. Secular opposition confronted the *haredim*, who sought to create not only a segregated sacred space inhabited by a holy community but also a holy city.

Each group justified its claims to the land by appealing to moral arguments. While confronting the Palestinians, the Israelis relied on symbolic claims based upon historical association with Jerusalem, continuous worshipping, symbolic ties and long presence in the city. The Palestinians have also pointed to their long presence in the city and to the central role it has played in their culture and religion. The *haredim* developed their own set of claims associated with Jerusalem as the holy city and the city of the temple. The secular Jews, on the other hand, pointed to the connections between Jerusalem as the capital city of a state that regards itself as democratic and liberal.

Unable to reach an agreement that would reconcile between the conflicting moral-political claims, the different parties resorted to the use of power and violence. This raises some serious questions with regard to political-moral theory. If different national and cultural groups have incompatible moral claims to the same territory, how can a just solution be reached, and what criteria should be used to guide such a decision? Failing to answer this question might perpetuate the status quo, legitimizing those in power.

Moral Debates

To answer these questions one has to seriously consider several ethical approaches and territorial solutions and to confront them with the power approach. The power approach, exemplified through the two cases explored here, relates to the other as an adversary who can be either defeated or transformed into some other irrelevant political opponent. From a territorial point of view this implies either full Israeli control over the city or enforcement of the *haredi* rules on the other side. The problem in Jerusalem is that neither option seems feasible. As the previous discussion clearly indicates, such measures are bound to exacerbate the problems, leading to further partiality, harassment and counter-activities.

The alternative to the power approach would be an ethical-political approach, which aims at a realist solution. This solution rests on two basic assumptions: (a) no side is going to win and thus achieve its goals by imposing its will on the other; (b) the other side is not going to go away – it is in Jerusalem to stay and to be dealt with. Hence, the alternative to the use of power is an ongoing dialogue whose aim is not about doing away with differences but about discovering ways to live with differences. In the long run some of these differences might be resolved, but a more realistic goal is simply to find a way to temper their importance.

Such an approach may not benefit from the old biblical teaching, already cited above, 'Thou shalt love thy neighbour as thyself'. Throughout its control over East Jerusalem, Israel has shown no care for the Palestinians, and the *haredi* care for their secular brethren left the latter more miserable. Perhaps, instead of caring for the other as we care for ourselves, we may wish the other side what they want for themselves. Following this line of reasoning, an alternative ethical principle to guide the relations between the different groups in Jerusalem is the one postulated by the sage Hillel the Elder. In response to a would-be proselyte who demanded to be taught the entire Torah while standing on one leg, Hillel said: 'What is hateful to you do not do unto your neighbour. That is the entire Torah. All the rest is commentary, go and study' (B. T. Shabbath 31a).

Although Hillel's moral principle has been quite often equated with 'love thy neighbour as thyself', I think the two differ in a remarkable way. Whereas the latter turns to what one should do to the other, the former turns to what one should not do to the other. Hillel's rule implies that we should limit our own actions so as not to interfere directly with the other side's pursuit of its goals. It thus comes close, in my view, to Isaiah Berlin's (1969) concept of negative rights, those that give us the right to exercise our freedom of choice without any external intervention as long as we don't violate the other's rights. While this lowering of the bar reduces considerably the impact of compromise, it may prove more realistic in the end. Such compromise does not necessarily entail benevolent or charitable ideals. What it requires, as Avishai Margalit (1996) contends, is a non-humiliating approach that accords the others control over their own lives and affairs.

Territorial Implications

The ideal of a non-humiliating approach suggests a territorial solution to Jerusalem's problems that entails respect for national and cultural differences through territorial separation. Once this has been achieved, the different groups may engage in a counter-process which emphasizes their sameness. Secured in their territories, diverse groups may seek new ways of sharing the city space by pursuing co-operation across national and cultural boundaries. A just approach to the Israeli–Palestinian conflict is therefore a two-capital solution, while a just solution to the secular–*haredi* conflict would be the borough system.

These political-territorial solutions may not fully respond to the aspirations of the opposing sides, and may be criticized by those who adhere to idealist (neoliberal) solutions based upon power sharing. As Timothy Sisk (1996) clarifies, power sharing is a set of practices and institutions that result in broad-based governing coalitions generally inclusive of all major groups. He identifies the principal approaches to power sharing as including autonomy, federations and proportional electoral systems. Indeed power-sharing solutions of different kinds and forms have been occasionally promoted with the aim of ending the territorial conflict in Jerusalem, including a joint municipality, metropolitan government or a bi-national capital. In my view, the power-sharing solution as far as the Israeli–Palestinian conflict is concerned seems to be detached from the specific political problem it seeks to resolve. An increased sense of nationalism coupled with the current geo-political crisis in the Middle East and the soaring tensions between Israelis and Palestinians make the power-sharing proposal extremely unrealistic.

Under these geo-political circumstances it is not clear why Israelis and Palestinians should adopt a power-sharing solution of joint sovereignty and co-management that requires a high measure of trust and confidence. Why should they seriously consider any solution which is less than full sovereignty? The power-sharing answer is that joint sovereignty and co-management will ultimately enhance confidence and trust building. But this answer is insufficient insofar as it presupposes a sense of trust and norms of co-operation that do not exist. From where will these norms and values appear? What is the mechanism required for trust building?

Power sharing in the case of the *haredi*–secular conflict is more complex an issue. Actually the current political system is based on power sharing, at-large elections, and, until recently, a broad-based city coalition. This structure was seriously shattered in the 2003 municipal elections when a *haredi* man was elected Mayor of Jerusalem and the orthodox parties became a majority in the city council, dominating the city coalition. This situation hides a serious deficit in local democracy and various forms of intolerance and discrimination against the secular population. The *haredi* minority is over-represented in the city council due to a high turnout of the *haredi* electorate, and controls most of the senior positions and portfolios in the city council, including the City Mayor's position. This enables *haredi* council members to discriminate against the non-orthodox public in various spheres, including payment of taxes, allocation of public resources and planning (Hasson, 2001).

I entirely endorse the view that the solution to Jerusalem's problems must go against the grain, calling into question long-established conceptions and beliefs. But no matter how daring and courageous the solution is, it cannot be detached from the political, economic and cultural context which it seeks to rectify. Given the current tensions, mistrust and conflicts, it is recommended to favour varied forms of territorial solution to any power-sharing resolutions, and limit power sharing to places or services that cannot be divided. In this view, political power sharing and economic co-operation will follow a territorial solution. Border delineation, international recognition in the Israeli–Palestinian conflict and judicial and administrative arrangements in the secular–*haredi* case should precede, to be followed later by political, regional, economic and technical co-operation.

The proposed solutions offer prospects for a realistic settlement as they respect the national and cultural differences and enable each group to maintain its identity. Once separation is established and rights of the different groups have been secured the different parties should forge co-operation and openness that transcend national and cultural boundaries. This may be reflected in the mobility of the labour force, tourism, co-operation in the development of physical infrastructure, protection of the environment and planning. Choice of residence across national boundaries would be limited to respect the principle of a two-state solution. In the case of *haredi* and secular Jews, an agreement should be struck to respect the unique culture, freedom and way of life of each group. Past experience has shown that secular Jews do not move into *haredi* areas; *haredi* individuals would be free to move into secular neighbourhoods if they chose to do so, but would have to respect the local culture and its rules. Transcendence of national and cultural barriers is especially needed in the Old City of Jerusalem, which must be left as a cosmopolitan centre shared by the three monotheistic religions.

Conclusions

The city of Jerusalem is engulfed by deep national and cultural conflicts, which are grounded in specific political, cultural and territorial contexts. At the centre of these conflicts are opposing moral-political claims to land.

Two options suggest themselves at this point: to resolve the conflicts through the exercise of power or to seek a solution based upon ethical discourse. The study presented here clearly shows that the adversaries opt for the power-conflict approach. Each group in Jerusalem – Israelis, Palestinians, secular and *haredi* Jews – has a partial-closed value system that justifies its own position and disregards the other. Partiality and disregard for the other have bred political and social tensions, which so far have been dealt with by resorting to power. However, the use of power only helped to exacerbate the problems and intensify partiality in terms of the value system. Under these circumstances it appears that the only plausible way to stop this vicious circle is by turning away from partiality and use of power to a moral-political approach, which is predicated on a universal principle of respect for the other. Specifically, a moral principle has been recommended which does not impose one's values on the other, but rather wishes the other to realize what they want for themselves.

The territorial implications of this moral principle are twofold: (a) territorial separation that would enable different identity groups to forge and develop their distinctive ways of life and pursue their interests; and (b) spatial sharing of the city which would enable equal access to economic resources, acquaintance with the other, tolerance and economic efficiency in the provision of physical infrastructure, planning and environmental protection.

These territorial solutions, which take the form of two national capitals and cultural-based boroughs, are predicated on respect for the other's rights. They are based on recognition of national and cultural differences and the need to maintain them through territorial separation. Territory is thus conceived as a resource to be cherished and enjoyed, as it is associated with memories, a sense of belonging and identity. Indeed, the national and cultural groups discussed here strive to define a territory of their own where they can set up their political institutions and forge their cultural and social way of life.

Recognizing the value of territory does not necessarily entail a parochial approach which leads to exclusion. Territorial separation might limit freedom of movement and access to resources, and on certain occasions might be used as a tool of control and oppression. The striving for national identity and closure might often collide with freedom of movement and economic mobility, as the former is linked with boundaries and control over movement and the latter is associated with transcendence of boundaries and free movement.

The approach presented here utterly rejects a parochial approach of exclusion and seeks to enable openness and recognition of sameness through social and spatial interaction. In so doing, it challenges the idealist benevolent approach of power sharing, which seems to be detached from the specific political and cultural context of Jerusalem, and refuses to succumb to the politics of power struggle. It suggests that nations (Jews and Palestinians) and cultural groups (*haredi* and secular Jews) must search for a balance between closure and openness, inclusion and seclusion, difference and sameness. And this balance has to be struck against the specific conditions which groups and nations find themselves in. As is quite often the case, there is no easy solution to this problem, as every nation or cultural group that wishes to maintain its identity has to strike the appropriate balance between contradictory elements: national identity or cosmopolitan citizenship, particularistic or universalistic culture.

REFERENCES

Abu-Amr, Z. (1995) 'The significance of Jerusalem: a Muslim perspective', *Palestine–Israel Journal* 2, 23–31.

Berlin, I. (1969) *Four Essays on Liberty*, London and New York: Oxford University Press.

Friedman, M. (1991) *The Haredi (Haredim) Society: Sources, Trends and Processes*, Jerusalem: The Jerusalem Institute for Israel Studies.

Gonen, A. (2000) *From Yeshiva to Work: The American Experience and Lessons for Israel*, Jerusalem: The Floersheimer Institute for Policy Studies.

Hasson, S. (1996a) 'Local politics and split citizenship in Jerusalem', *International Journal of Urban and Regional Research* 20, 116–33.

Hasson, S. (1996b) *The Cultural Struggle over Jerusalem: Accommodations, Scenarios and Lesson*, Jerusalem: The Floersheimer Institute for Policy Studies.

Hasson, S. (2001) *The Struggle for Hegemony in Jerusalem: Secular and Ultra-orthodox in Urban Politics*, Jerusalem: The Floersheimer Institute for Policy Studies.

Hasson, S. and Gonen, A. (1997) *The Cultural Tension within Jerusalem's Jewish Population*, Jerusalem: The Floersheimer Institute for Policy Studies.

Jospe, R. (1995) 'The significance of Jerusalem: a Jewish perspective', *Palestine–Israel Journal* 2, 32–40.

Khalidi, W. (1983) Address to the Middle East Consultation, the Carter Center, Emory University, Atlanta, Georgia, 9 November.

Margalit, A. (1996) *The Decent Society*, Cambridge, Mass.: Harvard University Press.

Shilhav, Y. (1983) 'Community conflict in Jerusalem – the spread of ultra-orthodox neighbourhoods', in N. Kliot and S. Waterman (eds), *Pluralism and Political Geography: People, Territory and State*, London: Croom Helm, pp. 100–13.

Shilhav, Y. (1991) *A 'Shtetel' (Small Town) within a Modern City: A Geography of Segregation and Acceptance*, Jerusalem: The Jerusalem Institute for Israel Studies.

Sisk, T. D. (1996) *Power Sharing and Internal Mediation in Ethnic Conflicts*, Washington, DC: Carnegie Commission on Preventing Deadly Conflict.

Smith, D. M. (2000) *Moral Geographies: Ethics in a World of Difference*, Edinburgh: Edinburgh University Press.

Tamari, S. (1998) 'Conflictual and consensual social patterns in Jerusalem: an essay on social infrastructure', paper presented at the Jerusalem Seminar, Stockholm, 28 July.

Walzer, M. (1997) *On Toleration*, New Haven: Yale University Press.

11

Land Reform Policy in Post-Apartheid South Africa: The Elusive Quest for Social Justice?

Brij Maharaj

Introduction

Debates about the rights and access to land can be traced back to the beginnings of civilization. Human beings have developed a propensity for territorial affiliation with the place in which they have been nurtured, as well as a tendency to defend their rights to remain on that land (World Council of Churches, 1983). A number of mechanisms have influenced the allocation of land, and these include rules pertaining to 'gender, kinship and inheritance, membership of local or racial communities and national citizenship, rights of occupation and property ownership' (Williams, 1994, p. 5). Indeed, against a background of

> conflicts over the appropriation of land by some and the dispossession of others, land acquires a powerful symbolic meaning. Claims to 'land' are claims to the country. Claims to repossess the land are claims to all the resources from which the dispossessed have been excluded. The land question is central to the politics of states and of communities, and also to the politics of kin groups and households. (Williams, 1994, p. 5)

In South Africa the apartheid state played an important role in influencing distribution of land and the spatial and social organization of society. As David M. Smith (1982, p. 258) has emphasized, the geographical landscape in South Africa (physical, social and economic) has been profoundly influenced by the policy of apartheid, which constitutes an unparalleled example of state-directed socio-spatial structuring and 'has a special fascination for the geographer.... Indeed, it would not be too much of an exaggeration to describe apartheid as the most ambitious contemporary exercise in applied geography.'

Although a number of processes have been responsible for the inequitable distribution of political power and wealth in South Africa, the dispossession of land was the most important for the majority of black communities. This was because their economic and social structure depended on the distribution of land, and this was typical of most agrarian communities. In South Africa the land question revolves around the fact that 80 per cent of the population live on 13 per cent of the land. A major challenge facing the new Government of National Unity is to adopt a land reform strategy which is efficient, and also addresses the historical legacy of dispossession (Smith, 1994).

In a period of political transition and transformation, land reform and redistribution is 'thought to provide the key to solving poverty and inequality, and is seen as the starting point in any real debate about redistributing wealth' (James, 2001, p. 93). However, it has been suggested that 'private property restitution is controversial, raising as it does questions of prioritising for one group in society at the expense of others' (Blacksell and Born, 2002, p. 183). David M. Smith (1995) has expressed concern about whether the replacement of apartheid by a non-racial democracy will contribute to social justice in South Africa.

This chapter critically examines the policies and mechanisms which have been developed to address the issue of land reform in post-apartheid South Africa. The chapter is divided into five sections. The first section briefly contextualizes the land question in South Africa. The major debates influencing the development of land reform legislation are assessed in the second section. The third section analyses the shift to a market-orientated land reform programme. Land reform and restitution are the focus of the fourth part, followed by critical reflections in the final section.

Land Dispossession in South Africa

There is a symbolic, moral force to the land question in South Africa that is linked to race, colonialism and apartheid (Hart, 2003). The development of mechanisms of spatial and social segregation ensured the exploitation and servility of blacks. The present inequitable distribution of land in South Africa can be traced back to the Native Land Act of 1913 (Bundy, 1979), the Urban Areas Act of 1923 (Rich, 1978) and the Group Areas Act of 1950 (Western, 1981; Maharaj, 1997).

A key factor in the structural and coercive dominance over blacks was white attempts to dispossess the former of their land and livelihood. During the early colonial period Africans were still predominantly subsistence pastoralists – some very successful who were competing with white farmers. The 1913 Land Act destroyed the economic independence of the African peasantry and 'intensified the process which was transforming them into landless wage labourers or labour tenants' (Davies, O'Meara and Dlamini, 1987, p. 106). In terms of the 1913 Land Act, Africans could only own land in traditional reserves, which comprised 8 per cent of South Africa. In 1936 this was increased to 13 per cent. The Land Act legalized the dispossession of African land that had commenced 200 years earlier (Platzky and Walker, 1985). To survive, males were forced into the migrant labour circuit.

The emergence of a coercive labour system did not deal with the problems of how the workers were to be accommodated in mines and in industrial areas, and how they were to be regulated and controlled to meet the needs of the economy (Mabin, 1986). The Natives (Urban Areas) Act of 1923 represented the first Union attempt to control, manage and segregate urban Africans. The rationale for the legislation was based on the findings of the Stallard Commission, initiated in 1922, which contended that the Native should only enter urban areas 'when he is willing to administer to the needs of the white man, and should depart therefrom when he ceases so to administer' (Hellmann, 1961, pp. 121–2). The Urban Areas Act constituted five basic principles for urban segregation which were later revised and consolidated under the apartheid regime: the influx of blacks into urban areas via a controlled labour system; the establishment of segregated townships; the self-financing of certain means of collective consumption through a separate revenue account administered by local authorities; the imposition of constraints on land ownership; and the denial of political rights to blacks in urban areas (Bloch and Wilkinson, 1982).

The peculiar feature of the apartheid era was the imposition of more austere, all-embracing and rigidly imposed regulation over blacks in terms of their migration to cities, and in their work and housing opportunities. The Nationalists viewed the geographical separation of the different race groups as vital to continued white domination, especially since it eliminated blacks competing with whites in all spheres. The Group Areas Act (1950) emphasized separate residential areas, educational services and other amenities for the different race groups. The implementation of apartheid in South Africa centred to a large extent on the control of residential location. This spatial segregation and segmentation of residential areas for whites, coloureds, Indians and Africans expressed the impact of apartheid most acutely (Maharaj, 1997). Consequently, about 3.5 million blacks were forcibly removed off their land and business sites with little or no compensation (Platzky and Walker, 1985).

There was a great deal of resistance to forced removals in urban as well as rural areas (Claasens, 1990a; Maharaj, 1999, 2001). Conflict over land has played an important role in mobilizing and organizing the dispossessed, and this has been emphasized by Claasens (1990b, p. 11): 'Land is the flashpoint for ongoing struggles, whether by the urban homeless in "squatter camps" or by rural communities defending themselves from eviction and taking occupation of land. Millions of black people have defied a barrage of legislation to live in and sometimes farm land illegally.'

As the democratic transition proceeded in South Africa in the early 1990s, the inequitable land distribution was a startling reality: about 55,000 white commercial farmers had access to 102 million hectares, and 1.2 million black households only had access to 17 million hectares of land in the former Bantustans (Marcus, Eales and Wildschut, 1996, p. 97).

Debates About Socially Just Land Redistribution and Restitution

The debate on land redistribution and property rights was one of the most contentious issues at the negotiations leading up to the democratic transition in 1994 (Walker, 1997a). The African National Congress (ANC) argued that the existing unequal distribution of land in South Africa was the result of dispossession, and the fact that the black majority have been denied rights and access to land. The mere repeal of racial laws was unlikely to reverse the situation, and legislative intervention would be required. There were two key elements in the ANC's land policy: 'restitution for those who were dispossessed by apartheid forced removals, and a process of redistribution of land to deal with land hunger and the unequal distribution of land' (ANC, 1994, p. 1).

While acknowledging that the market had a role to play in land reform, the ANC argued that it would hardly address the problem. As a result of apartheid, the majority of the dispossessed did not have the capacity to buy land. Under these circumstances the market was likely to exacerbate existing inequalities (Maharaj, 1996). The ANC therefore emphasized the role of the state in the acquisition of land. The state would be empowered to acquire land in a number of ways, including expropriation with compensation. The ANC intended imposing a ceiling on land ownership and multiple ownership of farms, and the following categories of land would be made available for redistribution by the state: land held for speculation; under-utilized land or unused land with a productive potential; land which was being degraded; and hopelessly indebted land (ANC, 1992, p. 17).

The ANC also emphasized that any land policy had to address the legacy of forced removals. It envisaged 'the creation of an independent, non-racial, non-sexist and representative land claims court to preside over and make the necessary adjudications with regard to claims to land' (ANC, 1992, p. 18). Interestingly, an ANC-commissioned study on the feasibility of such a process conducted by the Centre for Applied Legal Studies concluded in

1993 that 'a Court is not an appropriate mechanism for handling claims since the judicial process and courts are conservative and court processes are slow, expensive and complicated' (Levin, 1997, p. 242). The study also recommended that a legal mechanism to redress land claims arising from rural forced removals only could be handled by a court. Political solutions were more appropriate in the other instances of dispossession, especially urban land claims. There was concern that a court would go no further than adjudicating existing claims and would not address the problems of land-lessness and the redistribution of land.

The ANC believed that the successes of the court in New Zealand and Canada could be replicated in South Africa (Claasens, 1991). It was thought that a court would empower the landless, ensure that decision-making would be more open and accountable, and legitimize ownership for all (Maharaj, 1996). Successful submissions to the court would depend on equitable access to essential legal services. In this regard David M. Smith (1994, p. 237) warned that a land claims court 'would have to guard against the possibility, intrinsic to land reform in general, of favouring those with the resources to plead the most convincing case'. However, there was a significant shift in the ANC's land policy from a socially just redistributive strategy as a result of the influence of the World Bank.

Capitulation to Markets

The World Bank had a major role in changing the ANC government's approach to land reform from a comprehensive interventionist approach to a neoliberal market-driven land reform process (Sihlongonyane, 1997). While the Constitution was being developed, the Land and Agricultural Policy Centre (LAPC) was established as the ANC's think tank on its land and agrarian policy. The LAPC immediately called for a World Bank-funded policy investigation project which significantly re-orientated the ANC's land policy.

The following recommendations of the World Bank, supporting a market-driven land reform programme, were subsequently adopted as South Africa's land reform policy:

i) the poor should be given government grants and land bank loans to *buy* commercial farmland from *willing sellers* [emphasis added];

ii) there could be no direct government intervention by expropriating or purchasing white-owned land;

iii) there would be a judicial settlement for the dispossessed; and

iv) current land owners should be compensated at market-related rates through a market-assisted land reform process (Minaar, 1994, p. 43).

By forming a close working relationship with the LAPC, the World Bank ensured that its hegemonic approach to rural restructuring remained unchallenged in Sub-Saharan Africa (Sihlongonyane, 1997). According to Sihlongonyane (1997, p. 119), these neoliberal reforms imposed by the World Bank in Sub-Saharan African countries implied that the continent was being 'recolonised under the guise of Western-prescribed structural adjustments and policy dialogue'. The World Bank had a similar influence in other African, Asian and Latin American countries, which added to their foreign debt (Manji, 2001).

Venter and Anderson (1993) illustrated the failure of land policies in African countries where the property clause was included in the Constitution. Budlender (1992, p. 304) maintained that the entrenchment of the property clause would 'disable any attempt at substantial redistribution of land'. The Minister of Land Affairs stated that the ANC agreed to the inclusion of the property clause in the Constitution as a compromise to ally white fears of expropriation of their land without compensation (*Sunday Times*, 10 September 1995).

According to Khosa (1994), the land reform process was a compromise between the ANC, the National Party, current white landowners and international capital. The reasons for this change in position was 'the necessity to create a stable environment for investment and the desirability of creating a secure system of property rights' (Claasens, 1993, p. 57). This ignored the argument that the role of the market should be limited in the South African context since it would be unable to provide mechanisms for equitable redistribution. Most blacks would be inhibited from obtaining land because of the high price and the existing skewed distribution of wealth (Moore, 1992).

In contrast to its traditional approach to consult with communities, the ANC relied on 'technical experts' from the World Bank in developing land reform policies (Sihlongonyane, 1997). The limited consultation with the landless and a reliance on technical experts was also a major shortcoming that contributed to the failure of the Zimbabwean land reform programme (Palmer, 1990; Cousins and Robins, 1993).

Land Reform and Restitution

The South African land reform programme had three key elements, namely the restitution of property to people dispossessed of land rights after 19 June 1913 in terms of racially discriminatory laws or practices; the redistribution of land and provision of land for the disadvantaged and poor for residential and productive purposes; and tenure reforms that would improve tenure security for all South Africans (Republic of South Africa, 1997). The aim of the land reform policy was to 'redress the injustices of apartheid; build national reconciliation and stability; support economic growth and improve household welfare and reduce poverty' (LAPC, 1996, p. 2). The Restitution of Land Rights Act provided for the establishment of an independent Commission with regional offices to investigate and mediate claims, and a Land Claims Court with jurisdiction to determine restitution of such rights.

However, as early as August 1994, there were concerns about delays in the land reform process. The Minister of Land Affairs in the Government of National Unity, Derek Hanekom, stated that he was aware that people were becoming impatient, and mainained that the land redistribution project would be completed in five years:

> There is impatience. People have started reoccupying their land. They don't understand the delay. People have suffered an injustice and they want justice to be done as quickly as possible. What we plan to do is to ensure that people who have been forced off their land will be able to return. Those who were denied access to land will benefit. We want land used productively and want people secure on the land they occupy. (*Sunday Tribune*, 21 August 1994)

Initially, three organizations were tasked with implementing the land restitution programme: the Commission on Restitution of Land Rights, the Department of Land Affairs (DLA) and the Land Claims Court.

Commission on Restitution of Land Rights

There were five regional Commissions where claimants initially had until April 1998 to lodge their claims. However, the cut-off date was later extended to December 1998. The task of the Commission was to investigate claims by doing archival, deeds and other research. Investigations included determining the present value of the land and the compensation received upon dispossession. Valid claims were published in the *Government Gazette* and submissions in favour of, or objections to, the claims were considered. The Commission then invited all interested parties to negotiate a solution to the claim. The negotiated settlements were referred to the Land Claims Court for ratification. Claims that could not be solved by the Commission were referred for mediation and then to the Court.

The policy for settling claims was that if the property that was claimed was vacant, the original land was restored to the successful claimant. If the land was developed, claimants could either receive alternate land; monetary compensation; a combination of both forms of relief; or priority access to state resources in the allocation and development of housing and land (Republic of South Africa, 1994). Other creative forms of restitution included upgrading tenure and living conditions in areas presently occupied by claimants, tax and rate rebates, and 'symbolic' restitution. The settlement could also include access to one of the Department's land reform financial assistance packages. Awards took into account the compensation claimants received at the time of their dispossession, which would be deducted from the total to be paid to the claimant (Khosa, 1994).

Department of Land Affairs

The Department of Land Affairs' Restitution Directorate was charged with making restitution policy and negotiating settlements to claims. The lack of capacity for restitution in the provincial department offices led to a bottleneck of cases to be investigated and negotiated. It also had a national research department, which often duplicated investigations done by the Commission. This led to a great deal of 'tensions and ambiguities' over the two organizations' roles in the management of the restitution process. The Department of Land Affairs also controlled the budget to settle claims.

The Land Claims Court

The Land Claims Court functioned at the level of the Supreme Court with a panel of five judges. The Court was empowered to order the transfer of state land and the expropriation or purchase of property which had passed into private ownership. If privately owned land was expropriated, the state was obliged to compensate the current landowners at market value. However, the history of the property's acquisition, its current market value and use, and the interests of the parties involved had to be taken into account. The Court could also upgrade the rights held by people at the time of dispossession. Appeals against the Court's decision would be referred to the Constitutional Court (Republic of South Africa, 1994).

Critical Reflections

The compromises reached by the national liberation forces at the Kempton Park negotiations contributed to the slow delivery of far-reaching land redistribution. The programme was described as being very ambitious considering the dichotomy between financial constraints and popular need and demand for land (Walker, 1997a). After 1995, communities became impatient and disillusioned with the process and incidences of land invasions increased. Finance and resource constraints were the main cause for the slow pace of delivery, and this was dictated by a neoliberal growth agenda that placed 'economic growth ahead of social justice' (Greenberg, 2003, p. 2). Basically, 'the quality of land settlement and restorative justice have been sacrificed in the interests of neo-liberal, macro-economic objectives' (Hargreaves and Eveleth, 2003, p. 79). Hence the redistribution of resources is determined by the market. Levin and Weiner (1997, p. 291) warned that 'a market-led reform programme in the context of a neo-liberal macro-economic planning framework would exclude most of apartheid's rural victims'.

The land reform programme was allocated a limited budget. Three billion Rands was estimated to be the fiscal requirement to ensure far-reaching land reform, but the Department of Land Affairs was only allocated 0.3 per cent of the national budget (*Land Update*, March 1997). This raised questions about the government's commitment to the land reform programme. The exorbitant cost of market-related compensation for current landowners might have contributed to the state not prioritizing land reform over other pressing social needs. The lack of urgency given to the land reform programme contributed to its slow delivery rate. There was also serious lack of capacity to implement the programme. Most of the structure and systems had to be created from scratch. Much of the 1995–7 period was spent on building and developing the organizations to implement the programme.

The scope of a market-led process was limited and had been unsuccessful in other African countries such as Zimbabwe, Matabeleland and Nigeria (Palmer, 1990; Alexander, 1991; Williams, 1992). Zimbabwe's land reform programme provided a good illustration of the failure of the 'willing seller–willing buyer' principle to redistribute land to the landless (Palmer, 1990; Cousins and Robins, 1993).

It was argued that the 'willing seller–willing buyer' principle would benefit the current landowners, who could dictate the sale and price of land. This would leave the landless and the government's finances at the mercy of the current landowners. In contrast, the R16,000 grant per household for beneficiaries of the Settlement/Land Acquisition Grant (SLAG) was perceived by communities to be insufficient. Many households had to pool their grants to buy farms. The grant only allowed the poor to acquire some property but neither productive land nor the resources for development (*Land Update*, November 1996). This seriously affected the rapid transfer of property to the landless majority. By the year 2000, 484 projects were approved in terms of the SLAG programme, and 55,383 households received 780,407 hectares of land. Only 1.3 per cent of land had been redistributed between 1994 and 2001 (Lyne and Durroch, 2003). In the period 1994–9 the government's target had been to transfer 30 per cent of agricultural land to black farmers (Manji, 2001). In 1999 a Department of Land Affair's sponsored

> quality of life report indicated that the apartheid pattern of dumping people in rural areas with no means of earning livelihoods was being replicated in many land redistribution projects. Not only were beneficiaries not trained or supported in carrying on economic activities once they were settled, but basic services like water, sanitation, health care, electricity and educational facilities were not provided. (Greenberg, 2003, p. 14)

The land reform programme committed itself to gender equality and identified women as a major category of beneficiaries of the programme (Republic of South Africa, 1997, p. ix). Women envisaged access to land as an important factor which would contribute to their role in social reproduction and the domestic economy. However, South African rural women were 'systematically marginalised from access to, and control over, land as a result of the interaction of past racial land and labour policies with patriarchal structures of authority' (Walker, 1997b, p. 1). Walker (1996) argued that women should have land rights, access to land, inheritance rights (including chieftainship), the right to participate in land claims, the right to alienate matrimonial property without a man's permission, and that matrimonial property should be divided equally on divorce. This would require 'the removal of legal restrictions on women's access to land, the use of procedures which promote women's active participation in decision-making and the registration of land assets in the name of household members and not household heads' (Walker, 1997b, p. 6). It was essential that these policies were implemented to ensure gender equity in land reform and the removal of discrimination against women in access to land and in tenure systems (Walker, 1997b). However, with the small budget allocated to the Gender Commission, it was questionable whether it had the capacity or resources to monitor the land reform programme. Agarwal (1994) illustrated in the South Asian context that although gender was included in laws, it did not ensure that its implementation promoted gender equality. Although the land reform policies constantly referred to women's access to land, so far there had been no practical indications as to how it was going to be achieved.

In the restitution process, the trauma of losing one's property rights, sources of livelihood and the costs of physical removal were not being taken into account. There was no financial formula that could compensate communities for the loss of religious sites, schools, burial grounds, and so on. These had cultural and emotional value that could not be assessed in material terms. The social and psychological costs of forced removals could not be quantified.

A controversial section of the Restitution of Land Rights Act was the Section 34 'block-out clause', which allowed local authorities to apply to the Land Claims Court for land not to be restored to original landowners. This application was to be considered by local authorities when development projects in the area were threatened by the restoration of land (Republic of South Africa, 1994). In lieu, restoration claimants would have to consider other forms of restitution, like alternate land and cash compensation. Restitution claimants argued that Section 34 was unconstitutional since it denied the dispossessed a right to restoration of land. Restitution was also a public right. The appropriateness of Section 34 to settle urban land claims needed to be investigated. Restitution was perceived as an obstacle to development in urban areas, even by provincial governments, local authorities and other government departments (Maharaj and Ramballi, 1997). The government also had the responsibility for developing vacant land to provide houses, employment and economic opportunities. Finding a balance between the two issues was difficult since social and economic rights were enshrined in the Constitution. In many urban areas,

> there was a conflict between those who lost rights of access to land and housing (i.e. the claimants) and those that never had this access under apartheid (i.e. the landless and homeless). In urban areas, a top-down technocratic model of urban land planning and settlement is shaped by the desire to attract large-scale capitalist development. It has inflamed conflict between planners and resource-poor communities who find themselves in the path of a development agenda that has no space for them. (Greenberg, 2003, p. 1)

The Section 34 process was adversarial in practice and made high demands on scarce resources. The process was confusing to the public and claimants and was also disempowering, bureaucratic and inaccessible to resource-poor claimants. Negotiations and mediation could lead to a more amicable solution to urban land restitution claims than resorting to Section 34 (Ramballi and Maharaj, 2002).

The Restitution Act only catered for people who were dispossessed of their land after 1913. During this period land rights were already highly circumscribed and unequal (Walker, 1997a). Land conquest and official forms of segregation were already entrenched prior to 1913 (Sihlongonyane, 1997). Historical claims which were rooted in tribal identities and traditional authorities were rejected. Land claimants argued that historical claims should be considered since land dispossession started with the colonial conquests. They were of the opinion that the 1913 cut-off date was 'a denial of the historical processes through which people lost their land and thus a denial of people's loss' (*Land Update*, July 1996, p. 15). The Act was criticized as being exclusionary and limiting the scope of the restitution process.

By the end of the 31 December 1998 deadline, 68,878 claims were lodged with the Land Claims Commission. By September 2000, only 18 per cent of these claims were settled. By October 2002 more than half of the claims were settled, of which 80 per cent were in urban areas (Lyne and Durroch, 2003). However, the tendency for

> restitution claims to be 'settled' through financial compensation rather than land, has provided a statistical escape mechanism to a state eager to deflect criticism of the failure of the country's World Bank-styled land reform programme. It has now become standard fare for government officials to conflate 'land reform' with 'land restitution', and to quote claim settlement statistics as evidence of the progress made in land reform, while quietly ignoring the realities of 'cheque-book restitution'. (Hargreaves and Eveleth, 2003, p. 92)

Cash compensation for land claims, which cannot be sustained, will result in issues relating to land restoration, access and equity not being addressed (De Villiers, 2003). The scale of landlessness and homelessness is enormous in South Africa and the expectations for delivery are high. Budlender (1992, p. 304) warned ominously that the failure to respond to these needs and expectations would compel people 'to revert to the traditional South African land claims process – land occupation'. There have indeed been several incidents of land invasion in different parts of the country, the most well known of which is the case of Braudel.

Conclusion

The land question 'lies at the very root of some of the most fundamental, important and controversial aspects in the creation of the new South Africa' (Olivier, 1992, p. 6). In an era of reconstruction, development and planning, land reform, restitution and redistribution can be regarded as an opportunity to heal the scars resulting from apartheid planning and forced removals. The Restitution of Land Rights Act proposed a restructuring programme to address historical injustice in land allocation. However, the framework for restitution was judicial, very elaborate and technical, with many institutional role players. Restitution applied strict judicial procedure to what was in essence a political problem. It dealt with the loss in right to land without dealing with the moral and emotional pain and suffering caused by forced removals.

The political comprises negotiated during the political transition resulted in the adoption of a market approach to land reform which disadvantaged those who had been dispossessed. Wealth distribution was skewed as a result of apartheid. The fact that millions of South Africans were poor and landless meant that they would be excluded from the land reform process. In 1995 David M. Smith warned prophetically that as long as the unequal apartheid distribution of wealth and income persists, social and economic injustice will be perpetuated in the new South Africa. Hence, the need for redistribution of land on a far larger scale than has presently occurred. Otherwise, land reform policy in post-apartheid South Africa is likely to remain an elusive quest for social justice.

REFERENCES

Agarwal, B. (1994) *A Field of One's Own: Gender and Land Rights in South Asia*, Cambridge: Cambridge University Press.

Alexander, J. (1991) 'The unsettled land: the politics of land redistribution in Matabeleland, 1980–1990', *Journal of Southern African Studies* 17 (4), 581–610.

ANC (1992) *Ready to Govern*, ANC policy guidelines for a democratic South Africa adopted at the National Conference, 28–31 May.

ANC (1994) *Policy on the Restitution of Land Rights*, Johannesburg.

Blacksell, M. and Born, K. M. (2002) 'Private property restitution: the geographical consequences of official government policies in Central and Eastern Europe', *The Geographical Journal* 168, 178–90.

Bloch, R. and Wilkinson, P. (1982) 'Urban control and popular struggle: a survey of state union policy 1920–1970', *Africa Perspective* 20, 2–40.

Budlender, G. (1992) 'The right to equitable access to land', *South African Journal on Human Rights* 8, 295–304.

Bundy, C. (1979) *The Rise and Fall of the South African Peasantry*, London: Heinemann.

Claasens, A. (1990a) 'Rural land struggles in the Transvaal in the 1980s', in C. Murray and C. O'Regan (eds), *No Place to Rest: Forced Removals and the Law in South Africa*, Cape Town: Oxford University Press, pp. 27–65.

Claasens, A. (1990b) 'Land policy: seeking a common framework in local struggles', *Sash – Journal of the Black Sash* (May), 10–14.

Claasens, A. (1991) 'Who owns South Africa? Can the repeal of the Land Acts De-racialise Land Ownership in South Africa?', *Monitor – The Journal of the Human Rights Trusts*, 66–77.

Claasens, A. (1993) 'Compensation for expropriation: the political and economic parameters', in M. Venter and M. Anderson (eds), *Land, Property Rights and the New Constitution*, Community Law Centre, University of Western Cape, pp. 55–60.

Cousins, B. and Robins, S. (1993) 'Institutions for financing land reform', paper presented at the Land Redistribution Options conference, Johannesburg, 12–15 October.

Davies, R., O'Meara, D. and Dlamini, S. (1987) 'The development of racial capitalism', in D. Mermelstein (ed.), *The Anti-Apartheid Reader*, New York: Grove Press, pp. 99–112.

De Villiers, B. (2003) *Land Reform: Issues and Challenges*, Johannesburg: Konrad-Adenauer-Stiftung.

Greenberg, S. (2003) 'Redistribution and access in a market-driven economy', *Development Update* 4, 1–26.

Hargreaves, S. and Eveleth, A. (2003) 'The land restitution programme: advancing real reform or delaying it?', *Development Update* 4, 95–126.

Hart, J. (2003) 'Land: critical choices for South Africa', paper presented at the Wolpe Lecture Series, University of Natal, Durban.

Hellmann, E. (1961) 'The application of the concept of separate development to urban areas in the Union of South Africa', in K. Kirkwood (ed.), *St. Anthony's Papers Volume 10, African Affairs*, pp. 120–46.

James, D. (2001) 'Land for the landless: conflicting images of rural and urban in South Africa's land reform programme', *Journal of Contemporary African Studies* 19, 93–109.

Khosa, M. M. (1994) 'Whose land is it anyway?', *Indicator South Africa* 12 (1), 50–6.

LAPC (1996) *A Guide to the Department of Land Affairs' Land Reform Programme*, Johannesburg.

Levin, R. (1997) 'Land restitution and democracy', in R. Levin and D. Weiner (eds), *'No More Tears': Struggles for Land in Mpumalanga, South Africa*, Trenton, NJ: Africa World Press, pp. 233–51.

Levin, R. and Weiner, D. (1997) 'Conclusion', in R. Levin and D. Weiner (eds), *'No More Tears': Struggles for Land in Mpumalanga, South Africa*, Trenton, NJ: Africa World Press, pp. 291–300.

Lyne, M. C. and Durroch, M. A. G. (2003) 'Land redistribution in KwaZulu-Natal, South Africa: five census surveys of farmland transactions 1997–2001', University of Natal, Pietermaritzburg.

Mabin, A. (1986) 'Labour, capital, class struggle and the origins of residential segregation in Kimberley, 1880–1920', *Journal of Historical Geography* 12, 4–26.

Maharaj, B. (1996) 'Land reparations in South Africa: a preliminary analysis', in R. B. Singh (ed.), *Disasters, Environment and Development*, Oxford and New Delhi: IBH Publishers, pp. 467–78.

Maharaj, B. (1997) 'Apartheid, urban segregation and the local state: Durban and the Group Areas Act in South Africa', *Urban Geography* 18, 135–54.

Maharaj, B. (1999) 'The integrated community apartheid could not destroy: the Warwick Avenue Triangle in Durban', *Journal of Southern African Studies* 25, 245–62.

Maharaj, B. (2001) 'Politics, community displacement and planning: Cato Manor – past, present, future', in C. de Wet and R. Fox (eds), *Understanding Changing Patterns of Settlement and Resettlement in Southern Africa*, Edinburgh: University of Edinburgh Press, pp. 133–46.

Maharaj, B. and Ramballi, K. (1997) 'Urban land claims – contested terrain: the Case of Cato Manor', paper presented at the Conference on Land Surveying and Land Tenure, Durban, August.

Manji, A. (2001) 'Land reform in the shadow of the state: the implementation of new land laws in Sub-Saharan Africa', *Third World Quarterly* 22, 327–42.

Marcus, T., Eales, K. and Wildschut, A. (1996) *Down to Earth: Land Demand in the New South Africa*, Durban: Indicator Press.

Minaar, A. (1994) 'The dynamics of land in rural areas: 1990 and onwards', in A. Minaar (ed.), *Access and Affordability of Land in South Africa: The Challenge of Land Reform in the 1990s*, Pretoria: HSRC, pp. 27–60.

Moore, B. (1992) 'The case for a land tax: from entitlement to restitution', *Indicator South Africa* 9 (2), 25–9.

Olivier, N. J. (1992) 'Land: drastic change is inevitable', *Reality* 24, 6–8.

Palmer, R. (1990) 'Land reform in Zimbabwe, 1980–1990', *African Affairs* 89, 163–81.

Platzky, L. and Walker, C. (1985) *The Surplus People: Forced Removals in South Africa*, Johannesburg: Ravan Press.

Ramballi, K. and Maharaj, B. (2002) 'Land reform and restitution in the New South Africa: a critical review', in R. Donaldson and L. Marais (eds), *Transforming Rural and Urban Spaces in South Africa during the 1990s: Reform, Restitution, Restructuring*, Pretoria: Africa Institute of South Africa, pp. 29–52.

Republic of South Africa (1994) *The Restitution of Land Rights Act 22 of 1994*, Cape Town: Government Printer.

Republic of South Africa (1997) *White Paper on Land Reform*, Cape Town: Government Printer.

Rich, P. B. (1978) 'Ministering to the white man's needs: the development of urban segregation in South Africa', *African Studies* 37, 177–91.

Sihlongonyane, M. (1997) 'What has gone wrong with land reform?', *Debate* 3, 118–29.

Smith, D. M. (ed.) (1982) *Living under Apartheid: Aspects of Urbanization and Social Change in South Africa*, London: George Allen and Unwin.

Smith, D. M. (1994) *Geography and Social Justice*, Oxford: Blackwell.

Smith, D. M. (1995) 'Geography, social justice and the new South Africa', *South African Geographical Journal* 77, 1–5.

Venter, M. and Anderson, M. (eds) (1993) *Land, Property Rights and the New Constitution*, Community Law Centre, University of Western Cape.

Walker, C. (1996) 'Re-settling old scores: land restitution in KwaZulu/Natal', *Indicator South Africa* 13, 46–50.

Walker, C. (1997a) 'The restitution of land rights in South Africa: the challenges, the claims, the Commission', paper presented at the iKusasa Conference on Land Surveying and Land Tenure 1997, International Convention Centre, Durban, 27 August.

Walker, C. (1997b) 'Land reform and gender in post-apartheid South Africa', paper presented at the International Workshop on Gender, Poverty and Well-being: Indicators and Strategies, Trivandrum, Kerela, India, 24–7 November.

Western, J. (1981) *Outcast Cape Town*, Johannesburg: Human and Rousseau.

Williams, D. C. (1992) 'Measuring the impact of land reform policy in Nigeria', *Journal of Modern African Studies* 30 (4), 587–608.

Williams, G. (1994) 'Land and freedom: an outline', CSDS Working Paper No. 12, University of Natal, Durban.

World Council of Churches (1983) *Land Rights for Indigenous People*, Programme Unit on Justice and Service Commission to Combat Racism.

Part III

Moral Geographies in Place

The moral significance of place has attracted attention in recent years. For example, Michael Curry (1999) points out that, because places are basic sites of human activity, a central function is to define what is possible and allowable within their boundaries. Places are thus fundamentally normative, concerned with what is right and good conduct and where. To say 'That's how we do things here' captures a form of place-specific moral justification which is subject to spatial differentiation. Robert Sack (2003) has provided an extended account of the moral 'power of place'. He recognizes that we create places to transform reality according to ideas and images of what we think it ought to be. He demonstrates the capacity of place to weave together the moral elements of truth, justice and the natural, and the empirical elements of meaning, social relations and nature, leading to different outcomes. While situatedness may restrict our vision, we are never completely the victims of particular places and their localized moralities; we have the imaginative capacity to think ourselves out of them.

The moral significance of place thus raises again the issues of universalism and particularism raised in the Introduction. Respect for diversity and pluralism, in the spirit of such contemporary intellectual (or political) currents as multiculturalism and postmodernism, can find a place for moral absolutism. Suspicion of universalism can similarly make room for relativism. Navigating between these extremes is crucial to normative ethics, otherwise there are no grounds for critique of local values and practices. This involves recognition of the importance of context, and of the interaction of the cultural and the material within particular historical geographical situations.

This task is exemplified in Chapter 12, where Stuart Corbridge looks at local practices of queueing (or waiting in line). He notes that in rural India this is regulated not by the precepts of human equality but by hierarchy, which favours some members of society over others. However, while propensity to jump the queue might be attributed to culture, to different moral understanding of personal worth and the rights of others, he prefers an interpretation which recognizes the production of scarcity. These material conditions should be subject to critique, and to public policy intervention.

In Chapter 13 Gill Valentine examines the notion of 'sexual citizenship', in the context of particular places. She considers the space of the school as a heteronormative environment, in which lesbian and gay young people may be victimized. She describes the attempt of the Scottish parliament to repeal section 28 of the Local Government Act in Britain (which bans the promotion of homosexuality in schools), and the way in which business, the church, politicians and campaign groups have drawn on different moral discourses about Scottishness to argue their cases for or against the legislation.

According to Jean Hillier (Chapter 14), traditional theoretical approaches suggest that local land-use planning decisions follow a utilitarian premise, of planning officers making technical, objective recommendations to elected representatives who take neutral, balanced decisions. She looks at planning practice as actually encountered in local authorities in Western Australia, suggesting that decision-making may be exercised with little distinct or overt logic. She asks whether those concerned act consequentially, or whether their behaviour is rights-based or deontological. Rather than conforming to such general ethical codes, she finds moral improvisation in messy, highly politicized planning decision-making practice – in how they do things here.

And so back to the realities of geographical context. How things are done here or there reflects not merely the characteristics embedded in particular territories but also the mutual transformations between territorial spaces and topological relations stretched across space. Such geographies are acutely apparent in questions of morality and ethics, as may be demonstrated, for example, by the transnational and highly mobile anti-globalization movements. These draw upon a moral resistance – albeit often incoherent and multiple in form – to what is understood as a set of ideas, institutions and practices which are transforming a moral landscape in unacceptable ways. What may or may not be acceptable is an ethical question bound up with social circumstance. It is, therefore, profoundly geographical, and so the surprise is that an ethical turn has come so recently in geography and for geographers.

REFERENCES

Curry, M. (1999) 'Hereness and the normativity of place', in J. D. Proctor and D. M. Smith (eds), *Geography and Ethics: Journeys in a Moral Terrain*, London: Routledge, pp. 95–105.

Sack, R. (2003) *A Geographical Guide to the Real and the Good*, New York and London: Routledge.

12

Waiting in Line, or the Moral and Material Geographies of Queue-Jumping

Stuart Corbridge

Introduction

In this chapter I want to tack back and forth between political economy and moral geography, two areas in which David Smith has made lasting contributions in a long and distinguished career. I will do so by offering some first thoughts on the causes and significance of queueing, or what Americans call 'waiting in line'. Queueing is something that practically everyone has done at one time or another. The queue is a quintessentially geographical phenomenon that orders time and space. This is true even when the queue is imposed electronically or telephonically, as when we are told to wait for the next available operator, who turns out to be working not locally in London or Miami, but in Glasgow, Phoenix or even Bangalore. I also want to consider the practice of queue-jumping. What causes some people to barge in front of others, and why do we seem to observe such behaviour more often in countries like India or Italy than in the UK and parts of the US? Is this mainly a result of different moral understandings of the rights of others? This is one possible explanation, and it sits easily with the important recent work of Jean-Philippe Platteau (1994) on 'generalized morality'. I shall discuss this explanation first. Or might it have more to do with the production of scarcity, in both the economic and the political realms? This explanation sits more comfortably with Albert Hirschman's enduring work on 'exit, voice and loyalty' (Hirschman, 1970), and I shall discuss it secondly. My answer, for what it is worth, is that the truth lies closer to Hirschman, and that therein lies a lesson for what we might call 'the responsibilities of critique' – a lesson, I shall contend, that David Smith has taught us many times before.

Moral Geographies and Queue-Jumping

Over the past few years I have worked with several colleagues on questions relating to state performance in eastern India, particularly from the point of view of the rural poor. In the course of our research we have become interested in the question of how different individuals and groups within the rural poor 'see' the state (see Corbridge, Williams, Srivastava and Véron, 2005). For the most part, such people do not 'see' the state at a fixed time, through an appointment for example, nor do they always get to see a government servant in his or her official place of work. Government business is also transacted on the verandah of an officer's house, in the process ensuring that the boundaries between the 'everyday state and society' in India become blurred.[1] Nevertheless, many poorer people – and poor women especially – can be seen waiting patiently outside government buildings like the Block Development Office, hoping perhaps to register a name or to receive a pension. It is not unusual for them to be kept waiting for hours, and sometimes for days. During the course of this wait they will often see local political bosses (*netas*) storm into the office of the highest ranking local government official to demand an audience. Even when women are lucky enough to see the Block Development Officer, or one of his/her subordinates, the meeting might have to be set up by a male relative or local fixer (*dalaal*), and it is entirely likely that it will be interrupted by somebody with social clout. Waiting is something that poorer people do, and more than once we witnessed *adivasi* (tribal) women standing in the sun or rain for hours waiting their turn to see '*sarkar*' (government), sometimes refusing to go for lunch in case they 'lost their place'.

Now, most of us have queue-jumped at some point or another, even if it is simply to cut in front of another car at a motorway intersection or off-ramp. Some of us will also get around queues by purchasing a service with a credit card or on-line, a point I will come back to later. But for those of us brought up in England, a country in which queueing is supposedly valued, the behaviour I have just described would surely provoke a response. Take the case of a barbershop on a Saturday morning when trade is brisk. Every man or boy who takes a seat there forms a mental map of where he stands in line and of who was there before him. If he jumps in the barber's chair out of turn he must expect a rebuke. If he misses his place by just one person he might get off with a polite warning: 'it's my turn next', someone might say. But if he is foolish enough to jump ahead of three or four people he'll be asked 'what do you think you are doing?', or, more tellingly, 'who do you think you are?' This last question forces both parties to confront the question of social equality. Culturally, at least, the ethics of the queue, and of correct queueing behaviour, would seem to be strongly egalitarian.

Even in the breach this observation is confirmed, as my colleague Ian Gordon reminds me with an example. English readers will recognize the truth of his suggestion that train commuters observe a strange and tacit micro-ethics of queueing behaviour when they arrive at their home stations after work and begin searching for a taxi. Take a look at a commuter station at around 7 p.m. and you will see men and women running past fellow commuters to get a better position in the line for cabs. But once these commuters spill out of the station proper into the forecourt a sense of decorum takes over. Only the 'rudest' or 'most selfish' people want to be seen to overtake a fellow passenger in the highly visible space of ten or twenty yards that lies between the station entrance and the line of taxis. 'Morality' is suddenly restored and geography re-ordered.

So why are matters different in rural eastern India? One answer is that the conduct of social life there is regulated by the precepts not of *Homo aequalis* but of *Homo hierarchicus*. Louis Dumont (1972) argued this point in his classic account of the 'caste system and its implications'. In *Homo Hierarchicus* he suggested that secular power in traditional Hindu society is encompassed by and subordinate to religious values. The Kshatriya gives way to the Brahman within a system that encourages everyone to know their place, or that of their caste or *jati* (roughly, sub-caste). Asymmetrical relationships are religiously sanctioned, and the practices of everyday life are produced in accordance with a cosmology which marks individuals, families and social groups as more or less pure (the Brahmans, who embody the priestly qualities of reason and reflection that spring from the head of the supreme being; also the Kshatriyas, who take his shoulders and the kingly qualities of valour and leadership), and more or less impure (the Shudras, the peasants who toil in the fields; and the erstwhile Untouchables [now Harijans – Gandhi's Children of God, or Dalits – the oppressed, or Scheduled Castes], whose very presence can pollute the bodily integrity of members of the twice-born communities). To expect Western standards of 'civility' or balanced social intercourse in these circumstances, Dumont argues, is to fall victim to a form of Eurocentrism which refuses to recognize that different cultures dance to different beats.

Several aspects of Dumont's account have been critiqued by his fellow Indologists. The so-called neo-Hocartians, for example, including Gloria Raheja and Declan Quigley, prefer to think of 'the caste system' in core–periphery terms, with various castes (including Brahmans) entering into service relationships with dominant land-holding castes drawn from the Kshatriya community (Raheja, 1988; Quigley, 1993). Nick Dirks and others have gone further and argued that what we think of today as 'the caste system', with all its rigidities, was called into existence by colonial forms of governmentality, including, most notably, the decennial Census of British India that was begun in 1872. 'What we take now as caste is, in fact, the precipitate of a history that selected caste as the single and systematic category to name, and thereby contain, the Indian social order' (Dirks, 2001, p. 13).

Be this as it may, there is still considerable support for the view that 'the caste system' has helped to produce a sense of community that Satish Saberwal (1996) has described as cellular and fundamentally constrained in its sense of humanity at large. Saberwal argues that the caste Hindu gains his or her sense of self almost entirely with regard to the family, and the lineage or caste in which that family is situated. This sense of self is reproduced through tightly constrained marriage patterns, as well as by social taboos that make it difficult for members of some castes to eat food or share water together. The fact that Harijan *tolas* (hamlets) are usually separate from the main village – often to the south, the direction of death – is further evidence of this fractured sense of 'we-ness', as indeed is the propensity of some middle-class urbanites to throw garbage over the wall of their house into the street alongside.[2] A sense of public space is apparently as underdeveloped as is a sense of shared humanity or Indian-ness, and it should come as no surprise that some Indians will jump queues with little or no sense that they are 'doing wrong'. Members of the upper castes (mainly men, it should be said) simply do not recognize the claims to equality that standing in line would seem to imply. Just as importantly, nor do many government officers. Sudipta Kaviraj (1984, p. 227) has argued that the fundamental conceit of Nehruvian forms of rule in India has been to assume that the men and women charged with carrying out the will of New Delhi see the world in the same ways as their English-educated superiors. On the whole, says Kaviraj, they do not. The instructions of New Delhi are translated by men and women who might not share central government's stated concerns for the rights of formally equal human beings, or about the perils of nepotism or outright corruption. Very often, Kaviraj suggests, their local practices ensure that the modern state is grounded in vernacular feet of clay.[3]

Such arguments about the 'traditional autonomy of segmental codes', and the difficulty of ensuring 'an extensively binding normative order' in India (Saberwal, 1996, p. 65), have also been broached by Platteau and given greater reach. In an important paper published in the *Journal of Development Studies* (significantly), Platteau argued that the sorts of asymmetrical exchanges that one sees in India are far from being abnormal. In his view, indeed, it is 'the West' that is exceptional, for it is only in certain parts of north-western Europe, as well as in some of its ex-settler colonies and in post-Tokugawa Japan, that individuals have been produced as 'abstract actors in the sense that they are not socially differentiated before entering into the exchange process' (Platteau, 1994, p. 539). It is only in these regions, Platteau contends (following Max Weber), that the institutional bases of modern capitalism are fully provided, and that market societies can solve questions of trust on the basis of legal regimes rather than on the basis of personal reputations or force. What Platteau calls 'generalized morality' becomes the glue that allows some countries to 'prevent [the] enforcement costs of the rules of honesty from being excessively high – perhaps to the point of making the system unworkable' (p. 756). In countries that fail to develop the 'virtues of civic humanism' (p. 769), moralities remain limited to segmented social groups or ethnies, and the development of long-distance trade and divisions of labour becomes more difficult.

It would surely be consistent with Platteau's wider arguments about development to maintain that the rules of queueing will be adhered to most closely in societies that have 'shattered the fetters of the kinship group' (p. 769, after Weber, 1958, p. 237). Only in these societies are individuals constructed as persons of potentially equal worth, with equal rights that need to be respected by all other persons, regardless of their social connections. The sorts of behaviour that we witness in an orderly line, then, far from being trivial, might be counted as geographical markers of the production of political democracy.[4] This, I think, is the second major lesson that Platteau points us toward when he claims that

> if limited-group morality is understood as morally restricted to *concrete* people with whom one has close identification while generalized morality is morals applicable to abstract people (to whom one is not necessarily tied through personal, family or ethnic links), there is good sense in arguing that *the western world has a somewhat unique history rooted in a culture of individualism pervaded by norms of generalized morality.* (p. 770, emphases in the original)

Scarcity and Queueing Behaviour

Platteau is too good an economist to maintain that queues will *not* form in Africa or Asia, and I should be careful about putting words in his mouth here. Nevertheless, the thrust of his remarks is to suggest that queue-jumping will be the norm in societies that fail to establish a culture of generalized morality or civic humanism. If we care about such things as orderly and egalitarian queues, we are likely to be disappointed if we expect progress any time soon.

But is this really the case? A moment's reflection suggests that matters are more complicated. I have several times set down at Howrah (Calcutta) or New Delhi Railway Stations and found myself in long and orderly lines for taxis. It is true that most of my fellow queuers were members of the Indian middle class: we were waiting for cars, not auto-rickshaws. But if class is such an important factor, it suggests that an explanation of queueing behaviour based upon religiosity or some other deep-seated cultural variable needs considerable qualification. Moral systems collide and overlap more often than Platteau's model allows. Just as importantly, I have had many chances to observe how commuters to London behave in the rush hour when they are trying to get home. Trains for Cambridge leave King's Cross every thirty minutes at this time, but there are still not enough seats to meet demand. People who get to the station twenty or twenty-five minutes ahead of time know that they should stand on the platform at those points where X literally marks the spot. All being well, these are the points where the doors will open on an incoming train. Later arrivals will form a penumbra around the first two or three individuals, leaving strange gaps between the Xs (strange, at any rate, to someone not used to the scramble for seats at this time). And when the train does arrive, it is not uncommon for English 'civility' or phlegm to disappear. Although people know perfectly well who was at the track-side before them, this knowledge doesn't seem to count for a lot. In the barbershop there is always the fear of reproach, or of being shamed in front of other people. But here the crowd dissolves into anonymity and large numbers of people will start shoving. Being old or frail sometimes makes a difference, and some people will remember their 'manners', but this is not to be counted on. For the most part, behaviour becomes competitive and selfish, and far removed from the canons of generalized morality.

Why is this? The simple answer is that queueing behaviour is highly contextual. I am most likely to queue patiently when certain conditions are met. If I arrive at Cambridge station at 8 a.m. and see a single line snaking towards the ticket counter, I am more likely to consider this fair than when I see six lines making their way to six ticket counters. What if I end up in the wrong line, behind someone who is booking fifteen different tickets or who has an itinerary that needs discussion with the booking agent? I am also likely to behave calmly when I can see ticket machines in the booking hall. If I have a credit card with me, these provide me with choice, and work to keep the main line shorter. And if I arrive at 11 a.m., I know that I will have no difficulty getting a seat on a direct train to London. Waiting in the ticket hall for five minutes isn't a big deal. In addition, but very importantly, when I queue at Cambridge station, or at city hall to get a parking permit, I do so in the expectation that I will be treated fairly and with respect. Personalities differ, of course, and we can all have bad days, but for the most part I don't have to worry about someone doing their job, or simply disappearing for a while when I am trying to talk to them. Nor do I worry about that person's relatives or close friends pushing ahead of me. And if this should happen, I can do something about it. I can protest or appeal, and expect to be listened to. I have a sense of my rights, and of the accountability of public officials. These rights also extend to the right not to be shamed in public, as Adam Smith once put it: not to be humiliated or treated with disrespect. Civility comes fairly easily in these circumstances, just as it can disappear when I am anxious to get home on Monday night to watch football, and when I don't want to stand all the way from London to Cambridge. Never mind English reserve when everyone else is maximizing his or her self-interest.

Now consider parts of Africa, or India, or even southern Italy or Miami. It probably is the case that one observes 'anti-social' behaviour there more often than one does in Wisconsin or Cheshire, at least when it comes to driving standards or queueing/queue-jumping. But we should be wary of ascribing this to culture in some 'fixed' or primordial sense. Cultures are more open and mobile than stereotypes suggest, and the production of cultural rules has a good deal to do with economic pressures and systems of governmentality. Albert Hirschman (1967) recognized this long ago when he pondered the inefficiency of the Nigerian railway system. What interested him was the fact that the Nigerian Railway Corporation performed so badly even though it was faced with competition from long-distance road haulage companies. In his view, this paradox was explicable only in terms of the peculiar combination of exit and voice that he found in Nigeria: 'exit did not have its usual attention-focusing effect because the loss of revenue was not a matter of gravity for management [which could dip into the public treasury in times of deficit], while voice was not aroused and therefore the potentially most vocal customers were the first ones to abandon the railroads for the trucks' (Hirschman, 1970, p. 45). Fellow Nigerians were then saddled with an inefficient and over-subsidized public railway system, and an arena of exchanges between officialdom and ordinary citizens which encouraged 'an oppression of the weak by the incompetent and an exploitation of the poor by the lazy' (p. 59). The endless delays that railway users encountered, which began with long and perhaps raucous queues to get tickets in the first place, were caused, finally, by a 'combination of exit and voice [that] was particularly noxious' (p. 45) and which made civil behaviour unlikely.

Hirschman, in other words, sought to understand the behaviour of government officials, and by implication the behaviour of people queueing to see government employees, in terms of a resolutely materialist account of the production of public mores. The weak and the poor were oppressed by the lazy and the incompetent not because of a lack of generalized morality, but because of a lack of political will at the highest levels. The managers of the railway system in Nigeria were no more called to account for their behaviour (in terms of fiscal probity) than were their employees on the tracks, in the trains, and in the ticket booths. Lack of accountability led directly, Hirschman suggests, to a lack of efficiency and courtesy, and this in turn would have caused the customers of the railway system to respond, quite rationally, with a similar lack of civility. Men and (some) women will burst in on public servants when they feel this will work, or when they see others doing it. They will also be minded to queue-jump in this way when they are in a hurry, and in recognition of the fact that 'the state' commands little respect – either for its efficiency or for its fairness.[5] Queueing shouldn't always be seen in the romantic and solidaristic terms with which I began this chapter. It's one thing to spend the odd night on the streets of Birmingham, England, queueing with friends in the 1970s to see Led Zeppelin or the Rolling Stones at the city's Odeon Theatre, but it's quite another matter to spend large parts of a working day obtaining permits or even basic goods from government offices or state-run shops. When the state appears as an enemy or deadweight, it is almost inevitable that people will seek to hide from it, or to engage it as rapidly as possible. Alan Bleasdale made this point very powerfully in *Boys From the Blackstuff*, his dramatization of how certain Liverpudlians survived by 'milking the system' during the Thatcher administrations of the 1980s. And we see it vividly in contemporary India, or in parts of post-debt crisis Latin America, where middle-class families routinely employ people to queue for them. Only poor people queue, we said before, and there is a good deal of truth to this. But if better-off people aren't queueing, this isn't only because of their rudeness or their willingness to disregard the rights of others; it is also because they *can* circumvent some lines, and have strong economic reasons for doing so.

On still other occasions, queues take shape in the wake of the 'absolute' scarcity of the state or service provider. Queues always form in relation to some measure of scarcity, of course. When we are made to stand in line at a post office in the UK it is because there aren't as many open windows as customers. But most of us accept this as a fact of life, and recognize that it would be absurd for the Post Office to employ thousands more counter staff to meet the surges of people that will occur from time to time. (That said, take a look at a post office queue early on a benefits day like Thursday: what you will see is far from a random cross-section of British society.) Matters are very different, however, in some Blocks of Ranchi District, Jharkhand, where I have been working for over twenty years. In Lapong Block the state has been reduced to an unpainted shell of a building that houses the Block Development Officer (BDO) and two or three support staff. Most of the files that should be in the Block Office, and which would speed the business of state, have gone missing. Given the lack of electricity and of a local school, too, it is unlikely that the BDO will spend as much time in his office as he might otherwise, or as his contract might require of him.

Even in neighbouring Bihar, where the infrastructures of rule are sometimes in better supply, there can still be chronic problems of state scarcity at the level of personnel. It is common nowadays for agencies like the World Bank to talk about the inefficiency of public sector workers, and for good reason in some cases. But even with the best will in the world it is difficult for the men and women who run the Block Development Office in Sahar Block, Bhojpur District, or Bidupur Block, Vaishali District, to keep up with the flood of government schemes that have been announced since the end of the 1970s. Much like the pen-pushing schoolteachers and police officers of Blairite Britain, these government employees are simply required to do too much. By 1999, the Block Offices in Sahar and Bidupur were receiving six to eight times the funds flow they would have dealt with in 1979. Each Block Office was required to run 100–30 food for work (JRY) or employment assurance schemes, as well as to provide 1,000 new homes annually under the Indira Awas scheme and 500 wells under the Million Wells scheme. This was in addition to the usual work of administering pensions, responding to disputes, and so on, and the work had to be carried out, in Sahar Block, across fifty-five villages in twelve *panchayats* (councils), many of which are very difficult to access, and some of which are unreachable in the rainy season. (The Block Office in Vaishali has to serve 133 villages in 24 *panchayats*, but communications are rather better, and the BDO is not faced by a left-wing insurgency [the Naxalite movement] or the private armies [*Senas*] of the upper castes.) The BDO is helped by a Head Assistant, two Assistants and an Accountant (*Nazir*), as well as by two Junior Engineers and an Assistant Engineer on the technical side, and nine Village-Level Workers and twenty-four *panchayat sewaks* (council volunteers). Together, they have to serve the interests of perhaps 30,000 to 50,000 people, something which can't be done. Not surprisingly, people with power or money do what they can to 'capture' the state (including meeting with the BDO) as and when they need to, which can be quite often given the heavily bureaucratized nature of civilian life in India. The scarcity of the state, then, as much as its inefficiency and monopolistic powers, helps to produce forms of behaviour that exclude the poorest and which seemingly can be read as evidence of different (possibly 'worse') cultural standards.

The Responsibilities of Critique

There is much more that could be said about queueing behaviour in different contexts. It is a hugely under-researched subject (try typing the word into Amazon's list of books), and yet I suspect it has a lot to teach us about the conduct of everyday life, as well as about the construction of a sense of self, the other, the state, and even of modernity. There is a well-respected tradition of social science that tends to work downwards from large concepts like 'globalization', or the 'world city' or the 'world system'. Geography is then presented as the working out of these primeval forces. But we should not lose sight of an inductivist tradition which investigates the making of modern life through more discrete topics like the geography of offshore banking (Hudson, 1996), or the history of commodities like marijuana, salt or tea (Davenport-Hines, 2002; Kurlansky, 2003; MacFarlane and MacFarlane, 2003), or the moral panics surrounding masturbation (Lacqueur, 2003). We could produce interesting multi-scalar geographies by focusing on the production and consumption of chewing gum or guns, for example, just as we might illuminate the histories of post-war England or the Soviet Union by pressing more firmly on their local histories of queueing. In some countries, perhaps, the queue will become a site of resistance, or of public order concerns. And in practically all countries it offers a peculiarly public performance of governmentality, or what Foucault called the ethical government of the self (see Dean, 1999, Chap. 1).

Rather than follow this lead, however, I want to close this chapter by looking at queue-jumping from a public policy perspective. One of the things I find admirable in David Smith's work is its seriousness when it comes to public policy. In the 1970s and 1980s it became fashionable in some parts of human geography to blame everything on capitalism. In the 1990s it was modernity that took a pounding in some quarters, along with the idea of 'development'. And it is easy to see why. It is not difficult to show that capitalism is associated with the production of entrenched inequalities at all spatial scales, or with the privatization of space, or with a necessary tendency to boom and bust. By the same token, it is not hard to see why Arturo Escobar (1995, p. 4) writes that: 'The debt crisis, the Sahelian famine, increasing poverty, malnutrition, and violence are only the most pathetic signs of the failure of forty years of development.' It is also true that geography has gained enormously from the 'critical' turns of the past thirty or so years, and that our understandings of the world have been deepened substantially by David Harvey's (1982) work on the limits to capital, or Michael Watts' (1983) work on the silent violence of commoditization in northern Nigeria, or Felix Driver's (2000) work on the colonial origins of modern academic geography. Driver's work, indeed, seems to provide precisely that sort of inside-out reading of the production of technologies of rule that I alluded to earlier. In much of this work, too, we get a sense that things might be different, and this is important. Public intellectuals need to have a sense of alternatives, and perhaps even of utopias. At any rate, they need to take seriously Max Weber's injunction that 'the true function of social science is to render problematic that which is conventionally self-evident'.[6]

We might want to tread carefully, however, before offering forms of critique that are 'covering' and/or 'associational' in form, or which fail to specify the costs of their own (implicit or explicit) public policy (or political) proposals. By a covering critique I mean a form of argument which refuses the possibility of reform in object x by insisting that all forms of x (capitalism, say, or modernity or development) are equally as bad, and take shape under the cover of similar laws or tendencies. In this way, Escobar can write off 'development' by reference to the work of Walt Rostow or US aid policy in Colombia in the 1950s. A more recent concern for participatory development or sustainable development apparently counts for little when set against the essentially imitative and colonial nature of Development with a capital D. By an associational argument I mean a form of reasoning which is able to show that capitalism (in this case) is associated with the production of a, b and c (pollution, inequality and instability), but which fails to consider whether these same consequences might be produced under non-capitalist forms of production and exchange. It also fails to list the benefits that might be particular to certain types of capitalism. Associational arguments are often linked with a reluctance to specify the opportunity costs of the actions they are proposing: of organizing a socialist society, for example, or of delinking from the world system in order to create a zone for post-developmentalist alternatives. Yet any argument for socialism must be weakened to the extent that one could show that it is associated with problems d, e and f, as well as with a and c. Likewise, people might be less persuaded of the merits of post-developmentalism if they were apprised of its likely costs. They might prefer to fight for greater control over the *very diverse* circuits, practices and institutions that make for what we conventionally (and for convenience) call 'development'.

I think this perspective is one that David Smith might share, for it is one that I have encountered in several of his writings. In the 1970s David wrote extensively on questions of inequality and welfare (Smith, 1973, 1977, 1979). Unlike David Harvey, however, who wrote penetratingly on the laws of motion of capitalism, he refused to jump to the conclusion that 'liberal' views of the city (or of other sites of inequality) had to be ditched in favour of a 'scientific' Marxism which insisted that: 'It remains for revolutionary theory to chart the path from an urbanism based in exploitation to an urbanism appropriate for the human species' (Harvey, 1973, p. 314). And in this judgement he was surely right. For all its brilliance, Harvey's call for a 'revolutionary practice [that would] accomplish such a transformation' must have seemed not just romantic but also disturbingly thin on details (not to mention costs).

Reading David Smith's work, in contrast, one gets a strong sense of the 'raw nerve of outrage' being kept alive, to borrow E. P. Thompson's felicitious phrase (not least in his work on apartheid South Africa: Smith, 1985), even as one is reminded of the enormous difficulties of formulating practical policies for dealing with such matters as health care reform in the

UK (Smith, 1995). Suggesting that life might be better under a non-capitalist regime does not always make for sound public policy. David's willingness to link moral reasoning to determinate policy suggestions might also usefully inform an approach to the 'problem' of queue-jumping with which I began this chapter. When I said in the introduction that I leaned more to Hirschman than to Platteau it was with public policy in mind. We can learn a great deal about 'theory' and 'models' by attending to the policy implications that are thought (or which might be said) to flow from them.

I read Platteau much as I read Putnam on the formation of social capital (Putnam with Leonardo and Nanetti, 1993). 'Cultures' take on a sedimentary quality in these accounts, and are difficult to shift as a result. While politicians might read Putnam in terms of a discourse of social engineering – let's build up dense networks of trust and social interaction in a few short years – the real thrust of his work on social capital in Italy is to highlight an extraordinary degree of path dependence: north and south have supposedly been on different trajectories for a millennium. Platteau might be read and critiqued in similar terms. While it is clear that behaviour is learned, and that we need to respect 'cultural differences' (cf. Dumont), we should be wary of assuming that 'cultures' are set in stone, or that moral principles are distributed between countries on an either/or (generalized/limited) basis.

The willingness of more powerful people in India to jump queues might well be bound up with a lack of respect for some of their fellow 'in-liners', and perhaps even with a limited sense of fellowship itself. One can't help feeling, however, that the sort of anti-social behaviour that queue-jumping represents can be tackled quite directly, and without resort to cultural generalizations. In Miami, for example, where some motorists will 'cheat' on a daily basis when approaching the one-lane off-ramp from the Palmetto Expressway to Interstate 75, apparently ingrained behaviour could be changed by linking a system of fines to a robust system of surveillance. There is no need to invoke stereotypes about 'Latino' driving habits. Meanwhile, in rural India, the often humiliating positions in which poorer people are placed when dealing with 'the state' could be improved by a range of tangible actions, the net effect of which would be to challenge the very culture of hierarchy and disrespect which Dumont sees as the bedrock of Hindu culture.

The World Bank likes to place emphasis here on public service reforms, and not without reason. Public officials might be provided with material and other incentives for respecting queues, or for treating poorer people with dignity. On occasions, too, the state might be asked to take on a more regulatory role. Sanjay Kumar and I have documented the fact that in Jharkhand, in the mid-1990s, a poor tribal villager had to make contact with state officials on forty-five occasions to obtain a permit to cut down ten jackfruit trees on his private (homestead) land (Corbridge and Kumar, 2002). He was often made to wait for several hours, and treated with disrespect. He also had to hand over small bribes or commissions, and several times witnessed more powerful men jump in front of him (or the *dalaal* working for him) in what passed for a queue. In this case, it would make sense to scrap the system of permits and to encourage the Forest Department, instead, to regulate a quasi-privatized trade in some timbers. Queue-jumping would not then be an issue. On other occasions the appropriate response might be to build up state capacity, as I indicated would be necessary in Lapong Block, Ranchi District, Jharkhand. Some queues, and thus some incentives to jump queues, are encouraged by the relative scarcity of the state, whether in terms of personnel, training, record keeping or technology. Finally, and not unrelatedly, I should mention that a non-governmental organization in Rajasthan, western India, the Mazdoor Kisan Shakti Sangathan (MKSS), has made major inroads into a culture of queue-jumping, by providing poorer people with information about their rights vis-à-vis the state (Jenkins and Goetz, 1999). The apparently simple act of providing citizens with access to a photocopier has helped here, for it has enabled poorer people to compare the way they are treated by the state with what the statute book says should be the case. With paper memory comes accountability, or at least a battle for accountability. And with that, one might hope, comes a battle also for equality of treatment under the law, and a challenge to a 'culture' (or what I would call an existing set of rules and incentives) that allows queue-jumping.

Such changes are slowly being brought about in India, and they provide testimony to the importance of combining moral and material discourses in a discriminating and determinate fashion.[7] David Smith has rightly insisted on the importance of the normative in human geography, but he has also shown us that little is to be gained (indeed much can be lost) by indulging in sweeping and moralistic denunciations of capitalism, or development, or modernity. This brief study of queueing and queue-jumping has tried to make the same point, albeit in a lesser register. Social scientists should not give up the right to be judgmental. Queue-jumping is not on a par with inflicting bodily harm, but it is overwhelmingly an affront to the poor (and poorer women especially), and it is roundly condemned by the poor themselves. At the same time, however, we should be wary of invoking an overly generalized account of the causes of queue-jumping, such as we might expect to find in Dumont or Platteau. The fact that queue-jumping might effectively be addressed by material and institutional changes points up once more the dangers of conflating moral geographies and politically romantic geographies, and of disregarding the lessons of public policy analysis.[8] David Smith's career has shown us how much we gain from not taking this road.

NOTES

1   See Gupta (1995, 1998) on blurred boundaries, and Fuller and Benei (2001) for an excellent collection of essays on the everyday state and society in modern India.

2   For an interesting discussion of 'garbage, modernity and the citizen's gaze', see Chakrabarty (2002, Chap. 5). Chakrabarty offers a typically sensitive account of the ways in which 'dirty spaces' were produced within both colonial and nationalist discourses, but his concluding remarks come close to valorizing dirt as a form of resistance to Westernization. 'Through what historical process of subject formation', he asks, 'did long life, good health, more money, small families, and modern science come to appear so natural and God given?' (p. 79). Equally relevant questions might be these: 'who tips rubbish on whom?'; and 'what evidence is there to suggest that most poor people don't value good sanitation or longer life?'

3   For sympathetic critiques, see Corbridge and Harriss (2000), and Osella and Osella (2001).

4   Albeit at a limited spatial scale. The production of seemingly endless, if often orderly, queues in the Soviet Union was a result of excessive state regulation and the absence of countervailing voices.

5   I am grateful to Pilar Saborio for prompting on this point.

6   This has long been one of my favourite quotes, and I owe it to Derek Gregory. If truth be told, though, I have yet to locate it in Weber's writings! On the matter of utopias, while I salute the intention of the Appendix to David Harvey's (2000) book *Spaces of Hope*, I do think his discussion of utopias betrays an unwillingness to deal with practical politics that speaks to, and calls into question, his brilliant and yet essentialized account of capitalism and its supposed effects. I deal with what I call the 'associational fallacy' in the next paragraph. See also Corbridge (1998).

7   Like all such proposals, these are not costless. Deregulating the trade in certain timbers, for example, might lead to the production of private monopolies or excessive deforestation. Increasing the pay of government servants might lead to less spending on capital projects. And so on. My point, simply, is that this is where the hard work of politics – and of theory, importantly – begins. Disdain for detail can lead to forms of theory and politics that are transcendentalist, and/or which offer overly enchanted readings of the possibilities of empowerment. Hardt and Negri's (2001) account of *Empire* is an obvious case in point (see Corbridge, 2003).

8   Max Weber described with great clarity the duties of an intellectual who stands in the service of 'moral forces'. He said these duties are bound up with attempts to make clear 'what is at stake when we try to govern in a particular way... [it entails] an analytics of government [that] allows us to accept a sense of responsibility for the consequences and effects of thinking and acting in certain ways' (Dean, 1999, p. 36, developing Weber, 1972). Quite so.

REFERENCES

Chakrabarty, D. (2002) *Habitations of Modernity: Essays in the Wake of Subaltern Studies*, Chicago: University of Chicago Press.

Corbridge, S. (1998) ' "Beneath the pavement only soil": the poverty of post-development', *Journal of Development Studies* 34 (6), 138–48.

Corbridge, S. (2003), 'Countering Empire', *Antipode* 35, 184–90.

Corbridge, S. and Harriss, J. (2000) *Reinventing India: Liberalization, Hindu Nationalism and Popular Democracy*, Cambridge: Polity.

Corbridge, S. and Kumar, S. (2002) 'Community, corruption, landscape: tales from the tree trade', *Political Geography* 21, 765–88.

Corbridge, S., Williams, G., Srivastava, M. and Véron, R. (2005) *Seeing the State: Governance and Governmentality in Rural India*, Cambridge: Cambridge University Press.

Davenport-Hines, R. (2002) *The Pursuit of Oblivion: A Global History of Narcotics*, New York: Norton.

Dean, M. (1999) *Governmentality: Power and Rule in Modern Society*, London: Sage.

Dirks, N. (2001) *Castes of Mind: Colonialism and the Making of Modern India*, Princeton: Princeton University Press.

Driver, F. (2000) *Geography Militant: Cultures of Exploration and Empire*, Oxford: Blackwell.

Dumont, L. (1972) *Homo Hierarchicus: The Caste System and Its Implications*, London: Paladin.

Escobar, A. (1995) *Encountering Development: The Making and Unmaking of the Third World*, Princeton: Princeton University Press.

Fuller, C. and Benei, V. (eds) (2001) *The Everyday State and Society in Modern India*, London: Hurst and Company.

Gupta, A. (1995) 'Blurred boundaries: the discourse of corruption, the culture of politics and the imagined state', *American Ethnologist* 22, 375–402.

Gupta, A. (1998) *Postcolonial Developments: Agriculture in the Making of Modern India*, Durham, NC: University of North Carolina Press.

Hardt, M. and Negri, A. (2001) *Empire*, Cambridge, Mass.: Harvard University Press.

Harvey, D. (1973) *Social Justice and the City*, London: Edward Arnold.

Harvey, D. (1982) *The Limits to Capital*, Oxford: Blackwell.

Harvey, D. (2000) *Spaces of Hope*, Berkeley: University of California Press.

Hirschman, A. (1967) *Development Projects Observed*, Washington, DC: Brookings Institution.

Hirschman, A. (1970) *Exit, Voice and Loyalty*, Cambridge, Mass.: Harvard University Press.

Hudson, A. (1996) *Nation-States in a Globalizing Economy: Offshore Banking in the Bahamas and Cayman Islands*, unpublished PhD dissertation, University of Cambridge.

Jenkins, R. and Goetz, A.-M. (1999) 'Accounts and accountability: theoretical implications of the right to information movement in India', *Third World Quarterly* 20, 589–608.

Kaviraj, S. (1984) 'On the crisis of political institutions in India', *Contributions to Indian Sociology* 18, 223–43.

Kurlansky, M. (2003) *Salt: A World History*, New York: Penguin.

Lacqueur, T. W. (2003) *Solitary Sex: A Cultural History of Masturbation*, New York: Zone Books.

MacFarlane, A. and MacFarlane, I. (2003) *Green Gold: The Empire of Tea*, London: Ebury Press.

Osella, F. and Osella, C. (2001) 'The return of King Mahabali: the politics of morality in Kerala', in C. Fuller and V. Benei (eds), *The Everyday State and Society in Modern India*, London: Hurst and Company, pp. 137–62.

Platteau, J.-P. (1994) 'Behind the market stage where real societies exist, parts I and II', *Journal of Development Studies* 30, 533–77, 753–817.

Putnam, R. with Leonardo, R. and Nanetti, R. (1993) *Making Democracy Work: Civic Traditions in Modern Italy*, Princeton: Princeton University Press.

Quigley, D. (1993) *The Interpretation of Caste*, Oxford: Clarendon Press.

Raheja, G. G. (1988) 'India: caste, kingship and dominance reconsidered', *Annual Review of Anthropology* 17, 497–522.

Saberwal, S. (1996) *The Roots of Crisis: Interpreting Contemporary Indian Society*, Delhi: Oxford University Press.

Smith, D. M. (1973) *The Geography of Social Well-Being in the United States: An Introduction to Territorial Social Indicators*, New York: McGraw-Hill.

Smith, D. M. (1977) *Human Geography: A Welfare Approach*, London: Edward Arnold.

Smith, D. M. (1979) *Where the Grass is Greener: Living in an Unequal World*, Harmondsworth: Penguin.

Smith, D. M. (1985) *Apartheid in South Africa*, Cambridge: Cambridge University Press.

Smith, D. M. (1995) 'Geography, health and social justice: looking for the "right theory"', *Critical Public Health* 6 (3), 5–11.

Watts, M. (1983) *Silent Violence: Food, Famine and Peasantry in Northern Nigeria*, Berkeley: University of California Press.

Weber, M. (1958) *The Religion of China: Confucianism and Taoism* (trans. H. H. Gerth), Glencoe, Ill.: Free Press.

Weber, M. (1972) *From Max Weber: Essays in Sociology* (ed. and trans. H. H. Gerth and C. W. Mills), London: Routledge and Kegan Paul.

13

Moral Geographies of Sexual Citizenship

Gill Valentine

Introduction

Since the late twentieth century the length of time that young people are legally defined as dependent on their parent(s) has tended to be extended, by an increase in the school leaving age and by more stringent benefits entitlements. Paradoxically, however, this period has also been marked by popular anxiety that the length of childhood is in practice contracting. The media, fashion industry and technology have all been accused of undermining children's innocence, and blurring the boundaries between adults and children. In particular, some commentators have argued that the growing commodification of young people is eroding childhood as a distinctive stage, as young people are taking on all of the trappings of adulthood at an earlier age, from wearing clothes seen as fashionable or provocative, consumption of drugs, drink, and so on, to physical relationships, and in the process are being sexualized prematurely (Postman, 1982). Diduck (1999), for example, suggests that the increasing numbers of children acting in unchildlike ways is causing a contemporary debate about what constitutes childhood. This chapter focuses on one aspect of this general moral concern about the sexualization of childhood: young people's sex education. It explores the debates about whether childhood should be a protected space free from the allegedly pernicious influences of the adult sexual world by considering the specific case of the introduction, and subsequent attempts to repeal, legislation in the UK that sought to regulate young people's awareness of homosexuality.

In 1988 the then Conservative government of the UK, led by Margaret Thatcher, passed a new Local Government Act. This sparked a national moral debate because of the inclusion of section 28, which stated that '[a] local authority shall not intentionally promote homosexuality or publish material with the intention of promoting homosexuality'. In 1997 and again in 2001, when Tony Blair's Labour government was returned to power, amongst its pledges was a commitment to lesbian and gay rights. Recent initiatives to equalize the age of consent for heterosexuals and lesbians and gay men at 16, and to enable lesbians and gay men to be members of the armed forces, were followed by attempts to repeal section 28 of the Local Government Act 1988 (successfully in the Scottish parliament in 2000, and eventually in the UK parliament in 2003). In the process old wounds were reopened about the role of the school in moral education, about boundaries between public and private moralities, the creation of a safe/unsafe space for 'childhood', and about the relationship between morality and national identity. In the following sections of this chapter I explore each of these diverse geographies of morality, beginning with consideration of the way that morality is constituted through the specific space of the school.

Public Morality: The Space of the School as a Site of Moral Engineering

Despite the fact that sex is often popularly imagined to be a private matter, it is the subject of much public concern, debate and legislation. Weeks (1985, p. 4) describes sex as 'a contested zone, a moral and political battlefield'. The school is the site where these skirmishes are often played out because it offers universal access to the citizens of the future. It is in this public space that hegemonic or official representations of personal and public morality can be instilled.

Indeed, the origins of mass schooling in the UK lie in part in the concerns of middle-class Victorians to inculcate morality and discipline into working-class children at a time when the brutal exploitation of child labour in factories and the absence of a welfare system meant that children were being dehumanized. Takanshi (1978, p. 13) describes how in the nineteenth century 'ragged unsupervised children roved the streets in small bands, sometimes stealing and breaking store windows'. With juvenile delinquency emerging as a perceived threat to moral and social stability '[s]chools were to act as "moral hospitals" and provide corrective training' (May, 1973, p. 12). In particular, schools were to civilize children by instilling in them particular forms of bodily control, comportment and moral values that would eventually allow them to be admitted into adult society (Elias, 1939). Although not a school per se, the playground movement, in the nineteenth-century United States, was, likewise, regarded as a solution to a perceived loss of morality brought about by the onset of modernity. The belief was that through physical discipline and control, immigrant children in particular would develop the normative gender qualities and moral behaviour necessary to become appropriate US citizens (Gagen, 2000). Despite the fact that in the twenty-first century moral codes of behaviour are perhaps less explicitly articulated, schools are still a 'hotbed of moral geographies', with conventions about how children ought to learn and behave being embedded in contemporary classrooms (Fielding, 2000).

The specific origins of school sex education have been shown by historians to be rooted in moralist and eugenic concerns about: the breakdown of the family; changing roles/expectations of women; differential birth rates across the social classes; and racial purity (Mort, 1987; Thomson, 1993). Sex education was therefore introduced to define and reinforce normative definitions of appropriate sexuality, particularly the moral 'norms' to which individuals should conform; and to address the negative consequences of immoral sexuality (such as unwanted pregnancy, venereal disease, etc.). Foucault's (1981) *History of Sexuality* clearly demonstrates that there is nothing 'natural' or 'normal' about sexual practices; rather, in different places, and at different historical periods, common agreement about what is 'normal' and what is offensive have varied considerably. However, the persistent dominant discourse is that heterosexuality is 'natural' and homosexuality is 'deviant'. This is the prescriptive model that is reproduced and confirmed through sex education.

School sex education in general, and specifically the debates about the repeal of section 28, which prohibited the promotion of homosexuality, contains a whole raft of assumptions: about childhood; sexuality; the relationship between public and private; and about the space of the school.

Historically, there have been two dominant, and competing, sets of ideas about childhood, which Jenks (1996) dubs Dionysian and Apollonian. Dionysian understandings of childhood drew on the notion of original sin, regarding the child as primitive or already fallen. Apollonian views of childhood imagined the child as fundamentally pure and innocent, drawing heavily on Rousseau's romantic portraits of children's natural virtues and talents. These contested notions of childhood gradually combined to produce the powerful ideal of the twentieth-/twenty-first-century child as innocent of the adult world (particularly in relation to sex) but potentially corruptible and so in need of protection (Valentine, 1996a). This understanding underpins the notion of sex education. Children are assumed to be uncomplicatedly asexual. Indeed, historically, and in many contemporary homes, there is a conspiracy of silence about sex in front of young children. Instead, schools are usually regarded as the best place for sexual knowledge to be made available to the young as the gap is closed between childhood and adulthood because teachers are understood as best placed to judge when and how children should be enlightened (Wyness, 1997; Jackson and

Scott, 1999; Valentine, 2004). Yet, at the same time, schools themselves are imagined to be desexualized environments.

Although section 28 did not ban the inclusion of lesbian and gay issues within sex education, the political climate within which it was introduced was very conservative. The assumption was that knowledge about homosexuality should not be made accessible to children as this would be tantamount to encouraging or inciting them to experiment with their sexuality. In the mid- to late 1980s the Department of Education (now Department for Education and Skills) fired off various circulars to schools stressing the need for them to help pupils understand the 'benefits of stable married and family life and the responsibilities of parenthood' (Moran, 2001, p. 78). One such circular stated that 'there is no place in any school in any circumstance for teaching which advocates homosexual behaviour, which presents it as the "norm" or which encourages homosexual experimentation by pupils' (Moran, 2001, p. 78). Although section 28 was never put to the judicial test because no prosecution was ever made in connection with it, and indeed it was badly drafted and probably unenforceable, nonetheless it was symbolically very important because it showed official and legal disapproval of homosexuality (Epstein, 2000). Local authorities and schools were scared to risk breaching the act, and as such it 'had an affective life and a symbolic affect of far more importance than its legal, institutional power' (Moran, 2001, p. 74). When Tony Blair's Labour government initiated attempts to repeal section 28, it caused a moral panic amongst right-wing politicians, commentators and some church leaders,[1] who argued that legislative change might threaten children's innocence by exposing them to inappropriate information (Moran, 2001). For example, in parliamentary debates about the repeal of section 28 its opponents conjured up a vision of children being force-fed gay sex education at school and of taxpayers' money being spent on promoting homosexuality and teaching children that homosexuality is the same as marriage (*Hansard*, 23 March 2000 and 30 March 2000, cited in Moran, 2001, p. 81). In particular, church leaders were angry at the prospect of schools representing a moral equivalence between heterosexuality and homosexuality (Brown and Sullivan, 2000).

Embedded in both the original conception of section 28, and the fears about its repeal, was an assumption that teenage sexuality is emergent rather than predetermined and thus, if 'innocent' young people are subject to 'undesirable' influences before what Epstein, Johnson and Steinberg (2000, p. 17) term the 'age of fixation', they might be 'turned' lesbian or gay. Moreover, some commentators argued that if young people's sexual identities are unsettled during adolescence and they make the 'wrong' choice at this stage of life, it is irreversible. For example, in a House of Commons debate about the age of consent, the Conservative MP Ann

Widdecombe argued that: '[it is] wrong...that a young person of 16 should be free in law to embark on a course of action that might lead to a lifestyle that would separate him, perhaps permanently, from the mainstream life of marriage and family' (*Hansard*, 10 February 2000, cited in Moran, 2001, p. 83). At the same time, some lesbian and gay groups claimed that young people's sexuality is not fluid but rather is fixed, arguing that section 28 is unnecessary because individuals are born lesbian and gay or heterosexual so that the 'promotion of homosexuality' will not 'corrupt' children. Somewhat paradoxically, therefore, debates about the repeal of section 28 tried to suppress ideas about childhood sexuality through recourse to notions of innocence, while at the same time creating it as a public problem (Moran, 2001).

There was also an implicit spatiality to the representation of sexualities in these debates, in that section 28 represented a return to a narrow expectation that public spaces, such as the school, are the space of 'the normal' (although at the same time it is rarely acknowledged that this space is sexualized, or rather heterosexualized); and that homosexuality is only to be tolerated when it is articulated in private and is therefore hidden (Valentine, 2003). When homosexuality is made visible in 'public' space (such as through sex education in schools or other forms of public knowledge, or what might be regarded as 'promotion'), it is assumed to threaten heterosexuality, which is represented as inherently unstable and fragile. Indeed, in debates around section 28, lesbians and gay men have variously been accused of having the power to undermine the social order by corrupting the young, destroying the family, eroding the nation's morality and even threatening its competitiveness in a global economy (Epstein et al., 2000). At the same time, the moral panic around the introduction of section 28 in terms of the dangers of public knowledge about homosexuality also helped to deflect attention from the growing public awareness about domestic violence and child sex abuse and therefore from opening up questions about the private space of the family home and 'normality' (Thomson, 1993).

Finally, the debates about the repeal of section 28 generated assumptions about the space of the school and about children's lack of agency. Implicit in the desire to limit children's information about homosexuality is an assumption, noted above, that schools are asexual environments, and that despite the porosity of these spaces in the globalized age of the Internet, children can still be protected from uncomfortable 'secrets' until it is appropriate for them to be enlightened through education. Yet '[s]chools are sites in which sexualities and sexual identities are developed, practiced and actively produced through daily routines' (Lahelma, Palmu and Gordon, 2000, p. 463). Heterosexuality (in terms of reference to marriage, gender roles, etc.) is taught implicitly and explicitly from an early age, while reference to homosexuality in the curriculum is usually minimal or only in negative terms (Rogers, 1994; Wallis and VanEvery, 2000). Indeed, HIV/AIDS education, while making visible gay lifestyles and practices that were not previously acknowledged in sex education, has tended to align the disease with gay men rather than with sexual practices *per se*, thus further stigmatizing homosexuality (Stacey, 1991; Thomson, 1993; Quinvalen, 1996).

Children's own peer group cultures are saturated with the pressure to conform to gender identities defined within a heterosexual matrix (Valentine, 2000; Holloway and Valentine, 2003). As social actors in their own right, young people, especially boys, actively seek out sexual information from television, newspapers, magazines and the Internet, and are critical of adults' naïvety about their sexual knowledges (Holloway and Valentine, 2003). Sex and sexuality are therefore important in a whole repertoire of pupil–pupil interactions and even pupil–teacher interactions, including dress codes, name calling, flirting and harassment (Haywood and Mac an Ghaill, 1995; Lahelma et al., 2000; Valentine, 2000). Indeed, accusations of being gay and general homophobic abuse are actively used by children to police each other's identities (and indeed those of teachers) and to mark out those who do not conform (Haywood and Mac an Ghaill, 1995; Holloway, Valentine and Bingham, 2000). Thus, schools, rather than being gatekeepers of children's sex knowledge, are actually sites where sexuality and sexual information are pervasive, and moralities are not merely instilled but actively constituted by adults and children alike.

Rather than protecting children's innocence by limiting their access to sexual knowledge, section 28 actually served to permit children's own homophobic peer group cultures to go unchallenged. A number of studies have demonstrated that young people who come out as lesbian and gay, who are suspected by their peers to be lesbian or gay, or who do not fit in with hegemonic understandings of masculinity and femininity for other reasons are subject to bullying, intimidation and violence (Khayatt, 1994; Haywood and Mac an Ghaill, 1995; McNamee, Valentine, Skelton and Butler, 2003). Yet section 28 tied the hands of many schools who felt unable to deal adequately with such homophobia because of fears of prosecution. In one survey, four out of five teachers questioned reported that section 28 made it difficult for them to meet the needs of lesbian, gay and bisexual pupils (Douglas, Warwick, Kemp and Whitty, 1998). In this way, section 28, while intended to protect 'innocent' children, actually served in practice to make schools a less safe space for some 'vulnerable' young people.

In the following section I consider a different moral geography of section 28, by examining how the debate between pro- and anti-repealers was played out within the specific geographical context of Scotland.

Contested Terrain: Nationhood and Citizenship

The debate around the repeal of section 28 in Scotland took place in 2000, only one year after Scottish devolution. It was particularly interesting because of the way it became entangled with wider debates about democracy, citizenship and nationhood, such that it effectively became represented as a fight for the soul of Scotland between pro- and anti-repealers. Both sides tried to align themselves with the concept of democracy, and to mobilize a particular vision of Scottish national identity in the new millennium.

The anti-repealers included Conservative members of the Scottish parliament, some dissident Labour backbenchers, and church leaders, such as Cardinal Thomas Winning, head of the Catholic Church in Scotland, and Reverend Kenneth Macleod, Moderator of the Free Church of Scotland. However, the figurehead of the movement effectively became Brian Souter, the multi-millionaire owner of Stagecoach Transport. He pledged half a million pounds to fight the repeal of section 28.

The anti-repeal campaign reproduced the sort of imaginings outlined in the previous section of children as innocent and in need of protection from lesbians and gay men who might corrupt their emerging sexuality. For example, Brian Souter funded a billboard campaign and media advertisements under the slogan 'Protect Our Children' which implied that young children might be forced to have gay sex lessons. Through such messages the 'Keep the Clause'[2] campaigners also constructed a particular imagining of national identity wherein Scotland was represented as a nation with a long history and tradition in which the family was crucial to the fabric of its society. As such, these campaigners argued that Scottish people's traditional family values would be eroded by the repeal of section 28, and implicitly that this would threaten the very basis of the nation. For example, Cardinal Winning and Reverend Macleod wrote an open letter to Donald Dewar, then Secretary of State for Scotland, stating: 'We sincerely believe that nothing less than the soul of Scotland is at stake. We cannot stand silently by as this foundation [marriage] is undermined' (*Daily Record*, 28 March 2000; Noone, 2000). Brian Souter, who was often described as a father of four, and pictured as a model citizen doing charitable work for others (most notably disabled children), echoed this view in his public statements, in which he often mobilized visions of a moral majority fighting for a democracy being overrun by minorities. In the Scottish newspaper the *Daily Record* he made the plea that: 'I would like all the politicians to stop in their tracks and listen to what the PEOPLE are saying' (15 January 2000).

In such ways the 'Keep the Clause' campaign effectively imagined lesbians and gay men as not belonging to a nation predicated on the heterosexual family unit, and therefore as not 'real' citizens. Moreover, in arguing that spending any money on educational materials about non-heterosexual relations and identities would be an abuse of taxpayers' money, the campaigners drew a discursive distinction between lesbians and gay men and taxpayers. Epstein et al. (2000, p. 14) argue that such discursive distinctions 'symbolically dislocate lesbian and gay people from full civil status, even though empirically lesbian and gay people pay taxes'.

The pro-repeal campaigners (Labour Scottish members of parliament, lesbian and gay activists, some teachers and journalists) imagined a very different Scotland. They argued that section 28 was counter to the fundamentals of a democratic society where everyone should be treated as equals, without discrimination. For example, the Communities Minister, Wendy Alexander, symbolically embraced lesbians and gay men as citizens when she described section 28 as an 'ugly restraint on the ability of local government to support all members of the community' (Associated Press, 21 June 2000). Highlighting the significance of Scottish devolution (achieved in 1999), the pro-repeal campaigners claimed that as Scotland entered a new millennium the nation should be looking forward, not back, and leaving old prejudices behind. If the nation was truly to come of age it would need to be an open, tolerant society. For example, the journalist Ian MacWhirter, writing in the *Herald* (19 January 2000) newspaper, argued that '[t]here is frankly an ingrained prejudice among sections of Scottish society, born of an instinctive fear of people with a different sexuality', and that a vote against repeal would be pandering to such prejudices and 'returning to the dark ages' (Noone, 2000).

Lesbian and gay activists also challenged the morality of Brian Souter's 'Keep the Clause' campaign. As well as personally funding the 'Protect Our Children' media campaign, discussed above, he also financed an unofficial referendum that purported to show a majority of Scots against repeal of section 28. The activists argued that Souter's use of personal wealth was chequebook democracy, enabling him single-handedly to manipulate the media in an attempt to buy public opinion and determine the moral agenda of the nation, and that such power was an anathema in a devolved Scotland. Unable to compete financially with Brian Souter, lesbians and gay activists nonetheless publicly contested his moral authoritarianism, mounting a Posterwatch campaign to identify 'Keep the Clause' posters and sabotage them by spray-painting them or ripping them down as soon as they appeared on the streets. They also sought to make their cause visible by taking up public space through other means, such as marches for equality. Indeed, taking to the streets is a well-established tactic used by lesbians and gay men to symbolically challenge and disrupt heterosexual hegemony in public space (Davis, 1995; Valentine, 1996b, 2003).

This bitter campaign for the soul of Scotland in which both sides claimed the right to articulate and defend their own moral position, and used morality as a justification for particular forms of social action, was finally brought to an end when Scottish members of parliament passed the Ethical Standards in Public Life bill in June 2000. The corresponding bill to repeal section 28 in England and Wales had a more turbulent time, being defeated for the second time in the House of Lords in July 2001. It was eventually repeated in September 2003 when the Local Government bill received the Royal Assent.

Conclusion

There is a growing body of work on moral geographies concerned with the evaluation of human conduct (in terms of what is right and wrong, good and bad, what people ought to do or not do) and with what kinds of people and behaviour belong where (Smith, 1997, 2001). This chapter has focused on sexual moralities, and the specific question of the sexualization of childhood, by examining debates about the repeal of section 28 of the Local Government Act 1988. In doing so I have highlighted a tension between the moral traditionalism or absolutism of those who believe that homosexuality is wrong and are committed to safeguarding this moral stance; and the respect for social diversity and pluralism that is evident among those who fought to repeal section 28.

Such debates about universalism and relativism have a geography in that they are played out in specific everyday sites and in particular political and social contexts. In the first half of the chapter I demonstrated how questions of sexual morality have been constituted through the specific space of the school. Here I illustrated the role of the school in instilling particular moral codes of behaviour in children and reflected on the assumptions implicit in the debates about the repeal of section 28 about sexuality and the creation of a safe/unsafe space for 'childhood'. In the second half of the chapter I focused on the relationship between morality and national identity by examining how concerns about section 28 were played out in the specific context of Scotland, which had recently been granted its own devolved parliament.

As such this chapter has also raised broader moral questions about the sexualization of childhood and ultimately children's competence and agency to make choices about their own lives in their own best interests. The debate about what children ought or ought not to know about, which has been central to this chapter, is inherently adultist in its assumption of the possibility of protecting the uncomplicatedly asexual child from a rising tide of sexualization. Children are not walled off from the everyday world in which they live but are always and inextricably part of the adult world. As such we need to recognize that children are moral subjects in their own right who will make their own choices – albeit ones that as adults we might judge to be 'good' or 'bad', 'right' or 'wrong'.

NOTES

I am grateful for a Philip Leverhulme prize fellowship that enabled me to work on this chapter. My focus on this theme was inspired in part through the work of Margaret Noone and Kathryn Morris Roberts, postgraduates at the University of Sheffield. I wish to thank Roger Lee and David Smith for their editorial work. But above all I wish to acknowledge the support and encouragement I have received from David Smith throughout my career.
1   Although the moral credibility of the Christian church has been somewhat undermined by publicity about cases in which priests and clergymen have sexually abused children.
2   In the draft Local Government bill that was put out for consultation prior to becoming law, section 28 was known first as clause 27 and then clause 28. Many campaigns around this issue began at this point; as a result, some campaigns and campaigners continued to refer to section 28 as clause 28.

REFERENCES

Brown, C. and Sullivan, J. (2000) 'Church protest forces Blair to shelve Section 28 vote', *Independent*, 25 January, p. 1.
Davis, T. (1995) 'The diversity of Queer politics and the redefinition of sexual identity and community in urban spaces', in D. Bell and G. Valentine (eds), *Mapping Desire*, London: Routledge, pp. 284–303.
Diduck, A. (1999) 'Justice and childhood: reflections on refashioning boundaries', in M. King (ed.), *Moral Agendas for Children's Welfare*, London: Routledge, pp. 120–37.
Douglas, N., Warwick. I., Kemp, S. and Whitty, G. (1998) *Playing It Safe: Responses of Secondary School Teachers to Lesbian, Gay and Bisexual Pupils, Bullying, HIV and AIDS Education and Section 28*, London: Institute of Education.
Elias, N. (1939) *The Civilizing Process: The History of Manners and State Formation and Civilization* (trans. E. Jephcott), Oxford: Blackwell, 1994.
Epstein, D. (2000) 'Sexualities and education: catch 28', *Sexualities* 3, 387–94.
Epstein, D., Johnson, R. and Steinberg, D. L. (2000) 'Twice told tales: transformation, recuperation and emergence in the age of consent debates 1998', *Sexualities* 3, 5–30.
Fielding, S. (2000) 'Walk on the left! Children's geographies and the primary school', in S. L. Holloway and G. Valentine (eds), *Children's Geographies: Playing, Living, Learning*, London: Routledge, pp. 230–44.

Foucault, M. (1981) *The History of Sexuality, Vol. 1: An Introduction* (trans. A. Sheridan Smith), Harmondsworth: Penguin.

Gagen, E. (2000) 'Playing the part: performing gender in America's playground', in S. L. Holloway and G. Valentine (eds), *Children's Geographies: Playing, Living, Learning*, London: Routledge, pp. 213–29.

Haywood, C. and Mac an Ghaill, M. (1995) 'The sexual politics of the curriculum: contesting values', *International Studies in Sociology of Education* 5, 221–36.

Holloway, S. L. and Valentine, G. (2003) *Cyberkids: Children in the Information Age*, London: FalmerRoutledge.

Holloway, S. L., Valentine, G. and Bingham, N. (2000) 'Institutionalised technologies: masculinities, femininities and the heterosexual economy of the IT classroom', *Environment and Planning A* 32, 617–33.

Jackson, S. and Scott, S. (1999) 'Risk anxiety and the social construction of childhood', in D. Lupton (ed.), *Risk and Social Cultural Theory*, Cambridge: Cambridge University Press, pp. 86–107.

Jenks, C. (1996) *Childhood*, London: Routledge.

Khayatt, D. (1994) 'Surviving school as a lesbian student', *Gender & Education* 6, 47–61.

Lahelma, E., Palmu, T. and Gordon, T. (2000) 'Intersecting power relations in teachers' experiences of being sexualized or harassed by students', *Sexualities* 3, 463–81.

May, M. (1973) 'Innocence and experience: the evolution of the concept of juvenile delinquency in the mid-19th century', *Victorian Studies* 17, 7–29.

McNamee, S., Valentine, G., Skelton, T. and Butler, R. (eds) 'Negotiating difference: lesbian and gay transitions to adulthood', in G. Allan and G. Jones (eds), *Social Relations and the Lifecourse*, Basingstoke: Palgrave Macmillan, pp. 120–34.

Moran, J. (2001) 'Childhood sexuality and education: the case of section 28', *Sexualities* 4, 73–89.

Mort, F. (1987) *Dangerous Sexualities: Medico-moral Politics in England since 1830*, London: Routledge.

Noone, M. (2000) *How Media Representations during the Clause 28 Debate Affected the Lives of Scottish Gays and Lesbians*, unpublished Masters dissertation, University of Sheffield.

Postman, N. (1982) *The Disappareance of Childhood*, New York: Delacourt Press.

Quinvalen, K. (1996) 'Claiming an identity they taught me to despire: lesbian students respond to the regulation of same-sex desire', *Women's Studies Journal* 12, 100–13.

Rogers, M. (1994) 'Growing up lesbian: the role of the school', in D. Epstein (ed.), *Challenging Lesbian and Gay Inequalities in Education*, Buckingham: Open University Press, pp. 31–48.

Smith, D. M. (1997) 'Geography and ethics: a moral turn?', *Progress in Human Geography* 21, 583–90.

Smith, D.M. (2001) 'Geography and ethics: progress, or more of the same?', *Progress in Human Geography* 25, 261–8.

Stacey, J. (1991) 'Promoting normality: section 28 and the regulation of sexuality', in S. Franklin, C. Lury and J. Stacey (eds), *Off-centre: Feminism and Cultural Studies*, London: HarperCollins, pp. 284–320.

Takanishi, R. (1978) 'Childhood as a social issue: historical roots of contemporary child advocacy movements', *Journal of Social Issues* 34, 8–27.

Thomson, R. (1993) 'Unholy alliances: the recent politics of sex education', in J. Bristow and A. Wilson (eds), *Activating Theory: Lesbian, Gay and Bisexual Politics*, London: Lawrence and Wishart, pp. 219–45.

Valentine, G. (1996a) 'Angels and devils: moral landscapes of childhood', *Environment and Planning D: Society and Space* 14, 581–99.

Valentine, G. (1996b) '(Re)negotiating the heterosexual street', in N. Duncan (ed.), *Bodyspace: Destabilizing Geographies of Gender and Sexuality*, London: Routledge, pp. 146–55.

Valentine, G. (2000) 'Exploring children and young people's narratives of identity', *Geoforum* 31, 257–67.

Valentine, G. (2003) 'Sexual politics', in J. Agnew, K. Mitchell and G. Toal (eds), *A Companion to Political Geography*, Oxford: Blackwell, pp. 408–20.

Valentine, G. (2004) *Public Space and the Culture of Childhood*, London: Ashgate.

Wallis, A. and VanEvery, J. (2000) 'Sexuality in the primary school: policy and practice in England and Wales', *Sexualities* 3, 409–23.

Weeks, J. (1985) *Sexuality and Its Discontents: Meanings, Myths and Modern Sexualities*, London: Routledge and Kegan Paul.

Wyness, M. (1997) 'Parental responsibilities, social policy and the maintenance of boundaries', *Sociological Review* 45, 305–24.

14

'But Tight Jeans Are Better!': Moral Improvisation and Ethical Judgement in Local Planning Decision-Making

Jean Hillier

Decision first, rationalization after.

Flyvbjerg, *Rationality and Power* (1998), p. 20

Introduction

In a world where waging war against Iraq has been justified to citizens on possibly politically 'cherry-picked' intelligence contrary to the spirit of several civil servants' interpretations, it is unsurprising that in Britain and the US, at least, public trust in politicians' ethics is at an all-time low (Hume, 2003). A long tradition of some mistrust has been replaced, in the twenty-first century, by an almost automatic assumption that politicians 'spin' issues for the benefit of themselves, their friends and allies.

This lack of trust permeates all scales of politics from international affairs to local issues of rates, roads, rubbish and land uses. Far from demonstrating implementation of a legal regulatory system in a broadly utilitarian notion of 'the public interest', in which planning officers make technical, objective recommendations to elected representatives who take neutral, balanced decisions, recent theoretical and empirically based discussions consider the power-plays which occur in these highly uncertain, politicized decision-making arenas. Most authors, however, tend to focus on the roles of planning officers as they face situations of political uncertainty. In this chapter, I address planning practice as it is encountered in the worlds of politically elected representatives (ERs). Analysis of instances where officer recommendations are ignored, or where ERs change their minds, suggests that actual decision-making may be exercised in ways which are contingent, complex and organized with little distinct or overt logic. In the gap between officer recommendation and ER decision lies the political: the often seemingly irrational, questionably unethical, overturning or ignoring of officers' hard-worked advice. The nexus between political representatives and the public is fraught with possibilities of impressionability on both sides. Opinions may change and decisions may be taken in council chambers, as indicated below, influenced by the emotional tears of an inconsolable grandmother or the appeal of a young blonde wearing tight jeans. Do ERs act consequentially: pragmatically or teleologically? Is their behaviour rights-based or deontological?

My focus here is not on ethics as a formalized system of standards, rules or codes, but as 'better or worse practice' (Forester, 1999). What does it mean to act well or badly where moral practical issues are concerned? I seek to uncover the communicative behaviours which precede and are construed in the ritualized formal process of political decision-making and which form a face of power that may remain invisible to practitioners and the public. Such instances of communication form the hidden transcripts of decision-making; they constitute an underlying logic of democratic practice.

I seek to interrogate such logic; to bring into hearing various dialogical techniques and devices of communication, modes of authority and subjectifications and the *telos* of strategies and ambitions. I stray a long way from rules and codes towards moral improvisation and ethical judgement in messy, highly politicized local planning decision-making practice.

If ERs were to be publicly accountable for their actions (other than through the relatively ineffective mechanism of the ballot box) and decisions were taken transparently, there would be increased pressure for ERs (and planning officers) to take responsibility for their responsibilities. Levels of public trust and respect for politicians could be enhanced, perhaps reflected in higher turnouts at local and national elections, although damage caused by 'fallout' from the 2003 war in Iraq may be substantial.

Ethical Planning in Theory

Public policy decisions are inherently moral decisions.[1] Local land-use decisions, either individually or collectively, may have enormous ethical, social and environmental impacts. A decision to locate a new highway, for instance, can severely blight an area. It can sever people's access to facilities only some 200 metres away. It can destroy important wetlands and ecosystems irreparably. A proposal for a waste dump, vociferously opposed by middle-class NIMBYs, may well end up next to an area of poor immigrants from non-English-speaking backgrounds or (in Australia) Aboriginal residents. These examples of distributive ethics emphasize the ends or outcomes of planning practice. Alternatively, we can examine issues of procedural ethics: the manner in which planning decisions are taken. Procedural ethics frames the discussion below.

What would ethical planning practice look like in theory? I agree with John Forester (1999, p. ix) that it entails attempting to 'act more effectively in the face of political inequality, racism, turf wars, and the systematic marginalization and exclusion of the poor'.

But this is only one definition, and a fairly left-wing one at that. Others will vehemently disagree, suggesting that ethical planning involves abiding by the statutory rules and professional Codes of Practice to facilitate development according to market preferences.

Planning decision-making is fraught with tensions and contradictory values, often between the 'good' (that which is thought to be intrinsically valuable) and the 'right' (that which one ought to do), between teleological and deontological ethics. To explain further, teleological ethics is concerned with end results, whereas deontological approaches focus on the rightness of the actions themselves according to sets of rules and rights, regardless of the consequences which result.

Planning practice in reality tends to be a messy combination of approaches. Planning officers may state that they plan 'in the public interest' (for the greatest good of the greatest number, in a famous utilitarian teleological formulation), but that they also abide by the rules and the inviolability of property rights. ERs tend to emphasize rules, rights and duties as influencing their decisions. However, they are also conscious of the anticipated consequences of their actions on their capacity to gain votes and be returned to office at the next election. Teleologically, many officers and ERs would agree that the 'correct' land-use decision is that which generates the greatest *quantity* of value. But what about *quality*? Whose good is to be maximized? Who benefits from the value generated? And, perhaps, more importantly, who does not?

Bauman (1993, p. 10) suggests that humans are morally ambivalent. He states that notions of humans as being essentially good or essentially bad are both wrong. Our actions vary, depending on the particular circumstances in which we find ourselves. There is no universal definition of 'good' behaviour for all times and places. We may act well or badly, often not through rational choice, but on impulse; of the moment.

To most people, acting without reasoned thought may be of little consequence. Nevertheless, for ERs, in positions of representative responsibility, an impulsive action may have extensive ramifications for a considerable number. The notion of government thus encompasses not only how planning officers and ERs exercise authority over others (local residents, developers, and so on), but also how they govern and exercise authority over themselves. Gutmann and Thompson (1996) offer the principles of publicity and accountability[2] as constituting the moral core of democracy. Publicity involves transparency of action with full, public justification. Accountability comprises taking responsibility for one's actions and being generally accountable for them.

In the 'game' of planning decision-making, a certain number of regular patterns of behaviour result from conformation to codified, recognized rules. However, other, generally political, patterns of decision behaviour do not appear explicable either by the invocation of rules or in terms of brute causality or spontaneity. They are products of a 'feel for the game' or 'practical sense'.

My aim in this chapter is to add some sense of the political to ethical theory. I seek to uncover the how and why of those seemingly errant decisions when ERs ignore officer recommendations or change their minds. I focus on the mechanisms through which politics influences what ERs want, 'what they regard as possible and even who they are' (Edelman, 1964, p. 20). I do not pretend to offer an exhaustive range of possible reasons. However, I believe that if planning practitioners are to act ethically and effectively in John Forester's sense, they cannot afford to ignore or to misconstrue the contingent and dynamic nature of political decision-making. They may then also be able to gain a feel for the game, to anticipate reactions to their recommendations and to take steps accordingly.

In what follows, I utilize these ideas as a framework for thinking about the linkages between questions of planning decision-making, authority and politics and questions of identity, self and person. The work is grounded in the practice stories of ERs and planning officers. By listening to such stories we can learn about what may be important to politicians, to what practitioners could pay attention, and what may be really at stake behind the fictions of rational decision-making.

Methodological context

I seek to theorize practice; to step down from an objectivist viewpoint to situate myself in 'real activity', in practical relation to the world of local planning decision-making. In order to do this I have conducted conversational interviews with several currently serving and ex-politicians at local government level in Western Australia (WA) from metropolitan and country town authorities, in capacities ranging from member or Chair of the Planning Committee to Mayor[3] of their jurisdictions.[4] In this way, the stories which ERs tell can reveal 'political judgements about opportunities and constraints, about more and less responsible efforts, about more and less supposedly legitimate mandates, about relevant history to be respected and learned, relevant concerns, interests, and commitments to be honored' (Forester, 1999, p. 47).

I have also interviewed several current and former public planning officers in senior positions from metropolitan authorities who are widely regarded as exemplars of astute practitioners with integrity and participatory track records, and who are motivated by concerns for social justice.

As stated before, I am concerned here only with those decisions of planning committees and full council which are taken contrary to planning officers' recommendations and those which represent an endogenous change of mind between the decision of the planning committee and its 'ratification' by full council;[5] what Bohman and Rehg (1997, p. xviii) might term 'the relation between reason and politics'. Given the percentage of decisions taken under officer-delegated authority and general agreement between officer recommendation and ERs, we are concerned with a relatively small amount of planning decisions, but which, nevertheless, tend to be those which are most controversial and potentially could have substantial impact on a local community.

I seek to uncover the 'hidden transcripts' (Scott, 1990) which influence ERs behind the scenes and those less hidden acts of communication which take place in public committee meetings; the transcripts which result in what would appear on the surface to be largely irrational decision-making. In what follows I am not going to be judgemental. I tell the stories as I heard them, at face value. I do this so that, in Forester's (1999, p. 34) words, 'these stories might nurture a critical understanding by illuminating not only the dance of the rational and the idiosyncratic, but also the particular values being suppressed through the euphemisms, the rationalizations, the political theories and "truths" of the powerful'. I attempt to uncover the various types of frames through which ERs might view issues, but make no claims as to its being anywhere near an exhaustive list.

Planning in Practice: Elected Representatives and Decision-Making

Planning is the art of persuasion. Whether it is officers persuading ERs of a technical recommendation or constituents persuading their representatives of a particular opinion, the constructive use of persuasion is important. Persuasion involves 'the proper framing of arguments, the presentation of vivid supporting evidence, and the effort to find the correct emotional match with your audience' (Conger, 1998, p. 86).

In what follows I am not interested in instances of large-scale lobbying by interest groups (Hillier, 2000a, 2000b) or in exposing corruption.[6] I distinguish between what I term public and private actions. Public actions take place in open committee and council meetings which set the stage for performances and drama. Private actions take place backstage, often informally via meetings, telephone or email conversations. The public transcript of the committee or council decision, then, does not tell the whole story. It ignores the hidden transcripts of backstage communication. It is to these which I turn as I outline possible reasons for ERs' behaviour.

Private

Personal gain

I term as personal gain those decisions in which an ER directly stands to gain financially or has other interests in the outcome. I emphasize that my research suggests that such behaviour in 1999 was very limited in WA: 'it's not pecuniary interest on the whole. Few come on Council specifically for that' (Mayor, rural LA).

Ian Alexander (1992) has written, as an ex-member of the council concerned, about the kinds of backstage deals and favours taking place on Perth City Council during the early 1980s. He indicates that between 1982 and 1985 some ninety projects were considered by the local authority planning committee in which ERs declared some form of interest (averaging three projects per meeting). No less than eleven of the thirteen councillors who served on the Town Planning Committee in those years were involved in development projects under consideration by the authority.

More recently, the Inquiry into the City of Cockburn (1999–2000) has been particularly concerned that 'the council has allowed itself to be manipulated by [the Mayor], a dominant personality who had been pursuing his own interests' (Hunter, 1999a, p. 33) over development of a parcel of land owned by his family company, of which he is a Director. Evidence was also given to the Inquiry that a motion had been adopted by the council to delete certain items from its Code of Conduct. The deleted items included: 'Councillors will ensure that there is no actual (or perceived) conflict of interest in the impartial and independent fulfilment of their civic duties' and 'Councillors (staff) will not take advantage of their position to improperly influence (other) Councillors or (other) staff in the performance of their duties or functions, in order to gain undue or improper (direct or indirect) advantage or gain for themselves or for any other person or body' (Department of Local Government, 1999, p. 11).

Clearly some ERs do put pressure on planning officers to make recommendations in their interests or persuade their council colleagues to overturn officer recommendations accordingly, but these are in a small minority. More difficult to discern is the receipt of gifts.

Gifts

The issue of gifts is complex. Bourdieu (1990, p. 100) suggests that receipt of a gift implies 'the possibility of a continuation, a reply, a riposte, a return gift'. However, as Iris Marion Young (1997, p. 355) points out, a true gift should not entail the expectation of something in return or any consideration of the recipient 'owing' the donor.

It is, then, as Bourdieu (1990) comments, all a matter of style. The choice of occasion, timing, cultural circumstances, and so on, of the gift can have different implications and meanings, which the ERs themselves need to understand.

Favours

There may also be some expectation of reciprocity when doing favours for others. It seems in WA that ERs might occasionally perform favours of permitting/refusing a particular development application, for example, for people in the community who have supported them in some manner in the past or who might be called upon some time in the future: 'a standing in good stead – In case – you know. Future favours' (Mayor, rural local authority [LA]). There would appear to be almost a logging or 'clocking up' (metropolitan LA planning officer) of favours in certain instances.

Favours might take the form of votes traded between council colleagues – 'you scratch my back and I'll scratch yours' (ex-ER, metropolitan LA); 'part of the pervading business culture of exchange of favours and corporate dealings' (ex-ER, metropolitan LA) – or favours performed for the wider community: 'the Freemasonry connection, etc.' (Mayor, metropolitan LA).

Pressure for favours is even greater in small, close-knit rural communities where everyone knows and may even be related to almost everyone else. In such circumstances the need for decisions to be made on valid planning reasons increases: 'there is constituent pressure, neighbour pressure, especially when they're personal friends, but I remind people of the Acts and the sections on valid planning reasons and impartiality' (Mayor, rural LA). With applications from friends, however, 'You obviously try to help, you know. You might give them quiet advice on how to improve their application or to withdraw it' (Mayor, rural LA).

Factions

There are factions, alliances or caucuses in many groups and institutions. As Flyvbjerg (1998, p. 138) writes, 'alliances are an important part of the rationality of power', and Roelofs (1967, pp. 252–3) defines a caucus as being 'usually private, certainly informal, and often marked by that some-what stylized bonhomie typical of relations between men who, even if not friends, know that they need each other.' Factions in WA cross partisan lines of political party, ethnicity and gender. Communication is private, often by untraceable meeting or telephone call.

In WA, 'purple circles' (ex-planning officer, metropolitan LA) exist in most local authorities, in which there are 'tacit agreements' to vote simi-larly, even to the extent that 'people go against their own ideals to vote with the faction' (ex-planning officer, metropolitan LA)

> It's their 'duty' to go along. (ex-ER metropolitan LA)
> There's logrolling. Any particular development is automatically good if it's supported by one of the inner sanctum. (ex-ER metropolitan LA)

What matters in co-ordinating 'beliefs' and votes is not what those beliefs are, but rather who holds them. The issue is exacerbated if the faction leader is also the local mayor. In WA several Department of Local Govern-ment investigations have found mayors to dominate proceedings rather than being impartial Chairs, which thus 'denies the community fair, proper and open debate' (Department of Local Government, 1999, p. 20).

Culture

Australia is a multi-cultural country and WA is no exception. Apart from a large Angloethnic population, there are significant communities of Italian, Serbian, Croatian, Chinese and increasingly Vietnamese, Iraqi and Afghani people living in WA. Each community may have different cultural personal values and ways of working. In some Asian cultures, for instance, the significance of gift-giving as a mark of respect is important. Such gifts are not intended as bribes, but are a cultural aspect of business relationships.

People's life experiences can also shape the ways they interact with ERs and officers of governance. Many migrants have arrived in WA from coun-tries which do not have democratic systems in the Western sense. Ballot-boxes and ERs are unfamiliar, if not alien, concepts, as are open committee and council meetings for people who have never had opportunities to voice their concerns publicly. Other migrants have arrived from countries which did not have a planning system. Such people tend to hold certain expect-ations that they can do whatever they like with their land. Having to submit planning applications which are then refused can be confusing and bewildering.

Local residents may thus find themselves caught in an interstitial position between two or even more cultural ways of working. It should not be surprising, therefore, that people from particular cultural groups should seek out any ERs on council from that group, irrespective of whether that person is the relevant ward councillor or not; that some people give ERs gifts as a token of respect for those in authority; and that ERs from different cultural groups tend to 'look after their own' (ER, metropolitan LA).

My argument is that ERs from such cultural groups may not believe that they are acting unethically in receiving gifts, helping kinspeople, and so on. The Mayor of Cockburn, a Croatian, 'did not believe that he was doing anything wrong' (Hunter, 1999b, p. 37) in using his position to influence council decisions. As another mayor suggested, the British-based planning system in WA is 'culturally insensitive to various ethnic needs' (Mayor, metropolitan LA).

At the same time, however, members of frustrated cultural minority groups see apparent favours and privileges given to 'the old school tie, Western suburbs private school "mates"' (Mayor, metropolitan LA) who seem to work covertly in similar fashions. 'That's the *real* Mafia' (Italian constituent, metropolitan LA).

The WA planning system is 'a template which doesn't fit local needs' (Mayor, metropolitan LA). ERs are often not deliberately acting wrongfully but are resisting an inappropriate system. Whether the way forward is to change the system or to 'educate' ERs and the public as to what constitutes correct and incorrect conduct is a matter for debate.

Public

Populism – posturing, grandstanding, benevolence and vote-winning

In public arenas such as planning committees and full council meetings, political debate is overtly rhetorical and emotional on all sides, including ERs and members of the public gallery. ERs tend to be guilty of political impression management: posturing and 'grandstanding in front of the public' (Mayor, rural LA), especially in the lead-up to local elections, when they are eager to create a good image as concerned, involved representatives worthy of being voted back into office. One ex-metropolitan planning officer commented that: 'committees are like circuses' as ERs 'bend to the whims of the most vocal element', to 'whoever turns up or who they happened to hear from last' (planning officer, metropolitan LA).

A survey in WA by Stubbs (2002) explored ERs' rationales for rejecting planning officer recommendations. Politicians claimed to be far more 'in tune' with the local population than are planners, who 'have little appreciation of community views, pursuing policy not supported by the community' (R6 in Stubbs, 2002, p. 43); 'go by the letter of the law – regardless of public opinion' (R9, pp. 45–6); 'work with policies and books – they're not in the real world' (R14, p. 48); whilst 'our political noses tell us that a recommendation will not be acceptable to the community' (R18, p. 51); and 'Councillors are in a better position to judge community values than officers' (R6, p. 43).

In many situations, ERs react to direct action, lobbying and presentations to committee or council meetings by applicants and/or objectors. Politics is performance wherein participants perform roles through which they enact their positions, as humble petitioner, as oppressed victim (members of the public) or as all-powerful and/or benevolent provider (ERs). Meetings come to resemble Bakhtinian carnivalesque or Debordian spectacles. Yet, as Debord (1994) points out and Tony Blair in Britain has demonstrated, the spectacle is also 'the locus of illusion' (p. 12), where, 'in a world that really has been turned on its head, truth is a moment of falsehood' (p. 14).

ERs generally like to be seen supporting their ward constituents. In particular, they seem keen to appease the local Ratepayers' Association, which is often their powerbase in the constituency: 'If the Ratepayers' Society says jump, they jump' (planning officer, metropolitan LA). This may involve, as Kitchen (1997, p. 41) indicates, speaking out against something or voting against an application, even when they know that in terms of council policies, which they themselves approved, it should be accepted.

Public perceptions of benevolence lead to populism,[7] in addition to making the ERs involved feel good about themselves. Politicians would appear to be 'suckers for hearts and flowers arguments' (Mayor, metropolitan LA) in 'weak-willed acts of going with the grain' or PAP (Pragmatism And Populism) (Powell, 2000, p. 53). Virtually every interviewee recalled stories of people in the public gallery winning over ERs on decisions contrary to officer recommendation. Whether it is the small child with a ventilator in a wheelchair, the elderly grandmother silently weeping or the attractive young woman bursting into tears, ERs seem to change their minds about issues, often to the frustration of planning officers whose reasoned, technical arguments get discarded. As one officer grumbled after a particularly difficult recommendation was overturned by ERs following a public appeal by a young blonde woman wearing a revealing tee-shirt and tight trousers: 'grovelling is good, tears are good, but tight jeans are better'.

Members of the public who play emotional strategies are often successful. They may use potent symbols of helplessness, such as wheelchairs and tears, to achieve their own goals. These goals may well be contrary to the good of the majority of the local population and especially of more marginalized groups in society, such as the unemployed, the Indigenous, and so on. In Brittain's (1996) words, such 'democracy by the majority can jeopardise the civil rights of minority or other powerless groups'. Moreover, given the domination of local authority participation strategies by a few vociferous members of ratepayer or other interest groups, decision-making which takes into account only comments made during formal participation processes may well be tyranny by a minority rather than a majority.

Sometimes, however, people's strategies may misfire and serve to antagonize ERs rather than inveigle them. Behaviour such as making force-based threats and name-calling is counter-productive, as is dogmatically telling ERs that they are wrong: 'grovelling is good, begging for mercy is good, telling them they're wrong is not good' (planning officer, metropolitan LA). Such activities may generate 'planning by petulance' (Mayor, metropolitan LA) against the people concerned. This may also result in decisions taken against officer recommendation and serve to reinforce ERs' feelings of omnipotence.

It could appear from the above that 'parochialism and populism rule OK' (ex-planning officer, metropolitan LA) in WA, but I emphasize that it is a relatively low proportion of planning decisions which are influenced in these ways. Kitchen (1997) estimated that in his British local authority, it was in only 20 per cent of cases where public speaking rights had been exercised that the planning committee decision was different from that of the officer recommendation. Even so, the resulting 'organicist' populism is unlikely to favour strategies of social or environmental justice.

Summing up: 'There goes the mob! I am their leader, I must follow them'

Are ERs simply puppets of populism, or can we begin to discern more about the exercise of political will? We need to consider new ideas of planning decision-making, those which account for the gap between officer recommendation and council decision. We need to accept that rationality is context-dependent and that what we may have traditionally regarded as rationality could actually be *post-facto* rationalization (see Flyvbjerg, 1998).

ERs may be swayed by rhetoric rather than argument. The presence of an audience in the public gallery may lead to populist posturing and acts of benevolence or petulance as ERs jump on passing bandwagons of public opinion: 'a vote is a tender plant; it needs to be tended, fed and watered, cozened and schmoozed' (MacCallum, 2002, p. 54). The spectacle of the committee meeting becomes a self-portrait of power in which perception of an immediate 'good' may override deontological right.

Local politicians like the social prestige their position invokes, but as Baxter (1972, p. 106) suggests, 'possibly more important is the prestige it brings to a councillor in his [sic] own eyes – the satisfaction of feeling important'. This may be through helping family, friends, constituents or cultural kin. Political decision-making involves far more than rationality, far more than simple marketplace trading. Decisions are taken according to a 'feel for the game' which is being played out in public and/or in private.

Rulebooks or Moral Improvisation?

Most planning decisions where ERs ignore officer advice can be traced to conflicting frames for viewing the issues concerned. The decisions illustrate the tension which exists in several jurisdictions between legislation which requires ERs to have 'due regard' only to technical planning considerations when making decisions (e.g. the WA Town Planning and Development Act 1928[8]) and other legislation which provides that part of the responsibilities of councillors is to 'represent the interests of the electors, ratepayers and residents of the district' (WA Local Government Act 1995). WA has yet to resolve these tensions.[9] On what basis, however, does one frame become preferable to another in the absence of universals of truth and objectivity?

It appears from the narratives cited above that, apart from any private reasons, ERs attach considerable importance to obtaining help for constituents who may appeal to them. ERs tend to respond to immediate electoral or political pressure and may thereby come into conflict with planners, who are professionally required to use a longer-term and wider-ranging frame to view the issue. I regard this as social role taking on the part of ERs rather than deception or corruption. Yet taking such a populist stance may serve to 'sweep aside' (Canovan, 1981, p. 183) both bureaucratic professionalism and the due process of planning law, with significant implications in terms of the spatial allocation of 'good' and 'bad' land-uses, and of environmental and social justice.

It amounts to a question of ethics or moral judgement. Yet moral judgement cannot be reduced to formulae or technical calculation. Part of such judgement involves an appreciation of what is at stake, and for whom, in any given case. There is a fine balance between the need for ERs to be responsive to the opinions of their constituents and the need for planning decisions to be made according to valid 'planning' criteria. Plentiful guidelines and 'rulebooks' or Codes of Conduct, Ethics and/or Practice exist to help planning officers and ERs keep their balance, especially following highly publicized instances of abuses of power (sleaze) in the UK and Australia.[10]

Moral judgement cannot be reduced either simply to 'applying the rules'. Rules can often be applied in several ways; they may be conflicting or ambiguous. Rules are not value-free, and if the ends are deemed sufficiently important, bending them may be acceptable. Rulebooks can also raise the question of what it actually means to understand a rule. ERs and planning officers may benefit from engaging practical sense or a feel for the game to guide their interpretation of the 'rules' in different circumstances.

Planning practice is therefore a form of spatial ethics (Upton, 2002) which necessitates continual interpretation and reinterpretation of what the rules really mean. The relation between rule and practice is reciprocal: various sets of rules (the statutory planning system, cultural traditions, etc.) inform practice and practice influences the interpretation of the rules. The rules are, at any given time, what practice has made them. There are no universal formulae, and to attempt to apply formulae as such could lead to disaster.

If planning officers are to practise 'good planning',[11] intuitive practical wisdom could be valuable in deciphering the hidden transcripts of their ERs. 'Without some access to the hidden transcript, planners will see only the bouncing ball, missing the forces that make it bounce' (Briggs, 1998, p. 9). Intuition and anticipation are key elements of being able to catch the ball: 'you can tell which decisions will be hot' (ex-planning officer, metropolitan LA).

Experienced practitioners should be able to reflect in action on the frame conflicts which might arise in relation to various development applications or policy suggestions. Schon and Rein (1994) stress the importance of practitioners 'getting into the heads' of likely actors (ERs, local residents, developers, etc.) to anticipate their reactions. This should then facilitate practitioners in designing their own actions (moral improvisation) so as to communicate the lessons they wish the other actors to draw; shaping their attention accordingly.

Of course there will be events which planners cannot anticipate, especially those instances when private deals and favours may have been struck. Overall, however, I believe that the predictive abilities of 'practical anticipations of ordinary experience' (Bourdieu, 1987, p. 96) should form a strong basis for 'good' effective practice.

Anticipation and moral improvisation are only the first steps however. Responsibility, accountability and publicity are also necessary, but in isolation insufficient, conditions of 'good' planning practice. As Bauman (1998, p. 18) reminds us, though, the way ahead is far from easy: 'there is but sailing between the reefs which punctuate the risky voyage of the modern self'. On one side lies the 'Scylla of Indifference', of washing one's hands of responsibility for potentially unethical behaviour and its implications. On the other side is the 'Charybdis of Oppression', of 'I know what is best for people'. Navigating between these two extremes becomes the fate of the moral practitioner or representative when he or she attempts to do 'good' planning. As Bauman (p. 18) continues, 'to add moral agony to fear of navigational error, the waters we sail are poorly charted and one never knows how far the ship is from foundering; the luxury of moral certainty arrives only after the ship has already sunk'.

I hope that my work here has helped to chart some of the murky and turbulent waters of local planning practice and to demonstrate the difference between moral or ethical responsibility and contractual obligation; a difference which Bauman (1998, p. 19) summarizes as 'one is obliged towards the strong. One is responsible for the weak.'

Conclusions: Are Tight Jeans Really Better?

Ethical practice involves more than moral reasoning. It involves being able to anticipate and identify ethical issues before they arise, being able to reflect on what issues are at stake, being able to improvise an appropriate course of action, and being able to implement or navigate that course.

ERs might ask themselves a series of questions before they give way to acts of impulsiveness. Such questions include who is in the relevant moral community on this issue (i.e. those people or things in the environment which could be affected by the decision)? What principles (such as publicity, transparency, accountability) should define our responsibility to the moral community? Should the rights of certain individuals be deemed to override the rights of others and of the natural environment?

In the messy complexity of local planning practice, morality is the 'drama of choice' (Bauman, 1998, p. 13). The drama may be acted out by ERs off- or on-stage, in private or in public. Decisions are often non-rational, taken on impulse, without consideration of any but immediate or short-term benefit. I have attempted to outline some of the reasons why decisions may be made contrary to planning officers' recommendations. Once they understand more about ERs' patterns of behaviour, officers may then begin to anticipate ERs' seemingly irrational actions and be able either to pre-empt or react to them. Planning decision-making is a complex mixture of hybrid processes – technical, collaborative, political (see Innes and Gruber, 1999) and ethical – all involving a range of values and ideals competing for decision-makers' attention.

Anticipation and moral improvisation are more important than recourse to rulebooks and Codes which regard issues in unambiguous black and white, leaving no grey area of ambivalence and multiple interpretation. Rules and Codes substitute the knowledge of rules for the moral self as constituted by responsibility. Moral improvisation involves having a feel for the game. It entails responding to the ends and means, norms and obligations, desires and needs of the often uniquely significant particularities that make each decision what it distinctively is.

Considering all the above, what, then, would constitute 'good' effective planning? It comprises far more than technical skill and includes astute observation, sensitivity to others' cultural traditions, their emotions and opinions, anticipation of reactions and reflective strategies to pre-empt or to counter such reactions. Effective planners are not left in frustration merely retrospectively monitoring the exercise of political will. They actively attempt to communicatively channel that will in specific directions.

Effective decision-making in the voices of my practice stories involves attempting 'to sort out instances of genuine need from the quick buck'. 'It's greatest challenge is to find the boundaries of legitimate interests' (both quotes, Mayor, metropolitan LA).

In this chapter I have tended to concentrate on the morality of local authority politicians rather than the morality of politics itself. I have told stories of local private and public actions, of personal ethics and morality rather than the wider ramifications of political power and the global morality they perpetuate. I make no excuse for dealing with localized worlds of planning decision-making in which rhetoric, emotions and tight jeans are everyday realities. I offer no simple solution, but concur with the wisdom of an ex-planner that 'any claim to have a "solution" in today's complexity is a bizarre overreach'.

NOTES

My thanks to all the planners and elected representatives with whom I talked and without whose stories this chapter would not have been possible.

1 See Campbell (2002) and Upton (2002) for recent discussion.
2 Gutmann and Thompson's concept of deliberative democracy also includes reciprocity as a fundamental principle. For simplicity I concentrate here on publicity and accountability.
3 I use the term 'Mayor' to denote the ER leader of the council or Shire President. There is no political alignment at local municipal authority level in WA, unlike in Britain, where local ERs may experience tensions between political group discipline and loyalty and case-specific demands of constituents (Copus, 2001).
4 Given the nature of the information sought, I only approached ERs whom I knew and who felt they could trust me with some ethically controversial material. This resulted in my interviewing only more 'honest' politicians, although I believe their stories of experience of others' dealings have been valuable.
5 Most, but not all, local authorities in WA have open planning committee and full council meetings at which the public is given opportunity to speak.
6 The WA Criminal Code, Section 83, defines an act of corruption as 'any public officer who, without lawful authority or a reasonable excuse, a) acts upon any knowledge or information obtained by reason of his office or employment . . . so as to gain a benefit, whether pecuniary or otherwise, for any person, or so as to

cause a detriment, whether pecuniary or otherwise' (cited in Department of Local Government, 1999, p. 12).

7   For further discussion of populism in a local planning context, see Hillier (2003).

8   The 1928 Act legislates that local authority planning decisions must be taken on sound planning principles. Aspects of market competition, impact on property values, morality, compassion, and so on, are not deemed planning principles.

9   The Blair administration has attempted to do so in England and Wales in the Local Government Act 2000 with its *Model Code of Conduct* for Councillors (Department of Transport, Local Government and the Regions, 2001).

10 Such as reported by the Nolan Committee (1995) in Britain and the Cockburn Inquiry in WA (Department of Local Government, 1999).

11 I interpret 'good planning' as transformative change for the benefit of the disadvantaged.

REFERENCES

Alexander, I. (1992) 'City centre planning: for public or private interest?', in O. Yiftachel and D. Hedgcock (eds), *Urban and Regional Planning in Western Australia,* Perth: Paradigm Press, pp. 79–91.

Bauman, Z. (1993) *Postmodern Ethics,* Oxford: Blackwell.

Bauman, Z. (1998) 'What prospects of morality in times of uncertainty', *Theory, Culture & Society* 15 (1), 11–22.

Baxter, R. (1972) 'The working class and Labour politics', *Political Studies* 20, 92–107.

Bohman, J. and Rehg, W. (1997) 'Introduction', in J. Bohman, and W. Rehg (eds), *Deliberative Democracy,* Cambridge, Mass.: MIT Press, pp. ix–xxx.

Bourdieu, P. (1987) *Choses Dites,* Paris: Éditions de Minuit.

Bourdieu, P. (1990) *The Logic of Practice* (trans. R. Nice), Stanford: Stanford University Press.

Briggs, X. de Sousa (1998) 'Doing democracy close-up: culture, power and communication in community building', *Journal of Planning Education Research* 18, 1–13.

Brittain, J. (1996) 'Direct democracy by the majority can jeopardise the civil rights of minority or other powerless groups', *Annual Survey of American Law* 3, 441–9.

Campbell, H. (2002) 'Planning: an idea of value', *Town Planning Review* 73 (3), 271–88.

Canovan, M. (1981) *Populism,* London: Junction Books.

Conger, J. (1998) 'The necessary art of persuasion', *Harvard Business Review* 76 (3), 84–95.

Copus, C. (2001) 'Citizen participation in local government: the influence of the political party group', *Local Governance* 27 (3), 151–63.

Debord, G. (1994) *The Society of the Spectacle* (trans. D. Nicholson-Smith), New York: Zone Books.

Department of Local Government (1999) *Report of the Inquiry into the City of Cockburn*, Perth: DLG.

Department of Transport, Local Government and the Regions (2001) *Model Code of Conduct* [online]. Available: *http://www.odpm.gov.uk/stellent/groups/odpm_localgov/documents/page/odpm_locgov_605150.pdf*

Edelman, M. (1964) *The Symbolic Uses of Politics*, Urbana: University of Illinois Press.

Flyvbjerg, B. (1998) *Rationality and Power*, Chicago: University of Chicago Press.

Forester, J. (1999) *The Deliberative Practitioner*, Cambridge, Mass.: MIT Press.

Gutmann, A. and Thompson, D. (1996) *Democracy and Disagreement*, Cambridge, Mass.: Harvard University Press.

Hillier, J. (2000a) 'Going round the back? Complex networks and informal action in local planning processes', *Environment & Planning A* 34, 33–54.

Hillier, J. (2000b) 'More than reason: interstitial politics and informal action in planning theory', in M. Tewdr-Jones and P. Allmendinger (eds) *Planning Futures: New Directions for Planning Theory*, London: Routledge, pp. 110–35.

Hillier, J. (2003) 'Puppets of populism?', *International Planning Studies* 8 (2), 157–66.

Hume, M. (2003) 'Why should we trust leaders who believe in nothing?', *Spiked Politics* [online]. Available: *http://www.spiked-online.com* [24 September].

Hunter, T. (1999a) 'Call to sack Cockburn councillors', *The West Australian* 21 December, p. 33.

Hunter, T. (1999b) 'Grljusich defends actions in land row with Council', *The West Australian* 7 December, p. 37.

Innes, J. and Gruber, J. (1999) 'Planning strategies in conflict: the case of regional transportation in the Bay area', AESOP conference paper, Bergen, 7–11 July.

Kitchen, T. (1997) *People, Politics, Policies and Plans*, London: Paul Chapman.

MacCallum, M. (2002) *How to be a Megalomaniac*, Sydney: Duffy & Snellgrove.

Nolan Committee (1995) *Standards in Public Life*, Cm 2850-I and Cm 2850-II, London: HMSO.

Powell, M. (2000) 'New Labour and the Third Way in the British welfare state: a new and distinctive approach', *Critical Social Policy* 20 (1), 39–60.

Roelofs, H. (1967) *The Language of Modern Politics*, Homewood, Ill: Dorsey Press.

Schon, D. and Rein, M. (1994) *Frame Reflection*, New York: Basic Books.

Scott, J. (1990) *Domination and the Arts of Resistance*, New Haven: Yale University Press.

Stubbs, R. (2002) 'An examination of the circumstances in which elected representatives of local governments feel justified in rejecting the recommendations made by professional planners', unpublished Planning Report for Postgraduate Diploma in Urban and Regional Planning, Perth: Curtin University.

Upton, R. (2002) 'Planning praxis: ethics, values and theory', *Town Planning Review* 73 (3), 253–69.

Young, I.M. (1997) 'Asymmetrical reciprocity: on moral respect, wonder and enlarged thought', *Constellations* 3 (3), 340–63.

Part IV

Geography and Ethics: Method and Practice

The engagement of geography with ethics has important implications for research method and practice. If our subject matter is to include moral values and their expression in human behaviour, and how they are understood as ethics, then the way in which these phenomena are investigated is likely to differ from studies of industrial location, for example; hence the increasing adoption of qualitative inquiry. In the early years of their application in geography, qualitative methods tended to be defined in contrast to quantitative methods, almost as a binary opposite to standard practice. However, speculation about qualities of nature, and of human life, has a history going back to the classical Greek philosophers. It was the advent of modernity, and the scientific approaches associated with it, which prioritized the material world of directly observable phenomena, along with a rather mechanical conception of causality. In geography this reached its apogee in the so-called 'quantitative revolution' and the era of human geography as spatial science, which dominated the 1960s and 1970s.

The introduction of qualitative methods in human geography in the 1980s was closely associated with (re)emergence of humanist perspectives. Cultural and social geographers were giving increasing attention to issues of race, ethnicity, gender, sexuality, illness and disability, analysis of which hardly lent itself to mere quantification. They began to look outwards, to such fields as ethnography, interpretative sociology and phenomenology, to find methods appropriate to new challenges (Eyles and Smith, 1988). The ethics of research practice were also hard to avoid, with the adoption of a widening range of qualitative methods. So when a collection of papers was published exploring the interface of geography and ethics (Proctor and Smith, 1999), the final part (comprising five chapters) was devoted to the subject of ethics and knowledge. This focused on relationships between researchers and researched, with positive value assigned to such qualities as empowerment, emancipation and participation, applied to what were often otherwise disadvantaged subjects of geographical inquiry.

In Chapter 15, William Lynn argues for the indispensability of qualitative inquiry. With the continuing reassertion of the importance of human subjectivity and agency, Lynn points to an interweaving of matter, perception and conception into 'maps of meaning'. His elaboration conveys something of the complex reality of human experience which requires qualitative inquiry. Qualitative approaches include an emphasis on multiple methods (or triangulation), and an interpretative focus on what Lynn describes as the meaningful, value-laden character of human action and cultural processes. He emphasizes the importance of case studies in applied ethics, revealing contextual details of particular normative issues under investigation.

The other contribution arises out of such a local case study. Lynn stresses the importance of ethics in both the practice of geography and its purpose, one aspect of which may be improving the lives of marginalized people. Priscilla Cunnan (Chapter 16) describes an investigation requiring particular sensitivity to vulnerable research subjects: poor female street traders in Durban, South Africa. She explains that her approach was influenced by feminist epistemology, including non-exploitative relations with interviewees, rapport building, and acknowledgement of the positionality of the researcher: strategies which have come to be associated with ethically informed and reflective research practice in general. Her purpose in studying this particular group of women carries its own ethical justification, in not only making their conditions more widely known, but also thereby hoping to contribute to the improvement of these hard-earned lives (to borrow a phrase from Cornwell, 1984). From the work of Jocelyn Cornwell with London's Eastenders to that of Priscilla Cunnan with the pavement people of Durban represents twenty years of qualitative research in the Queen Mary graduate school of geography. Certainly, it is the kind of scholarly commitment that is necessary if the forms of uneven development addressed in Part I of the book are to be exposed for what they are.

REFERENCES

Cornwell, J. (1984) *Hard-Earned Lives: Accounts of Health and Illness from East London,* London: Tavistock.

Eyles, J. and Smith, D. M. (eds) (1988) *Qualitative Methods in Human Geography,* Cambridge: Polity.

Proctor, J. D. and Smith, D. M. (eds) (1999) *Geography and Ethics: Journeys in a Moral Terrain,* London: Routledge.

15

The Quality of Ethics: Moral Causation, Method and Metatheory in the Interdisciplinary Science of Geography

William S. Lynn

Introduction

David Smith's influence on the field of ethics in geography is enormous. His contributions are topically broad, conceptually rich and illustrated with practical case studies. It is pioneering work that begins a conversation, invites the insights of others, and thereby sets research agendas. For many, he exemplifies how we should think about ethics and geography, providing a 'template', as it were, for moral reasoning about space.

Less appreciated, I think, are the presuppositions behind Smith's method of ethics, much less some implications of geography's engagement with ethics. The latter is the subject of this contribution. Using Smith's geographical ethics as a starting point, I explore the methodological connection between science, ethics and qualitative inquiry through the concept of 'moral causation'. I then turn to a metatheoretical discussion of the 'qualities' of our research phenomena (agents of inquiry and objects of analysis alike), to clarify why ethics and qualitative methods are indispensable to geography as an interdisciplinary science.

Making Space for Ethics

When I was a graduate student in the early 1990s, there was no 'discourse' or 'subfield' of ethics in geography. There was certainly a small discussion of professional ethics in the field, and the absence of an authoritative dialogue did not stop geographers from making normative claims, of varying degrees of self-conscious ethical reflection (for good examples, see

Harvey, 1973; Mitchell and Draper, 1982). And like all new disciplinary arenas of inquiry, the sledding could be rough-going. Ethics work was regarded by critics as a-theoretical (i.e 'not spatial enough'), unempirical (i.e. 'not quantitative enough') or simply 'not geography' ('remember, "if you can't map it, its not geography" '). I could go on typifying such marginalizing comments with examples from cartographers, feminists, Marxists, post-colonialists, social constructionist and more. All of these typifications are drawn from people who are now advocates for ethics in the field.

In North America, the solution to this marginalization was obvious. Scholars interested in geographical ethics needed a specialist group to champion their cause in the Association of American Geographers, as well as a journal to publish their research. With this goal in mind, a few of us created the Values, Ethics and Justice Specialty Group in the Association of American Geographers, and launched a new journal, *Ethics, Place and Environment*, which first appeared in 1998. Today, that publication is flourishing, ethically inflected research increasingly appears in established geography journals, and the number of geographers interested in ethics continues to grow. While the discourse of social construction has side-tracked geographers into the dead end of moral relativism regarding nature, we are doing far better in the human dimensions of the discipline, especially with regard to the intentions, practice and consequences of research.

An indispensable reason for the success of this moral turn is David Smith. In a series of cogent articles and books, he outlines the connections he sees between geography and ethics (Smith, 1994, 1997, 1998a, 1998b, 1998c, 1999a, 1999b, 2000a, 2000b, 2000c; Proctor and Smith, 1999). His own research on ethics, particularly questions of justice, is both theoretically rich and empirically focused. Moreover, he speaks the language of space with a moral accent, and in so doing, invites other geographers into the dialogue. Without his efforts, the moral turn in geography may not have taken hold, or if it had, we would certainly be the poorer.

A number of features characterize Smith's search for 'common ground' between geography and ethics. His search begins with an understanding of normative issues informed by ethical theories from philosophy. Questions that loom large here include metaethics (the logic of moral reasoning), normative ethics (theories of prescriptive moral claims), the tension between universalism and particularism in moral theory, and the difference between explanation in science and justification in ethics (to name a few). In terms of prescriptive theories of ethics, Smith's passion is justice, especially as it illuminates the responsibilities of global citizens for the health and well-being of distant others. These concerns lead Smith to consider ethics in international development, the spatial extent of our moral responsibilities, the moral dimensions of community, boundary making and exclusionary practices, and ethical rationales for entitlements to land and resources (for an especially cogent summarization, see Smith, 1998a).

A key feature in virtually all this work is the use of case studies to provide contextual details when applying Smith's ethical framework. This provides a thick description of the normative issues under investigation, and under-writes with evidence the conclusions reached by his moral reasoning. Moreover, the case studies feature questions of space and social theory – location, migration, space and place, globalization, social-spatial dialectics, and the like. This allows Smith not only to inform geography with moral philosophy, but also to spatialize the abstract theories of philosophical ethics. Overall, Smith's work exemplifies 'applied ethics' at its best. Borrowing insights and theories from moral philosophy, he uses these to inform the theories and practice of geography. At the same time, the spatial characteristics of geographical phenomena 'contextualize' abstract ethical theories so that questions of right and wrong have practical implications on the ground, and may improve the lives of marginalized people (for example, see Smith, 1994).

The conceptual analysis of insights from moral philosophy, when applied to case studies that contextualize and spatialize moral theory, thus consti-tutes the method Smith pursues in his research. There is real power here, a power to reveal the moral issues at stake in human endeavours, as well as to provide guidance on the ends and means of our striving for justice in particular, and the good life for all in general. Without gainsaying the power of Smith's approach to geographical ethics, I want to explore some of the presuppositions and ramifications raised by his and cognate endeav-ours. My intention here is not corrective. I am suspicious of totalizing or triumphal 'theories' and 'discourses' that promote the worst kinds of schol-arship and partisan bickering in the academy. Instead, I wish to comple-ment the approach of Smith and others by exploring the methodological implications for how we think about geography as an interdisciplinary science, the role of ethics in our science, and the metatheoretical reasons why qualitative inquiry is indispensable to ethics within geography.

Moral Causation: Science, Ethics and Qualitative Inquiry

There is an extensive literature on science and ethics, less on ethics and qualitative inquiry, and a paucity of work configuring all three. Because of the breadth and complexity of the subject, allow me to phrase the essential questions as a set of interrelated presuppositions.

First, science is a rigorous inquiry in the search for *explanatory* know-ledge. This knowledge may or may not be objective, certain or predictive, but it must adequately elucidate the causes of events. To do this it uses explanations and notions of causation that 'fit' the characteristics of the phenomena it studies. Thus we often distinguish between the natural and human sciences (a European distinction), or the physical and social sciences (an Anglo-American distinction). We do this because the methods, research design and theories of science should be adapted to the study of natural process or human agency, respectively. What the human and natural sciences share, then, is a common search for explanations, not a common set of methods, a common study design or common theories (Bhaskar, 1975, 1989; Silverman, 1993).

There is disagreement here, to be sure. In the Anglophone world, social science since the Second World War has often aped the methods and theories of the physical sciences. In geography, social physics and the gravity model are two examples. While most philosophies of science now recognize this as an error and a failure, departments of social science are frequently gripped by the 'ghost of positivism', with its outdated 'unity of science model (for a *mea culpa* on its folly, see Ayer, 1978; for a powerful statement of a bygone era, see Nagel, 1979; for a contemporary reaffirmation, see Wilson, 1998). By their very nature, ghosts are difficult to see. The ghost that grips geographic thought is not normally sighted in an explicit positivism, but in the obsession with space, quantitative techniques and/or cartographic visualization as definitive of the discipline.

Second, causal explanation in geography (and other interdisciplinary human and natural sciences) cannot depend on models and measuration alone, but must apprehend the meaning(s) embodied in human agency. Our individual and collective lives can only be described, explained or evaluated by accounting for people's motives, intentions, purposes, concepts, meanings, interpretations and communications. To do this we need to examine the natural languages, speech communities and discourses in which persons participate and through which they come to an understanding of the natural and social worlds. This emphasis on understanding contrasts with the explanations based on universal laws or social regularities that are more appropriate to the physical and engineering sciences, not the world of consciousness, social interaction and culture (Bernstein, 1991a, 1991b; Wallerstein and the Gulbenkian Commission, 1996).

Third, like other scientists, geographers are strongly informed by empirical observations of the natural and human worlds. This is all to the good, as this deepens our basic knowledge. Yet by participating in a shared history of scientific philosophy rooted in the mechanistic worldview of the physical sciences (e.g. empiricism, positivism, etc.), geographers often assume that the foundation of research is quantitative in nature, that is, measurement, modelling and visualization. Without taking anything away from the importance and insights of quantitative work, one critical element is overlooked by this presumption: some phenomena may be tangible and measurable (e.g. length, mass, velocity), while other phenomena are equally real but intangible and not measurable (e.g. ideas, concepts). We therefore need empirical sciences that study distinct kinds of phenomena (tangible or intangible), and this requires sciences with distinct theories and methods. Generally, those sciences that study tangible phenomena use 'quantitative' methods, and those that examine intangible phenomena use 'qualitative' methods (Rorty, 1967; Livingstone, 1992; Wallerstein, 2001).

Fourth, qualitative inquiry is indispensable to our scientific understanding of human beings. Being 'qualitative' encapsulates the methods, research design, hypotheses, theories and philosophies used to apprehend human understanding and action. This includes techniques of research (the methods), as well as the wider epistemological, ontological and axiological understandings that make research intelligible (Harvey, 1990; Silverman, 1993). Emerging from under the shadow of quantitative norms, qualitative methods are no longer regarded as 'merely' exploratory, biased, anecdotal or indicative of a science in search of its paradigm. Qualitative inquiry shares a heritage with much older traditions of interpretative inquiry that date back to the beginnings of philosophy, history and geography in the Mediterranean world (Mueller-Vollmer, 1989; Bruns, 1992). It is also a 'co-tradition' of concepts and practices, an interdisciplinary bridge between different fields and theoretical standpoints (Denzin and Lincoln, 2000).

As cognitive ethology is discovering, altruistic motives (one root of ethical sensibility) and qualitative methods are equally indispensable to the study of animal behaviour, although its salience varies as greatly between different animal species, as it does between human and non-humans. This plays havoc with settled notions that quantitative and qualitative research loosely mapped over the domains of nature and society, respectively. Wilhelm Dilthey, the German philosopher of the human sciences, was the classic exponent of this proposition (Rose, 1981; Makkreel, 1992). Yet the emerging understanding of animal agency (e.g. consciousness, sociality and culture) has birthed a revisionist ethology that is learning to incorporate 'ethnology' into its theories and methods (for examples of this, see Bekoff, 2002; Bekoff, Allen and Burghardt, 2002). The rediscovery of animal agency has strong implications in animal geography as well, motivating the hybridization of ethical and social theories that transgress the boundaries of the animal and human worlds (Lynn, 1998, 2002, 2004; Philo and Wilbert, 2000).

Certain features roughly characterize qualitative research. These include an emphasis on multiple methods and triangulation (e.g. participant-observation, interviews, textual analysis, semiotic analysis and case study), an interpretative focus on the meaningful, value-laden character of human action and cultural processes (e.g. caring, activism), a highlighting of the inadequacy of objectivist science (e.g. empiricism, positivism, critical rationalism) and quantitative inquiry (e.g. laboratory experimentation, surveys, statistical analysis) in many human inquiries, a suspicion of privileged epistemologies, totalizing theories and rigid ideologies of human ways of life (e.g. doctrinaire Marxisms; religious fundamentalism of any stripe), the importance of experience and narrative understandings in the constitution of both individual and group worldviews (e.g. personal biography, ethnic history), and an awareness of the ethics and power embedded in all human relations (Crabtree and Miller, 1992).

Fifth, qualitative research is a term used in contrast to (but not opposition with) quantitative research. Quantitative research's passion for measuration and mathematical techniques helps us redescribe phenomena, identify statistical correlations, posit causal relations and falsify conclusions (Bryman, 1988, Chap. 1; Barnes, 1994; Marshall and Rossman, 1995). These methods are well adjusted to the study of certain phenomena which are physically measurable, relatively enduring, have causal properties which are relatively stable, operate under known conditions, and exist in closed or demarcated systems. They are not well adjusted to the study of human (or animal) subjectivity that violates the domain boundaries of measurable, enduring, stable and well-characterized phenomena (Cloke, Philo and Sadler, 1991; Sayer, 1992).

Finally, ethics is indispensable in the practice of geography, and can be a form of qualitative research. Scholars frequently conceptualize ethics as radically different from science. Science, we are told, seeks *explanations* for natural and social phenomena, while ethics seeks *justifications* for our actions in the world. Whereas science asks questions such as 'What exists?' and 'What causes that?', ethics asks questions like 'How shall we live?' and 'What ought I do in this situation?' While this distinction is important, it does play into a rigid division of facts from values, reality from morality, reason from emotion. In the real world, justifications frequently motivate actions and thus serve as (partial) explanations in human affairs. You cannot understand why some people or communities do as they do until you understand the full range of their intentions, motivations and presuppositions. The ethical dimensions of these understandings are crucial. Moral norms frequently justify and guide our actions (for good or ill), and are the basis for critiques of oppression and injustice. Ethics is a form of discursive power which enables people to change the world around them via political action, social protest, legal manoeuvring and personal entreaties. In all these senses, then, ethics is a parallel and internal concern of science, helping us to describe, explain and/or justify the geographies of our lives (Bellah, Haan, Rabinow and Sullivan, 1983; Lynn, 2000).

Overall, the relationship between science, ethics and qualitative inquiry is rather simple. Because humans are sapient beings who act with individual and collective agency, qualitative inquiry is a requisite method for any human and social science. Because human agency may at times be explained by recourse to our moral sensibilities, *moral causation* is an indispensable force in human and environmental affairs. And because moral causation is best understood through qualitative methods, ethics is an indispensable mode of qualitative inquiry.

Qualities, Primary and Secondary

Beyond the methodological linkages just articulated, are there deeper metatheoretical connections between the scientific, ethical and methodological practice of geography? What do these connections have to do with the qualities of the phenomena (object, system, subject, agent) that we investigate? One answer to these questions is revealed in the intellectual history of qualitative inquiry.

Qualitators and quantitators – researchers using qualitative and quantitative methods, respectively – are accustomed to defining themselves against one another (Bauer and Gaskel, 2000, p. 7). This usually takes the form of reciprocally binary definitions, with the quantitators associated with mathematics, certainty, objectivity and causation in the 'hard' sciences, and the qualitators associated with words, images and performances, contingency, intersubjectivity and meaning in the 'soft' sciences (Guba and Lincoln, 1994, pp. 105–6; Schwandt, 2000). These sciences are presumably hard or soft based on the tangible and measurable nature of their objects of analysis. These binary definitions tend to reinforce a picture of qualitative as anti- or non-quantitative.

Not only are the histories of qualitative inquiry of little help in overcoming this dualism, but they also tend to see qualitative inquiry as a 'modern' practice. Denzin and Lincoln (2000, pp. 11–18) begin their periodization of the five historical 'moments' in qualitative research in the early modern period. Arthur Vidich and Stanford Lyman produce a more comprehensive periodization, but only give passing mention to ancient and medieval sources. Their full account begins with the eighteenth-century ethnographies of European colonialists (Vidich and Lyman, 2000). Lost to these modernist histories is the heritage of interpretative inquiries in geography and history, a heritage as old and respected as Herodotus' *History* (c. 450 BCE), Ibn Khaldun's the *Muqaddimah* (1377), Giovanni Vico's *Principles of a New Science* (1725) and von Humboldt's *Kosmos* (1845–62). To understand the meaning of quality for geography (and the other human and social sciences), we have to go back to the ancient Mediterranean philosophies that speculated on the 'qualities' of nature.

Empedocles (c. 450 BCE) articulated an elemental theory dividing the terrestrial world into the eternal elements of earth, air, fire and water.

Adopting Empedocles' division of the elements, Aristotle (c. 384–322 BCE) developed the theory of 'sensible qualities' to explain what he perceived to be the intrinsic characteristics of these elements. Aristotle postulated six sensible qualities – hot, cold, dry, wet, light and heavy – which in various combinations gave rise to each of the terrestrial elements. Thus earth is cold, dry and heavy; air is hot, wet and light; fire is hot, dry and light; and water is cold, wet and heavy. In addition, he theorized four causes by which to explain change in *both* natural and human phenomena – 'what it is made of (material cause), what it essentially is (formal cause), what brought it into being (efficient cause), and what its function or purpose is (final cause)' (Urmson and Rée, 1989, p. 26). Aristotle's theories about qualities and causes became the basis for Islamic and European science (Lindberg, 1992).

Early modern scientists rejected these theories about substance and causation. They adopted instead an atomistic theory of 'corpuscular' matter, causation in which was produced by the physical motion of matter, and they pursued a mathematically inclined and mechanistic model of 'natural philosophy'. Moreover, they believed the mechanistic worldview would guarantee universal and certain knowledge of cause and effect, thereby giving humans complete power over nature, and elucidate God's intentions through the study of creation (Glacken, 1967; Worster, 1985). Galileo Galilei (1564–1642) was an early proponent of this new atomistic and mechanistic science, and was the first modern to dichotomize *primary* and *secondary* qualities. Primary qualities (e.g. extension, mass, velocity) were inseparable from objects, while secondary qualities (e.g. colour, touch, sound) were the subjective effects of the senses, and, therefore, less real and fundamental (Dampier, 1984, pp. 127–34). Primary qualities, then, describe the materiality of the world, while secondary qualities name our sensorial experiences of the same.

This was a radical break from the ontology of the ancient, medieval and Islamic worlds. That ontology claimed human experience evidenced a continuum of material and spiritual substances, each with its own mix of qualities, all of which were equally 'sensible'. Thus, the material, experiential and spiritual were equally real and objective (e.g. external to the knowing subject). The colour of an evergreen tree was as real and embodied in the tree as its size or mass. The sensation of colour was a direct, somehow corporeal experience of the object in one's sight. Colour was simply one aspect of the sensible qualities in matter. Early modern scientists broke with this ontology in a decisive fashion, and they would only accept primary qualities as candidates for causal explanation. To return to the example of colour, it was theorized as a wavelength of reflected light that human eyes are adapted to seeing. Thus, colour was rendered a secondary quality and did not have a causal role in vision. Moreover, since the primary qualities were the quantifiable aspects of nature, science became identified with the measuration of nature and mathematization of scientific theory, in a word, with quantification (Dampier, 1984, Chap. 4). Science increasingly embraced objective, causal and certain knowledge, gleaned through the empirical and quantifiable study of nature. What distinguishes the social from the physical sciences was not their theories or methods *per se*, but the units of analysis they investigated, the so-called 'unity of science' hypothesis.

The worldview of mechanistic science did produce substantial intellectual progress, and the technological ability to transform nature is a testament to its (partial) insights. There was a price to pay, however, in adopting this vision of science. It systematically erased from scientific research those phenomena that were not quantifiable. Non-material experiences and social relations either had to be theoretically reduced to materialist causation, or dropped from scientific studies altogether, and explanation in human affairs increasingly marginalized human subjectivity and agency (Rorty, 1979; Toulmin, 1990; Sorell, 1991).

Tertiary Qualities and the Sources of Moral Causation

Few of us would argue against the importance of primary qualities. They are critical to an understanding of material causation. Even so, people are sapient beings, distinctive for their ability to think and feel with self-awareness. Because of this, we are agents of our own lives, capable of acting with volition, empowered by our interpretations and motivations to produce our own intrinsic, non-materialistic 'causes' for action. These other characteristics are associated not solely with secondary qualities and raw experience (although I am not ruling these out), but with what I term tertiary qualities. *Tertiary qualities* are the cognitive, cultural and social elements of human life – sapience (self-awareness), emotion, reason, interpretation, education, individual and collective action, politics, and the like. They name those aspects of an intangible but still very real and empirical world, one generated and transformed through human consciousness and cultural traditions. This makes material causation inadequate to the task of explaining human action, and primary qualities only one characteristic to consider when trying to understand the human and social worlds. Indeed, it is scarcely possible to describe ourselves, much less explain or understand our thoughts and conduct, without taking tertiary qualities into account (Taylor, 1985; Wachterhauser, 1986, 1994).

Examples are readily at hand. Consider one's sense of touch. A touch can be experienced as a caress, a sharing of friendship, or a sexual assault. It is not experienced as a touch first, then passed through an algorithm to produce its meaning. On the contrary, our prior understandings and current interpretation constitute what a touch may mean. We may be drawn to, comforted by, or repelled from someone's touch. We can consider a deforested landscape in the same way. It is a complex interweaving of matter, perception and conception – of primary, secondary and tertiary qualities – into maps of meaning. One element in these maps is the moral value(s) we recognize in the landscape, and different moral outlooks will produce different descriptions and experience of deforestation. The junk-bond trader who is clueless or careless about intrinsic moral value may see trees as proto-timber, fungible capital in natural wealth, and not even recognize the loss to individual, species and ecosystem values on the landscape. The orthodox Marxist, who considers nature as valuable only in relation to the well-being of humans, may see the forest as humankind's external body, and the metabolization of the landscape as an intrinsically valuable increase in material well-being. The radical environmentalist, who considers all of nature laden with intrinsic moral value, may see arrogance, slaughter and rape, evidence of our indifference to other forms of life.

In this sense, primary and secondary qualities are mediated and given significance by tertiary qualities, that is, perception and experience is given form and meaning by personal and cultural understandings. Together, the primary, secondary and tertiary qualities point us towards a wholistic consideration of the material and cultural dimensions of human existence. Ontologically our existence, experience and sapience are simultaneous and reciprocal. Epistemologically, however, primary, secondary and tertiary qualities name distinctions that differentiate and highlight the plural and interlaced context of our lives.

Conclusion

Tertiary qualities are the link between science, ethics and qualitative research. This is so in all interdisciplinary sciences studying human and natural phenomena. If we take science to be a rigourous inquiry in the search for explanatory causal knowledge, then this knowledge may be derived from sources having primary, secondary or tertiary qualities. What this means, of course, is that good science adapts its methodology to appropriately fit the characteristics of the phenomena under study. In the case of the human and social sciences, the methods, research design and theories must be adapted to the study of human agency and subjectivity.

As for qualitative inquiry, we can confidently say John Stuart Mill was wrong when in 1872 he stated, 'The backward state of the moral sciences can only be remedied by applying to them the methods of physical science, duly extended and generalized' (Mill, 1987, p. 19). There are multiple kinds of phenomena manifesting different qualities. Qualitative and quantitative methodologies are both legitimate modes of research, appropriately adapted to understanding the distinctive qualities of differing phenomena. As an interdisciplinary science with physical and human components, geography should incorporate both forms of inquiry. Still, many of us endure the mutual recriminations between qualitators and quantitators, between claims that one kind of geography is about objective facts, while the other is about subjective values. One reason for this conflict is the under-theorization of 'quality', depriving us of the conceptual tools needed to appreciate the legitimate reasons for multiple methodologies in geography.

Finally, ethics is a tertiary quality of human life. This is true whether ethics takes the form of abstract theory or felt sensibility. When geographers investigate moral values, they are recovering some of the tertiary qualities erased by early mechanistic science in its search for primary qualities. In so doing, they deepen our causal understanding of the world, for to describe, explain or justify our world, we must apprehend the ethics that partially constitute those understandings. It is for this reason that ethics can never only be an external arbiter of research practices, although it should help us practice as best we can. Rather our moral sensibilities are intrinsic to the purposes and subject matter of geographic research. Ethics is a constitutive element of geography, and explanations that inappropriately exclude tertiary qualities like ethics are, fundamentally, no explanation at all.

ACKNOWLEDGEMENT

Parts of this chapter draw on materials from a book manuscript in preparation, *Practical Ethics: Moral Understanding in a More Than Human World*, itself an outgrowth of my dissertation (Lynn, 2000).

REFERENCES

Ayer, A. J. (1978) 'Logical positivism and its legacy: dialogue with A. J. Ayer', in B. Magee (ed.), *Men of Ideas*, New York: Viking, pp. 119–33.

Barnes, T. J. (1994) 'Qualitative methods', in R. J. Johnston, D. Gregory and D. M. Smith (eds), *The Dictionary of Human Geography* (3rd edition), Oxford: Blackwell, pp. 493–4.

Bauer, M. W. and Gaskel, G. (2000) *Qualitative Researching with Text, Image and Sound: A Practical Handbook*, Thousand Oaks, Calif.: Sage.

Bekoff, M. (2002) *Minding Animals: Awareness, Emotions, and Heart*, New York: Oxford University Press.

Bekoff, M., Allen, C. and Burghardt, G. (eds) (2002) *The Cognitive Animal: Empirical and Theoretical Perspectives on Animal Cognition*, Cambridge, Mass.: MIT Press.

Bellah, R. N., Haan, N., Rabinow, P. and Sullivan, W. (1983) *Social Science as Moral Inquiry*, New York: Columbia University Press.

Bernstein, R. J. (1991a) *Beyond Objectivism and Relativism: Science, Hermeneutics and Praxis*, Philadelphia: University of Pennsylvania Press.

Bernstein, R. J. (1991b) *The New Constellation: The Ethical-Political Horizons of Modernity/Postmodernity*, Cambridge, Mass.: MIT Press.

Bhaskar, R. (1975) *A Realist Theory of Science*, Leeds: Leeds Books.

Bhaskar, R. (1989) *Reclaiming Reality: A Critical Introduction to Contemporary Philosophy*, London: Verso.

Bruns, G. L. (1992) *Hermeneutics Ancient and Modern*, New Haven: Yale University Press.

Bryman, A. (1988) *Quantity and Quality in Social Research*, London: Unwin Hyman.

Cloke, P., Philo, C. and Sadler, D. (1991) *Approaching Human Geography: An Introduction to Contemporary Theoretical Debates*, New York: Guilford Press.

Crabtree, B. F. and Miller, W. L. (1992) 'Introduction', in B. F. Crabtree and W. L. Miller (eds), *Doing Qualitative Research*, Newbury Park, Calif.: Sage, pp. 3–28.

Dampier, W. C. (1984) *A History of Science, and Its Relations with Philosophy and Religion*, Cambridge: Cambridge University Press.

Denzin, N. K. and Lincoln, Y. S. (2000) 'The discipline and practice of qualitative research', in N. K. Denzin and Y. Lincoln (eds), *Handbook of Qualitative Research* (2nd edition), Thousand Oaks, Calif.: Sage, pp. 1–28.

Glacken, C. J. (1967) *Traces on the Rhodian Shore: Nature and Culture in Western Thought from Ancient Times to the End of the Eighteenth Century*, Berkeley: University of California Press.

Guba, E. G. and Lincoln, Y. S. (1994) 'Competing paradigms in qualitative research', in N. K. Denzin and Y. S. Lincoln (eds), *Handbook of Qualitative Research*, Thousand Oaks, Calif.: Sage, pp. 105–17.

Harvey, D. (1973) *Social Justice and the City*, London: Edward Arnold.

Harvey, L. (1990) *Critical Social Research*, London: Unwin Hyman.

Lindberg, D. C. (1992) *The Beginnings of Western Science: The European Scientific Tradition in Philosophical, Religious, and Institutional Context, 600 BC to AD 1450*, Chicago: University of Chicago Press.

Livingstone, D. N. (1992) *The Geographical Tradition: Episodes in the History of a Contested Discipline*, Oxford: Blackwell.

Lynn, W. S. (1998) 'Contested moralities: animals and moral value in the Dear/Symanski debate', *Ethics, Place and Environment* 1, 223–42.

Lynn, W. S. (2000) *Geoethics: Ethics, Geography and Moral Understanding*, Doctoral dissertation, Department of Geography, University of Minnesota, Minneapolis.

Lynn, W. S. (2002) '*Canis lupus cosmopolis*: wolves in a cosmopolitan worldview', *Worldviews* 6 (3), 300–27.

Lynn, W. S. (2004) Animals: a more-than-human world', in S. Harrison, S. Pile and N. Thrift (eds), *Patterned Ground: Entanglements of Nature and Culture*, London: Reaktion Press, pp. 258–60.

Makkreel, R. A. (1992) *Dilthey: Philosopher of the Human Studies*, Princeton: Princeton University Press.

Marshall, C. and Rossman, G. B. (1995) *Designing Qualitative Research* (2nd edition), Newbury Park, Calif.: Sage.

Mill, J. S. (1987 [1872]) *The Logic of the Moral Sciences*, La Salle, Ill.: Open Court.

Mitchell, B. and Draper, D. (1982) *Relevance and Ethics in Geography*, New York: Longman.

Mueller-Vollmer, K. (1989) *The Hermeneutics Reader: Texts of the German Tradition from the Enlightenment to the Present*, New York: Continuum.

Nagel, E. (1979) *The Structure of Science: Problems In the Logic of Scientific Explanation*, Cambridge, Mass.: Hackett.

Philo, C. and Wilbert, C. (eds) (2000) *Animal Spaces, Beastly Places: New Geographies of Human–Animal Relations*, London: Routledge.

Proctor, J. D. and Smith, D. M. (eds) (1999) *Geography and Ethics: Journeys in a Moral Terrain*, New York: Routledge.

Rorty, R. (ed.) (1967) *The Linguistic Turn: Recent Essays in Philosophical Method*, Chicago: University of Chicago Press.

Rorty, R. (1979) *Philosophy and the Mirror of Nature*, Princeton: Princeton University Press.

Rose, C. (1981) 'Wilhelm Dilthey's philosophy of historical understanding: a neglected heritage of contemporary humanistic geography', in D. R. Stoddart (ed.), *Geography, Ideology and Social Concern*, Totowa, NJ: Barnes & Noble Books, pp. 99–133.

Sayer, A. (1992) *Method in Social Science: A Realist Approach* (2nd edition), London: Routledge.

Schwandt, T. A. (2000) 'Three epistemological stances for qualitative inquiry: interpretivism, hermeneutics and social constructionism', in N. K. Denzin and Y. S. Guba (eds), *Handbook of Qualitative Research* (2nd edition), Thousand Oaks, Calif.: Sage, pp. 189–213.

Silverman, D. (1993) *Interpreting Qualitative Data: Methods for Analysing Talk, Text and Interaction*, Newbury Park, Calif.: Sage.

Smith, D. M. (1994) *Geography and Social Justice*, Oxford: Blackwell.

Smith, D. M. (1997) 'Geography and ethics: a moral turn', *Progress in Human Geography* 21, 596–603.

Smith, D. M. (1998a) 'Geography and moral philosophy: some common ground', *Ethics, Place and Environment* 1, 7–34.

Smith, D. M. (1998b) 'Geography, morality and community', *Environment and Planning A* 31, 19–35.

Smith, D. M. (1998c) 'How far should we care? On the spatial scope of beneficience', *Progress in Human Geography* 22, 15–38.

Smith, D. M. (1999a) 'Geography and ethics: how far should we go?' *Progress in Human Geography* 23, 119–25.

Smith, D. M. (1999b) 'Social justice and the ethics of development in post-apartheid South Africa', *Ethics, Place and Environment* 2, 157–77.

Smith, D. M. (2000a) *Moral Geographies: Ethics in a World of Difference*, Edinburgh: Edinburgh University Press.

Smith, D. M. (2000b) 'Moral progress in human geography', *Progress in Human Geography* 24, 1–18.

Smith, D. M. (2000c) 'Social justice revisited', *Environment and Planning A* 32, 1149–62.

Sorell, T. (1991) *Scientism: Philosophy and the Infatuation with Science*, London: Routledge.

Taylor, C. (1985) *Philosophy and the Human Sciences: Philosophical Papers 2*, Cambridge: Cambridge University Press.

Toulmin, S. (1990) *Cosmopolis: The Hidden Agenda of Modernity*, New York: Free Press.

Urmson, J.O. and Rée, J. (eds) (1989) *The Concise Encyclopedia of Western Philosophy and Philosophers* (new and completely rev. edition), Cambridge: Unwin Hyman.

Vidich, A. J. and Lyman. S. M. (2000) 'Qualitative methods: their history in sociology and anthropology', in N. K. Denzin and Y. S. Lincoln (eds), *Handbook of Qualitative Research* (2nd edition), Thousand Oaks, Calif.: Sage, pp. 37–84.

Wachterhauser, B. R. (ed.) (1986) *Hermeneutics and Modern Philosophy*, Albany: State University of New York Press.

Wachterhauser, B. R. (ed.) (1994) *Hermeneutics and Truth*, Evanston, Ill.: Northwestern University Press.

Wallerstein, I. (2001) *Unthinking Social Science: The Limits of Nineteenth-Century Paradigms* (2nd edition), Philadelphia: Temple University Press.

Wallerstein, I. and the Gulbenkian Commission (1996) *Open the Social Sciences: Report of the Gulbenkian Commission on the Restructuring of the Social Sciences*, Stanford: Stanford University Press.

Wilson, E. O. (1998) *Consilience: The Unity of Knowledge*, New York: Alfred A. Knopf.

Worster, D. (1985) *Nature's Economy: A History of Ecological Ideas* (2nd edition), Cambridge: Cambridge University Press.

16

On the Pavement: Reflections on Fieldwork with Urban Poor Black Women Street Traders in Durban, South Africa

Priscilla Cunnan

Introduction

The South African government's strategy for Growth, Employment and Redistribution (GEAR) implemented in June 1996 had the negative consequences of increasing unemployment and under-employment. Owing to a lack of employment opportunity, many of the newly urbanized are compelled to resort to the informal sector. In July 1997 the Department of Small Business and Informal Trade estimated that there were 4,000 street traders in the Durban central business district (CBD) at any one time.[1] Sixty-two per cent of all informal traders in South Africa are women, the majority of whom are black.

This chapter is based on my fieldwork with urban poor black women street traders in the city of Durban[2] for a PhD thesis on their self-reported health and access to health care (Cunnan, 2002). When I commenced the study in 1997, the only published data available on street traders in the CBD of Durban were the Durban City Engineers Report (1984) and a working paper of the project Women in Informal Employment: Globalizing and Organizing, subsequently published as Lund and Skinner (1998). The former was a quantitative study mainly pertaining to income earning details, since its prime objective was controlling the 'infiltration' (original text) of street traders into the CBD of Durban. The latter was a qualitative study also focusing mainly on the traders' paid labour conditions. Neither study made a distinction regarding the gender of the traders, nor did these studies consider their health and well-being. Thus my study was reliant only on original data.

My priority for the accumulation of data was to utilize a non-exploitative, empowering approach. Essentially, I would not be manipulative or lie to the women, even if it meant not accumulating the desired data. I also intended to explain the concept of informed consent so that they would know their rights while working with me and other researchers. In addition, I would give them the opportunity to learn from me in terms of gender rights and other information that would help them in the city. Furthermore, I acknowledged my non-neutrality as a researcher (Rose, 1997) and the power relations between the street traders and myself. Therefore I found a feminist epistemology most relevant to the present study. While there is no specific feminist methodology (see, for example, England, 1994; Gilbert, 1994; Katz, 1994; Kobayashi, 1994; Nast, 1994; Staebeli and Lawson, 1994; Lawson, 1995; McLafferty, 1995; Mattingly and Falconer-al-Hindi, 1995; Moss, 1995; WGSG, 1997), over the years particular practices have come to be associated with feminist research (Doyle, 1999). This includes forming non-exploitative relationships with the interviewees, rapport building, reflexivity, considerations of ethics and the acknowledgement of the impact of the positionality of the researcher on both data collection and writing. To reduce the possibility of misinterpretation, I resolved to use triangulation or multiple methods both in the data collection and in the analysis.

Another important influencing factor in the research strategy was that I was based in London and, for family reasons, had to undertake the fieldwork in South Africa during the British summer holidays.[3] I did not require long periods to get accustomed to the area or situation, as I have worked with deprived black communities in KwaZulu/Natal in a voluntary capacity since 1981 and in a research capacity since 1992 (Cunnan, 1993; Cunnan and Maharaj, 2000). However, this decision had the effect of ten-week concentrated periods of fieldwork between stages of analysis undertaken in London. This limited the scope for extended pilot work and also meant that the qualitative work had to be completed before much analysis of the quantitative data was undertaken.

Pilot Fieldwork

In the summer of 1997, I spent the first of three weeks of pilot fieldwork observing the street traders in various sites of the Durban CBD. Initially, my observation ranged from covert to detached. In the latter approach I did not interact with all the women but they knew that I was a researcher taking notes (Robson, 1993). My objective was to accumulate information on how the traders worked – for example what they sold, the numbers of hours worked, and frequency of rest periods or trips to the toilet – before I interacted with them.

At the end of the first week I decided to 'talk' and interact with the traders because I felt that I had accumulated adequate information to ask relatively informed questions. To negotiate access, Peace (1993, p. 31) advocated using established or powerful groups within a society or community. Thus I approached the Secretary of the Self-Employed Women's Union (SEWU) and the Director of the Department of Small Business and Informal Trade, thinking that they might be the gatekeepers. After obtaining 'grassroots' information from the SEWU, and a more bureaucratic view from the latter, I spoke informally to eight traders from three sites with the highest concentration of traders, namely the Beach area, Warwick Avenue and Durban Railway Station. Beach traders catered mainly for foreign and local tourists, generally selling souvenirs, handmade produce and imported trinkets. Warwick Avenue traders worked in a situation of a high volume of people and vehicle traffic, selling mainly fresh produce, cooked food and traditional medicinal goods. Durban Station traders lived on-site in varying makeshift structures constructed from cardboard and plastic and catered for a low-income cliental selling a variety of hand made produce which relied on their traditional skills of beadwork and basket weaving. Using what Preston-Whyte (1982, p. 43) referred to as an informal schedule ('*aide memoire*'), my questions and our discussions concerned the women's experiences of trading, where they lived, their use of health facilities and finally their health problems. One interviewee was a supervisor who liaised with the SEWU and the Department of Small Business and Informal Trade in negotiations on behalf of the traders and thus was able to provide key background information. Another key informant was a 72-year-old trader who has been trading in the Beach area since 1978. One of the initial traders, she related how they first started trading and some of the difficulties encountered during the apartheid era, for example regular confiscation of goods and imposition of fines.

I spent the remaining two weeks observing and talking intermittently with various traders from the three sites. These discussions informed the compilation of the questionnaire for the survey conducted in the following year. At the end of the pilot work, the three sites previously chosen for the pilot work were confirmed as study sites for the main data generation process on the premise that the traders from these sites were fairly typical of traders throughout the Durban CBD. The traders sold different wares at the three sites but they had similar working conditions and not dissimilar life experiences.

Quantitative Data Collection

A questionnaire survey was considered the most efficient method of obtaining initial original data from a relatively large sample taking into account financial and time constraints (Roberts, 1990). The questionnaire was used as a precursor to the qualitative work and hence was used to get a sense of the general response from the women traders, as they were the majority. Thus the quantitative responses helped me to prepare for the subsequent qualitative work. I opted to stop after completing 200 questionnaires because I felt that 'saturation level' had been reached, in the sense of repetition of similar responses, rather than the number of questionnaires being a representative sample.

Taking into account my limited three weeks of initial pilot fieldwork and that it was not possible for me to return to South Africa to pilot a questionnaire before the questionnaire survey, I decided to compose a questionnaire using a collection of well-established and -validated questions from existing questionnaires.[4] However, my past experience researching the experiences of deprived black people made me realize that the original wording of some questions would be too complicated or easily misinterpreted upon translation. Further, adapting Northern-based instruments for use in a Southern country meant that I needed to be reflexive when developing the adapted questions. One of my foremost concerns was using words that are taken for granted in Northern countries but which do not exist in the Zulu society to which the women belonged. For example, there is only one Zulu word for illness and disease; there is no distinction. Thus the translation of the question needed slightly more elaboration to draw out the distinction intended in the validated question. Here I used the names of common local illnesses and diseases as examples instead of giving them my understanding of illness and disease. I discussed each translated and simplified question of the English and Zulu version of the questionnaire with two Zulu student nurses to check the clarity of the questions and that the same meaning and intention of the validated questions were maintained. This enabled me to include views and ideas which, although generally insignificant, were sometimes crucial in improving the overall feasibility of the questionnaire.

The majority of the questions were in a pre-coded multiple choice format with many requiring a simple yes/no response. Realizing that this might constrain the kind of information collected, I also included the category of 'other' and recorded all explanations or elaboration for this choice. Interviewees were encouraged to 'digress' and elaborate, as I saw it as an opportunity to collect important data which would be followed up by qualitative work (Yeandle, 1984). These additional notes ranged from a couple of sentences to several pages. The latter occurred especially when a question prompted a group discussion involving the women sitting closest to the trader being interviewed. One disadvantage of covering almost all the aspects of the study in the questionnaire was the eventual length of twelve pages. The whole process from initial contact to the completion of the questionnaire took from one to one and a half hours. None of the women complained about the length or the time taken to complete the question-naire.

The three chosen sites had an estimated total of 1,000 traders at any one time. I chose a sampling fraction of one fifth of the women traders with the intention of reviewing that once completing 200 questionnaires. I chose a starting point at each site and subsequently chose any one of the first five traders and then every fifth trader thereafter. At the end of the day I made a note of the physical spot where I had interviewed last with the intention of resuming the sample from there.

It was not possible to conduct the interview in private, but since the sites were so noisy it was possible to conduct an interview at a certain pitch which excluded the neighbouring traders. However, on many occasions the woman would repeat the question to the other traders and verify her answer before answering me. Administering the questionnaire highlighted that field roles cannot be entirely controlled by the researcher and are often dictated by the researched (Burgess, 1982, p. 16). After the initial intro-duction my behaviour towards the traders very much depended on the age and the disposition of the women. I cajoled and joked with the more urbanized and/or younger women but was more reserved, sympathetic and restrained with the older and/or rural women.

Generally, the women were friendly and accommodating. Although the interview was a one-off situation, when I went back to the sites the women who were previously interviewed would shout greetings such as 'Hello my friend, you are back today!' or '*Unjani Sisi?*' (how are you, sister). Similar to the experiences of Finch (1996) and Oakley (1981), the women were disarmingly enthusiastic about telling me their story. Often I was offered their comfortable patch on the pavement and sometimes I was offered tea. In one instance I was invited to sit on a clean space. After chatting to the women I asked if I could interview one woman in particular and was informed that I was already sitting *in* her 'house'. For those who lived on the pavements in *mjondoles* (a makeshift structure commonly called a shack), I was invited into their homes. So I was treated as a guest rather than just tolerated (Finch, 1996, p. 167).

As a result of their enthusiasm to help me, the women usually went on to explain more than what was required in response to the question and sometimes they offered information which they felt was necessary even though I had neglected to ask. Thrilled to be so enthusiastically received, I was also mindful of the possible negative consequences of these women receiving my attention and discussing issues which were sometimes very personal (Patai, 1991; Stacey, 1991). I adopted the role of supplicant, whereby I exposed my dependence on them for vital information, empha-sizing that without their co-operation I would be unable to continue my research, thereby shifting the power over to them (England, 1994, p. 82). Yet, I also reminded them that I was visiting South Africa for a short period and that it would be a year before I saw them again, if ever. Thus I did not encourage them to elaborate on painful experiences such as the previous high incidence of rape at the Durban Station because I felt that I would not be able to provide support once the woman disclosed her experience.

Qualitative Data Collection

Generally, research in the past has neglected to ask black people what they think and feel about their own lives and health (Donovan, 1986, p. 121). However, in approximately the past two decades it has been acknowledged that it is no longer appropriate to talk about, and on behalf of, black women but that it is time for the women to articulate their own stories (Funani, 1992, p. 67). In the second part of my fieldwork I used qualitative methods to generate intensive data on issues which had arisen from the question-naire survey and also to acquire information on what the women thought and felt about their health in a less structured manner. By using qualitative methods I hoped to be able to contribute towards devising what Funani (1992, p. 67) called strategies to facilitate the need for oppressed women to articulate their own stories. I used two methods, namely group discussions and individual interviews. Owing to the noticeably hostile atmosphere at Durban Station and Warwick Avenue (as explained below under problems encountered), it took four weeks for me to familiarize myself with the situation and re-negotiate access. I conducted a total of three group discus-sions and twenty individual interviews during the remaining five weeks.

Group discussions provided the opportunity to discuss a series of par-ticular questions with several women simultaneously (Fontanna and Frey, 1994, p. 364; Goss, 1996). My intention of using the group discussions was to test the feasibility of the schedule of questions that I intended to use for the individual interviews and also to ascertain if there were other questions which needed to be added to the schedule. The groups ranged from four to six women. Two group discussions were conducted at Durban Station and one at the Beach area. The situation in Warwick Avenue precluded having a group discussion there. The discussion took the form of participants answering semi-structured questions. Sometimes the discussions deviated slightly from the format, especially when varying health beliefs for the same symptoms were being discussed. Group discussions took on average two to two and a half hours.

Given the long trading hours and the nature of the sites, I realized that it was not realistic to plan the group discussions in an indoor setting close to where the women worked. Thus all the group discussions were conducted at the trading sites during trading hours. Usually, traders at Durban Station and the Beach sit in a position which allows them to talk to one another while working. I used this situation to facilitate a group discussion. This had some disadvantages, such as the noise level from passing traffic and when the discussion had to be interrupted because a customer needed attention. Another disadvantage was that traders from the three sites were not able to come together for a combined group discussion so traders from each site formed independent group discussions. The most significant disadvantage was in terms of recording the data generated. Although I had a tape recorder that was designed to record in outdoor situations, it was quite ineffective given the background noise. Thus I had to resort to writing shorthand notes during the discussion. This had obvious limitations such as not being able after the discussion to review the subtle dialogues of voice inflections (Burgess, Limb and Harrison, 1988a, p. 458). To combat this I made detailed fieldnotes about the group dynamics and any observations during the discussion. I also wrote detailed descriptions on all the participants which prompted my memory in the analysis of the transcripts. The advantages included that the women were in familiar settings with friends and appeared to be relaxed. The intimacy of the group also allowed participants to share their feelings with one another even though this was a once-only group discussion. Knowing each other also helped to prompt memory, for example 'remember when you were angry with that nurse for being rude ... ' (group discussion 1), which prompted the woman to remember an unpleasant experience of health care delivery. The disadvantage of using pre-existing groups was that it was not possible to control for group dynamics (Burgess, Limb and Harrison, 1988b). In all the groups there were one or two dominant women. I tactfully drew other women into the discussion when I realized that one woman was dominating the discussion, but sometimes especially at Durban Station the group dynamic was overwhelming. I also have to acknowledge that the women did not openly challenge their friends. I was alerted to their disagreement by suppressed giggles or smiles. On enquiry they explained their views but were always mindful to acknowledge that the other could be correct.

To obtain my sample for the individual interviews I used the same sampling method as in the questionnaire survey. Twenty-five women were approached and twenty consented. The total of twenty consisted of seven traders from the Beach area, seven from Durban Station and six from Warwick Avenue. Although it was possible to tape-record the individual interviews, the majority of the women were very nervous about their voice being recorded. For those who did consent to being recorded, I perceived that they were very self-conscious and almost always were much more relaxed when the recorder was switched off. Thus I adopted a similar technique to the group discussions and had to write notes throughout the interview. This prolonged the length of the interview and on average these interviews took almost two hours. The interviews were conducted mainly in English but often lapsed into Zulu. Six interviews were conducted entirely in Zulu. I wrote the notes in Zulu and translated it into English prior to returning to Britain. This afforded the opportunity for both sets to be reviewed by a lecturer in the Department of Zulu at the University of Durban-Westville. He verified that my translation was correct.

Individual interviews were conducted around the same schedule of topics which were used in the group discussions. There were some standard questions that were administered to all interviewees but I also developed questions specifically as the interview progressed. Further, while I attempted to cover as many topics as possible, I also let the women direct the course of the interview, as in the instance when I interviewed a woman who had recently been diagnosed with AIDS.

Although the women were very co-operative and cordial I also felt that regarding some questions that I was given a 'public account'. Public accounts are sets of meanings which are reproduced since they are considered legitimate and acceptable in society (Cornwell, 1984, p.15). This was especially so when the interview concerned the use of traditional medicine. However, I have to concede that the majority of the women were disarmingly candid about their lives and feelings and often related private details to illustrate their answers. Although I did not do repeat interviews, many of the women said that they knew me from my previous fieldwork trips even if I didn't work with them. They often related their thoughts and feelings in a story form as if I was an old familiar friend. When some women explained their health beliefs, they sometimes added that it was a cultural belief or 'that's what we grew up believing'. Thus they shared private accounts while being aware that I might not find it acceptable or believe in it. Therefore even if a few women might have given me a public account, I believe that an overwhelming majority of the women gave me private accounts of their health and health beliefs.

Negotiating Access and the Influence of My Positionality

I anticipated problems of access during the implementation of the questionnaire survey in the summer of 1998 since the traders were being bombarded with changes in the laws and regulations regarding trading in the Durban CBD from the winter of 1997 (SEWU, 1997). This created a fragile and suspicious community of traders which was relatively closed to outsiders, especially if the person was from another race group.

While I consider myself a black South African, many of the women whom I worked with initially saw me as 'Indian' and probably continued to do so. I was the 'correct' gender and have had not dissimilar experiences to the women in terms of apartheid oppression but I still did not fit in the situation completely because I did not belong to the same race group. The policy of apartheid, which spatially and mentally separated the four race groups in South Africa, has created a situation where race is prioritized before nationality. I probably have more insight into the life experiences of black South Africans compared to a white South African. However, I must also acknowledge that apartheid has controlled our lives to the extent that the three race groups classified as 'non-white' had varied experiences of apartheid. Thus my Indian descent rendered me as 'other' in a situation where all the traders belonged to the African race group.

Differences, whether cultural, socio-economic or political, are an essential aspect of all social interactions (Nast, 1994, p. 57). Hence the metaphor of 'betweenness' (Kobayashi, 1994), which basically denotes some issues of commonality between researcher and researched depending on the context of time and place. Kobayashi (1994) advised that it is more constructive to acknowledge the differences and inequalities between the researcher and the researched and to work in imaginative ways to overcome the situation. She (p. 78) recommended focusing on the personal attributes of the researcher, such as the researcher's history of involvement with the researched and the researcher's understanding of that particular social milieu. My background knowledge of deprived black communities obtained over the past twenty years reassured the women that I was not a complete novice (Peace, 1993, p. 32). Yet I have to concede to Funani's (1992, p. 4) assertion that we have to question the meaning of our 'knowing', since collecting, analysing and reporting data is not the same as living it.

I was also particularly cautious not to create a situation of 'contagious' polite refusal. As Parpart (2000, p. 5) cautioned, 'Knowledge is not something that just exists out there, ready to be discovered. It is embedded in social contexts and attached to different power positions....' In addition, control over knowledge, even through silence, may be an essential survival strategy for marginalized people (Parpart, 2000, p. 5). In my experience, people working among deprived black communities in KwaZulu/Natal who begin in an authoritarian manner, or in any way which threatens or frightens persons in these communities, have encountered complete or partial, yet polite, silence. Very often if a person in a deprived community is unsure about a person's motives, whatever they are asked, the reply will be 'Ungas', which, loosely translated from Zulu, means 'I don't know, I have no idea.' The Durban Station and Warwick Avenue sites were also notorious for a high crime rate. Thus for security reasons as well as to increase my chances of acceptance into the three sites, I decided to have an African woman accompany me. However, after four weeks I chose to work alone as

I had become familiar with and confident in what I had previously assumed would be trouble areas. Furthermore, I was able to achieve a rapport with the traders more easily than I had anticipated. Rapport is used in the context of developing a relationship of understanding and responsibility on both sides (Gilligan, 1982, p. 19) instead of as previously implied in quantitative research, that is, the task of the interviewee accepting the research goals and actively providing relevant information (Oakley, 1981, p. 35). I dressed in old, faded, casual clothes which allowed me to merge into the area and sit comfortably on the pavement. Unlike the researchers in McDowell and Court (1994), who had to carefully choose their dress and language to demonstrate their competence, I had to be very careful that my dress and language did not intimidate the traders.

My physical appearance also facilitated my access. My small stature was often mistaken for youth. Explanations that I was older than I looked generally served to create a relaxed jovial atmosphere, since it was almost always followed by bawdy jokes which initiated the power sharing. My small physical size was also perceived as a sign of relative weakness. The women at Durban Station adopted a protective attitude, calling me 'Umtanuwam' (little one). Dominant women in Warwick Avenue perceived me as harmless because of my size and were less confrontational. Judging from the frequent incidence of verbal abuse and physical violence amongst the traders at Durban Station and Warwick Avenue, I was definitely treated with less vigour.

Similar to Oakley (1981), I was asked a variety of questions extending from questions about the research and myself, to advice and information. At Durban Station mainly younger women were curious to know more about me, and when they saw my daughter they enquired about her father. I believe it was their way of trying to 'place' me since I was asking them personal questions (Oakley, 1981; Finch, 1996). Following the empathetic mode of interviewing (Oakley, 1981; Winchester, 1996), I choose to divulge that I was a lone parent. This had a most unexpected response. While they acknowledged that I was in a more secure position financially, they still felt that I needed protecting and assistance because of my physical stature. So rather than my divulgence having the effect which allowed them to feel that I was able to empathize with them, it had an unexpected effect where the women took on a more protective role towards me. Often when a researcher works continuously with a community the person may become emotionally involved with that community, but in this situation the involvement appeared to be from both sides.

The woman were approached with greetings and enquires about their well-being before being asked whether I could disturb them. Initially, my explanation of the study was lengthy because I was concerned to obtain informed consent (Punch, 1994, p. 90). However, I found that after a few days at the sites, the lengthy elaboration was not necessary because of the ultra-efficient network. Since the traders do not have access to mass media, they rely on 'news' from others. The presence of an outsider in that community, especially if the person belongs to another race group, generally causes much anxiety, thus the women rely on 'word of mouth' to be informed or to alleviate fears. Eventually, all that was required was to introduce myself as a student researching women's health before the woman reassured me that she had previously seen or heard of me. Consequently, I tried to briefly yet succinctly cover all details which I considered important. These included the women's right to refuse to be interviewed, withdrawal of consent at any stage of the interview and their right to decline to answer a question if they found it embarrassing or upsetting, since some health issues can be quite personal. Further, I tried to explain the various possible uses of the data to be collected. Yet, ultimately, I don't believe I received a fully informed consent because my perception is that they did not completely understand the many possible audiences to whom the data could be presented. I am not able to completely protect the anonymity of my participants. Thus, since the information was given so enthusiastically and freely it will be my responsibility to devise ways to ensure that it is not used detrimentally against the collective interests of the women traders (Finch, 1996, p. 176).

Problems in the Field

All women interviewed for the questionnaire survey in 1998 offered their time and assistance for the planned qualitative data collection in 1999. However, it was not possible to collect qualitative data from the women previously interviewed. While most of the women have been trading at those particular sites for extended periods, their exact location at the site varies. During the quantitative fieldwork I was sometimes unable to trace the women whom I had interviewed four weeks previously. Occasionally, I took photographs of a site that included a trader and offered to give the woman a copy. However, when I tried to find her I encountered problems. At the Beach and Warwick Avenue sites her daily trading site was determined by the time she arrived each morning. Hence she could either be on the same spot or a few hundred metres away, which was very difficult to locate in the chaos of the market area. The women gave me their names but I soon realized that they were called completely different-sounding nicknames when I tried to trace some of them at the end of the fieldwork. At Durban Station, although the women slept on the spot where they traded, it was still difficult to trace them. While the area is small and it seems like a small number of traders, the actual turnover of traders was very frequent.

When the woman went home, she could spend a weekend to two months way from the site. Traders did not reserve their places and used any spot that was available on their return.

The hostility and distrust among the traders due to the changes in the laws and regulations in the winter of 1997 were exacerbated by the Durban City Council's decision to move some traders from Durban Station and Warwick Avenue in the spring of 1999. Many of the traders had incorrectly rationalized that the information which they had given me had been used against them, and were very angry with me. Being far away from them also made matters worse as I was unable to sympathize with and console them during the move. Thus I experienced some difficulty convincing them in the summer of 1999 that I was on their side and that what they had told me was confidential and for the use of my thesis instead of City Council plans.

Reflections on Personal Interaction in the Research Process

I found that using and acknowledging common mannerisms, both verbal and non-verbal, greatly facilitated my access to the community as the women took this as an indication that I was familiar with and respected their culture.

Among these mannerisms was the tilt of one's head with the simultaneous nodding or movement of head from side to side with closed eyes, with a pained expression on one's face, hunched shoulders and the emitting of an 'Awoa' sound. This generally signifies empathy in local communities. When I empathized in this manner, the women often elaborated beyond the answer of the question, thus providing rich ethnographic data.

Eye contact with the traders varied depending on which area I was working in. At the Beach area, traders were more familiar with looking into the faces of their customers and therefore looked at me when I spoke to them, while traders at Durban Station who were more recently urbanized did not look at me and instead looked away. According to Zulu custom, it is rude to look into the eyes of another person while talking, especially for women. However, it could also have been an indication of boredom and disinterest (Mason, 1996). Thus if the situation seemed ambivalent, I enquired if it was okay to continue just to confirm if the woman was still interested. None of the women indicated disinterest and were embarrassed that they might have made me feel that they were bored.

Language is part of a culture. Yet, it is often assumed to be fairly simple to communicate with clients whose first language is not English but who speak and understand English (Schott and Henley, 1996, p. 69). Often, as in the case of South Africa, people speak a variety of dialects of English that have been influenced by other languages and have developed aspects of their own grammar, intonations, rhythm, accent and vocabulary. Also in most European languages it is common to state the main point of an argument first, and then to illustrate or expand upon it (d'Ardenne and Mahtani, 1989). Zulu culture differs. Traders sometimes related a long story before they finally answered my question. If one is not accustomed to this type of behaviour, it is easy to interrupt, reiterate the question or ask another question, fearing that the woman has lost track of the original question.

In Western society a conversation requires people to take turns and it is considered polite for only one person to speak at a time. However, among the traders it was considered very normal to talk or comment while the other person was speaking. If I listened attentively without commenting (which would be the polite thing to do in Western society), the woman became self-conscious and gradually responded in monosyllables.

The traders generally, but more especially at Durban Station and Warwick Avenue, did not talk softly and often shouted from where they were sitting or standing to someone metres away, to have a conversation. They also had no problem with other people, who happen to overhear, contributing. Pons (1982, p. 31) posited that when people are literally thrown together, as is the case of most informal trading or living, privacy and anonymity are virtually impossible. Often, my comment or enquiry to what I had overheard would be relayed loudly by the trader whom I was interviewing, ending with 'the visitor said' or 'Priscilla wants to know'. Initially, I was embarrassed and expected them to get angry but the response was always jovial. Often the person would shout back an answer and I would shout back a response, maintaining a conversation with someone fifty metres away. Thus I was often included in conversations with people whom I did not know, which helped to increase my network.

I did not use first names to address the women but instead used traditional terms of address. For example, I referred to a young married woman as *Mokoti* (new bride or married woman with young children), a middle aged woman with grown children as *Mama* (a mother) and an elderly woman as *Gogo* (granny). This made the women feel respected and endeared me to them.

The form in which data are collected has an impact on the relationship between the researchers and the researched (Bell and Roberts, 1984; Martin, 1990). My decision not to carry my camera with me every day for security reasons sometimes meant a lost opportunity. I was also cautious about taking photographs, as I did not want to contribute to aerial distance, allowing the unacceptable situation of poor living conditions to be made picturesque (Martin, 1996). Thus I always asked permission. Since I commenced my work displaying respect and gratitude, I did not want to ruin the relationship. These decisions had a positive and negative effect.

The negative consequence was that I could not take photographs of what I knew would be significant in my discussions of their health, for example their cooking utensils or water receptacles, because the women would not consent. They explained that they were embarrassed to live in such conditions and did not want people 'overseas' to see that. The positive effect was that the women were able to relax and knew that I respected their views.

A formal written copy of the data collected was not presented to the traders for feedback because most of the traders cannot read English. On a personal trip to South Africa in July 2000 I tried to present the data to the traders while they sat in the groups that I had used for my group discussions. The women declined my offer. Although they were willing to provide further information, they felt that it was a waste of time to discuss what I had previously collected. They also said that they were mainly uneducated and could not understand what people did at universities. Furthermore, they said that if they had not trusted me to 'take down the information correctly' and to treat what they said to me with respect, they would not have spoken to me. Thus it is my responsibility to the traders to analyse the data in a way that I hope would meet with their approval if they ever read it.

Conclusion

The research reported here was guided by a relational ethics, grounded in respect for the subjects of my investigation. The values involved included the importance of empowering and non-exploitative relations with interviewees, rapport building and acknowledging the positionality of the researcher. A detailed account of method and practice makes these values explicit, and helps to reveal something of the demands of this kind of ethically informed inquiry.

NOTES

1   Personal communication with Alan Wheeler of the Department of Small Business and Informal Trade in Durban (1997).
2   Durban is the largest city in the predominantly rural province of KwaZulu/Natal, which is one of the most densely populated regions of the country and also one of the poorer of South Africa's nine provinces (Bonnin, 1997).
3   I had to accommodate my daughter's school terms, as I am a lone parent.
4   The three surveys used were the Urban Poverty and Social Policy in the Context of Adjustment UPA study (Moser, Gatheouse and Garcia, 1996a, 1996b), General Household Survey (1972) and Health Survey for England (1995).

REFERENCES

Bell, C. and Roberts, H. (eds) (1984) *Social Researching: Politics, Problems, Practice*, London: Routledge and Kegan Paul.

Bonnin, D. (1997) 'Lwalulukhulu usizi la – political violence and poverty in Kwa Zulu Natal', *Agenda* 33, 64–7.

Burgess, J., Limb, M. and Harrison, C. M. (1988a) 'Explaining environment values through the medium of small groups: 2. Illustrations of a group at work', *Environment and Planning A* 20, 457–76.

Burgess, J., Limb, M. and Harrison, C. M. (1988b) 'Explaining environment values through the medium of small groups: 1. Theory and practice', *Environment and Planning A* 20, 309–26.

Burgess, R. (1982) *Field Research: A Sourcebook and Field Manual*, London: Allen and Unwin.

Cornwell, J. (1984) *Hard-Earned Lives: Accounts of Health and Illness from East London*, London: Tavistock.

Cunnan, P. (1993) *Primary Health Care Need, Use and Provision in Informal Settlements: The Case of Canaan, Durban*, unpublished MA dissertation, University of Durban-Westville, South Africa.

Cunnan, P. (2002) *The Health of Urban Poor Black Women Street Traders in Durban, South Africa*, unpublished PhD thesis, Queen Mary, University of London.

Cunnan, P. and Maharaj, B. (2000) 'Against the odds: health care in an informal settlement in Durban', *Development Southern Africa* 17, 667–86.

d'Ardenne, P. and Mahtani, A. (1989) *Transcultural Counselling in Action*, London: Sage.

Donovan, J. (1986) 'Black people's health: a different approach', in T. Rathewell and D. Phillips (eds), *Health, Race and Ethnicity*, London: Croom Helm, pp. 117–36.

Doyle, L. (1999) 'The big issue: empowering homeless women through academic research', *Area* 31, 239–46.

Durban City Engineers Department (1984) *The Hawker Report: A Geography of Street Trading in central Durban*, Durban: Durban City Council.

England, K. V. L. (1994) 'Getting personal: reflexivity, positionality, and feminist research', *Professional Geographer* 46, 80–9.

Finch, J. (1996) 'It's great to have someone to talk to: ethics and politics of interviewing women', in M. Hammersley (ed.), *Social Research: Philosophy, Politics and Practice*, London: Sage, pp. 116–80.

Fontana, A. and Frey, J. H. (1994) 'Interviewing – the art of science', in N. K. Denzin and Y. S. Lincoln (eds), *Handbook of Qualitative Research*, London: Sage, pp. 361–76.

Funani, L. (1992) 'Nigerian Conference revisited', *Agenda* 15, 63–8.

General Household Survey (1972) *Office of Population Censuses and Surveys*, London: Social Survey Division, HMSO.

Gilbert, M. R. (1994) 'The politics of location: doing feminist research at "home"', *Professional Geographer* 46, 90–5.

Gilligan, C. (1982) *In a Different Voice: Psychological Theory and Women's Development*, Cambridge, Mass.: Harvard University Press.

Goss, J. D. (1996) 'Introduction to focus groups', *Area* 28, 113–14.

Health Survey for England (1995) London: Great Britain Department of Health, Stationery Office.

Katz, C. (1994) 'Playing the field: questions of fieldwork in geography', *Professional Geographer* 46, 67–72.

Kobayashi, A. (1994) 'Colouring the field: gender, "race", and the politics of fieldwork', *Professional Geographer* 46, 73–9.

Lawson, V. (1995) 'The politics of difference in examining the quantitative/qualitative dualism in post-structuralist feminist research', *Professional Geographer* 47, 449–57.

Lund, F. and Skinner, C. (1998) 'Women traders in Durban: life on the streets', *Indicator South Africa* 15 (4), 17–24.

McDowell, L. and Court, G. (1994) 'Performing work: bodily representations in merchant banks', *Environment and Planning* 12, 727–50.

McLafferty, S. L. (1995) 'Counting for women', *Professional Geographer* 47, 436–41.

Martin, C. (1990) 'How do you count maternal satisfaction? A user-commissioned survey of maternity services', in H. Roberts (ed.), *Women's Health Counts*, London: Routledge, pp. 144–66.

Martin, J. R. (1996) 'Aerial distance, esotericism and other closely related traps', *Signs: Journal of Women in Culture and Society* 21, 584–614.

Mason, J. (1996) *Qualitative Researching*, London: Sage.

Mattingly, D.F. and Falconer-al-Hindi (1995) 'Should women count? A context of debate', *Professional Geographer* 47, 427–35.

Moser, C., Gatehouse, M. and Garcia, H. (1996a) *Urban Poverty Research Sourcebook Module I: Sub-city Level Household Survey*, UMP Working Paper Series 5, Washington, DC: World Bank.

Moser, C., Gatehouse, M. and Garcia, H. (1996b) *Urban Poverty Research Sourcebook Module II: Indicators of Urban Poverty*, UMP Working Paper Series 5, Washington, DC: World Bank.

Moss, P. (1995) 'Embeddness in practice, numbers in context: the politics of knowing and doing', *Professional Geographer* 47, 442–8.

Nast, H. J. (1994) 'Opening remarks on "Women in the field"', *Professional Geographer* 46, 54-66.

Oakley, A. (1981) 'Interviewing women: a contradiction in terms', in H. Roberts (ed.), *Doing Feminist Research*, London: Routledge and Kegan Paul, pp. 30–61.

Parpart, J. L. (2000) 'Rethinking participation, empowerment and development from a gender perspective', in J. Freedman (ed.), *Transforming Development*, Toronto: University of Toronto Press, pp. 89–102.

Patai, D. (1991) 'US academics and third world women: is ethical research possible?', in S. B. Gluck and D. Patai, D. (eds), *Women's Words: The Feminist Practice of Oral History*, London: Routledge, 137–54.

Peace, S. (1993) 'Negotiating', in P. Shakespeare, D. Atkinson and S. French (eds), *Reflecting on Research Practice: Issues in Health and Social Welfare*, Buckinghamshire: Open University Press, pp. 25–35.

Pons, V. (1982) 'Launching a neighbourhood study in an African Town', in R. Burgess (ed.), *Field Research: A Sourcebook and Field Manual*, London: Allen and Unwin, pp. 31–42.

Preston-Whyte, E. (1982) *Why Questionnaires are Not the Answer: Comments and Suggestions Based on a Pilot Study on the Rural Informal Sector in KwaZulu - Questionnaires are No Short Cut*, Working Paper 48, Durban: SALDRU.

Punch, M. (1994) 'Politics and ethics in qualitative research', in N. K. Denzin and Y. S. Lincoln (eds.), *Handbook of Qualitative Research*, London: Sage, pp. 83–98.

Roberts, H. (ed.) (1990) *Women's Health Counts*, London: Routledge.

Robson, C. (1993) *Real World Research: A Resource for Social Scientists and Practitioner-Researchers*, Oxford: Blackwell.

Rose, G. (1997) 'Situating knowledge: positionality, reflexivities and other tactics', *Progress in Human Geography* 21, 305–20.

Schott, J and Henley, A. (1996) *Culture, Religion and Childbearing in a Multiracial Society: A Handbook for Health Professionals*, Oxford: Butterworth-Heinemann.

SEWU (Self-Employed Women's Union) (1997) 'A labour policy for all', *Agenda* 35, 51–4.

Stacey, J. (1991) 'Can there be a feminist ethnography?', in S. B. Gluck and D. Patai (eds), *Women's Words: The Feminist Practice of Oral History*, London: Routledge, 111–20.

Staebeli, L. A. and Lawson, V. A. (1994) 'A discussion of "women in the field" – the politics of feminist research', *Professional Geographer* 46, 96–102.

WGSG (Women in Geography Study Group) (1997) *Feminist Geographies: Explorations in Diversity and Difference*, Harlow: Longman.

Winchester, H. P. M. (1996) 'Ethical issues in interviewing as a research method in human geography', *Australian Geographer* 2, 117–31.

Yeandle, S. (1984) *Women's Working Lives: Patterns and Strategies*, New York: Tavistock.

Part V

Moral Context and Professional Practice in Geography

The history of geographical concepts and practice has for long fascinated a discipline which seems unusually introspective. Few of the academic profession will have evaded an undergraduate course or postgraduate seminar dignified by such labels as 'nature and methods' or 'the philosophy of geography'. David Smith recalls reading the classic by Richard Hartshorne (1939) cover to cover, in preparation for his final examinations in 1958, and later exposure to the thoughts of his Manchester colleague Walter Freeman (1961). Contemporary reviews include one by David Livingstone (1992), and the regularly revised modern classic by Ron Johnston (1997). The treatments in these books all have their own particularity, as signalled in sub-titles (see references below), including the notions of a developing science, current thought illuminated by the past, and a contested enterprise. The contest, like the interpretation, will inevitable involve moral values concerning what kind of discipline geography ought to be – a debate which will continue as long as there are geographers to engage it.

Johnston's explicit limitation to the Anglo-American realm, which the other books largely share, is a reminder of the geographical limitations of our profession. Not only are we, in the Anglo-American world, somewhat isolated from much of the rest (if only by language), so geographers in many of these other countries are not integrated into what we regard as the mainstream. In the first of the two contributions to this concluding part of the book, Ron Johnston (Chapter 17) considers the significance of networks in the career paths from which the discipline develops. Planned or chance encounters and collaborations with particular others, at particular times and places, have been highly influential; as he reminds us, place matters, context is crucial.

The origins of contributors to this volume give some indication of the particularity of one such network: that of David Smith's professional associates. Roughly half of the authors are from outside Britain: three from the United States, three from Eastern Europe (including the writer of the Foreword), two from South Africa, one from Israel, and one has spent a substantial time in Australia. Hence our claims to provide international perspectives, selective though they will inevitably be.

Many contributors to this volume have commented on David Smith's work, with a generosity which they must have regarded as fitting for a project initiated in his honour. It therefore seems appropriate to conclude with more substantial reviews. The intention is not to add further plaudits, nor to balance these with heavy critique. The purpose is to see what might be found of more general interest from this example of professional geographical practice set in a moral context. As Ron Johnston emphasizes, personal biographies can be important supplements to the published record in understanding disciplinary change.

These two chapters require little further introduction. Ron Johnston's interpretation is set imaginatively, within his approach to disciplinary change, with its emphasis on paradigm shifts and the question of whether these reflect revolution or evolution. Whatever it might be, values are deeply implicated. David Smith's account of his own career (Chapter 18), played out very much on the discipline's fringe, stresses concern with the normative as its guiding theme, from location theory to moral philosophy. He concludes with a reassertion of his professional ethics, involving the spatial extension of mutually supportive networks, which challenges aspects of contemporary practice. And here we are back to the essentially ethical and moral point of academic work.

REFERENCES

Freeman, T. W. (1961) *A Hundred Years of Geography: A Historical and Biographical Survey of Geography as a Developing Science*, Chicago: Aldine Publishing Company.

Hartshorne, R. (1939) *The Nature of Geography: A Critical Survey of Current Thought in the Light of the Past*, Lancaster, Penn.: The Association of American Geographers.

Johnston, R. J. (1997) *Geography and Geographers: Anglo-American Human Geography since 1945* (5th edition), London: Edward Arnold.

Livingstone, D. L. (1992) *The Geographical Tradition: Episodes in the History of a Contested Enterprise*, Oxford: Blackwell.

17

Disciplinary Change and Career Paths

Ron Johnston

... if there is any coherence to my personal professional journey, it was certainly not planned. Chance encounters with particular people, places and publications tended to pull me one way rather than another, along with a far from clear vision of a better world that scholarship might help to create. And I suspect this is how most of us work.

Smith, 'On performing geography' (2001), p. 146

For some geographers, a concern with the history of their discipline is unnecessary, a diversion from the imperatives of today and tomorrow (Barnett, 1995; Thrift, 2002). To others, however, ignorance of where we have come from – both collectively and individually – impoverishes both our understanding of the present and our ability to address the future. But how do we advance that understanding? What methods and sources are needed? Many recent attempts draw very heavily on published works, the great majority of which are research papers. Thus to a considerable extent the history of geography is an account of what was being published, when, where and how, of the debates over different approaches and practices, and of the influence of particular individuals and groups – as indexed, for example, by secondary data such as citations. From such accounts, explanatory descriptions have been assembled.

Although informative and valuable in providing overviews of disciplinary change and expansion (even 'progress', if that value-laden term is allowed: Bassett, 1999), such analyses ignore much of the detail and tell us more about the products of geographic scholarship than they do of the production processes. To appreciate the latter, we need to be more aware of details of the academic lives of the individuals involved – the how, why, what and where of their careers and scholarly decision-making. This calls for biographical material, of which there is a paucity in geography, other than (relatively brief) obituaries: despite some efforts (notably in the *Geographers: Biobibliographic Studies* series, all of whose essays related to deceased geographers), we know relatively little of the influences on many of the discipline's key individuals.

This lack of detailed appreciation of the conditions within which our bodies of knowledge have been produced is perhaps particularly important for geographers because so much of their discipline's corpus of scholarship has been produced over the last few decades, with many of the most distinguished contributors still active practitioners. Appreciating the details of their career trajectories – as against those of geography's founders, most of whose works have little direct contemporary relevance – is to some extent being extended by autobiographical essays (e.g. Haggett, 1990; Gould and Pitts, 2002), although their value will almost certainly be enhanced when that material is reworked into wider appreciations. Even so, such essays merely skim the surface of the large volume of hidden – much of it unwritten – material relevant to appreciating disciplinary history and formulating more general appreciations of the conditions and nature of knowledge-production in geography.

One of the intriguing features about work on the history of geography is that it illustrates one of the discipline's own canons – places matter! As Livingstone (2003) has argued for science in general, context is crucial to knowledge-production: much of it occurs in locales where individuals interact, places that have their own cultural norms and accepted practices into which individuals are socialized – and against which they sometimes react, even rebel! Disciplinary histories are forged in those locales. They are not fixed, however; rather they change with their membership, and as people move between locales so they diffuse ideas and practices. Furthermore, their relatively dense systems of inter-personal contact are associated with impersonal interactions. Most knowledge is deposited in repositories – mainly books and journals – and has an existence beyond its producers', being permanently available for consultation and interpretation. Scholars constantly interact with this vast store of knowledge, whilst extending the foundation for their own work, discovering evidence and arguments both for and against their own views and thereby enhancing their inter-personal interactions, as well their interpretations of the world outside academia.

Appreciating the history of geography as an academic discipline therefore calls for study of the geography of its knowledge-production. Such an enterprise will provide deeper understanding of the reasons why geographers have done particular types of work (when and where), and why, in some cases, they have shifted the orientation of their activities. To succeed, it needs biographical studies set within a framework of the general context for academic production – which itself varies over space and time. The present chapter is one such brief contribution to that effort, examining the career of David M. Smith with a general 'model' of how academic geography operates.

Geographers and Kuhn: Revolutions No but Paradigms Yes!

In the 1960s and 1970s a number of geographers were seduced by the terminology of Kuhn's (1962) model of changes in scientific disciplines, even though he made it clear – especially in his later writings (Kuhn, 1991) – that his model did not apply to disciplines that were in what he called a pre-paradigmatic state. Kuhn never mentioned geography by name, but it certainly fell into that pre-paradigmatic category then – and still does.

Nevertheless, the model was bewitching, especially two of its terms – revolution and paradigm. A *revolution* in a Kuhnian sense involves a switch in a discipline's nature brought about by the perceived failures of one set of practices and their replacement by another, accepted as superior; the switch requires a statement of faith by those involved, since the two sets of practices are incommensurate and evaluation of their relative merits entails subjective rather than objective judgements. As their critics have argued (Stoddart, 1986; Livingstone, 1992), many of the geographers did not deploy the term in a descriptive-analytical sense as essayed by Kuhn, but rather as a form of boosterism for their view of disciplinary practice, which was at odds with the 'conventional wisdom'.

Such boosters were promoting an alternative *paradigm*, using this part of Kuhn's terminology in its accepted sense as a shared set of beliefs about knowledge and its production. A paradigm is an academic culture, a means of operating whereby the adherents (members of an academic community akin to a village, according to Geertz, 1983) agree on issues of epistemology, ontology and methodology within a defined sphere of academic activity – usually a sub-discipline rather than an entire discipline, as Kuhn made clear in his later writings. Students are socialized into a paradigm with which they may remain throughout their subsequent careers. They may transfer their allegiance to another, however, rejecting previously held views; this may involve a change in academic interests, perhaps associated with changes in the scholars interacted with (i.e. in the communities to which they belonged), both directly and indirectly, and perhaps also with one of more of epistemology, ontology or methodology. Choice of paradigm – or community (the terms are used interchangeably here) – involves decisions about academic work and life that cannot be divorced from wider considerations, such as political and ethical views (in the broadest sense); the case study here certainly illustrates that.[1]

A third Kuhnian term also deployed, though neither as frequently nor with as much fervour as the previous two, is *normal science*. To Kuhn, normal science is what a paradigm's adherents do. They accept the relevant community definitions of what is known and how new knowledge is produced, and they then proceed in a linear fashion, adding new knowledge to the portfolio using accepted procedures. For most of the time, normal science within an agreed paradigm characterizes most scholarly activity: knowledge accretes within accepted frameworks to which challenges are infrequent – and out of which revolutions rarely emerge.

Does any of this help us to understand changes in the discipline of geography over the last five decades (since David Smith became an undergraduate at the University of Nottingham in 1955)? Certainly the concepts of paradigm and normal science are of value, to the extent that they indicate that scholars are socialized and then work within communities with shared values and practices. But how about revolutions? There have certainly been major shifts in geographical practices during that period – some involving individuals switching from one paradigm to a very different blueprint – but many doubt that these have been revolutionary in any sense, let alone the Kuhnian.

Recently, for example, Gauthier and Taaffe (2003) identified three major switches within American geography during the twentieth century, which they term revolutions because they meet six (relatively vague) criteria – type of change; pace of change; intensity of accompanying debate; operational characteristics (or core concepts); impact of the change; and context for the change. Their conclusion was more circumspect, however, with a summary description of a

> continuity model with surges superimposed to represent the three 'revolutions'. During the surges the weaknesses of the previous paradigm are usually stressed and caricatured. . . . Later, as the surge subsides, we begin hearing more about hapless conceptual babies being thrown out with the bathwater of the old paradigm. The merits of some aspects of the previous paradigm are discussed and recognized, and a certain amount of continuity sets in – perhaps only leading to a wave of enthusiasm about a new paradigm. (p. 523)

What stimulated those surges? What conditions created a milieu within which change could occur? What contingent circumstances meant that it happened in some places rather than others? And what were the roles of particular individuals in all of that? Extensive changes there certainly have been (as documented, for example, by Johnston and Sidaway, 2004), but in most cases these have not involved paradigm replacement (revolutionary or otherwise). Instead the range and variety of geographical practices have increased, and the number of separate (though somewhat overlapping and far from independent) communities of practitioners has expanded substantially. Answering the questions posed above is thus a major task whose scope is well beyond a single chapter. Furthermore, as will be argued here, it is wrong to assume that there is a common model which applies to all change events, let alone to all geographers involved in them. This is illustrated here by focusing on just one geographer – David Smith – whose career covers a turbulent set of decades in the history of geography as an academic discipline. That career is set within the framework of an introductory discussion of academic networks.

Networks of Geographers

Very little – if any – scientific progress is made in a vacuum: it involves scholars interacting with each other, and with each other's ideas, as well as with a wide range of other sources, fixed and mobile, animate and inanimate. Those interactions occur through networks, within which the communities of scholars discussed above are embedded. Such networks have a number of components, including the individual scholars, the places where, and the media through which, they interact.

Individuals join, or are enlisted into, networks of scholars when they become practitioners within an academic discipline, usually by their 'teachers' and fellow-students. Such networks may be dense and located in a particular place – as in a large graduate school; others may be much sparser (with a 'lone scholar' as a polar type, for example) and/or 'placeless' – as with Internet chat-rooms and discussion groups. As scholars' careers develop, so their networks expand, especially those that are not associated with a particular place – the scholar's 'home location'. Much network expansion involves movement to other places, either on solo visits to another institution to meet with one or a few like-minded individuals, or to a designated meeting-place, such as a conference venue. From contacts there, both intentional and serendipitous, working relationships are forged and patterns of connectedness within academia and its myriad sub-communities stimulated. (Direct personal connections with potential co-workers are not necessary, however: an increasing number of collaborations – including the writing of books and papers – involve individuals who have never physically encountered each other and whose only interactions are via the Internet.)

Such networks are immensely complex and subject to rapid change, as people move jobs, students enter and leave graduate schools, scholars visit other institutions, and conferences and other meetings, large and small, are convened. Mapping them out in detail would be a massive and largely unproductive task, although understanding the details of many individuals' careers can be much assisted by knowledge of their time-space trajectories, as illustrated by Pred's (1979) deployment of Hägerstrand's time geography to his own career and Clout's (2003; Clout and Gosme, 2003) discussion of the linkages based around the writing of the UK government's *Admiralty Handbooks* at the Oxford and Cambridge geography departments during the Second World War. As the recent history of geography shows, many major innovations have stemmed from productive collaborations of groups (often far from self-selecting) located at a particular place at a fortuitous time (and perhaps with a range of other propitious circumstances: Johnston, 2004).

But not all innovations have emerged in that way, by any means. Others are produced by scholars working in relative isolation, perhaps at institutions where there are no others with like interests and few, if any, graduate students. They may operate relatively independently from others, in that they lack direct person-to-person contacts with 'collaborators'. Instead, their intra-community interactions are via what Popper termed 'World Three' – the world of ideas as inscribed in the written word (on which see Bird, 1975). This world is infinitely more voluminous than that of inter-personal networks, though its density also varies considerably over space as well as time. The items that it comprises – predominantly, though far from solely, books and academic journals – are themselves mobile, like the individuals who produce them, but are almost always consulted in a place where they are located – usually a library or a scholar's study (as too are the increasing number of 'placeless' documents available on the Internet, which most readers 'download' and print rather than read them on-screen).

Individuals are influenced – both negatively and positively – by the items that they read, so that understanding the evolution of disciplinary ideas and practices involves appreciating both the flow of such materials and the uptake of their contents. But scholars must be selective in what they choose to read – increasingly so, because of the volume and range available: some items may be accessed serendipitously (a book purchased from an airport shop, for example, or an article in a journal read to fill in unexpected time on a train journey), but most are chosen deliberately – because of their subject matter (as indicated by title and, perhaps, abstract), or their author (certain writers' works are favoured), or because they have been recommended by somebody else (either directly or by some other means – such as book reviews).

Appreciating the evolution of a discipline involves studying the multiplicity of interactions through these networks – the operation of paradigms during periods of normal science and the promotion of 'revolutions' or other forms of change. Furthermore, those networks cannot be studied in isolation. As historians of science (e.g. Livingstone, 1992, 2003) stress, academic disciplines operate within much wider social networks, involving links to both other disciplines and the society beyond their (relative) 'ivory towers'. Academics respond to those external worlds, and indeed are involved in their reconfiguration, through continuous processes of structuration: how they practise their disciplines may reflect direct 'diktats' from external bodies, but are much more likely to emerge from their observations and interpretations of the worlds in which they act out their daily lives.

Tracing the history of a discipline therefore involves a wide range of components. Many essays focus almost entirely on disciplinary outputs – notably books and journal articles. Relatively little attention – especially in studies of recent history – is devoted to other aspects, such as the conferences, seminars and informal meetings and conversations where the ideas that eventually result in the published outputs are rehearsed and honed.[2] Furthermore, there is relatively little biographical and autobiographical work done (though it has increased recently, often without any clear formulation of intent other than to 'tell the story as you see it'), with full obituaries and memoirs becoming confined – in geography at least – to a relatively few eminent scholars only. In sum, we know relatively little about many (if not most) of the individual career paths that collectively comprise the history of our, or almost any other, discipline, other than what they have published.[3]

Career Paths and Disciplinary Change

Geography experienced five decades of turbulence during the second half of the twentieth century, a period when its number of practitioners increased very substantially and the volume of research and publication much more so. A number of 'revolutions' were promoted by would-be change-agents within the discipline, and others were recognized by commentators on changes within the discipline. None of them were revolutions in the true Kuhnian sense, however, involving wholesale replacement of disciplinary practices. Instead, new sets of practices were grafted onto those already existing. In a number of cases, such new sets became central activities within the disciplinary portfolio, attracting adherents from recent recruits to the profession and, in some cases, 'converts' from other paradigms. But hegemony was never established; instead, an increasing number of competing and co-existing paradigms came to characterize the discipline, with the number depending on the scale at which they were identified (Johnston and Sidaway, 2004).

At a macro-scale, Sheppard (1995) identified two major paradigms within human geography over the last thirty to forty years – spatial analysis and social theory. The former preceded the latter in its formulation and, according to Sheppard, won over several influential individuals who were schooled and did their first work as spatial analysts. He took as his indicator of influence those who were heavily cited within the discipline's literature, and selected twenty-four individuals. Comparing their number of citations over two periods (1981–5 and 1986–90), he identified ten who had become less influential, all but two of whom he could readily identify as 'spatial analysts'. Of the twelve 'social theorists' identified, eight were categorized as 'social theoretic critics of spatial analysis ... [who were] dissidents from within its own ranks' (p. 288). They were divided into three separate cohorts: the first contained those who had written classic works within the spatial analysis tradition (such as David Harvey and Allen Scott); the second comprised individuals whose early work was in spatial analysis but who shifted their orientation before mid-career (people such as Doreen Massey, Richard Peet and Nigel Thrift); and the third included individuals trained as spatial analysts but who quickly shifted their attention (as was the case, he claims, with Gordon Clark). Those who remained with spatial analysis either continued to promote that cause (as with Berry, 2002: see Yeates, 2001), though to smaller audiences, or, presumably, became less active.

Paradigm Shifts and a Career Path: David M. Smith

One of the individuals identified by Sheppard as a spatial analyst with a declining citation count was David Smith, yet by the mid-1980s David would certainly not have identified himself as a spatial analyst – if he ever had done previously! He had, of course, written books in the spatial analysis mould, with major texts on both spatial theory (*Industrial Location: An Economic Geographical Analysis*: Smith, 1971b, 1981) and quantitative spatial analysis (*Patterns in Human Geography: An Introduction to Numerical Methods*: Smith, 1975), as well as a research monograph deploying those methods (*The Geography of Social Well-Being in the United States*: Smith, 1973). By the mid-1980s, however, his attention had been refocused onto aspects of what became known as 'welfare geography' (*Human Geography: A Welfare Approach*; *Where the Grass is Greener*: Smith, 1977, 1979) and non-quantitative methods (*Qualitative Methods in Human Geography*: Eyles and Smith, 1988); it later turned to issues of justice and ethics (*Geography and Social Justice*; *Geography and Ethics*; *Moral Geographies*: Smith 1994a, 2000a; Proctor and Smith, 1999). In terms of Sheppard's categorization, David Smith was clearly somebody who had written classic works in the spatial analysis tradition but had then switched to other paradigms. As such, his career path provides us with an important case study of individual trajectories within a changing discipline, and how the system of networks and places operates.

The career

David Smith was born, raised and educated in the English Midlands, culminating in his BA (1958) and PhD (1961) degrees at the University of Nottingham. After two years as a planning assistant for Staffordshire County Council, during which he did independent fieldwork on industrial archaeology (*The Industrial Archaeology of the East Midlands* was published in 1965), he joined the staff of the Department of Geography at the University of Manchester. He resigned from this post in 1966 (in part because the University would not grant him a year's leave of absence) and subsequently held posts at Southern Illinois University and the University of Florida. He left the United States in 1972, occupying visiting positions at the Universities of Natal, the Witwatersrand and New England (New South Wales) before being appointed to a chair in geography at Queen Mary College, University of London, where he remained until his retirement in 2001 (serving for periods as head of that Department and as Dean of Social Studies).

Apart from a spell of three years as an elected member of the Council of the Institute of British Geographers (1977–9), David has not been a major participant in the discipline's large-scale formal structures. He has, however, been an organiser of and major participant in smaller-scale activities, notably in twelve joint 'Anglo-' seminars (most of them organized through the Institute of British Geographers) with Soviet/Russian geographers, three with Georgian geographers, two each with Polish and Israeli geographers and one with both Georgian and Polish geographers. He has also held a number of short-term visiting positions, in Australia, Israel, Poland, Russia and South Africa as well as the United States. He has developed a wide international network of contacts and conducted research in a number of countries which are off-the-beaten track for most Anglo-American human geographers. He may be marginal to the dominant networks of that community in terms of personal contacts (though he has attended many major conferences in both the UK and the USA), but he was by no means a 'lone scholar' during his career: he may not have led large research groups, winning substantial grant and contract income, but he acted as an important stimulus for students, colleagues and those who established working relationships within a variety of contexts and milieux (and the Health Research Group that he established at Queen Mary in the late 1970s and directed for about a decade obtained grants/contracts totalling c.£0.5m during that period). Furthermore, he has published widely, particularly book-length works (both texts and monographs), and is widely cited and influential through those media.

But do the shifts in his career represent anything akin to 'revolutions' as Kuhn defined them and some commentators have claimed characterized geography during that period? Certainly there have been major shifts in the nature of his work. As he records, his undergraduate education took place in a 'pre-quantitative-and-theoretical-revolution' context, with a 'dull succession of regional courses', although those which he took in economics exposed him to an 'analytical discipline' which had important later implications for his work (Smith, 1984, p. 121). There was, however, a course by Eric Rawstron which, in effect, introduced location theory – and for which he had to read Lösch as the basis for a seminar presentation. He was stimulated by Rawstron's enthusiasm (on which see Rawstron, 2002) and by Lösch's claimed 'sense of duty "not to explain our sorry reality but to improve it"' (p. 121). But this had only a marginal impact on his PhD work, a regional study of industrial location which focused on the role of the hosiery industry alongside others in the economic development of the East Midlands. When he obtained a lectureship at Manchester, he realized that geography was changing: he could readily come to terms with the economic theory being adopted and adapted, but he had to struggle to assimilate the 'quantitative revolution', and eventually decided to go to the USA, because that was 'where it was at' in the development of location theory (and where his 'struggle' with quantitative methods was exacerbated when teaching them at Southern Illinois University).

So was this a 'revolution', away from 'historical, regional industrial geography' and towards theoretical economic geography associated with quantitative, empirical studies? It was certainly a major shift – presaged in an early paper (Smith, 1966) and extended in his 1971 and 1975 books. (The latter book was initially part of the former, which was too long to be accepted as a single volume: Smith, 1984, p. 127.) But 'as a major preoccupation ... [it] lasted barely five years' (p. 128): 'a new wind of change was beginning to blow through US geography: the message was "social relevance", and its direction towards public policy issues'; he wrote about one of his initial encounters with this at the 1971 Association of American Geographers Conference (Smith, 1971a). Most importantly, however, this academic exposure was grafted onto everyday experience of American social problems in southern Illinois and elsewhere, which led him to establish 'my new research field as the geography of social problems' (p. 129), which led to the 1973 book, among other things – including the influence of his wife, Margaret, who was then teaching social problems in the Department of Sociology at Southern Illinois University.

So, was this another revolution at the individual scale – although Smith (1984, p. 131) claims that with the 1973 book he 'failed to break out of the tradition of pattern recognition, albeit aided by modern methods of numerical description including the inevitable factor analysis'? Or was it, instead, merely the steady evolution of ideas and substantive interests, in which relatively little of previously acquired methods and approaches was discarded.[4] Neoclassical economic theories retained their attraction, extending to welfare economics while he was working in South Africa – where he 'found solace in the asocial and ahistorical abstraction of utility functions and welfare contours' while experiencing 'a sense of personal impotence in the face of South Africa's extreme racism and blatantly exploitive economy' (Smith, 1984, pp. 130–1), before he was later attracted to Marxian economics. This interpretation is sustained by the brief final chapter of *Industrial Location* (Smith, 1971b). After over 500 pages on location theory and issues of regional development, he appended a six-page discussion of 'the relative merits of the market-regulated economic system as against one which is centrally planned' (p. 511). This led, first, to a conclusion that market-regulated systems were unlikely to result in equilibria, let alone optimal location patterns, and that some form of state intervention may be justified 'if only in the interests of national self-preservation' (p. 514). Further,

> When considerations of social justice and the Christian ethic of responsibility to society's weaker brethren are added, the case becomes overwhelming. The only question that remains is the form government intervention should take and how far it should lead a nation along the continuum from unencumbered capitalism to complete state planning. (p. 514)

Turning to issues of regional variations in prosperity, he concluded that:

> It is difficult to see how the major problems of regional economic revival, environmental pollution, and minority unemployment in the American city can be solved except by a much greater input of social considerations in the plant location decision. Experience suggests that this input can seldom be left to the businessman. (p. 517)

Not a 'revolutionary shift' to equate with that announced by David Harvey (1973) two years later, certainly, but nevertheless a clear statement that the limits of location theory and its applications had been identified: if welfare is your concern, look elsewhere. Interestingly, that brief chapter was omitted from the book's second edition (Smith, 1981), though a brief epilogue addresses the same issues. Instead we are told that:

> If there is any substantial shift of emphasis in this edition, it is in making the broader societal context of industry more integral to the text as a whole, in the spirit of the past decade's growing preoccupation with issues of human well-being. (p. 3)

That epilogue was very similar to the first edition's discussion of the balance between free-market and centrally planned economies. In it,

Smith clearly hadn't moved as far as Harvey and others. His final paragraph read:

> The discussion of industrial location thus leads directly to some of the major issues facing contemporary society. If this field of inquiry has any meaning outside the pages of academic publications and the abstractions of the class-room, it is in its capacity to help build a new society through the development of new spatial forms of economic activity. As August Lösch, the most percep-tive of the great space economists, wrote in his *Economics of Location*, 'Not in explaining that which has grown, but where man himself is the creator, lies the real sphere of applicability for the laws of nature and of economics he has discovered.' So it is in the study of industrial location. (p. 458)

Published in 1981, this conclusion, after more than a decade of studying the geography of social well-being, suggests that David Smith still had a residual faith in the power of normative models to change the world for the betterment of all; there was certainly no immediate 'revolutionary paradigm switch' in his work. Much of his writing from 1973 on focused on the 'degree of inequality in human life chances' that characterizes capitalism (Smith, 1996b, p. 788), with his background foundation in economics leading him to focus (as in Smith, 1977) on technical critiques of the free market and its neoclassical underpinnings. However, his work in both the USA and South Africa encouraged consideration of the impact of local contexts on how the market system was operated – with particular reference to racism, as illustrated in his work on Atlanta (Smith, 1985; Smith and Pile, 1993) as well as in a collection of essays on urban problems in the second edition of which he concluded that, despite massive changes in the socio-economic and political context – with the emphasis on markets and self-reliance that characterized 'Thatcherism' and 'Reaganism' over the preceding decade – there was continuing evidence of '*a social problem of injustice* no more clearly expressed anywhere than in the city' (Smith, 1989, p. 396, his emphasis). Furthermore, work in the USSR, Poland and else-where 'behind the Iron Curtain' from 1976 on showed that inequality was not confined to capitalist societies, certainly not even in their post-socialist condition (Smith, 1994b, 1996c).

The shift to 'welfare geography' that apparently paralleled David's changing view of industrial location theory was strongly influenced by a number of factors, many of them personal – reflecting not only the 'who was where' aspects of his career but also continuing encounters with 'the real world' (notably in the USA and South Africa); these are set out in a retrospective essay on welfare geography, in which he describes an intellec-tual innovation as the likely 'product of a lengthy gestation, with the final outcome involving subtle interaction between the individual scholar and the context within which he or she works' (Smith, 1988a, p. 139). But the individual can influence that context, as David did by his work in and on the Soviet Union and Eastern Europe, and later on Israel, to complement that on the UK, the USA, and South Africa. By this deliberate navigation of the geography of his later career course, he was able to produce a 'popular' book – *Where the Grass is Greener: Living in an Unequal World* (Smith, 1979) – that conveyed his ideas to a wider audience than that of textbooks, and treated spatial inequality under communism and socialism as well as various 'stages' of capitalism. But the portrayal of inequality was not enough, nor were the attempts to account for its existence and geography through economic and other theory – important though those were. They had to be partially displaced from their central positions within human geography by a humanistic approach that revealed

> a world of experience, in which the meaning of things and places, and of life itself, is far from self-evident, yet in which commonsense and lay beliefs are as legitimate, as real, as findings of science. It is a world in which human volition is neither determined nor unconstrained, neither predictably responsive to stimuli nor totally lacking in logic or rationality. A world in which people can contradict themselves as well as others, giving different accounts of their lives in different circumstances – different versions of the truth. This world is a far cry from that of location theory's optimizing entrepreneurs, distance-minimizing consumers, place-utility maximizers and the like, and it is worth a brief reminder of how at least some of us reached it – how our own paths (or understanding of them) changed in the unfolding drama of disciplinary development. (Smith, 1988b, p. 258)

In recognizing this, there was no intention 'to proclaim yet another revolution in geography', although '[t]hat a new movement is taking shape is clear' (p. 266).

And the re-shaping continued. Much of it, as Smith (2003, p. 625) records, involved 'aspects of the search for human betterment' with its normative connotations 'shifting the focus from how things actually are to the way they ought to be'. Consideration of the 'ought' – now separated from the simplistic economic models of the 1960s – involved geographers in a 'moral turn'. Contacts between geographers and moral philosophers and/or ethicists were virtually non-existent, but recognition of the need for such links saw a growing interest in 'moral geographies', and the particular spatial issues that concerns over justice, equity and equality raise (see also Sack, 1997, and Miller and Hashmi, 2001). For Smith (2003, pp. 634–5), students of ethics have an 'abiding predilection towards philosophical abstraction'; geographers must argue for and illustrate the 'importance of context to the way in which real people act, in actual geographical and historical circumstances, in pursuit of the right and the good as they understand morality'. His own book (Smith, 2000a) illustrated the importance of the discipline's key concepts – landscape, location and place, proximity, distance, community, space, territory, development and nature – in the appreciation of moral geographies, and in 'working towards a universal theory of the right and good, however thin it might be, in a dialectical relationship with understanding actual human conduct in context' (Smith, 2003, p. 635), which has involved him in debates over ethical practices within academia in general and British geography in particular (Smith, 1988a, 1995a, 1996a, 2000b), as well as advancing the case for addressing moral issues directly within undergraduate teaching (Smith, 1995b).

Conclusions

> ... as scholars we are to a large extent creatures of our times. We react, to a greater or lesser degree, to contemporary professional fashion – itself moulded by the wider societal context. A new 'revolution' takes shape, the bandwagon begins to roll, and we push or jump on rather than be left behind. Some seek fame (even fortune), some professional eminence, power or status, some simply like the sound of their own voice or the sight of their own prose. We seek personal identity in an individualistic societal milieu. We use the talents at our disposal within our chosen (or chance) institutional setting of professional geography. A few stand aside from the crowd, ignoring the bandwagon (or falling off), pursuing scrupulous scholarship as they understand it, avoiding involvement in institutional structures, keeping off the committees, or simply turning in their lectures and going home to the gardening. Yet they may be no less captive than the rest of us – trapped in their narrow and unquestioned paradigms, idle, or just plain dull.
>
> Smith, 'Recollections of a random variable' (1984), p. 131

So what does David Smith's career – as illustrated by his journeys and writings, and especially his reflections – tell us about 'progress' in an academic discipline? Certainly it is hard to find too many echoes of it in the above quote. While at the beginning of his formal academic career – at Manchester and then Carbondale – David did approach, if not jump on, the fast-moving bandwagons, but from then on it is clear that he set a determined career goal, closely linked to personal concerns. How the detailed trajectory towards that goal evolved – from the mapping of inequality through attempts at explanation to issues of ethics and moral philosophy, and how it led him to question his work on, first, classical location theory and, then, welfare economics applied spatially[5] – certainly had some random elements in it. Though it was in no sense teleological, however, the direction was clear. His approach broadened as a result of myriad encounters, professional and otherwise, with landscapes and published sources as well as with people, but there is little evidence of 'revolutions' – and certainly not of him being trapped in a narrow paradigm, let alone dull.

But as he makes clear in his more personal, biographical essays – and in the chapter that follows this one – it was chance (or, at least, unplanned) encounters that in many cases widened his horizons and stimulated him to move in different directions: those mentioned include colleagues at Manchester and Carbondale, the Witwatersrand and (not surprisingly, given his thirty years there) Queen Mary. Such encounters, which illustrate embeddedness within locally based communities, initiated not only new academic directions but also exposure to new social conditions, which in many ways appear to have stimulated him more than some of his academic contacts. He responded by incorporating them into his career trajectory, along with the influences he had gained from wide and deep immersion in the impersonal academic worlds of library and study. Academic change involves the collective accumulation of the outputs of such individual journeys, involving periods of close interaction within particular communities – many, though certainly not all, of them locally situated, if having changing memberships – but also of much individual endeavour, interacting with animate and inanimate worlds and responding accordingly.

The degree to which different types of encounter influence any one individual's trajectory will vary considerably – some participate more than others in conferences large and small, for example; and some take a greater part in the role of institutions in the promotion of academic goals. The result is a congeries of different career paths through what, to paraphrase Hägerstrand, we might term the academic diorama. Generalization about the nature of those individual paths through the networks identified earlier in this chapter is far from straightforward – if either desirable or feasible – and there is no reason to suggest that the nature of David Smith's distinguished personal academic trajectory since he began his undergraduate career in 1955 is a paradigm case. It is only by appreciating his own encounters, and how they influenced not only that trajectory but also those of the many others he has come into contact with – both directly (not least through his teaching) and indirectly, through his publications (we can only be grateful that he loves 'the creative process of writing': Smith, 1984, p. 131) – that we can fully appreciate the genesis of his many contributions to geography's 'progress'. And it is only by studying the trajectories of a large number of others that we can piece together the history of the discipline. Fortunately, in a number of essays David Smith has provided us with important insights to that trajectory that other sources do not reveal; without them, we have to rely on published academic works, most of which provide but partial access to the influences and nature of an academic career. Autobiographical and biographical reports, along with the recording of oral history (much of which may soon be lost) about our fairly recent past, are necessary for full appreciation of disciplinary history – not least to illustrate what tangled webs we weave through our various networks and the virtual impossibility of capturing the complexity of contingency and constraint, chance and cartography, that evade the simplifications of any model-building strategy of other than the grossest over-simplification.

NOTES

1   Some have rejected the use of paradigm to describe the nature of academic communities because of its implication with revolutions in Kuhn's model, suggesting that to accept part of the language means an adherence to the entire model. This is not my position. I believe that the concept of a paradigm is valuable to appreciating how academic disciplines are structured even if that of revolution does not: 'Paradigms yes; revolutions no. Discuss with reference to the recent history of geography in the UK' is offered as a potential exam question!

2   One potential such locale was the IGU Symposium on Urban Geography held at Lund in 1962, at which 'more traditional' practitioners of urban geography came into close contact with the ideas of those promoting the 'quantitative revolution' – especially those emerging from the community at the University of Washington, Seattle, which was central to that enterprise. Although occasionally mentioned as a key event in the discipline's history, its nature and impact have not been explored in any detail.

3   A strong case can be made that we know less about geographers than scholars in many other disciplines. In the latest edition of the *International Encyclopaedia of the Social and Behavioral Sciences* (Smelser and Baltes, 2001), for example, only one geographer – Carl Sauer – was deemed worthy of a separate, bibliographic entry.

4   Though note his comment that '[m]ost geography is inconsequential claptrap, and never more so than during the "quantitative revolution"' (Smith, 1984, p. 132).

5   The 1977 book – *Human Geography: A Welfare Approach* – illustrates the evolutionary rather than revolutionary element of David's switch away from his roots in neoclassical economics, but it was, in effect, an attempt to deploy that tradition in new directions and, perhaps as a consequence, but also (and probably more importantly) because it didn't display the rhetoric of many contemporary 'radical geographers', failed to have a substantial impact on professional practice.

REFERENCES

Barnett, C. (1995) 'Awakening the dead: who needs the history of geography?', *Transactions of the Institute of British Geographers* (NS) 20, 417–19.

Bassett, K. (1999) 'Is there progress in human geography? The problem of progress in the light of recent work in the philosophy and sociology of science', *Progress in Human Geography* 23, 27–47.

Berry, B. J. L. (2002) 'Paradigm lost', *Urban Geography* 23, 441–5.

Bird, J. H. (1975) 'Methodological implications for geography from the philosophy of K. R. Popper', *Scottish Geographical Magazine* 91, 153–63.

Clout, H. (2003) 'Place description, regional geography and area studies: the chorographic inheritance', in R. J. Johnston and M. Williams (eds), *A Century of British Geography*, Oxford: Oxford University Press for the British Academy, pp. 247–74.

Clout, H. and Gosme, C. (2003) 'The Naval Intelligence Handbooks: a monument in geographical writing', *Progress in Human Geography* 27, 153–73.

Eyles, J. and Smith, D. M. (eds) (1988) *Qualitative Methods in Human Geography.* Cambridge: Polity.

Gauthier, H. L. and Taaffe, E. J. (2003) 'Three 20th century "revolutions" in American geography', *Urban Geography* 23, 503–27.

Geertz, C. (1983) *Local Knowledge: Further Essays in Interpretive Anthropology,* New York: Basic Books.

Gould, P. R. and Pitts, F. R. (eds) (2002) *Geographical Voices: Fourteen Autobiographical Essays,* Syracuse, NY: Syracuse University Press.

Haggett, P. (1990) *The Geographer's Art,* Oxford: Blackwell.

Harvey, D. (1973) *Social Justice and the City,* London: Edward Arnold.

Johnston, R. J. (2004) 'Communications technology and the production of geographical knowledge', in S. D. Brunn, S. L. Cutter and J. W. Harrington (eds), *Technoearth,* New York: Kluwer, pp. 17–36.

Johnston, R. J. and Sidaway, J. D. (2004) *Geography and Geographers: Anglo-American Human Geography since 1945,* London: Edward Arnold.

Kuhn, T. S. (1962) *The Structure of Scientific Revolutions,* Chicago: University of Chicago Press.

Kuhn, T. S. (1991) 'The natural and the human sciences', in D. J. Hiley, R. Bohman and R. Shusterman (eds), *The Interpretative Turn: Philosophy, Science, Culture,* Ithaca, NY: Cornell University Press, pp. 17–24.

Livingstone, D. N. (1992) *The Geographical Tradition: Episodes in the History of a Contested Enterprise,* Oxford: Blackwell.

Livingstone, D. N. (2003) *Putting Science in its Place: Geographies of Scientific Knowledge,* Chicago: University of Chicago Press.

Miller, D. and Hashmi, S. H. (eds) (2001) *Boundaries and Justice: Diverse Ethical Perspectives,* Princeton: Princeton University Press.

Pred, A. R. (1979) 'The academic past through a time-geographic looking glass', *Annals of the Association of American Geographers* 69, 175–80.

Proctor, J. D. and Smith, D. M. (eds) (1999) *Geography and Ethics: Journeys in a Moral Terrain,* London: Routledge.

Rawstron, E. M. (2002) 'Textbooks that moved generations', *Progress in Human Geography* 26, 831–6.

Sack, R. D. (1997) *Homo Geographicus: A Framework for Action, Awareness and Moral Concern,* Baltimore: Johns Hopkins University Press.

Sheppard, E. S. (1995) 'Dissenting from spatial analysis', *Urban Geography* 16, 283–303.

Smelser, N. J. and Baltes, P. B. (eds) (2001) *International Encyclopaedia of the Social and Behavioural Sciences*, Oxford: Elsevier.

Smith, D. M. (1965) *The Industrial Archaeology of the East Midlands*, Newton Abbot: David & Charles.

Smith, D. M. (1966) 'A theoretical framework for geographical studies of industrial location', *Economic Geography* 42, 95–113.

Smith, D. M. (1971a) 'America, America? Views on a pot melting. 2. Radical geography – the next revolution?', *Area* 3, 153–7.

Smith, D. M. (1971b) *Industrial Location: An Economic Geographical Analysis*, New York: John Wiley.

Smith, D. M. (1973) *The Geography of Social Well-being in the United States*, New York: McGraw Hill

Smith, D. M. (1975) *Patterns in Human Geography: An Introduction to Numerical Methods*, Newton Abbot: David & Charles.

Smith, D. M. (1977) *Human Geography: A Welfare Approach*, London: Edward Arnold.

Smith, D. M. (1979) *Where the Grass is Greener: Living in an Unequal World*, Harmondsworth: Penguin.

Smith, D. M. (1981) *Industrial Location: An Economic Geographical Analysis* (2nd edition), New York: John Wiley.

Smith, D. M. (1984) 'Recollections of a random variable', in M. Billinge, D. Gregory and R. Martin (eds), *Recollections of a Revolution: Geography as Spatial Science*, London: Macmillan, pp. 117–33.

Smith, D. M. (1985) 'Social aspects of urban problems: inequality in the American city – the case of Atlanta, Georgia, 1960–1980', *Geographica Polonica* 51, 65–83.

Smith, D. M. (1988a) 'On academic performance', *Area* 20, 3–13.

Smith, D. M. (1988b) 'Towards an interpretative human geography', in J. Eyles and D. M. Smith (eds), *Qualitative Methods in Human Geography*, Cambridge: Polity, 255–67.

Smith, D. M. (1989) 'Conclusion: from social problems and the city to the social problem of injustice', in D. T. Herbert and D. M. Smith (eds), *Social Problems and the City* (2nd edition), Oxford: Oxford University Press, pp. 387–96.

Smith, D. M. (1994a) *Geography and Social Justice*, Oxford: Blackwell.

Smith, D. M. (1994b) 'Social justice and the post-socialist city', *Urban Geography* 15, 612–27.

Smith, D. M. (1995a) 'Against differential research funding', *Area* 27, 79–83.

Smith, D. M. (1995b) 'Moral teaching in geography', *Journal of Geography in Higher Education* 19, 271–83.

Smith, D. M. (1996a) 'Reply to Rhind – value for money, the continuing debate', *Area* 28, 97–101.

Smith, D. M. (1996b) 'The quality of life: human welfare and social justice', in I. Douglas, R. Huggett and M. Robinson (eds), *Encyclopedia of Geography*, London: Routledge, pp. 772–90.

Smith, D. M. (1996c) 'The socialist city', in G. Andrusz, M. Harloe and I. Szelenyi (eds), *Cities after Socialism: Urban and Regional Change and Conflict in Post-socialist Societies*, Oxford: Blackwell, pp. 70–99.

Smith, D. M. (2000a) *Moral Geographies: Ethics in a World of Difference*, Edinburgh: Edinburgh University Press.

Smith, D. M. (2000b) 'Moral progress in human geography: transcending the place of good fortune', *Progress in Human Geography* 24, 1–18.

Smith, D. M. (2001) 'On performing geography', *Antipode* 33, 142–6.

Smith, D. M. (2003) 'Geographers, ethics and social concern', in R. J. Johnston and M. Williams (eds), *A Century of British Geography*, Oxford: Oxford University Press for the British Academy, pp. 625–42.

Smith, D. M. and Pile, S. J. (1993) 'Inequality in the American city: some evidence from the South', *Geographica Polonica* 61, 433–58.

Stoddart, D. R. (1986) *On Geography and its History*, Oxford: Blackwell.

Thrift, N. J. (2002) 'The future of geography', *Geoforum* 33, 291–8.

Yeates, M. H. (2001) 'Yesterday as tomorrow's song: the contribution of the 1960s "Chicago School" to urban geography', *Urban Geography* 22, 514–29.

18

From Location Theory to Moral Philosophy: Views from the Fringe

David M. Smith

> The real duty of the economist is not to explain our sorry reality, but to improve it.
>
> Lösch, *The Economics of Location* (1954), p. 4

> The point of morality is not to mirror the world, but to change it.
>
> Williams, *Morality: An Introduction to Ethics* (1972), p. 47

It may seem a long way from location theory to moral philosophy, even within the span of an academic lifetime. I have already written reflectively on aspects of this experience (Smith, 1984, 1988a, 2001), and Ron Johnston (above, Chapter 17) has set my career within his framework for interpreting disciplinary change. This contribution relates features of personal biography to my own understanding of the development of academic geography, from the first engagement with location theory in the 1950s to the contemporary exploration of the interface with moral philosophy. If there is any connecting thread to be found, it is concern with the normative: with the role of scholarship in seeking to identify and create a better world. Yet this aspiration is itself problematic, pushing the power of geography to its limits, and beyond, as we seek guidance from others in understanding such concepts as development and justice. These excursions to the fringe of our discipline are by no means one-way, however. They also help to highlight special contributions that geography can make to the work of others, revealing the importance of place manifest in local (regional or national) specificity, contingency and context.

I see my professional activity as involving an ongoing interaction between theory and practice. The search has been for what John Rawls (1971) described as reflective equilibrium, in the sense of trying to bring theoretical expectations and observed human conduct into some coherent structure. The theory has taken me into other disciplines, originally the economics that spawned location theory and regional science and most recently ethics or moral philosophy: beyond the fringe of even the most generous definition of geography. The practice has taken me into the field, to such diverse places as the former Soviet Union and South Africa: to the fringe in another sense – of the Anglo-American realm which tends to dominate the subject matter and profession of geography.

I have never felt comfortable within the confines of the Anglo-American world, far less as a member of the institution of 'British Geography': again, on the fringe, or margin as Ron Johnston puts it. In concluding with some reflections on personal and professional ethics, I argue for a more expansive and supportive international engagement with sometimes far distant others. Trying to make a difference in the creation of a better world, through writing, research and occasional consultancy, requires greater optimism that I can at times muster. But reaching out to fellow geographical practitioners elsewhere, assisting them in their scholarship, is a moral imperative if we are not merely to promote parochial self-interest. In the process, we may rediscover an ethics based on mutuality and reciprocity rather than on competition, to help us through hard times ahead.

Discoveries of Location Theory

I arrived at Nottingham University in 1955 fascinated by coastlines, and impressed by the order of the Davisian erosion cycle. I might have become a coastal geomorphologist, had it not been for the baffling formulae with which Cuchlaine King embellished her oceanography lectures. It was inspiration from two other quarters that led me in a different direction. The first was the economics I chose as a subsidiary subject: the first two years of an honours course. The second was the final-year option in economic geography taught by Eric Rawstron, which introduced the novel field of industrial location theory.

I have written of this experience elsewhere (Smith, 1984), so confine myself here to what I consider to have been the two most important discoveries. The first was realization of the interdependence of location theory and production theory. Rawstron (1958) had devised the 'spatial margin to profitability', defining the area within which plant viability was possible by virtue of total revenue exceeding total cost of production. I recognized this device as the equivalent of what my economics textbook termed the 'break-even points', which defined the upper and lower limits to the scale of production which would yield a profit. A few more technical twists showed that optimality with respect to location had simultaneously to be at optimal scale, within a given demand situation. While Rawstron's exposition had been largely intuitive, I translated the concept of the spatial margin, with space cost and revenue curves (or surfaces), into the kind of graphic models deployed in economics. It took a few years to gain the confidence to turn the sketches of a third-year undergraduate into a publishable paper (Smith, 1966), and a few more to flesh the analysis out at book length (Smith, 1971). Whatever the other merits of this work, industrial location in geography could never again be divorced from economic theory.

The second discovery was August Lösch's book *The Economics of Location* (1954). Rawstron was familiar with this and other contemporary classics of location theory, and distributed them to his students for seminars. That I got Lösch could hardly have been more fortunate. I was captivated by the order and regularity of his now-familiar economic landscape. I warmed to the rigour of his analysis, and the elegance of his prose. But what was most impressive to me was his explicit normative stance, captured in the axiom that the real duty is not to explain reality but to improve it: 'The question of the best location is far more dignified than determination of the actual one' (Lösch, 1954, p. 4). This contradicted the conventional preoccupation of industrial geography with describing and explaining actual location patterns. He went further: 'Wherever something new is being created, and thus in settlement and spatial planning also, the laws revealed through theory are the sole economic guide to what *should* take place' (p. 359). Whatever the limits of my grasp of Lösch's technical analysis, I learned that the creation of a better world required not only ideals but also the construction of normative models – of society, its institutions and its spatial form.

Excursions in Industrial Archaeology

My next move was rather odd for an aspirant location theorist, but understandable in the context of place and time. I had embarked on postgraduate research, intending to apply location theory to the industrial development of the East Midlands. But realization of the difficulty, accompanied by growing fascination with the region's economic history, prompted field encounters with relics of the industrial past. Numerous excursions led my future wife Margaret and I to exciting discoveries, ranging from the cotton mills and company townships built by the Arkwrights and Strutts in Derbyshire's Derwent Valley to the framework knitters' cottages with their distinctive elongated windows dating back to the days of domestic production. I began to see myself as a student of industrial landscape. The inspiration was less traditional geography than two contemporary series of books from outside the field: W. G. Hoskins's *The Making of the English Landscape* and Nikolaus Pevsner's *The Buildings of*

England. Both broke with convention in recognizing the significance of industrial features.

Completion of my PhD in 1961 further consolidated an interest in what would today be referred to as industrial heritage. Impending marriage required me to find work; failing to get a lectureship, I accepted a post in Staffordshire County Planning Department. Exploring new industrial landscapes, of the Potteries, Cheshire and Shropshire, provided escape from a job I found tedious. I began writing on the industrial landscape, combining background from the thesis with my extensive photographic record. An advertisement for a series of books in the nascent field of industrial archaeology led me to approach the publishers David & Charles. They accepted a proposal for my first book: *The Industrial Archaeology of the East Midlands* (1965).

As at the interface of economics, I saw mutual advantages working at this new fringe. While I learned something from the approaches of archaeology and architectural history, I argued that the geographer had a broadening contribution to make to a field which could be unduly preoccupied with buildings and machinery. I concluded: 'Industrial archaeology is, of course, ultimately concerned with people rather than things. . . . Those responsible for the birth of our modern industrial society erected their own monuments. It is for us to attempt to read and interpret the inscriptions' (Smith, 1965, p. 191). I was to return to this task more than thirty years later, in a moral reading of textile mill complexes and other monuments to human enterprise and suffering in a Polish city (see below).

Towards a Welfare Approach

In 1963 I obtained the much coveted lectureship, at the University of Manchester. I found the enormity of the local landscape too daunting for much further industrial archaeology. A return to location theory was augmented by a more applied interest in industrial development and regional planning (this at least I gained from the Staffordshire experience). An agreement to edit a series of regional studies of industry led to my second book, on the North West of England (Smith, 1969), the conclusion of which combined an endorsement of the social purpose of regional planning with a critique of piecemeal policies.

Having settled into Manchester's Geography Department, along with suburban domesticity, nothing could have been more out of character than to give it all up for a sojourn in the United States. But the new geography associated with the quantitative revolution, model-building and the like seemed to require American experience, and I obtained the offer of a one-year post at Southern Illinois University (SIU). However, the promised leave of absence from Manchester was unexpectedly refused, so I resigned in the summer of 1966 – an agonizing decision which turned out to be one of the best we ever made. Once we had settled in Carbondale, SIU were quick to offer me a tenured appointment and a post in Sociology for Margaret, so America became home.

Plans for a text on industrial location had been taking shape before I left Manchester. The Geography Department at SIU provided a supportive environment in which to undertake this project (Smith, 1971). Ease of computer access, in particular, facilitated what would have been impossible in Manchester, as well as encouraging over-indulgence in quantification. But the main significance of the US experience was to turn my interests in yet another direction, onto yet another fringe. The latter part of the 1960s was a period of turmoil in American society, the injustice of which soon became clear. My broadening perspective was reflected in the final chapter of the 1971 book, which stressed the relationship between industrial development and issues of political economy and social well-being, and argued for state involvement well beyond the prevailing conception of regional planning.

By the end of the 1960s I was being drawn towards the embryonic radical geography movement. I was redefining my interests as the geography of social problems: such conditions as poverty, hunger, ill-health and crime, hitherto largely neglected in geography. Margaret was teaching a course on social problems, and I could draw on her books as well as her knowledge. This change of direction was consolidated by moving to a joint appointment in the Geography Department and Urban Studies Bureau at the University of Florida, Gainesville, in 1970. Still the theorist at heart, I looked for a framework to give structure to what might otherwise have been indiscriminate mapping of the incidence of social problems. This was provided by the social indicators movement, in which practitioners of other disciplines, mainly economics and political science, were attempting to measure social progress in ways that challenged the conventional reliance on economic growth.

As with my earlier interactions on the fringe of geography, I found benefits both ways. I was influenced by how others were attempting to give both theoretical grounding and empirical substance to such concepts as social performance and the quality of life, within a public policy context. For my own part, I argued for the disaggregation of national-scale data, pointing to the importance of regional and local variations; I coined the term 'territorial social indicators' to stress the geographical perspective. This led to the inevitable book, identifying the geography of social well-being in the United States at different spatial scales (Smith, 1973). Among challenges to traditional regional terminology was my recognition of a 'southern region of social deprivation' in place of the old 'cotton belt'.

Working at a more practical level, as consultant to the City of Tampa, I applied the concept of territorial social indicators to the identification of target areas for a successor to the federal Model Cities programme.

As in Carbondale, my changing perspective was influenced by Margaret's activities. While pursuing independent professional lives, we did collaborate on a book on the United States for a popular audience (Smith and Smith, 1973). When we moved to Florida she declined a post in Sociology for voluntary work, mainly with the Gainesville Women for Equal Rights, a bi-racial pressure group for the unionization of black domestic servants and similar causes. Her involvement is still remembered in the city. As a former colleague wrote after Margaret died, it was 'as though she had been fighting racism all her life. These were dangerous times and probably more so for a "foreigner", yet she dived right in, and we never stopped loving her for it' (Jean Chalmers, personal communication, 3 February 2003). Not working so close to the front line, I did not need her courage, but still found Florida increasingly uncomfortable for my growing radicalism. By 1972 it was time to move on.

When applications for posts in the UK failed, the offer of a four-month appointment at the University of Natal in South Africa provided both escape and opportunity. I was becoming increasingly interested in race as a source of oppression, and felt ready to engage the extreme case of apartheid. The need for further employment was resolved by moving on to the University of the Witwatersrand, to complete the year. I soon realized that my emerging political activism would be far more dangerous in South Africa than in the American South, and found safety as well as solace in another bout of theory.

I have already written about the development of a welfare approach (Smith, 1988a), including those chance encounters which influenced the process. The most significant aspect, in the context of my present account, was re-exploration of the interface between geography and economics, turning to welfare theory in the neoclassical tradition. Welfare economics provided a more analytical framework than social indicators within which to set my concern with spatial inequality in social well-being. A monograph written at Wits provided an outline for what would become *Human Geography: A Welfare Approach* (Smith, 1977), the gestation of which was assisted by moving on to a six-month appointment at the University of New England in Australia with minimal teaching responsibilities.

Inequality and Social Justice

Returning to Britain, to a chair at Queen Mary College, London, coincided with publication of David Harvey's *Social Justice and the City* (1973).

I realized that I had some catching up to do: my colleague Roger Lee was critically examining neoclassical economics, as was Doreen Massey my beloved location theory. I read Marxian economics, and introduced elements into the welfare approach. Reservations about this, and other aspects of the 1977 book, are summarised elsewhere (Smith, 1988a, 1995). In retrospect, the real significance of this volume for my changing perspective was not the overall welfare framework itself, but the first step towards what would eventually become a more satisfying approach to the central normative issue underlying so much of my work since the late 1960s. This was the question of social justice, explored in a preliminary way in a chapter on judging distributions.

But before taking social justice more seriously, I had another empirical phase to work through. While convinced that there must be a better form of society than capitalism, I was not impressed by the rhetoric of the blunter edges of radical geography, or by uncritical advocacy of some ill-defined socialist alternative. By the time I had settled back into Britain, the realization that few self-styled radical geographers knew anything about socialism as actually practised stimulated my own curiosity. The International Geographical Union meetings in the Soviet Union in 1976 provided an opportunity to see something for myself, in a pre-conference symposium on industrial systems in Siberia as well as the main venue in Moscow.

This led to a number of subsequent excursions to the Soviet Union, and to Poland. The purpose was to supplement what evidence was available in documentary sources on inequality under socialism, with particular reference to its spatial expression within cities. To the outcome of repeated visits to Warsaw, Moscow and Akademgorodok (the academic satellite of Novosibirsk) was added experience from such other Soviet cities as Alma Ata, Leningrad (now St Petersburg) and Tbilisi, as well as Cracow and Łódź in Poland. While the initial focus was on the identification of patterns of inequality, a framework for interpretation emerged which recognized the interdependence of political economy, structural inequality and its spatial expression.

I was keen to portray inequality under socialism in a comparative perspective. This involved the development of case studies of the United States city as exemplified by Atlanta, Georgia, later extended to Jacksonville, Miami and Tampa in Florida. Another case was provided by revisiting the distinctive disequalizing society of South Africa under apartheid, again with emphasis on the urban dimension. Seeking to communicate my findings as widely as possible, I chose publications aimed at a general readership (Smith, 1979), students (Smith, 1988b) and teachers (Smith, 1989).

Another aspect of my interest in the spatial expression of inequality was health care, mainly in Britain and the Soviet Union (Smith, 1979,

Chapter 5). This led to the development of the Health Research Group (later Centre) in the Geography Department at Queen Mary, which focused initially on local variations in the need for health care and the service response. Close working relationships with local health authorities were established, and are maintained by Sarah Curtis and colleagues. As well as involving interface with health care planning and practice, this research brought encounters on another fringe: with medical sociology. Of special significance was the work of one of our early post-graduate students, Jocelyn Cornwell (1984), whose ethnographic perspective helped us to introduce qualitative methods to our repertoire, and to encourage other geographers to do so (Eyles and Smith, 1988).

By the beginning of the 1990s it was time to turn to theory again. I recall meeting David Harvey in Oxford, with the two of us confessing to one another rather diffidently that we were going back to social justice. My approach was to engage the massive theoretical literature which had accumulated since Rawls (1971) and Harvey (1973) had written so influentially twenty years before. This took me much further into moral and political philosophy than I had ventured earlier: yet another view from the fringe to absorb and somehow bring back into geography. The resulting book, *Geography and Social Justice* (Smith, 1994a), involved a comparative review of alternative theories. I moved on to an exposition of my own perspective of justice as equalization, which commends moves in the direction of equality unless there is a morally compelling argument to the contrary, the most persuasive being Rawls's 'difference principle', which justifies inequalities if they benefit the worst-off. I then provided case studies of the application of aspects of theory, drawing on my international research, showing that this requires sensitivity to geographical (and historical) context.

I continued to write about social justice for some time (e.g. Smith, 2000c). However, I was increasingly aware of the dependence of conceptions of justice on broader considerations of the good (Smith, 1997a): of what it means to talk about that elusive notion of the quality of life to which I had attempted to give empirical identity in my social indicators phase. As Michael Walzer (1994, p. 24) succinctly put it: 'we are distributing lives of a certain sort, and what counts as justice in distribution depends on what that "sort" is'. This had implications for how I approached the problem of social justice in post-apartheid South Africa (e.g. Smith, 2002), asking how the sort of lives enjoyed by a privileged minority could possible be good if inaccessible to the vast majority of the population under any conceivable development scenario. But it also represented my increasing concern with broader issues of ethics and morality.

Engagement with Ethics: Moral Geographies

The notion of moral geographies had been abroad for a few years, before I proclaimed a 'moral turn' in the first review on geography and ethics for *Progress in Human Geography* (Smith, 1997b). I followed this with pieces on common ground between geography and moral philosophy (Smith, 1998a), and on the spatial scope of beneficence as a case in point (Smith, 1998b). When invited to give the *Progress in Human Geography* Lecture in 1999, I developed an argument grounding moral progress in human geography on the notion of transcending the place of good fortune (Smith, 2000a). Of course, I was by no means alone on this new frontier: of geography and ethics, or moral philosophy. Among other activity, a trans-Atlantic 'Geo-ethics' project took shape, meeting at AAG and RGS/IBG conferences to discuss papers which came together in an edited collection (Proctor and Smith, 1999).

A book of my own was the inevitable outcome of my final excursion to the disciplinary fringe. In *Moral Geographies: Ethics in a World of Difference* (Smith, 2000b), I elaborate the significance of ethics (as theory) and morality (as practice) to geographical inquiry, and explain how a geographical perspective can contribute to moral philosophy. I try to navigate between the ideal of universal principles and the particularity of how actual people, located in time as well as space, understand and practise morality. Above all, I stress, yet again, the importance of context, in developing what I describe as a geographically sensitive ethics. While reviewers whom I respect have been generous to this volume, it is too early to see whether its impact might be greater than that of my welfare approach. All I care to say is that I got enormous satisfaction from writing the book, which I consider my best. If some of the content gives me special pleasure, it is for particular personal reasons. Delving into the role of place in the Jewish fate of murder and rescue during the Holocaust brought together some of my most poignant experiences in both Israel and Poland. Most deeply, my attempt at a moral reading of the landscape of the Polish industrial city of Łódź enabled me to take Margaret on my final fieldwork there, what turned out to be the last of so many such excursions we made together; her response to the awesome grandeur of the nineteenth-century mills brought full circle a journey we began with similar structures in the Derbyshire Dales more than forty years before.

I continue to explore ways in which ethics might illuminate geographical issues. Recent examples include urban fragmentation (Smith, 2003), and the challenge to open borders and free population movement raised by growing hostility to economic migration, political asylum and refuge (Smith, 2004). I hope for more such opportunities.

On Performing Geography: Personal and Professional Ethics

The message of my views from the fringe is quite simple. While many colleagues (like Roger Lee) may disagree, I have found the academic discipline of geography both limited and limiting, without consorting with others. I may have been promiscuous in my own extra-disciplinary liaisons, from economics and location theory to archaeology and architectural history, on to political science and sociology, and finally via social justice to moral philosophy. (Perhaps I should have taken in cultural studies on the way, but we have enough cultural geography without my involvement.) However, bringing in views from the fringe is only part of the project; the harder task is persuading those others to take geography seriously, understanding what our perspectives can offer them, and making something of it.

This leads to my last concern: that of professional ethics, or what it means to be a 'good geographer' in a normative sense. Implicit in my views from the fringe is the moral as well as academic imperative of engaging with others in mutually beneficial ways. It is not just a case of continuing trans-disciplinary research as a route to better scholarship, scientifically and socially. It also involves an ethics of professional responsibility to distant others in need (Smith, 1994b). What this means in practice is for those in resource-rich parts of the world, with well-endowed academic institutions, to extend some of their advantages to less fortunate colleagues elsewhere, on the fringes of our world of privilege.

For example, I have, over the years, tried to identify talented young scholars in Eastern Europe and South Africa, facilitating visits to Britain and other kinds of support (they are represented among the contributors to this volume). I have engaged in 'capacity building' in South Africa, in a university set up for a population group discriminated against under apartheid. I have helped to organize seminars, bringing British geographers together with those from the Republic of Georgia, Israel and Poland. And I have assisted colleagues from such places to publish their work in English. (Margaret's participation in numerous visits was important, as ever, helping to develop the personal relationships on which collaboration depends; she eventually made her own contribution, setting up social work training programmes in Armenia and the Ukraine with colleagues from the London School of Economics.) I make no claims to special virtue; many others engage in such activities, perhaps more effectively than I do.

The importance of all this would hardly require emphasis, if it was not for some growing impediments to the kind of exchanges which I value. These have to do with the cult of appraisal and performance assessment which has afflicted academic life in recent years. My critique will be familiar to anyone who followed a series of contributions to *Area*, or read an *Antipode*

'Intervention' on performing geography (Smith, 2001). Suffice it to note here that the focus on individual staff performance and departmental research standing, most notoriously in the Research Assessment Exercise (RAE) imposed on British universities, encourages consolidation of subject boundaries and institutional identities. It also breeds parochialism manifest in an exaggerated ethic of care for our own, at the expense of activity in support of more distant others which is unrecognized and unrewarded in conventional performance assessment.

The root of the problem is that methods of assessment currently adopted in Britain, for example, depend on a deeply flawed conception of academic activity. Sometimes referred to as the goal attainment model, it bears a strong resemblance to the planning framework of managerial rationality underpinning the social indicators movement of my American years. Individuals, and groups or institutions (academic departments and universities), are supposed to pursue goals (or targets), the attainment of which is somehow measurable. The way they do this is based (usually implicitly) on how the free market is supposed to operate in neoclassical economics, maximizing output for given expenditure. While this model may have validity in some walks of life, scholarship does not actually work this way. Universities are significantly different from factories: the creative process of scholarship is demeaned by the notion that it can be captured by a simple model or metric relating to quality of research and teaching.

The consequences are both practical and ethical. In practice, we do not know how to maximize research output, even if we knew how to measure it, with the reliability of industrial production theory. Ethically, it is wrong to claim such knowledge, and to run universities as though we had it. What universities should be, and how they should work, is a matter of proper public concern, and it is crucial that we critically engage the forces of darkness seeking to turn academic life into some gross parody of the competitive world of profit-seeking business; and that we do this not only by challenging alien understanding, but also by promoting alternative practice involving reaching out to others who would benefit from our involvement (as we would from theirs), in a spatially expansive and mutual ethics of care.

Epilogue: On Limits of Knowledge

There can be no ideal goal for human life. Any ideal goal means mechanization, materialism and nullity. There is no pulling open the buds to see what the blossom will be. Leaves must unroll, buds swell and open, and *then* the blossom. And even after that, when the flower dies and the leaves fall, *still* we shall not know. There will be more leaves, more buds, more blossom: and again, a blossom is an unfolding of the creative unknown. Impossible, utterly impossible to preconceive the uncreated blossom. You cannot forestall it from the last blossom. We know the flower of today, but the flower of tomorrow is beyond us all. Only in the material-mechanical world can man foresee, foreknow, calculate and establish laws.

Lawrence, 'Democracy' (1936), p. 321

Two early experiences drew my attention to the possible limits of know-ledge. One was a response to my standard lecture of the early 1960s, 'The textile mills of the Midlands', which I delivered with the conviction of the leading authority which I believed myself to be; after a presentation in Derby a member of the audience (wearing clerical collar) came up to me and said simply: 'The older I get, the less certain I am.' The other was a review of my book on industrial location in *The Economist*, where my repeated concessions that more research was required elicited the heading: 'What I don't know isn't knowledge'! Now, the more ethics I read, the less I seem to know; in this respect at least, moral philosophy resembles location theory, if not industrial archaeology.

The epigraph above, written by a product of the industrial East Midlands decades before postmodernism was invented, eloquently captures some of our contemporary uncertainties. (I used it to conclude my department's first submission to the RAE, before a more prudent colleague cut it out.) D. H. Lawrence's celebration of human spontaneity seems so much in tune with my own experience of creative scholarship, of performing geography (Smith, 2001), which has so little to do with the calculated rationality of goal attainment within a framework of academic planning. But do these sentiments really consign to the material-mechanical world August Lösch's laws revealed through theory, as the sole guide to what *should* take place? Perhaps they do, if we have in mind rigid structures based on certainty, scientific or moral. But if, to follow Bernard Williams, the point is to change the world rather than mirror it, we have to start with something. And if postmodernism has taught us anything, it is that knowledge can take different forms; something more limited and tentative than universal truth can be useful.

But there are things we know with certainty. To live a recognizably human life with some claims to the good requires basic subsistence needs to be satisfied, along with a minimum of security in which to plan and execute projects. And we know how hard it is for vast numbers of people to achieve this. If there is anything resembling moral truth, we also know that those of us with the capacity to do so have a responsibility to change the world, to the benefit of those less fortunately endowed. Thirty years ago I concluded my book on the geography of social well-being in the United

States with the rather simplistic idea that 'it takes good human beings to implement social reforms which help others to realize their own perceptions of the good life. Good people in leadership positions may yet prove to be the most important of our scarce resources' (Smith, 1973, p. 143). While prevailing structures of domination and oppression may seem unyielding to the most enlightened politicians and the most persuasive moral arguments, they are human creations and capable of challenge and change if not complete deconstruction.

The nearest I can get to a suggestion of what it may take to become good is in an epigraph I chose for the final chapter of my last book (Smith, 2000b): 'The wellspring of morality is the human capacity to put oneself in the place of others' (Paul, Miller and Paul, 1994, p. vii). This resonates with some familiar ethical formulations, from the 'Golden Rule' referred to in Chapter 1, to Immanuel Kant's categorical imperative, and on to John Rawls's veil of ignorance which 'forces us to put ourselves in the position of those people who, for no good reason, are less well off than ourselves' (Corbridge, 1993, p. 464). Nothing could be a greater challenge to our creative imagination than to assist the process of understanding and empathizing with unfortunate others elsewhere, as a prelude to trying to improve our sorry reality, to change the world. If I have come to know anything over these past forty years, it is that this would be 'good geography'.

REFERENCES

Corbridge, S. (1993) 'Marxisms, modernities and moralities: development praxis and the claims of distant strangers', *Environment and Planning D: Society and Space* 11, 449–72.
Cornwell, J. (1984) *Hard-Earned Lives: Accounts of Health and Illness from East London*, London: Tavistock.
Eyles, J. and Smith, D. M. (1988) *Qualitative Methods in Human Geography*, Cambridge: Polity.
Harvey, D. (1973) *Social Justice and the City*, London: Edward Arnold.
Lawrence, D. H. (1936) 'Democracy', in A. Arblaster and S. Lukes (eds), *The Good Society: A Book of Readings*, London: Methuen, 1971, pp. 320–5.
Lösch, A. (1954) *The Economics of Location*, New Haven: Yale University Press.
Paul, E. F., Miller, F. D. and Paul, J. (1994) 'Introduction', in E. F. Miller, F. D. Miller and J. Paul (eds), *Cultural Pluralism and Moral Knowledge*, Cambridge: Cambridge University Press, pp. vii–xiii.
Proctor, J. and Smith, D. M. (eds) (1999) *Geography and Ethics: Journeys in a Moral Terrain*, London: Routledge.
Rawls, J. (1971) *A Theory of Justice*, Cambridge, Mass.: Harvard University Press.
Rawstron, E. M. (1958) 'Three principles of industrial location', *Transactions and Papers, Institute of British Geographers* 25, 132–41.

Smith, D. M. (1965) *The Industrial Archaeology of the East Midlands*, Dawlish: David & Charles.

Smith, D. M. (1966) 'A theoretical framework for geographical studies of industrial location', *Economic Geography* 42, 95–113.

Smith, D. M. (1969) *Industrial Britain: The North West*, Newton Abbot: David & Charles.

Smith, D. M. (1971) *Industrial Location: An Economic Geographical Analysis*, New York: John Wiley; 2nd edition 1981.

Smith, D. M. (1973) *The Geography of Social Well-being in the United States: An Introduction to Territorial Social Indicators*, New York: McGraw-Hill.

Smith, D. M. (1977) *Human Geography: A Welfare Approach*, London: Edward Arnold.

Smith, D. M. (1979) *Where the Grass is Greener: Living in an Unequal World*, Harmondsworth: Penguin.

Smith, D. M. (1984) 'Recollections of a random variable', in M. Billinge, D. Gregory and R. Martin (eds), *Recollection of a Revolution: Geography as Spatial Science*, London: Macmillan, pp. 117–33.

Smith, D. M. (1988a) 'A welfare approach to human geography', in J. Eyles (ed.), *Research in Human Geography: Problem, Tactics and Opportunities*, Oxford: Blackwell, pp. 139–54.

Smith, D. M. (1988b) *Geography, Inequality and Society*, Cambridge: Cambridge University Press.

Smith, D. M. (1989) *Urban Inequality under Socialism: Case Studies from Eastern Europe and the Soviet Union*, Cambridge: Cambridge University Press.

Smith, D. M. (1994a) *Geography and Social Justice*, Oxford: Blackwell.

Smith, D. M. (1994b) 'On professional responsibility to distant others', *Area* 26, 359–67.

Smith, D. M. (with Chisholm, M. and Knox, P.) (1995) 'Classics in human geography revisited: Smith, D. M. 1977: *Human geography: a welfare approach*', *Progress in Human Geography* 19, 389–94.

Smith, D. M. (1997a) 'Back to the good life: towards an enlarged conception of social justice', *Environment and Planning D: Society and Space* 15, 19–35.

Smith, D. M. (1997b) 'Geography and ethics: a moral turn?', *Progress in Human Geography* 21, 596–603.

Smith, D. M. (1998a) 'Geography and moral philosophy: some common ground', *Ethics, Place and Environment* 1, 7–34.

Smith, D. M. (1998b) 'How far should we care? On the spatial scope of beneficence', *Progress in Human Geography* 22, 15–38.

Smith, D. M. (2000a) 'Moral progress in human geography: transcending the place of good fortune', *Progress in Human Geography* 24, 1–18.

Smith, D. M. (2000b) *Moral Geographies: Ethics in a World of Difference*, Edinburgh: Edinburgh University Press.

Smith, D. M. (2000c) 'Social justice revisited', *Environment and Planning A* 32, 1149–62.

Smith, D. M. (2001) 'On performing geography', *Antipode* 33, 142–6.

Smith, D. M. (2002) 'Social justice and the South African city', in J. Eade and C. Mele (eds), *Urban Studies: Contemporary and Future Perspectives*, Oxford: Blackwell, pp. 66–81.

Smith, D. M. (2003) 'Urban fragmentation, inequality and social justice: ethical perspectives', in R. Harrison, M. Huchzermeyer and M. Mayekiso (eds), *Confronting Fragmentation: Housing and Urban Policy in a Democratising Society*, Cape Town: Juta, pp. 26–39.

Smith, D. M. (2004) 'Open borders and free population movement: a challenge for liberalism', in C. Barnet and M. Low (eds), *Spaces of Democracy*, London: Sage, pp. 113–28.

Smith, M. R. and Smith, D. M. (1973) *The United States: How they Live and Work*, Newton Abbot: David & Charles.

Walzer, M. (1994) *Thick and Thin: Moral Argument at Home and Abroad*, Notre Dame, Ind. and London: University of Notre Dame Press.

Williams, B. (1972) *Morality: An Introduction to Ethics*, Cambridge: Cambridge University Press.

Index